Contents

Foreword

Our pleasure in publishing John Hattendorf's Newport Paper on maritime strategy arises from several sources. The Naval War College Press is pleased to republish and make more broadly available an essay that had become a standard reference work for those few fortunate enough to be both cleared for and fascinated by the evolution of postwar American strategy. This edition reproduces the Hattendorf analysis as it was first presented and published in 1989. The new elements—the now declassified NIE, the comprehensive updating by Peter Swartz of his earlier bibliographies, and the selective time line created by Yuri Zhukov under Hattendorf's direction—only enhance Hattendorf's original analytic core.

Even more important are the links between this essay and the Press's broader commitment to publishing and supporting the best work in maritime history. We have developed a notable series of naval biographies, most recently a splendid volume of Admiral H. Kent Hewitt's memoirs, edited by Evelyn Cherpak. We look forward to working with the materials developed by the project on the Cold War at Sea, a comprehensive effort led by John Hattendorf and Lyle Goldstein, with collaboration between the Naval War College, the Watson Institute of Brown University, and the Saratoga Foundation. We also hope for further historical efforts mounted by the new NWC Maritime History Department.

We appreciate the support we have received in declassifying the Hattendorf essay and obtaining the NIE from Peter Swartz and David Rosenberg, as well as the expert assistance of Ms. Jo-Ann Parks (JIL Information Systems) in the finalization of the manuscript. We express special appreciation also to Ms. Patricia Goodrich, guiding editor of the Newport Papers throughout much of the last decade, for this, her last hurrah.

Perhaps most important for the Press itself and for our readers, this essay sharpens our own sense of history. It recounts a fascinating story and also reflects the significant role that the Naval War College, the Strategic Studies Group, and individual leaders, past and present, played in this critical period of strategy making. It is rare to have as authoritative an account of the difficult, complex process of strategy making as that which Hattendorf produced within a very short time after the events themselves. Much has changed in the international context since then; but the fundamental tasks of conceptualization, assessment of ends and means, and focused implementation of strategy remain the challenges for all those who wish to secure their nation's safety and security. This essay provides a valuable guide to this critical enterprise.

CATHERINE McARDLE KELLEHER
Editor, Naval War College Press

April 2004

General Preface

To understand a series of events in the past, one needs to do more than just know a set of detailed and isolated facts. Historical understanding is a process to work out the best way to generalize accurately about something that has happened. It is an ongoing and never-ending discussion about what events mean, why they took place the way they did, and how and to what extent that past experience affects our present or provides a useful example for our general appreciation of our development over time. Historical understanding is an examination that involves attaching specifics to wide trends and broad ideas. In this, individual actors in history can be surprised to find that their actions involve trends and issues that they were not thinking about at the time they were involved in a past action as well as those that they do recognize and were thinking about at the time. It is the historian's job to look beyond specifics to see context and to make connections with trends that are not otherwise obvious.

The process of moving from recorded facts to a general understanding can be a long one. For events that take place within a government agency, such as the U.S. Navy, the process can not even begin until the information and key documents become public knowledge and can be disseminated widely enough to bring different viewpoints and wider perspectives to bear upon them.

This volume is published to help begin that process of wider historical understanding and generalization for the subject of strategic thinking in the U.S. Navy during the last phases of the Cold War. To facilitate this beginning, we offer here the now-declassified, full and original version of the official study that I undertook in 1986–1989, supplemented by three appendices. The study attempted to record the trends and ideas that we could see at the time, written on the basis of interviews with a range of the key individuals involved and on the working documents that were then still located in their original office locations, some of which have not survived or were not permanently retained in archival files. We publish it here as a document, as it was written, without attempting to bring it up to date.

To supplement this original study, we have appended the declassified version of the Central Intelligence Agency's National Intelligence Estimate of March 1982, which was a key analysis in understanding the Soviet Navy, provided a generally accepted consensus of American understanding at the time, and provided a basis around which to develop the U.S Navy's maritime strategy in this period. A second appendix is by Captain Peter Swartz, U.S. Navy (Ret.), and consists of his annotated bibliography of the public debate surrounding the formulation of the strategy in the 1980s, updated to include materials published through the end of 2003. And finally, Yuri M. Zhukov has created especially for this volume a timeline that lays out a chronology of events to better understand the sequence of events involved.

The study and the three appendices are materials that contribute toward a future historical understanding and do not, in themselves, constitute a definitive history, although they are published as valuable tools toward reaching that goal. To reach closer to a definitive understanding, there are a variety of new perceptions that need to be added over time. With the opening of archives on both sides of the world, and as scholarly discourse between Russians and Americans develop, one will be able to begin to compare and contrast perceptions with factual realities. As more time passes and we gain further distance and perspective in seeing the emerging broad trends, new approaches to the subject may become apparent. Simultaneously, new materials may be released from government archives that will enhance our understanding. New perceptions can also be expected from other quarters.

An example of this has already been made in a recent doctoral thesis completed at Kiel University in Germany. There, in late 2000, a retired German naval officer, Wilfried Stallmann, wrote a successful doctoral thesis on "U.S. Maritime Strategy after 1945: Development, Influence, and Affects on the Atlantic Alliance."[1] Working under the guidance of one of Germany's most prominent naval historians, Professor Dr. Michael Salewski, Stallmann used his wide personal experience as a German naval and NATO staff officer with his education as a graduate of both the Naval War College's Naval Staff College in 1974 and of its Naval Command College in 1988 to complement his academic studies in medieval and modern history, political science, and law. In his thesis, Stallmann made an unusual and important contribution in German academic practice by using data from maritime history to verify a thesis in political science that contrasted the substance of American strategy with the academic preparation given to professional officers. He concluded that the development of American maritime strategy over the fifty-year period of the Cold War conformed only in the exceptional case to the ideal and logical path of strategy making that is taught in U.S. and allied professional military colleges, as they link national interests, policy, strategy, and operations in a hierarchical way.

Stallmann's thesis is an important academic contribution that leads its readers to think about a historical situation, but also stimulates further practical questions for professionals to ask on the basis of a specific historical experience. His work poses a double-sided question for reflection. On the one hand, it leaves us to ask whether or not the U.S. Navy effectively uses appropriate educational insights as its officers engage in the process of formulating maritime strategy. On the other hand, one is left to ponder the quality and nature of what is formulated as strategy.

For a professional involved in either military education or in the development of national maritime strategy, these are very useful and profitable questions to pose in applying historical understanding to current issues. Materials such as those provided here can help lead to a critical understanding of historical events that may possibly result in improved professional performance and to better understanding in this professional realm for the future. In this particular case, one can weigh the relative importance and influence of organized educational institutions like the Naval War College and special groups like the CNO Strategic Studies Group.

This is an example of a very specialized and professional application of historical understanding, but it is not the only one that may arise. Examination of the process involved in the creation of the maritime strategy in this period can educate decision makers in government and in Congress as to the ways the Navy has used in formulating recent strategy.[2] Further, a case study such as this is interesting and useful to those in uniform within the naval service, as it recognizes individuals and their convictions, showing that they matter enormously during critical and important times in American naval history. Indeed, the study provides examples of innovation, leadership, and understanding that may make useful models for others interested in working toward intellectual and organizational change of the most fundamental dimensions.

To civilian academics, there are a wide range of possible uses for the type of information materials presented here. Among them, the story here shows how new, innovative understanding was introduced and propagated within a bureaucracy. The historical narrative can also provide some help in quite a different, but in an equally important, quest as one looks to see what motivated government officials to take certain actions and how they reacted to the Soviet Navy's challenge and to what degree they accurately interpreted Soviet intentions and actions.

For the general American public, a historical understanding of this same case involves another dimension, as it seeks to understand what the role of the U.S. Navy has been in the Cold War and what responsible government officials planned to do with the assets under their care. A narrative such as this can raise penetrating questions as to whether the ideas presented here were a wise use of national resources in peacetime or to insightful, counterfactual speculation as to what the judgment might have been if there had been an open conflict with the Soviet Union.

All such differing insights are to be found in the process by which we seek historical understanding and research, write, read, and study naval history. History is a tale of endless fascination. Not merely entertaining, it leads us to form our own understanding and our own convictions about the past that form our attitudes toward the present and the future.

Naval War College

Newport, Rhode Island
Center for Naval Warfare Studies
Originally published as
Newport Paper Number Six
The Evolution of the U.S. Navy's Maritime Strategy,
1977-1986 (U)
1989

The Evolution of the U.S. Navy's Maritime Strategy, 1977–1986

John B. Hattendorf, D. Phil.
Ernest J. King Professor of Maritime History
Naval War College

NAVAL WAR COLLEGE PRESS
Newport, Rhode Island
1989

Preface to the First Edition

This study is the sixth in a series of The Newport Papers published by the Center for Naval Warfare Studies, Naval War College, since 1981.[1] It is the full, classified version from which the author developed the unclassified, article-length version that was published in the *Naval War College Review* in 1988.[2]

The purpose of this history of "The Evolution of the U.S. Navy's Maritime Strategy, 1977–1986" is to provide a single study that summarizes some of the main trends in American naval strategic thinking over the past decade and that might serve as a useful starting point for those who are entering upon responsibilities in war planning. The emphasis of the study is on trying to understand the origins, the rationale, and the objectives of the people who put forward the various strategic ideas, noting how various contributions have complemented one another in a larger picture. The historian faced with a project such as this will encounter many pitfalls and cannot expect to write a definitive history so soon after the events. Indeed, as one pundit said, "those who follow the heels of history too closely may well be kicked in the teeth." Despite that warning, we have attempted to describe the issues dispassionately, to give credit where credit is due, and to avoid political squabbles while seeking to serve the larger purpose of contributing to strategic thought. Despite all efforts, we have not been able to interview everyone who was involved nor have we received responses from everyone to whom we sent the drafts for review. We have also not had access to all documents, and we have imposed our own limitation on the work by keeping it at the secret level of classification. In order to improve future understanding, readers are encouraged to report to the President of the Naval War College any factual corrections in the text and to provide documents and information on any aspect that may have been overlooked inadvertently.

October 1989   J. B. H.

Introduction

In relation to abstract analysis, this is a case study of the process by which a strategy was developed and applied within the present American defense establishment. As one reads this detailed study, he may evaluate the effort while bearing in mind the broad aspects involved in the rational development of a strategy through an understanding of national aims, technological and geographical constraints, and relative military abilities. As academic theorists have pointed out, these strictly rational calculations are commonly offset by institutional interests, bureaucratic politics, and conflict among decision makers. In addition, the complex task of war planning requires simplification and organization of concepts into a framework by which an organization's leaders can provide a basis for the education of new participants as well as guidelines for standard procedures and approaches to analysis. The process of using this conceptual framework can have a tendency to introduce elements of bias into a decision maker's perceptions and to influence his selection of choices. This may lead to a strategist ignoring issues that do not fit into his established categories or preferences.[1]

The American system of strategic planning is a pluralistic one that involves four levels at which people make statements of strategy:

- High policy established at the level of the President and modified or supported by Congress.

- War planning, the general conceptual plans for war, is done by the Joint Chiefs of Staff.

- Program planning, the system of coordinated weapons procurement, is accompanied by statements of strategy that define the rationale for the weapons involved and is done by each service and coordinated by the Secretary of Defense.

- Operational planning, the preparation of precise plans for wartime operations, is done by the various unified and specified commanders in chief.

In theory, the four levels of strategy making should directly complement one another with high policy establishing the goals and objectives for both program planning and war planning, while they, in turn, reflect operational planning. In practice, some academics argue that the theory has rarely, if ever, been achieved. Each level of strategy making has its own set of needs and constraints produced by the nature of the system, thereby producing the possibility for contradiction and disjunctions. Each decision-making element within each of the various levels of strategy making can be led away from a strictly rational calculation of strategy.[2] This is caused by the practical necessity to simplify complex issues involving a high degree of uncertainty and by the motivated bias created through the interaction of bureaucratic interests. These factors, which are present in nearly every system of governmental machinery, require constant reevaluation and adjustment in the effort to reach a rational application of strategy. That rational calculus is, however, forever changing as political events and technological developments alter the situation on the global stage. Thus, the development of strategy is a perpetual process of questioning, application, and reexamination.

CHAPTER ONE

The Evolution of Naval Thinking in the 1970s

The Ambiance of the 1970s

Writing in the mid-1970s, Admiral Thomas H. Moorer declared "the United States is crossing the threshold of the last quarter of the 20th century in a mood of apprehension and confusion—confusion over America's place in a rapidly changing world and over the correct path to a dimly perceived future."[1] This thought reflected the anguish and pessimism that had marked much of the previous decade for American servicemen. As former Under Secretary of the Navy Robert J. Murray later described it, "it is hard to think of a more chaotic decade than the period between the assassination of President Kennedy in 1963 and Nixon's resignation in 1974."[2] There was too much to think about during those years to deal with issues of broad national or naval strategy. Officers were "fragged," schools seemed to stop teaching, moral values were deprecated, children were disaffected. Adults as well as children found it difficult to find their way as they saw families collapsing, riots breaking out in cities, and even the sight of Washington, D.C., burning.

Then, after the United States withdrew from Vietnam, along came events in Ethiopia, Angola, Afghanistan, and Iran, which clearly demonstrated that the American position in international politics was not faring well, while the Soviet Union seemed to be having great success. As these events added insult to injury, they evoked a changing mood among leaders within the U.S. Government following the stabilizing influence of Gerald Ford's presidency. Beginning under President Jimmy Carter, the United States began to move outward again, using her armed forces to complement her foreign policy and establishing a clear trend in the use of U.S. naval and military force as a political instrument.[3]

Of the 71 incidents that occurred in the ten-year period between 1975 and 1984, 58, or 81 percent, involved the use of naval forces. Of those 58 incidents, 35 involved the use of aircraft carriers. During that same time frame, strategic nuclear forces seemed to play a declining and less obvious role, while conventional forces became much more

FIGURE 1

Incidents of uses of U.S. Armed Forces as a Political Instrument*

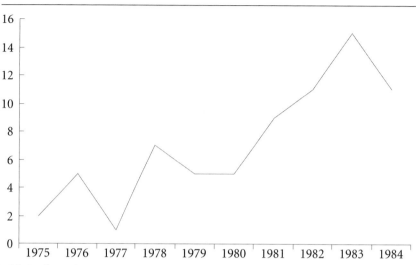

* Philip D. Zelikow, "The United States and the Use of Force: A Historical Summary." Draft. Unpublished.

important. In American foreign relations during the 30-year period 1946 to 1975, the presence of nuclear forces played a role on 19 different occasions. By contrast, there was no explicit political use of nuclear weapons for political purposes in the period from 1975 to 1984.[4]

These trends in American foreign policy were paralleled by a number of other separate, but interlocking, developments. First, there became evident visible signs that the confusion that had developed about naval theory was coming to an end. Secondly, there was a clear resurgence in general strategic thinking in many areas of the U.S. armed forces as well as in the academic world. Thirdly, the U.S. Navy had been engaged for a number of years in rebuilding its own forces to replace the block obsolescence of about half of the U.S. surface fleet. Finally, while these developments were in progress, the Soviet Navy had reached a new capability in its own dramatic development since 1962 and were now regarded as a global naval power. All these trends marked the central features of the ambiance in which new American naval thinking began to take shape.

Naval Theory Refined

Theory has never been an attractive area of study for naval officers, yet naval theorists work on an important subject that can both reflect and inform those whose concerns are strictly practical. Up to and including World War II, American naval strategists clearly based their fundamental theoretical concepts on the ideas that Alfred Thayer Mahan had expressed a half century earlier. The experience of World War II, particularly the decisive battles of the Pacific War, largely confirmed American faith in his ideas, but in the years following 1945, the challenge presented by new technology, particularly by nuclear weapons, missiles and electronics, seemed to make the old ideas inappropriate to a new and different era. Indeed the Cold War stressed the importance of an area which Mahan had not developed at all: the political uses of sea power in peacetime.[5] In America, the most widely read theoretical works on navies written in the postwar period were those by academic writers such as Laurence W. Martin, Edward Luttwak, Ken Booth, as well as the diplomat Sir James Cable, all of whom examined the political uses of navies—short of war.

A small, but less well-known group of thinkers centered at the Naval War College consistently devoted its effort to creating a thoroughly modern synthesis of major strategic ideas for wartime. The dominant figure in this work was Rear Admiral Henry E. Eccles, who was joined by Dr. Herbert Rosinski and Dr. William Reitzel, among others. Taken together, their work was designed to define with semantic precision the nature of naval strategy for modern warfare and to put in writing the core of what senior naval officers should understand intuitively and be prepared to develop into practical, operationally sound strategic plans for naval forces.[6]

Eccles expanded on Rosinski's definition that strategy is the comprehensive direction of power to control situations and areas in order to attain broad objectives. Since strategy is comprehensive, Eccles wrote, "it looks at the whole field of action. But since resources are always limited, the strategist must identify those minimum key areas and situations in relation to time and distance and the availability of tactical and logistics resources." As Eccles so distinctly defined the matter, in practical terms:

A strategic concept is a verbal statement of:

What to control

For what purpose

To what degree

When to initiate control

How long to control

And, in general, how to control in order to achieve the strategic objective.[7]

Another naval officer, Rear Admiral Joseph C. Wylie, took this concept one step further. For him, the common factor in all power struggles is the concept of control. "Military control, or military affairs in the broad sense, can seldom be taken up in isolation," Wylie wrote. "Military matters are inextricably woven into the whole social fabric. And that is why a general theory of strategy must, I believe, be a theory of power in all its forms, not just a theory of military power."[8]

Complementing these definitions, Eccles presaged much of what younger officers would attempt to do later in formulating the Maritime Strategy of the early 1980s. In Eccles's mind, the term naval strategy was a term too easily used for polemic purposes to enhance naval appropriations, the domestic political position of naval authorities, and to protect the navy from similar polemicists in the air force and the army. However, Eccles emphatically believed that the understanding of the naval aspects of an overall maritime strategy and of the creation and wide employment of naval forces is vitally important. Maritime power is but one of the elements of overall national power and of national strategy. "Maritime power is indispensable to the attainment and employment of purposeful 'great power,'" Eccles wrote. "Seapower cannot be understood save as a component of maritime power, and thus, naval strategy cannot stand alone."[9]

The work of naval theorists within the U.S. Navy concentrated on the uses of the navy in wartime, but extended their thinking to include not only peacetime political applications but also the relationships of naval strategy to the broader aspects of maritime and national power. There was a clear realization within the navy that naval force must be coordinated and related to other aspects of national power. Not the least important aspect in their thinking was the understanding that conventional naval forces had a role to play in a world of nuclear deterrence, parity of forces, and deterrence. The general trend in professional naval thought was to accept these factors as replacements for the traditional prenuclear idea of battles between fleets on a grand scale with no holds barred. The modern version of total war was a definition of nuclear war, yet professional thinkers had moved beyond total horror at that prospect and had begun to examine the nature of such conflicts. Clearly, there were variations in the way nuclear weapons might be used; they might be employed either massively, selectively, or after a preliminary phase of conventional warfare. In an age when continual crises seemed to exist and when regional tensions between political blocs were dealt with in the context of the strategic nuclear balance, there seemed to be a multiplicity of possible situations in which lower level conflicts might result.[10] These very situations heightened the importance for concepts of strategic control and for the interrelationship of naval forces with other types of national power.

This general trend in thinking was a significant alteration in American viewpoint. For nearly a quarter of a century, American military and naval thinking had been based on the notion that deterrence required the explicit threat of escalation to the nuclear level. That threat alone was once considered to be sufficient to preclude warfare. By the 1970s, military thinkers had returned to the idea that warfare was likely to be as frequent an occurrence in the future as it had been in the past. Moreover, the circumstances of conflict could involve a greater range and complexity than ever before.[11] This understanding implied that there was a large prospect for the use of substantial conventional forces, even in the nuclear age. While the opposing nuclear forces were about equal, thus even less useful for political purposes, conventional force seemed to gain utility not only in its relation to the nuclear balance and in terms of deterrence, but also as an increment of escalation. They contributed to the threat of escalation both horizontally through geographical positioning, and vertically through the threat of a prolonged conventional war in which economic and industrial strength would be the decisive factor.[12]

The Resurgence of Strategic Thinking in the U.S. Navy

The development of strategic thinking within the U.S. Navy goes back more than a century. For most of that time, the navy has maintained contingency plans and analyzed the ways in which naval power might be used in future wars. While there has never been a clearly identified cadre of officers given specific responsibility for developing naval strategy, the issues and ideas have been dealt with over the years by senior officials in Washington and by scattered groups of more or less intellectually inclined naval officers working at the Naval War College, in OpNav, and on the staffs of fleet commanders. The entire history of the Naval War College, in fact, has been the story of repeated efforts to promote broad strategic thinking within the naval officer corps to complement the ordinary, but incomplete, emphasis on technological developments and new weapons.

In the early 1970s (1970–1974), as Chief of Naval Operations (CNO), Admiral Elmo Zumwalt faced these same problems and took dramatic action to try to correct them. He established the Navy Net Assessment Group to create a gauge by which the U.S. Navy could measure its effectiveness against the Soviets and he sponsored "Project 2000" to provide a long-range review of policy beyond the five-year planning cycles initiated by Secretary of Defense Robert McNamara (21 January 1961–29 February 1968) in the previous decade. Paralleling this, Zumwalt fought to broaden naval thinking by revising the curriculum at the Naval War College.[13] Carrying out this mission, Vice Admiral Stansfield Turner noted a relatively new problem when he castigated the navy for "our increasing reliance on civilians and on 'think tanks' to do our thinking for us." While many people resented the implications of his remarks, he pointed to a serious issue when he said,

> We must be able to produce military men who are a match for the best of the civilian strategists or we will abdicate control of our profession. Moreover, I am persuaded that we can be a profession only as long as we ourselves are pushing the frontiers of knowledge.[14]

Despite the initiatives that Zumwalt and Turner made in this area, no dramatic change took place in terms of a permanent effect on the officer corps. Although the Naval War College's curriculum improved during Turner's tenure and was better prepared to make a long-term contribution, at that time the most influential and most promising officers were not being sent to Newport as students. Thus, its influence was limited. In Washington, at the same time, a few of the studies produced under Zumwalt's initiative began to have influence, particularly among those who had been involved with these studies and remained in service to work on similar projects at the end of the 1970s. Two projects in particular that were completed during Admiral Zumwalt's tenure had some impact on ideas developed later: *Future Maritime Strategy Study* (FUMAR) and "U.S. Strategy for the Pacific/Indian Ocean Area in the 1970s."[15]

These studies had their origins in late 1970. Following the issue of a Secretary of Defense memo on 16 December 1970 providing "Tentative Strategic Guidance," Admiral Zumwalt stated his desire to have a series of related regional studies and requested a plan for carrying them out. These studies, as well as others in progress, were designed to contribute to the future maritime strategy study sponsored in OpNav by OP-06. This study was designed to examine policy and strategy, both worldwide and regional, under conditions short of general war in the period 1975–1985.[16] Significantly, the study plan for FUMAR noted,

> Strategy has traditionally been associated with war, preparation for war, and the waging of war. As war and modern societies and politics have become more complicated, strategy of necessity has required increasing consideration of nonmilitary matters: economic, political, psychological and sociological. Thus strategy has become more than merely a military concept and tends toward the coordinated execution of statecraft.[17]

In May 1973, the Director of Navy Program Planning, (OP-090), Rear Admiral Thomas B. Hayward, promulgated the study. In his forwarding letter, he noted that the study had been designed to determine the complementary elements of U.S. national power and the role and relationship between types of general purpose military forces in advancing U.S. interests. Among other things, he noted that the study had concluded that "the optimum type of general purpose forces for the U.S. will be forces which are politically and strategically mobile and that are effectually linked to quick reaction strategic reserve forces and to the strategic nuclear force." Moreover, Hayward underscored the value of the study when he concluded that it "provides many imaginative and original concepts which can provide a basis for future analysis and refinement of naval strategic concepts."[18]

The second study, which followed on from this, was "U.S. Strategy for the Pacific–Indian Ocean Area in the 1970s." Personally tasked by Zumwalt and carried out in OP-605 by Captain William Cockell, who had also been heavily involved in the

FUMAR study as well. Cockell sought to look at the Pacific–Indian Ocean area as a single, strategic entity. Like FUMAR, the new study was broader than a military study. With the assistance of a contractor, Arthur D. Little Inc., economic and trade factors were included, as well as the problem of oil transport, well before international attention was focused on these issues. Simultaneously, the study provided support for the case of building up Diego Garcia as an Indian Ocean naval base, while at the same time looking at the entire strategic situation along the whole Asian littoral from the Persian Gulf to northeast Asia.

About the same time, Captain Cockell and Captain Curt Shellman carried out a third study for Zumwalt in OP-06. The subject of this study was to define the navy's nuclear strategy and force structure in the context of a sensible national strategy. Zumwalt saw this as an essential bit of groundwork to assist him in developing the navy's position in relation to the Strategic Arms Limitation area—following Senator [Henry M. "Scoop"] Jackson's criticism of the Joint Chiefs of Staff for not having done their homework for SALT I. The Cockell-Shellman study provided the concept for Fleet Ballistic Missile Submarine (SSBN) involvement with hard-kill capability and laid the groundwork for the Trident II (D-5) program, which was just then coming to fruition. Throughout, Zumwalt accepted the logic in the study, despite the fact that OP-96 and OP-90 opposed it, fearing that a major new submarine-launched ballistic missile (SLBM) program would drain resources from other important programs.

In the 1960s and 1970s, the official Department of Defense statement of naval missions did not change, yet within that same time frame, the long-term naval force goals that the navy used did change. In 1975, the goal was set at 575 ships by Secretary of Defense James Schlesinger (1973–1975); in 1976 Secretary of Defense Donald Rumsfeld (1975–1977) set it at 600; in 1977–1978, Secretary of Defense Harold Brown (1977–1981) set it at 425–500 ships. The variance in these number goals reflected the difference in judgment as to what was prudent for the country to plan for in facing the uncertainties of the future. The high numbers reflected estimates that focused on a future world war involving the Soviet Union. The low numbers, particularly the 400-ship figures used by the Carter administration in their 1977 DoD Consolidated Guidance, reflected the idea that the U.S. Navy's surface fleet should be designed for peacekeeping operations and for conflicts in which the Soviet Union chose not to be involved, while at the same time maintaining an edge of naval superiority over the Soviets.

In broad terms, the U.S. Navy's budget and its plans for the future had been sharply reduced in the period immediately following the Vietnam War. From 1962 to 1972, the navy had programmed the construction of 42 ships per year, but between 1968 and 1975 only 12 ships, or less than a third as many per year, were programmed. In 1975, given the age of ships already at sea, and the navy-expected service life for a warship of 25–30 years, the service anticipated retiring about 4 percent of the active fleet each year. With this in mind in 1975, Secretary of the Navy J. William Middendorf (1974–1977) declared, "looking ahead to 1980, for the navy to have a fleet of, say, 500 ships to carry out its missions, we would have to triple the current ship-building average or at least the ship-building average of the last 5, 6, 7 years."[19] In the previous ten years, the U.S. naval force had declined from 947 active ships to 478. In Fiscal Year 1976, total defense spending was 24.8 percent of the federal total, the lowest share since fiscal year 1940. Even so, President Gerald Ford's administration (1974–1977) was determined to maintain U.S. naval superiority. "We cannot and will not let any nation dominate the world seas. The United States must and it will," Ford declared.[20]

While President Ford was committed to a policy of reversing this decline in U.S. naval strength, Congress refused to approve all of his proposals. Expressing his concerns over the deficiencies in the legislation's authorization of $32.5 billion for procurement and for research and development programs, Ford stated:

> Congress has failed to authorize $1.7 billion requested for new ship programs that are needed to strengthen our maritime capabilities and assure freedom of the seas. In particular, they have denied funds for the lead ships for two essential production programs—the nuclear strike cruiser and the conventionally powered AEGIS destroyer—and for four modern frigates. The FY 1977 program was proposed as the first step of a sustained effort to assure that the United States, along with its allies, can maintain maritime defense, deterrence, and freedom of the seas. I plan to resubmit budget requests for FY 1977 to cover these essential ship building programs.[21]

Despite setbacks, Ford was able to establish a strong plan to rebuild the navy. This plan for new ships, however, was cut by the (President Jimmy) Carter administration (1977–1981).

Meanwhile within the navy staff under Chief of Naval Operations Admiral James L. Holloway III (1974–1978), thought was being given to long-range force levels and to the question of "how to size a navy." Studies were done for various naval force levels: 500, 600, 700, and 800 ships. Both the Atlantic and Pacific Fleets required a balanced force of combatant ships, amphibious assault lift capabilities, support ships and appropriate aircraft. The 500-ship navy corresponded to retaining the then-current fleet size with a reduction to 40 SSBNs and 12 carriers. The 800-ship figure corresponded to the 1984 fiscal year force objective recommended by the Joint Chiefs of Staff, while the 600 and 700-ship fleets were intermediate alternatives. The Five Year Defense Plan, which had already been programmed, corresponded to a 588-ship fleet by fiscal year 1983 and, when extrapolated to fiscal year 1985, would be a 600-ship navy.

A summary of the conclusion which the navy staff reached in these studies is shown in the Table of Sea-Control Capabilities.[22] Five task groups would be stretched at the 500-ship level, but

> The programmed force level [600 ships] will enable control of the Northeast Pacific, Indian Ocean, the Atlantic below the GIUK Gap, and the Western Mediterranean. It enables the U.S. to contest control of the South Pacific and the Arabian Sea. A 700-

TABLE OF SEA-CONTROL CAPABILITIES

SYMBOLS: +   *U.S. and Allied forces are likely to prevail.*
            ¤   *Outcome is uncertain for both sides.*
            -    *Enemy forces are likely to prevail.*

NOMINAL ACTIVE FLEET SIZE (SHIPS)	500	600	700	800
CASE 1: [NATO–WARSAW PACT WAR]				
Norwegian Sea	¤	¤	-	+
Mid-Atlantic CV operations #	+	+	+	+*
Atlantic SLOC (U.S.-Europe) #	¤	-	+	+*
Western Mediterranean	-	+	+	+*
Eastern Mediterranean	¤	¤	-	+
No Soviet bases in Mid East	¤	+	+	+
U.S. wartime oil SLOC	¤	¤	-	+
Philippines–Japan/Korea SLOC	¤	¤	-	+
Northeast Pacific & Valdez SLOC	-	+	+	+
Northeast Pacific	¤	¤	¤	+
South Pacific	¤	-	+	+
CASE 2: [US/PRC WAR IN ASIA]				
Not studied				
CASE 3: [US/USSR WAR OUTSIDE NATO REGION]				
Western Mediterranean	+	+	+	+
Eastern Mediterranean	¤	¤	-	+
Arabian Sea	¤	-	+	+
CASE 4: [UNILATERAL MILITARY ACTION BY U.S.]				
Middle East/Korea	¤	¤	-	+
Elsewhere	+	+	+	+
CASE 5: [PEACETIME PRESENCE]				
Generally	¤	-	-	+
CASE 1 and 4:	¤	¤	¤	-

* Most vital.

We have the capability to gain ultimate control of the Atlantic below the GIUK Gap, but below the 700 and 800-ship levels, lack sufficient surface combatants and V/STOL Support Ships to provide adequate protection of convoys during the 1–2 months of conflict (prior to the attrition of Soviet submarines).

Source: Sea Control CPAM, Ser 96/S59368, 15 May 1975, p.17.

ship force would enable control of the above plus contest control of the Eastern Mediterranean and the Norwegian Sea. A 35 percent increase above the programmed force level would provide an 800-ship navy which would enable control of the above plus the Eastern Mediterranean, Northwest Pacific, and the Norwegian Sea.[23]

In examining the general issues, the Joint Chiefs had agreed that the planned force levels would be inadequate for the United States to engage in unilateral military action while at the same time be engaged in a NATO War with the Soviet Union.

Clearly, in the navy's view, existing force levels were inadequate in 1975 to perform the navy's mission; however, increased funding to support the force levels already suggested by the Five Year Defense Plan would meet the very basic requirements, though without flexibility.

Continuing this analysis over the period of his term as Chief of Naval Operations, Admiral Holloway focused on the 600-ship goal as a general objective. The Department of Defense reported to Congress in January 1977 that over the following 15 years it would need almost $90 billion more than the amount funded. With a force reaching 568 ships by 1985, increasing to 638 in 1990, the navy could maintain both sea control and presence, but in the Indian Ocean this could not be done simultaneously with the other theaters. In reaching this conclusion, the report stressed the basic issue in relating force level budget decisions to strategy:

> The size of a navy depends upon the wartime sea-control capabilities and power projection capacity it must possess, the forward deployment it must sustain in peacetime, and the forces needed to maintain an appropriate U.S.-Soviet naval balance.[24]

To the public, it seemed as though the navy were a service in crisis, fending off zealous advocates of systems analysis who were trying to tailor a fleet to fit a shrinking budget. Secretary of Defense Brown seemed to be trying to bring the huge defense budget under control by strengthening NATO's land and air forces through reduction of the navy's role and budget. The Assistant Secretary of Defense for Program Analysis and Evaluation, Russell Murray, was quoted as saying that DoD's short-term objective was to ensure that NATO would not be overwhelmed in the first few weeks of a *blitzkrieg* war, and he advised that the navy should be concerned with local contingencies outside the NATO area.[25]

At the same time, it appeared to the public that the navy was torn within by discordant parochialism between aviators, submariners, and surface ship officers. Some observers commented that the aviators dominated the navy, and because of their presumed devotion to carrier task force operations had not maintained a balanced outlook in judgments on shipbuilding programs.[26] Under these circumstances, it was not surprising for academics to join the chorus. In a review of B. Mitchell Simpson's 1977 book, *War, Strategy and Maritime Power,*[27] a collection of essays culled from the first 25 years of the *Naval War College Review,* the well-known defense analyst Edward N. Luttwak asked, "What is a navy in the absence of a strategy? It is, in effect, a priesthood." Without strategy to inform and guide naval officers, Luttwak argued, it is all merely ritual and routine. "The United States," Luttwak declared,

> unavoidably needs a positive maritime strategy, i.e., a coherent statement of its own role in the world with a consequent delineation of the maritime requirements of this role. (Maritime rather than merely naval, because to a large extent naval *force* is merely the protective framework for the use of oceans in all its aspects.) The source of the problem is no mystery: we have no maritime strategy because we have no national strategy. But this in turn is no excuse for the failure of the U.S. Navy as a corporate body to formulate a coherent strategy. It merely means that the maritime strategy must be defined in terms of a *presumptive* national strategy in the hope that the nation will indeed accept the logic of the former, even if it does not fully acknowledge the latter. But this most basic of tasks continues to be evaded.[28]

These public criticisms were shared by many within the navy. Similar ideas were the basis for work that was just then getting started.

During the late 1970s, several developments occurred which had an impact on the transition to widespread offensive thinking within the naval officer corps. Admiral James L. Holloway III's emphasis on developing carrier battle groups and surface action groups were concepts that became the operational basis upon which later strategic concepts were formed. In the area of strategic thinking, there were two important early developments. Though sharing some qualities, their origins were different. One was the "Sea Strike Strategy" project developed by Admiral Thomas B. Hayward as Commander in Chief, Pacific Fleet, in 1977–1978. The other was "Sea Plan 2000," which originated in The Secretariat in Washington.

Sea Plan 2000

With the inauguration of President Jimmy Carter in January 1977, W. Graham Claytor Jr. took office as Secretary of the Navy. In the following month, R. James Woolsey became the Under Secretary. Upon taking up their responsibilities, both these men found difficulty in accepting the naval portion of Presidential Review Memorandum–10 (PRM–10), which outlined the Carter administration's defense policy. In their view, PRM–10 reflected incoherence in structure and assumptions as well as disagreements about different approaches and different naval force levels to implement strategy. Claytor and Woolsey believed "that a naval force structure plan should be done that draws a clear distinction between capabilities and requirements, and which uses the one to build on the other; that takes into account the full range of strategies and missions served by naval force; and that highlights the force posture implications of key assumptions about foreign policy (e.g., Chinese-Soviet hostility, availability of Allies forces and bases), the durability of NATO's flanks, and other factors."[29]

Specifically, they wanted a new study that would show the strategies and missions that forces then available could fulfill, the role of naval forces in a NATO war, intervention (with and without the need to confront the Soviets), crisis management, and peacetime presence. They wanted the study to be structured in a way that would allow the President, Secretary of Defense, and other senior national security policy makers to make explicit choices about national policy and to relate their choices to the contributions that naval forces could make. Believing that this approach, focusing on naval forces, cut less across military department lines than other types of issues, Claytor asked that the Navy Secretariat be given responsibility for coordinating a new study.[30]

On 1 August 1977, the Deputy Secretary of Defense directed the navy to undertake a naval force planning study which was "to examine the most probable range of tasks for Navy and Marine Corps forces for the balance of this century, and how well we would be able to perform these tasks with forces sized on reasonable funding assumptions." In his letter covering the resulting paper, Secretary of the Navy Graham Claytor emphasized, "The Study linked policy objectives with warfighting capability,"[31] and that is the essence of strategy.

Based in Washington, D.C., the Sea Plan 2000 Study Group was directed by Francis J. West, Jr., from the Center for Advanced Research, Naval War College. The group members included ten naval officers and two Marine Corps officers with technical assistance provided by Presearch-Incorporated. The study was completed in March 1978 and forwarded immediately to Secretary of Defense Harold Brown by Navy Secretary Claytor. In his forwarding letter, Claytor stated that "while the study group admits the difficulty of predicting the outcomes of wars we have not fought, I believe the insights it contains are substantial, balanced, and will serve you well."[32] In particular, Claytor noted four insights in the study that impressed him as valuable:

- In the next 30 years, U.S. naval forces will be far more constrained in carrying out their work than they have been used to in the years since World War II. The rise of the Soviet Navy as well as Third World forces has created capable opponents.

- Surface ships will become increasingly survivable through AEGIS and other new active and passive antisurface missile defense and antisubmarine warfare systems (ASW), although action must be taken to counter a potential air threat in the 1990s.

- It is important to have naval forces that are flexible and in balance for a wide range of operations. There is great value in maintaining an offensive option on means short of nuclear exchange and of carrying the war to the Soviets.

- Naval forces permit the President to respond to crises flexibly and to the degree appropriate to our arms and policies.[33]

Looking back on Sea Plan 2000, one is impressed by its continuity with several strategic concepts used in the Maritime Strategy, particularly with its points on deterrence of a major war, exerting pressure on the Soviets, reinforcement of allies, and the perception of the U.S.-Soviet naval balance.

Sea Plan 2000 pointed out the main policy-related measures that the U.S. Navy supported:[34]

Policy-Related Measures of Naval Capabilities

Maintain Stability

- Forward deployments

- Perceptions of naval power

Contain Crises

- Capability to affect outcome ashore

- Superiority at sea versus Soviets

Deter Global War

- Protection of sea-lanes

- Reinforce allies

- Pressure upon the Soviets

- Hedges against uncertainties

In discussing these issues in detail, Sea Plan 2000 noted in particular that the possible tasks for naval forces were interrelated. An offensive posture for American forces draws Soviet resources away from threatening Western sea-lanes.[35] Thus, putting pressure upon the Soviets through the threat of offensive action seemed to be an attractive option which could have impact on the equilibrium of the worldwide power balance as well as in the more remote possibility of an actual, global war.[36]

As Sea Plan 2000 stated the issue:

In any major war, the destruction of the Soviet fleet and denial to the Soviets of access to any ocean is a basic objective. This requires the close coordination of surface, submarine and sea-based air assets in an aggressive naval campaign. Denying the Soviets access to the oceans provides the allies with post-hostility negotiation leverage. The ability to achieve this objective has a significant impact on the attainment of other important objectives, e.g., maintenance of important SLOCs [sea lines of communication] and support for allies.[37]

The possibility of doing this depended largely on the ability of the U.S. Navy to maintain superiority, and the authors of Sea Plan 2000 noted ruefully, "The forward strategy linking the U.S. to other continents requires use of the seas. While the perception that the Soviets could deny the U.S. control of the seas is particularly damaging, such perception is not warranted by the projected trends in technology. Whether it will be warranted by a steady reduction in the size of the American fleet and the amount of forward deployment remains to be seen."[38]

After reviewing the general strategic picture, Sea Plan 2000 went on to outline three alternative options for U.S. naval force levels into the 1990s. Using President Carter's decision that the overall resources for national security would require a yearly real growth of 3 percent, the plan focused on this level, providing for 535 active ships by fiscal year 1984. Looking on either side of this base, the Sea Plan 2000 study group analyzed an option of 1 percent growth providing for 439 ships, and 4 percent growth providing for 585 ships. The study group determined that the 3 percent growth rate would result in a future navy more sophisticated and somewhat larger than current forces, but which only "hovers at the threshold of naval capability across the spectrum of possible uses, given the risks associated with technical and tactical uncertainties." The 4 percent option, however, provided "a high degree of versatility in the form of a wider range of military and political action at a moderate increase in cost."[39]

Within the navy, Sea Plan 2000 was considered a sound foundation for structuring the size and capability of its forces.[40] Outside, however, it came under considerable criticism. In 1979, the U.S. General Accounting Office (GAO) undertook an evaluation of the navy's work, entitled in draft, *How Good is Navy Force Planning?* This report concentrated on Sea Plan 2000 and a study entitled "Assessment of the Sea-Based Air Platform Project," as well as the then incomplete study entitled "The Sea-Based Air Master Study Plan." Severely criticizing Sea Plan 2000, the GAO report pointed out that none of the three force level and funding options it examined could be achieved because they were based on known unrealistic funding assumptions and that it was overly optimistic and shortsighted in considering present day and future Soviet threats postulated by the Defense Intelligence Agency (DIA). Moreover, GAO concluded that the assumptions behind the study were questionable or unrealistic.[41] Quoting from a speech at the Naval War College by Edward R. Jayne, the Associate Director for National Security and

International Affairs in the Office of Management and Budget, the report went on, "only if the Navy, applying its own goals and expertise, sets more realistic priorities can we hope to see a fully coherent and balanced Navy program in the future."[42] Rather than assume the carrier to be the centerpiece of future forces, GAO concluded that the navy's missions should be prioritized and analyses should be made of alternative ways to fulfill its mission through land-based aircraft and surface ships armed with cruise missiles.[43]

In September 1979, GAO sent a copy of its draft report to the Secretary of Defense. Assistant Secretary of Defense Fred P. Wacker replied that DoD believed that the GAO report could seriously mislead Congress because "it does not recognize that force planning efficiency can be properly evaluated only in the context of the Planning, Programming, and Budgeting System (PPBS) and the total force development process."[44] Sea Plan 2000 was written in a relatively short time by an *ad hoc* group convened by the Secretary of the Navy "for the purpose of examining a special set of options,"[45] Wacker pointed out. As a result of this letter, the GAO retitled its report. Instead of "How Good is Navy Force Planning?" it was labeled "How Good are Recent Navy Studies Regarding Future Forces?"

Project Sea Strike

Project Sea Strike had its origin in the thinking of Admiral Hayward when he was Commander, U.S. Seventh Fleet, in 1976–1977. During that period, Hayward became aware that it was not until the three-star level that a senior officer was faced with having to make strategic decisions. As a ship's commanding officer, one did not have the necessary knowledge, and in most other positions one did not have the time to prepare oneself. This insight gave Hayward the determination to do all that he could to encourage strategic thinking. As Seventh Fleet Commander, Hayward was disturbed that general war planning in his fleet was Single Integrated Operation Plan (SIOP) oriented. The Soviet Navy did not seem to be a major concern, and there seemed to be equally little concern for the geopolitical factors in the world situation.[46]

In 1977, Hayward became Commander in Chief, Pacific Fleet. There, he found a planning situation similar to that in the Seventh Fleet, and he set about in earnest to alter it. He reviewed Pacific Fleet war plans, and found that those then in place required the swing of forces from the Pacific into the Atlantic to concentrate our forces in the European Theater within the framework of NATO collective security, specifically for the concept of flexible response called for in NATO's MC 14/3. As Hayward reviewed the international situation in 1977, he came to the conclusion that forces in the NATO area were no longer strong enough to deter the Soviets. With nuclear parity, moreover, it seemed to him that it was unlikely that MC 14/3 could be executed. As CINCPACFLT, Hayward wanted to rethink naval strategy for the Pacific and in order to do this effectively, he reorganized his staff, reviving the concepts of organization and style that Nimitz had employed as CINCPAC/CINCPOA in 1942–1945.[47] Captain James M. Patton and Captain William Cockell were the key figures whom Hayward brought to the staff to deal with strategy and war plans. In addition, he brought along his Seventh Fleet science advisor, Dr. Al Brandstein, who played a major role in the analysis that underlay work in this area. Together, they faced a difficult task in trying to reorient national policy from the office of a distant fleet commander, but Hayward set out in 1977 by establishing a continuing project which he called "Sea Strike." Never a published study, it was a briefing that Hayward used to try to influence policy makers and get across his ideas to planners. Only one copy of the briefing was made, and Hayward and Patton together gave it about a dozen times, including presentations to CINCPAC, the Joint Chiefs, the Secretary of Defense, State Department, and to National Security Advisor Zbigniew Brzezinski in the White House.[48] Patton gave the presentation by himself to a number of other, working-level groups.

Hayward's objectives in Sea Strike were twofold. First he wanted to place the Pacific Fleet within a global U.S. naval strategy as the most effective means of developing plans for use in the event of war with the USSR. Secondly, he was concerned with the condition of the Pacific Fleet and its preparation for war. At that time there were no offensive naval war plans, only defensive plans. Hayward believed that for the sake of flexibility, if for no other reason, a credible offensive plan should be available.

The first idea that Hayward chose to analyze was a plan for an offensive strike against Soviet bases on Kamchatka and in eastern Siberia. This was "the easier plan to get an arm around," Hayward recalled, "easier than exploring the Soviet-PRC situation, and the easiest to think about in an isolated sense."[49] Hayward's idea was to get the planning process started by looking at the more isolated case of Kamchatka, then to move on to more complicated issues. In his view, the next easiest area to look at was the Indian Ocean and what might happen in Southwest Asia.

Sea Strike was developed initially as a plan for the Pacific Fleet in the case of conventional war with the Soviet Union. The scenario was an early offensive action against Petropavlovsk, Vladivostok, and the Kuriles, using forces then currently available. One force from the east and one from the south were to form up in a battle group at a point 500 miles from Petropavlovsk. Then four carriers would conduct air strikes in two attack waves which would put about 100 strike aircraft over the target giving a 50 percent possibility of target destruction.[50]

Although nominally an alternative plan to utilize the Pacific Fleet's conventional forces, it was also a strategy to justify not swinging Pacific forces to the Atlantic as required by general war plans. Pacific Fleet planners showed, with the help of the Intelligence

Center, Pacific, that the Soviets had the air capability to move quickly 101,000 men with their equipment, from the Soviet Far East to the NATO front. By using Sea Strike as a threat to the Soviet Union, Pacific Fleet planners argued that U.S. naval forces in the Pacific could make a strategic difference by preventing the move of Soviet Forces to Europe. Moreover, the plan could support America's commitment as a Pacific power, influencing the Chinese to deploy forces in a way that would further tie down the Soviets from reinforcing the European front. In the same way, they argued that Sea Strike would also influence Japanese policy makers to continue allowing the United States to have base privileges, which would allow strikes on the Soviet Union, rather than having Japan remain neutral. Finally, Sea Strike would allow for the immediate offensive use of Pacific Fleet forces, simultaneously protecting Alaska and the West Coast, instead of placing those forces in a largely ineffective status for the 30 days required to make the transit to the European Theater.[51]

The analyses of these forward, offensive operations using current capabilities revealed some deficiencies in the Pacific Fleet that were surprising to many. Among other things, they showed that there were too few F-14 aircraft. This resulted in Hayward's order to move up, by one year, plans to convert the carrier *Ranger* for handling F-14s. The importance of the Phoenix missile, as shown in the analyses, led to increasing the carrier loading capacity from 72 to more than 100 missiles. Further analyses showed that the E-2 aircraft did not offer enough of a warning, even at a range of 250 miles detection, for the carrier to launch aircraft effectively and to intercept bomber raids. This led eventually to an agreement between the Navy and the Air Force for using E-3 AWACS to obtain greater standoff detection ranges for carrier battle groups. Among other things, the Sea Strike analyses pointed out difficulties in the defense of the Aleutians. It showed the weakness of the Aleutians for land-based air to support antiair warfare during the withdrawal phase after attacks against Kamchatka. Secondly, it brought vividly to light the fact that Soviet attack and occupation of the western Aleutians would put the U.S. mainland under the arc of Soviet long-range air attack. Finally, it showed problems in conflicting operational control by various commands in defending the Aleutians. This led to a long-term but still unsuccessful attempt to rationalize Aleutian defense plans and command relationships. Most importantly, Sea Strike laid the basis for a reconsideration in the war-fighting strategy for the Pacific Command, which was based on a policy of not swinging Pacific area assets to Europe in the event of a war with the Soviet Union. These changes reflected a change in the national strategy, worked up by the National Security Council and eventually approved by the President. The work done at Pacific Fleet Headquarters was very influential in moving the national strategy in the direction it took. In the process of discussion and reflection which took place, some knowledgeable observers criticized Sea Strike as unrealistic.

Others argued that the losses occasioned by early, offensive strikes in the Pacific would make it an unprofitable course of action. To these criticisms, Admiral Hayward replied that Sea Strike was not a campaign plan but an analytical tool with which one could analyze Pacific Fleet employment in different, novel ways and assess the pros and cons of offensive fleet action in varying circumstances. Those involved in the study learned many lessons, both positive and negative, from the study. The result was mentioned in Sea Plan 2000, based on an early formulation of the results, then later put into the Pacific Command Campaign Plan and eventually incorporated into the Maritime Strategy.[52]

Conclusion

Sea Strike and the parallel work on Sea Plan 2000 were key parts in the development of the navy's opposition to the Carter administration's defense policy, which called for greater emphasis on the Central Front in a NATO–Warsaw Pact war, but a more constrained role for naval forces. The main point in the navy's criticism was that the Central Front could not be isolated from the European flanks. As F. J. West reported after a meeting in the Defense Department in December 1977,

> We highlighted our differences with PRM-10, which has assumed in a NATO war that Norway took care of itself and that the Italian and the French [navies] secured the Mediterranean. By definition under those assumptions, one needs a smaller U.S. Navy. I indicated, however, that also by definition such a U.S. plan would sound the death knell for NATO, insuring Italy and Norway would make other arrangements and converting the central front into a bilateral US/FRG treaty. Consequently, we showed a series of options for employing U.S. naval forces on the flanks as well as on the SLOC and in the Western Pacific.[53]

These strategic ideas clearly expressed the general direction in which naval thinking proceeded in the next decade.

In the mid-1970s, leaders such as Secretary of the Navy W. Graham Claytor, Jr., Under Secretary James Woolsey and Admiral James L. Holloway had clearly established a general consensus within the navy's Washington leadership that the service should strive for superiority at sea against the Soviets and, when examining the variety of possible wartime operations against the Soviet Navy, think in terms of forward, offensive operations as the most effective means to employ the navy to achieve the nation's broad defense policies. In promoting this view, the navy was reasserting a traditional view of its strategic role that not only is reflected in the strategic ideas that lay behind the establishment of NATO in the late 1940s, but also the long tradition of naval thinking embodied in the classical works of Alfred Thayer Mahan and Sir Julian Corbett. In the 1950s and 1960s, the overriding national emphasis of a defense strategy based on nuclear weapons had left doubt that these traditional ideas had any relevance at all in the nuclear age. On reflection, however, the Vietnam war, Afghanistan, and other events demonstrated that conventional weapons were not irrelevant to the nuclear age but must be reconsidered within the context of a broader spectrum of warfare. This change in perception created the need to adapt and refine older ideas for new conditions. While the more traditional ideas had never disappeared from the navy, the changing perception about the relevance of conventional weapons created a situation in which the full range of naval strategic thought could now be utilized. The seeds of development for further naval strategic thinking in the mid-1980s were sewn in the 1970s as the United States came to grips with the post–Vietnam war period and with the realities of political and military factors in international affairs. This changing ambience in the 1970s set the stage for a wide revival of strategic thinking within the naval officer corps.

CHAPTER TWO

Thinking About the Soviet Navy, 1967–1981

Any serious thinking about strategy must necessarily deal with the effect that the use of one's own forces has on an opponent. Moreover, how an enemy uses his forces is a critical factor in any strategic evaluation. Thus, when thinking about how one might employ one's own forces for achieving broad future goals in a war, one must also assess the probability of how an enemy might act or react, as well as examine everything that an enemy can do that may materially influence one's own courses of action.

From the early 1960s, when the growth of Soviet naval power became evident, the predominant view in America was that the Soviets were building a naval force with many capabilities similar to the United States Navy. Most importantly, the existence of a blue-water Soviet Navy seemed to emphasize, in American minds, the capability for peacetime power projection, the facility for wartime attack on U.S. and Western naval forces and sea lines of communication, as well as the ability to launch strategic nuclear strikes from the sea. Increasingly, Americans worried about the Soviet Navy as a sea-denial force that could deprive the West of the free use of the sea, thereby creating political, economic, and military disaster. In short, Americans tended to view the new Soviet naval capabilities in terms of mirror-imaging and refighting World War II.

The public discussion of the issue in Congress and the press as well as in the statements of senior naval officers stressed this interpretation. Simultaneously, however, there began to develop slowly an interpretation that attempted to move away from an ethnocentric view of the Soviets in American terms and rather toward an interpretation in Soviet terms on the basis of the Soviet Union's values and the views, aims, and objectives of its leaders. The first widely read book in America on this subject was Robert W. Herrick's *Soviet Naval Strategy: Fifty Years of Theory and Practice,* published by the U.S. Naval Institute in 1968. Herrick wrote much of the book while serving as staff intelligence officer at the Naval War College in 1963–1964, basing it on his own detailed reading of Soviet literature and his nearly 20 years of experience as an intelligence specialist in Soviet affairs. Herrick concluded that Soviet naval strategy, like Tsarist Russian naval strategy before it, was essentially defensive. This view was so greatly at variance with the commonly held official viewpoint, that the publisher added a preface to the volume and enclosed a printed bookmark which drew attention to this fact, calling for comments and articles expressing alternative views for publication in the U.S. Naval Institute's *Proceedings*.

It took a rather long time for a different attitude and interpretation to prevail within the U.S. Navy. This change did occur, however, at about the same time that the Maritime Strategy was being formulated in the late 1970s and early 1980s. The process by which the U.S. Navy changed its views can be seen most clearly in two places: on one hand in the work of the Center for Naval Analyses in the period 1967–1981, and on the other, within the Naval intelligence community.

The Work of the Center for Naval Analyses, 1967–1981

The conclusions that The Center for Naval Analyses (CNA) reached in its studies of Soviet naval strategy have often been at the center of the debate over Soviet intentions. Using a great deal of unclassified evidence, the bulk of which came from Soviet doctrinal writings supported by interpretations of Soviet exercises, deployments, and general capabilities, CNA developed a broad interpretation. It emphasized the primarily defensive role of the Soviet Navy in protecting its SSBNs as the Soviet Union's (USSR) reserve of strategic nuclear weapons. This conclusion was a controversial one which has not always sat easily with the intelligence community, but it is one which lies at the basis of The Maritime Strategy.[1]

As early as 1968, Robert Weinland pointed out that the Soviets might feel that their submarine nuclear deterrent would be threatened by a U.S. campaign to defend its sea lines of communication, even if the United States did not intend to attack the Soviet SSBN force. If the Soviet SSBNs were in the same immediate area as that used for Western sea lines of communication, the Soviet SSBNs ran the risk of becoming accidental or intentional victims of the conflict. If they withdrew to port or other safe areas, they might well compromise their own invulnerability and strike capability.[2]

In mid-1973, Bradford Dismukes cited evidence that the Soviets were increasingly concerned about the security of their SSBN force, pointing out that maintenance of SSBNs on station would be more important than attacking Western sea lines of communication. The linkage in the strategic situation between Western defense of its sea lines and Soviet SSBN security was the result of geographical and technological factors that are outside the immediate control of either side. Asking for a basic change in U.S. thinking, Dismukes wrote in 1973, "At the least, we should include pro- and anti-SSBN scenarios in our general purpose force planning or run the risk of structuring a force which might be ill-suited to the most important war-fighting tasks it may be called on to carry out."[3]

In 1972–1973, a series of eleven articles were published in *The Soviet Navy Journal* under the name of the navy's commander in chief, Admiral Sergei Gorshkov. The article bore the characteristic earmarks of new naval doctrine. CNA's work in analyzing these articles drew praise from the Director of Naval Intelligence, Rear Admiral E. F. Rectanus, U.S. Navy, and at the same time a request for further assistance from CNA.[4]

The result of Rectanus's request was a CNA draft to support preparation of the navy's input to a new National Intelligence Estimate on the Soviet Union (NIE-11-15-75). Prepared by members of the Institute for Naval Studies, comprised of Robert G. Weinland, James M. McConnell, and Bradford Dismukes, the CNA draft was a broad analysis that pointed out the significant changes in Soviet thinking, including "the apparent adoption of a strategic 'fleet in being' concept for at least a portion of their SSBN force."[5]

The unclassified Gorshkov series was an important source that seemed to reveal much about Soviet Naval thinking, but it was not easy to interpret. James M. McConnell, in a study prepared for the Office of the Chief of Naval Operations (OP-96) and the Office of Naval Research, listed what he considered to be the main points in what he called "Gorshkov's doctrine of coercive naval diplomacy."[6]

- The USSR is not only a formidable continental power but also a "mighty sea power."

- The importance of combat at sea in the "overall course of war" has grown, although Gorshkov avoids references to the role of the navy in "decisively defeating" the enemy.

- In war, navies are a powerful means of achieving the "political goals" for the armed struggle.

- The importance of fleets-in-being at the close of wars to influence the peace negotiations and achieve political goals is repeatedly emphasized through historical examples.

Gorshkov specifically endorses Jellicoe's strategy of holding back his forces at the battle of Jutland in World War I, thereby reversing previous Soviet naval historiography in its condemnation of the British Admiralty's "politico-strategic" rather than "military-strategic" approach to war, its "fleet-in-being" method, its "doctrine of conserving forces," and consequent reluctance to risk the main forces of the fleet in a "decisive clash" to achieve "complete victory," preferring instead to retain them "as an important factor at the moment of concluding peace and also for the postwar rivalry with erstwhile allies."

In World War II, although "military-geographic" conditions facilitated the British blockade, the Germans were successful, through diversion, in scattering British ASW forces throughout the Atlantic, creating a favorable situation for German naval operations "in the coastal waters of northern Europe."

Due, apparently, mainly to "military-geographic" conditions, Russian requirements for naval forces have differed from those of the West.

Although the USSR gives priority to submarines, they require air and surface support to ensure combat stability.

ASW is not very cost-effective against modern nuclear submarines, especially if the latter are supported by aviation and surface ships.

SSBNs are "more effective in deterrence" than land-based launch facilities, because of their "great survivability." This claim, made for the first time, occurs in a passage in which Gorshkov, if we are to take him literally, is treating "deterrence" as a "role in modern war." Elsewhere, when the discussion turns, explicitly or contextually, to deterrence "in peacetime," Gorshkov follows the traditional formula of coupling the Strategic Rocket Troops and the navy, in that order, as the main factors in demonstrating resolve.

The very first duty of the navy is to maintain a high state of "readiness" to carry out the mission of "defending" the USSR against possible attacks from the sea.

This "defense" mission is the "main task" for the navy, with the implication that "deterrence" and offsetting politico-military pressure is the main component of "defense."

Navies fulfill the important role of one of the instruments of state policy in "peacetime," including the protection of its "state interests" in the seas and oceans.

Tasks associated with protecting these state interests are "especially important" because of the many "local wars" that imperialism "leave behind in the wake of its policy."

Because of the "truly inexhaustible wealth" of the seas, they have become objects of contending "state interest"; and navies "cannot take a back seat in this struggle."

In addition to the Gorshkov series, note was also taken of points made by other Soviet naval specialists:

SSBNs specifically (and not just "submarines") are incapable of realizing their full potential "without appropriate support from their forces."

When the long-range Trident comes into operation in the U.S. Navy, SSBNs will be positioned in U.S. coastal waters, permitting the allocation of a "new function" to the main U.S. ASW forces—"guarding the strategic missile forces."[7]

By the end of 1974, the most controversial conclusion arising from analysis of the Gorshkov series, along with other evidence, concerned Soviet plans for the use of their SSBN force during a crisis. Everyone involved with the analysis of this problem agreed that it was a matter of inference from defective or presumptive evidence. The points could not be found explicitly in Gorshkov's writings, but the analysts made interpretations from what they saw as "latent content." At CNA, analysts believed that the Soviets would elect to use their *Kiev*-class ship with its capacity for aircraft operations and to employ her with other general purpose forces to protect their SSBNs. This was a centrally important task because the Soviets intended to withhold their submarine-launched ballistic missile (SLBM) force during the conventional stage of a war and during initial nuclear strikes in order to provide either a second strike capability or to retain a bargaining chip during negotiations.

Elaborating on this point, CNA analysts concluded in a draft "Study of Grand Soviet Maritime Strategy" being prepared for Commander N. V. Smith of OP-60N:

> It is likely that the Soviets intend to allocate some general purpose forces to the protection of SSBNs during the opening stages of a NATO–Warsaw Pact war. This priority would remain relatively high even if the war became prolonged. Only in the event of a clearly non-escalatory situation would pro-SSBN forces be reassigned to alternative missions.[8]

CNA's conclusions were quite different from those made at that time in the classified intelligence literature. While OP-60N endorsed the CNA conclusion, they were obliged to add qualifying language such as "this is an area about which we know little,"[9] anticipating intelligence community objections.

Continuing this work in the following years, CNA analyst James M. McConnell made a crucial contribution in 1977 in a draft, first chapter of *Soviet Naval Diplomacy,* which corroborated earlier interpretations of Soviet intentions to withhold their SLBMs. Developing evidence that the Soviet Union's SSBNs were under the direct control of the highest political leaders, and those forces would be used mainly in later periods of a war, McConnell wrote, "Wars might be won by other branches of the armed forces, Gorshkov seems to be saying, but surrenders and armistices are arranged from the sea; and beyond that, navies have a value in influencing the course of actual peacemaking."[10]

In an October 1977 contribution to James L. George's volume, *Problems of Sea Power as We Approach the Twenty-First Century,* McConnell went further and suggested that Soviet SSBNs would operate in defended, local sanctuaries in home waters, such as the Barents Sea for the Northern Fleet and the Sea of Okhotsk for the Pacific Ocean Fleet. These sanctuaries would be heavily guarded by mines and fixed underwater acoustic surveillance systems with the air defense and introspective cover for submarines, surface ships, and aircraft engaged in barrier operation.[11]

Looking to what the Soviets might do in a future war, McConnell wrote:

> I would not expect substantial forward deployments of platforms during the conventional phase of the war. Leaving aside escalation sensitivity, the counter-ASW environment would not be favorable and—given a perceived withholding strategy for the United States Navy to prosecute strategic ASW immediately upon entering the nuclear phase—these factors may explain Admiral Gorshkov's insistence that sea control is necessary for strategic defense as well as strategic offense.[12]

Throughout the late 1970s, CNA analysts expressed growing concern that U.S. Navy plans were giving insufficient attention to the implications of Soviet adoption of a withholding strategy for their SLBM force and the assignment of their general purpose navy to a protective mission for their SSBN force.[13] In March 1980, Bradford Dismukes reported the results of an initial investigation on the war termination mission of the U.S. Navy. This new topic arose from an attempt to assess the implication of the Soviet withholding strategy. In a briefing that reflected seminal ideas by James McConnell, Dismukes declared that "our nation's strategies require adjustment in reaction to a fundamental change that has occurred in maritime affairs."[14] The change that Dismukes saw was the emphasis that the Soviet Union put on the positive use of the sea for operating a strategic reserve of SSBNs and where security, in turn, was guaranteed by general purpose, Soviet naval forces. "If the U.S. Navy is to carry out its primary functions in deterrence, escalation control, and war fighting," Dismukes said, "it must attack Soviet strategy as effectively as Soviet weapons."[15] Dismukes suggested three areas that needed changes in the U.S. Navy. First, the further development of the U.S. Navy's capabilities to fight a sea-control campaign with conventional weapons in the context of a campaign involving all our forces against the Soviet nuclear-reserve SSBNs. Secondly, the U.S. Navy needed long-range, stand-off ASW weapons that would effectively enhance, in Soviet areas, the deterrent effect of the U.S. Navy's general purpose forces. Thirdly, the U.S. Navy must reevaluate its doctrines to take account of the Soviet nuclear reserve.

"What we're dealing with here is the capacity to deprive our opponent of his perceived requirement to answer last in the war," Dismukes said. While careful to point out that this strategy was not without risk, it might still be critical to have the option to use it if Soviet ground forces occupy Europe. A secure Soviet strategic reserve would ensure their dominance, but a threatened or insecure reserve would put them in a weaker position.[16]

Up until early 1981, CNA continued its role in the interpretation of Soviet intentions and its follow-on work in developing a naval strategy for the United States that could be used to attack Soviet strategy. In March 1981, as a part of a planned joint Naval War

College–CNA investigation, CNA prepared an initial estimate of the Soviets' probable response to a U.S. campaign against their SSBN reserve.[17] At this time, however, the Office of Naval Intelligence and the Office of the Chief of Naval Operations began to be concerned that for CNA to participate further, its analysts would begin handling intelligence material that could not be released to private contractors and analysts. Several intelligence collection efforts had begun to pay off, and because of the sensitivity of the sources, new classifications of "sensitive compartmented information" (SCI) were created; this information would be withheld in the future, available only to a small group of intelligence analysts and senior flag officers, not CNA or the navy at large.

There had always been a tension between CNA and the Office of Naval Intelligence (ONI) over differing interpretations, but this had often been regarded as a healthy and constructive difference of viewpoint. CNA analysts regretted that an exchange of views could no longer take place on the same terms, but CNA analysts Dismukes and McConnell continued their work after 1981 by assessing Soviet strategic responses to an anti-SSBN campaign. Some of this later work was commissioned by OpNav and ONI, but was not based on compartmented information. From 1981, the Office of Naval Intelligence carried out its own assessments based on this information dealing with Soviet naval force employment plans.[18]

The Development of Thinking within the Intelligence Community

In the mid-1970s, the naval intelligence community felt secure in its view of the Soviet Navy.[19] The prevailing wisdom explained the continuing Soviet naval buildup in terms of threats to Western sea lines of communication. Soviet exercises such as *OKEAN 1970* and *OKEAN 1975* seemed to emphasize the correctness of the interpretation that the Soviets thought primarily in terms of naval presence and in cutting Western sea lines. From this, American naval officers drew the conclusion that if war with the Soviet Union came, it would bring with it a battle of the North Atlantic and Northwest Pacific sea-lanes. By 1977–1979 however, the points that CNA was making paralleled evidence that the Intelligence community had already noticed suggesting that the Soviets did not seem to have made the typical preparation one would expect for a war on Western sea-lanes, in terms of their command and control arrangements, standby reserves, etc. Most importantly, the publication of the revised 1976 edition of Gorshkov's *Sea Power of the State* suggested clearly that the Soviets had a different set of priorities.[20]

In May 1977, CNA submitted to ONI a draft of its study by James M. McConnell, *Soviet Naval Diplomacy,* requesting that ONI review it and approve it for publication in an unclassified form. The main focus of the work was on Soviet peacetime, power projection, but chapter 1 was an essay dealing with Soviet naval wartime strategy and force employment concepts which did not agree with the official navy position on how the

Soviets would rationally employ their navy. In particular, the chapter discussed the Soviet concept of withholding SSBNs as a strategic reserve force in protected bastions. McConnell's work was based on an analysis of Soviet military and academic writings which were unfamiliar to the naval officers in the Estimates Branch of ONI.[21]

In response to this new material from CNA, ONI put together a special group of officers to evaluate McConnell's chapter. The group that was selected to do this had previously been given the task of analyzing the Gorshkov book, and consisted of ONI analyst Ted Neely, Commander Stephen Kime, and Captain William H. J. Manthorpe, Jr. Since the idea was new to them, they undertook the task of locating and reading all the recurrences that McConnell had used. This opened up an entirely new body of literature that had been previously little known and unexploited by naval intelligence. However, in the process of this investigation, the ONI group came to the conclusion that McConnell's work showed a pattern of misquotes, exaggerations, and unwarranted interpretations. Therefore, the group recommended to the Director of Naval Intelligence that the chapter containing McConnell's analysis on the Soviet concept of withholding SSBNs be deleted prior to ONI approval for publication. In 1979, discussions between CNA and ONI on this subject resulted in a much abbreviated chapter 1, without any reference to this matter. In this revised form, the McConnell study was published in 1977, but the substance of his ideas on the SSBN withholding strategy did not appear in an unclassified form until much later with McConnell's essay in James L. George's volume, *Problems of Sea Power as We Approach the Twenty-First Century.*[22]

McConnell had succeeded in introducing naval intelligence officers to the material they should be studying, but at the same time, the reception that his conclusions received had sowed the seeds of caution and disbelief for officials in dealing with the work of CNA. However, in the long run, McConnell's conclusions were born out by later evidence. The main problem at the heart of the issue was one of analysis. In retrospect, officers came to the conclusion that McConnell and others at CNA were doing their analysis and describing Soviet strategic plans on the basis of the literature of Soviet military science. This was academic and theoretical work designed to examine potential changes in future strategy and doctrine. It was not yet accepted or in use, but might possibly be an indication of a future direction or emphasis in those areas. While CNA was examining this theoretical literature, officers in naval intelligence were doing their analysis and description of Soviet strategy and fleet employment plans on the basis of observed Soviet fleet exercises. In contrast to the theoretical writings that CNA was examining, the exercises reflected past and current strategy, not future strategy. Reflecting on this dilemma for analysts of Soviet strategy, Captain W. H. J. Manthorpe, Jr., suggested that those who would try to predict whether the changes suggested by theory will actually occur are as likely to be wrong as right, since the transformation of military science into doctrine is as much a function of party and bureaucratic internal politics in the USSR as other factors. However, those who wait for the hard evidence from fleet exercises that strategy has actually changed are likely to be the last to recognize that the change has taken place. "The moral is," Manthorpe wrote, "if you want to be early you may be wrong, but if you want to be right you'll surely be late in recognizing changes to Soviet strategy."[23]

In the late 1970s, the best tentative conclusion that could be reached was that McConnell's ideas could well be right, but that actual practice did not confirm that any such change had taken place. Neither side in the debate had solid evidence to confirm their views on the actual course that Soviet strategy would follow, but as a result of the debate, each side took increasingly hard stands in the face of an opposing interpretation. The first good evidence that Soviet naval strategy had actually changed was the absence of a worldwide OKEAN exercise in 1980, similar to the ones that had occurred in 1970 and 1975; at the same time, several intelligence collection efforts paid off and sources were beginning to provide insight into Soviet naval force employment plans. At first, this data and the interpretation of it was incomplete and tentative, but during the latter half of 1980 and early 1981, a clear picture began to emerge through the compartmented information being used by ONI analysts. These analysts clearly appreciated the significance of the SSBN withholding strategy on the basis of the new evidence and saw its implications for American naval strategy.[24]

Meanwhile, the Director of Naval Intelligence, Rear Admiral Sumner Shapiro, decided that something should be done to resolve a second issue: the dichotomy between the apparent increase in Soviet naval deployment to challenge the U.S. Navy in peacetime and the suggestion that, in wartime, the Soviet Navy would be employed to defend Soviet SSBN bastions close to home waters. This raised the question as to whether the same Soviet forces could fulfill both roles without being placed in a disadvantageous position in the event of war, whether the Soviet Navy would expand its general purpose forces in order to carry out this dual role, or whether this dual role would limit Soviet peacetime deployment in order to be ready in the event of war. At the suggestion of Captain Thomas A. Brooks, Rear Admiral Shapiro convened the first of three annual summer symposia to discuss this issue. The first symposium met at the Naval Academy in Annapolis. The participants included among others, ONI analysts, CNA analysts, academic experts and representatives of the Central Intelligence Agency (CIA) and Defense Intelligence Agency. The discussions were held at the secret classification level, and the whole range of views about future Soviet navy employment were presented and discussed, while the conference was moderated by Captain Stephen Kime and summarized by Captain William Manthorpe.[25]

The consensus of the conference was that the Soviets planned to retain their general purpose forces close to home waters in wartime in order to defend the homeland as well as to protect the SSBN force. Because of this, the peacetime employment of Soviet general purpose forces would probably not increase significantly in the future. These conclusions were ones that would not be widely applauded within the U.S. Navy. The conclusions implied that there would be a lessened Soviet peacetime presence that needed to be matched by Soviet forces and that in wartime, there would be a lessened threat to Western sea lines of communication, the protection of which was the principal mission for the navy envisaged by the Carter administration.[26]

By the winter of 1980–1981, the available intelligence began to present a picture that confirmed these general conclusions. One could begin to see signs that the concept was in the early stages of introduction into the fleet as the strategy for the future. It showed clearly that the new pattern involved SSBN bastions in northern waters protected by the bulk of Soviet general purpose forces, and these concepts were being developed and tested in war games and in exercises. The dissemination of this compartmented intelligence was made on a very restricted basis, piece by piece as it arrived. It was restricted to senior flag officers, in particular, Rear Admiral Sumner Shapiro, the Director of Naval Intelligence; Admiral Thomas Hayward, the Chief of Naval Operations, and the Advanced Technology Panel (ATP), consisting of Admiral James Watkins, the Vice Chief of Naval Operations; Rear Admiral Kinnard McKee, the Director of the Office of Naval Warfare (OP-095); Rear Admiral Carlisle Trost, Director Navy Program Planning (OP-090); Vice Admiral Nils Thunman, the Deputy Chief of Naval Operations for Submarine Warfare (OP-02); and the Director of the Office of Research, Development, Test and Evaluation (OP-098). Also privy to this information was Captain William A. Cockell, Executive Assistant to Admiral Hayward. Cockell quickly recognized the implications of this intelligence for U.S. strategy and, with Captain Thomas A. Brooks, an intelligence specialist, drafted a memorandum for Admiral Hayward's signature directing the Office of Naval Intelligence to establish an organization for the continuing study of Soviet doctrine and strategy to complement the traditional ONI focus on equipment and capabilities. Captain Cockell was the catalyst within the organization that got the bureaucratic system moving to accommodate the new direction in intelligence analysis. His initiative was sustained by Rear Admiral Sumner Shapiro and his deputy Director of Naval Intelligence, Rear Admiral John Butts, through the creation of a new branch within the Office of Naval Intelligence, OP-009J, headed by Richard Haver with the assistance of Theodore Neely and Commander Michael Kramer. Paralleling this initiative, Rear Admiral Kinnard McKee saw that the new intelligence also had implications for the warfare capabilities of the U.S. Navy. In order to monitor these developments,

McKee created within OP-95 a special group, first called Team C, and later Team Z, for this purpose.[27]

During the winter of 1980–1981, ONI analysis of the new issues moved into high gear. Rear Admiral Shapiro clearly recognized that the analysis of Soviet intentions was an area that had been neglected and that the issue should be worked how the United States could learn to fight the Soviets most effectively. The focus of the new analytical effort was first directed by Captain Thomas A. Brooks, commanding officer of the newly established Naval Fleet Operational Intelligence Office at Fort Meade, and then shifted to the Pentagon under the direction of Richard Haver in OP-009J. By the spring of 1981, the initial ONI analysis had been completed, and by summer the first major presentations of the analysis and conclusions were made. As a result of this, Haver prepared a memorandum for Vice Admiral McKee to forward to the Chief of Naval Operations recommending new considerations for countering Soviet strategy. Shortly thereafter, in August 1981, Captain Brooks briefed the new analysis of Soviet strategy and force employment concepts to the Chief of Naval Operations and the Fleet Commanders in Chief at their conference in Annapolis. This briefing marked a critical turning point in the development of the analysis. After listening to the briefing, Admiral Hayward found the concepts of Soviet strategy so completely different that he expressed disbelief that the Soviets could possibly operate their navy in such a manner. Several of the other four-star officers, including Admiral Bobby Inman, Deputy Director of the CIA, shared Hayward's view and questioned the validity of the analysis. The most knowledgeable officers present, Vice Admiral McKee and Admiral James Watkins, previously the Vice Chief, but then the Commander in Chief, Pacific Fleet, did not speak up to defend the ONI analysis.[28]

On the day after the Fleet CINCs' conference, Rear Admiral Shapiro called in Haver, Manthorpe, and Brooks to assess the setback to their work and to discuss what to do about it. From these conversations, it was decided that the best arrangement would be to use Captain William Studeman, an intelligence specialist who had just become the executive assistant to the new Vice Chief, Admiral William N. Small, and to keep him fully informed. Small, through this connection, quickly saw the implications of the new intelligence and revitalized the largely dormant mechanism of the Advanced Technology Panel as the means of reviewing intelligence and endorsing analysis of it, then bringing it to the direct attention of the CNO. With this, a major effort began within the navy staff to educate key officers in the new appreciation of Soviet strategy. This effort took several forms. As initially planned between the fall of 1981 and spring of 1982, the Advanced Technology Panel was fully briefed on the evidence for change in the Soviet concept of naval force employment. Then Admiral Small, as senior member, was able to report to Admiral Hayward that the ATP had endorsed the ONI analysis and began to move forward in examining the de elopment of a U.S. "anti-SSBN strategy."[29]

In other areas, the intelligence analysis began to be worked into broader staff documents. For example, in the Navy Net Assessment, which had been prepared in the summer and fall and approved in December 1981, Captain Manthorpe had prepared a section which read:

> The principal additional role gained by the Soviet Navy . . . has been the responsibility for protecting submarine strategic strike forces while war proceeds at less than nuclear level or while those forces are being withheld from a limited nuclear exchange as a second strike force.[30]

At the same time, ONI set out to get the intelligence community to produce a National Intelligence estimate which would endorse the ONI analysis of Soviet force employment concepts. In November 1981, the Intelligence community completed an interagency Intelligence memorandum on "SOVIET INTENTIONS AND CAPABILITIES FOR INTERDICTING SEA LINES OF COMMUNICATION IN A WAR WITH NATO." This memorandum expressed the general agreement of Intelligence analysts that Soviet military planners regarded the wartime interdiction of NATO sea lines of communication as a secondary mission. According to the memorandum, a few submarines would be employed in attacking commerce in the North Atlantic in the opening stage of a NATO–Warsaw Pact war, but the majority of naval forces would be deployed close to the USSR to defend its SSBN force and to protect the homeland from NATO's nuclear-armed naval strike force.[31] Following on from this, Captain James Eglin and Mr. Charles Summerall of ONI were given the task of making the navy contribution to the National Intelligence Estimate. The estimate itself was drafted by Mr. Gene Sullivan of the Central Intelligence Agency and was ready for review in its first draft by March 1982. It was published in an SCI version in the fall of 1982, which was followed by a wider distribution at a lower classification. Paralleling these efforts, Rich Haver from ONI began a series of briefings to influential people in the Navy Department. Haver became, as Rear Admiral Thomas Brooks recalled, "the Saint Paul of the movement, going forth among the Gentiles (read unrestricted line) and preaching the gospel. The conversion rate was astounding."[32]

By December 1981, The Advanced Technology Panel had fully developed an interpretation of Soviet intentions, which cast serious doubts on the conventional U.S. Strategy based on Soviet attack of Western sea lines of communication. The new interpretation stressed the importance of the United States being able to defeat the mission of the Soviet Navy. Originally characterized as "anti-SSBN operations," Admiral Small broadened this definition so that the issue could be seen in terms of vital Soviet interests at sea as they used their general purpose navy to protect their SSBNs, and connecting this with the strategic situation in the key flank areas, the Norwegian Sea, and the eastern Mediterranean.[33] Over the next two years, between 1982–1984, the Vice Chief and the ATP focused their efforts on the creation of an "anti-SSBN" strategy both in terms of deterrence and war avoidance, and for war fighting. This work was based on continuing intelligence analysis and was supported by a number of other efforts. Admiral Small devoted much of his own time to assessing the pros and cons of the "anti-SSBN strategy." In connection with Small's personal interest, Vice Admiral Carlisle Trost commissioned a study from the Center for Naval Analyses entitled "Assessing Soviet responses [to an anti-SSBN campaign]." The study was directed by Rear Admiral W. J. Holland, director of the Strategic and Theater Nuclear Warfare Division (OP-65), and his deputy, Captain Linton Brooks, assisted by Richard Haver and Captain Manthorpe. Using the basic work of this study, Small, Holland, and Brooks held weekly meetings to continue to develop the strategy.[34]

The final step in the process of selling the new analysis of Soviet strategy was a series of war games, the most important of which were those sponsored by the ATP to assess various aspects of the "anti-SSBN strategy." Unlike some war games that are played, this was a "no holds barred, true all-source war game with the highest level of participation."[35] In April 1982, this dealt with anti-SSBN concepts; in October 1982 with anti-SSBN and SSN deployment concepts; and in February 1983 with anti-SSBN war termination concepts. During these games, many useful insights were obtained for the use of submarines that were directly used in the strategy. Another aspect of the games touched on the utilization of aircraft carriers. In this, these games found that the most significant utilization of the aircraft carrier was as a "tactical nuclear reserve" to tie down significant numbers of Soviet air assets while remaining beyond their effective reach just below the Greenland-Iceland-United Kingdom gap, until that point in a war when it became necessary to negotiate with the Soviet Union whether the war could be terminated or would escalate to a nuclear war. In this sense, the carriers became a nuclear bargaining chip. In the formulation of the strategy, however, the role of the carriers was overlooked, while most of the effort was concentrated on the submarine campaign.[36] Through this kind of tabletop war gaming with the participation of senior flag officers in positions of responsibility, the concepts behind the strategy and the relationship of intelligence analysis to strategy were clearly brought out and developed and integrated into other aspects of naval planning.

Following the April 1982 war game, Secretary of the Navy John F. Lehman became aware of this work while the debate was in progress over the desirability of a strategy against SSBNs. The idea was compatible with the forward strategy air strikes, the criticality of Japan, the employment of the Tomahawk missiles, Marine Corps thinking, and other considerations, but the skepticism of some made it clear that an anti-SSBN campaign could only be one of the options available for the navy, not its principal focus.[37]

As the process of strategy development continued, the security sensitivity of the associated intelligence information created some difficulty in handling, but Admiral James Watkins, the Chief of Naval Operations from June 1982 to June 1986, ordered that each major fleet staff set aside a cell cleared to know what was going on and to reflect as much as possible on this new thinking. It took time to do this, and for a period, certain commanders and certain staffs had the information while others did not. Not surprisingly, there were some imbalances. Vice Admiral Nils Thunman, as Deputy CNO for Submarine Warfare (OP-02) and a member of the ATP, moved quickly to set up the first cell on the staff of the Commander, Submarine Force, Atlantic. This, however, was in advance of the cell established on the staff of the Commander in Chief, Atlantic.

In July 1982, Captain Thomas A. Brooks was assigned to the staff of Admiral Harry Train, Commander in Chief, Atlantic. The new cell was activated within several months, but not fully manned until well into the first year of Admiral Wesley McDonald's tenure as CINCLANT. With the assistance of this cell, McDonald began to utilize the new intelligence data in flag level conferences and through special briefings. Similar cells were established in other fleet areas, at later dates. In the Atlantic Fleet, the initiation of an intelligence cell on the staff of Commander, Submarine Force, Atlantic, marked the beginning of reevaluation and rewriting of the existing war plans. Not surprisingly, this began with the submarine force, but shortly became widespread throughout the fleet. It quickly worked into the thinking of the navy in general through the various threads of changing personnel assignments among the key individuals involved, the discussions among the Fleet commanders in their annual strategy conferences, war games, and the discussions involved in the work of the CNO's Strategic Studies Group (SSG) based at the Naval War College.[38] In these ways, the new insights and analyses about Soviet naval force employment were spread throughout the navy and became a key element in strategic analysis.

CHAPTER THREE

From the CNO's Strategic Concepts to the Work of the SSG, 1978–1986

The appointment of Admiral Thomas B. Hayward as the 21st Chief of Naval Operations in June 1978 marks an important stage in the transition of thinking within the naval officer corps. Not only was it an affirmation of the strategic thinking that Hayward had done for the Pacific, but it marked the opportunity for different approaches to strategic problems within the navy. Up to this point, much of the debate about naval issues centered around the navy's budget. The confusing mass of unit costs and program alternatives tended to be confused with strategy. Unrealistic strategies were sometimes employed for no other reason than to justify larger shares of money for one program or another, and in this way the budget tended to drive strategic concepts. "This is why," Hayward explained, "academics and others say the Navy doesn't have a strategy."[1] To combat this problem and to remove the misperceptions, Hayward sought to change the terms of the debate from a budget battle to an analysis of the strategic issues for a global maritime power. Under Hayward, the navy's leadership agreed not to fight for particular force levels, but to work for a highly ready navy with adequate manning and to let Congress worry about how big the navy should be. In particular, Hayward put his priority on spare parts, ammunition, pay, and benefits as the means to increase readiness. Then, he went on to point out that the Central Front in Europe was not the only problem for the United States. The country needed a war-winning strategy.[2]

Hayward's most immediate strategic concern was to create a worldwide maritime strategy to provide the framework for such thinking within the navy. Hayward and his executive assistant, Captain William A. Cockell, worked together over a three-month period to develop an outline. Together they examined each principal maritime area, theater by theater, and produced a 20–30 page paper, in point-paper format, that dealt with significant strategic issues: the Soviet threat, U.S. naval capabilities, and appropriate naval operations for the U.S. Navy. The final thought for each section was to ask the question, "what difference would it make if the U.S. Navy were not able to succeed, and what complications for national strategy would flow from this?" In thinking through these questions, the most obvious problem was that there were not enough forces available. To deal with this, Hayward and Cockell developed the concept and coined the term "sequential operations."[3]

CNO Strategic Concepts

Hayward and Cockell completed their work in January 1979 and circulated the results in a memorandum entitled "CNO Strategic Concepts."[4] In his preface, Hayward made two important points.

> While he did not argue over the priority given to NATO, he hypothesized that the Carter administration's Central Front orientation failed to take into account the criticality of other regions of the world to NATO's vital interest. Moreover, war in Europe is the least likely contingency, and a broader based view of national security requirements is needed.

> The terms "sea control" and "power projection" were poorly understood by senior decision makers and were sometimes adroitly misapplied by analysts in order to hold down naval force requirements.

The CNO's strategic principles contained 17 major points, which may be summarized as follows:[5]

> A NATO–Warsaw Pact war will be global. The view that U.S. and Allied naval forces are needed solely to protect the sea-lanes to Europe is highly simplistic and seriously misleading.

> The U.S. Navy must be offensively capable. The Soviet Navy is sophisticated and highly capable, but the U.S. Navy can only assure control of essential sea areas by the destruction or neutralization of the Soviet Navy's capability to challenge that control. This requires taking the war to the enemy and retaining residual power after the battle.

> The U.S. Navy is clearly outnumbered and will remain so for the foreseeable future. Our present principal margin of superiority lies in carriers and in at-sea sustainability. To maintain this we must not mirror-image the Soviets, but develop further the capabilities this margin of superiority represents.

> The U.S. Navy must maintain technological superiority.

> The U.S. Navy must draw on sister services and allies.

> The U.S. must capitalize on the Soviet Union's geographical disadvantages and its defensive mentality. This means maintaining a potential U.S. Navy threat to the Soviet Union, making the Soviets understand that in a war there will be no sanctuaries, and

drawing the Soviets into a preoccupation with homeland defense and operations close to the Soviet Union which will preclude the availability of Soviet forces to attack Western sea lines of communication.

The U.S. Navy must plan to fight with what it has on hand; there will be no opportunity to mobilize reserves or to build or to activate major naval units.

The U.S. Navy must employ tactics that will ensure favorable attrition ratios. In order to maintain control over time, place, and the calculated risk of engagements, the U.S. Navy needs to have an offensive, not a reactive, strategy.

The northern flank of NATO represents a large land, sea, and air region which has a direct strategic impact on whether or not NATO has the ability to carry on successful defensive operations on the Central Front. The area is important not only in wartime, but also in peacetime to demonstrate that NATO has the will to operate in the most demanding of all maritime scenarios.

The Swing Strategy of reinforcing Europe by using forces from the Pacific is an anachronism dating from the time when Pacific Fleet force levels were higher and the importance of the People's Republic of China not as critical.

Present U.S. Navy force levels are not sufficient to permit simultaneous control over the Mediterranean, North Atlantic, Norwegian Sea, Western Pacific, and Indian Ocean, therefore the United States must put priorities on the key areas and choose an order for their sequential control.

Beyond these major points, there were some additional considerations. First, why and where a war starts could have a critical influence on the capability of the U.S. Navy to respond properly in a timely manner. The pattern in which the fleet is deployed at the time that a war breaks out might complicate American response, and therefore, the Soviets might attempt to draw the U.S. Navy into a maldeployment at such a critical point. Secondly, there is great uncertainty as to whether the Soviets would use tactical nuclear weapons at sea. The U.S. Navy needs to understand Soviet doctrine better in order to think through how we would deter the Soviet use of tactical nuclear weapons, or if necessary, how we would wage a war involving tactical nuclear weapons. Thirdly, the strategic concepts that Hayward and Cockell developed dealt with the role of conventional forces in a global war against the Soviet Union; it did not include a consideration of nuclear strategic forces or of contingencies involving other nations and areas.[6]

Flag Officers' Conferences on Strategy

In the spring of 1979, Admiral Hayward began to circulate his "Strategic Concepts." Among other approaches, he asked Rear Admiral Leland S. Kollmorgen, Director,

System Analysis Division (OP-96) to arrange a briefing for flag officers and to have a discussion with them. Five eight-hour seminars were held at the U.S. Naval Academy during the period between 7–11 May 1979. Each was chaired by an admiral or vice admiral and attended by 12 to 20 rear admirals, involving a total of about 100 flag officers from the Washington, D.C. area. In September–October 1979, similar sets of meetings were held in Norfolk, Pearl Harbor, and San Diego. The purpose of these meetings was to collect opinions and insights concerning both the CNO's strategic principles and the state of the navy.[7]

The results of these conferences demonstrated that flag officers throughout the navy were seriously concerned about the long-term trends and doubted that the United States could maintain its strength in the future. As one officer expressed it:

> Given the money situation, ship and aircraft levels are going to fall. We're going to get a lot smaller while the Soviets are going to be more capable. Our business-as-usual approach is not hacking it. We keep projecting we're going to get well through big bucks in the out-years. So we take marginal cuts across the board each budget year and kid ourselves about the cumulative effects by projecting large growth in funny-money out-year programs. It's time to get serious, take some painful vertical cuts and give up, or at least seriously reduce some missions.[8]

Yet, there seemed no agreement about how to reduce, or which programs to trade off. The only common thread in the discussion was that too much emphasis was being given to convoy protection for a long war, given Defense Department priority on a short war and the relative strength of the NATO allies in the convoy escort role. Over all, the general organization of the navy for strategy and procurement appeared to be in disarray to many flag officers. The OpNav staff seemed too busy, too large, and accomplishing too little, while only a few people, the CNO, the Vice CNO, OP-06, and OP-090 saw the overall view of the navy. Most believed that better integration was needed.

In considering the CNO's strategic concepts, most flag officers liked the idea of a set of principles that could provide rallying concepts for the navy, but they felt that the U.S. goal was naval superiority. This was a point upon which Hayward was in agreement, and the one that he made a central theme in his initial posture statement, submitted to Congress in January 1979. The principles that Hayward had provided were a step in the right direction, but they did not represent a complete theory. As a group, the flag officers felt that naval strategy should not start with a focus on a future NATO war but on the basic geographical fact that the United States is tied to a forward defense strategy, by culture, by trade, and by historical association to a set of nations in Europe and in Asia. "We seek an international balance of power, not just the defense of a region. If the United States is to be a world power and maintain links to Europe, she must control the sea when and where needed. Thus, naval superiority relates to perception in peacetime and performance in crisis, as much as it does to deterrence of a world war."[9]

Most flag officers agreed that a NATO war would be a global war. A few pointed out that it would be in the best interest of the Soviet Union to limit the war to the area in which it would be strongest, but the rejoinder to that observation was that the U.S. Navy could counter this by retaining the option of opening other theaters should it be in our best interest to do so. Basic national policy required forward deployment of naval forces, which had been done for many years. But these objectives had not been publicly stated by the State Department and other agencies so that the navy appeared to be using forward deployment merely as an excuse to build forces. The flag officers believed this should be changed. They emphasized that the public needed to perceive that the navy was responding to policy requirements.

All flag officers agreed that offensive capabilities for the navy were required. Because of the need for two battle fleets to operate in five theaters (Norwegian Sea, Atlantic, Mediterranean, Indian Ocean, and Western Pacific), many argued that the U.S. Navy must have a strong offensive capability in order to defeat the Soviets in one region, then shift to defeat them in another. However, as one participant in the Annapolis seminar noted, naval forces were essentially irrelevant if the national policy was limited to planning for a 30-day-long Central Front war in Germany. There was very little function for the navy in a short, nuclear, land war. The navy's major value lay in conducting a longer war with conventional weapons, employing forces in ways that caused the Soviets to divert resources from the Central Front. This concept of a future war was not at all what current national policy expressed. Most participants agreed that the CNO's strategic concepts could be rejected on these grounds, as they implied costs which clearly exceeded their worth in terms of national policy. Therefore, several participants pointed out that the navy must discuss its strategic perceptions more thoroughly with the Joint Chiefs and in the office of the Secretary of Defense to bring the options which the navy could provide into a direct reflection of national policy. From Hayward's point of view, this reasoning had the issues backward. His point was that national policy was nonexistent, and that was the situation that needed to be changed.

In the discussions, all the flag officer participants understood that in dealing with Soviet superiority in numbers, it was a matter of meeting it with U.S. and Allied quality. However, many felt that there was a need for more precision of expression, since in naval warfare, like forces do not fight like forces. Many expressed concern that the Soviets could, under current rules of engagement, make an effective surprise attack using weapons that would be of much less use once a war was well underway. However, all agreed that it was necessary to exploit Soviet disadvantages.[10]

Some participants in the discussion expressed strong skepticism that the concept of utilizing the capabilities of the Allies and other U.S. services could be relied upon for a significant contribution to navy needs. The other American services were viewed as being so overcommitted that they had to give low priority to naval missions. Some felt that the Allies lagged behind the United States in capabilities by 5–10 years in ASW and perhaps by more than that as Aegis became an effective antimissile defense. The NATO trend had been to increase land forces and decrease sea forces, and this had been compounded by the reluctance of the United States to transfer new technology to the Allies, because we feared compromising our capabilities and wished to reduce costs by procuring one-of-a-kind items. Since the Allies had largely moved toward convoy escorts, we had already planned to utilize their capabilities; however, the U.S. Navy remained America's worldwide instrument of naval power and must, therefore, retain independent capabilities. In general, the participants felt "that this principle may be a politically necessary nod toward Washington or DoD sensitivities. But it doesn't count for much in the real world."[11]

In addition, there was great skepticism among the flag offices that the U.S. Navy could fight a war on short notice, with existing forces. Most agreed that U.S. supply levels in 1979 were not sufficient. "Like a Greek chorus, the flag officers in the fleet kept saying, don't try it—you won't like the results."[12]

Combined with skepticism about supplies, many saw the idea of employing the navy with calculated risk as merely a means of offsetting criticism the navy was planning for some impossible mission, such as sailing into the Barents Sea on D-day. Some pointed out that when the idea of calculated risk was combined with the current rules of engagement, it would encourage timid behavior and defensive attitudes in peacetime. Since the U.S. Navy would fight in war as it had trained in peace, there were those who felt that this strategic concept could be counterproductive.

Hayward was pleased with the lively reaction of the flag community and felt that if they had accomplished nothing else, the symposia served the useful purpose of stimulating constructive thought about naval strategy in a community of officers not accustomed to thinking about such subjects. While recognizing that the response from the flag officers covered a wide range of diverse viewpoints, Hayward felt it was generally suggestive of the direction in which he was trying to take the navy. He encouraged flag officers to write to him directly with their thoughts on strategy and related topics, an invitation which a number of them accepted.[13]

Reinforced by the flag community response, Hayward continued to use his strategic concepts as the basis for thinking about naval force. He gave briefings to Congress, to the Joint Chiefs, the Defense Science Board, the CNO Executive Panel as well as other

groups, and used the concepts as the basis for the first part of his annual Posture Statement to Congress. An unclassified version was published in the U.S. Naval Institute's
Naval Review 1979 in an article by Hayward entitled, "The Future of U.S. Sea Power."[14]
Drafted for Hayward by Captain William Cockell, the article was based on Hayward's
unclassified Congressional Testimony, but cast in a new format. It was, as Cockell later
described it, "some simply stated principles . . . simple, not simplistic, and simple, by
design."[15] It lacked the sophistication and depth of the classified version, but the article
did express Hayward's basic concepts on how to think about naval force. For the readers of the *Naval Review,* Hayward made his point clear: classical naval theory is still
valid. Among those who commented on the article, William S. Lind, legislative assistant
to Senator Gary Hart, wrote "it signals a turn away from the historically French objectives of power projection and sea control and a return to Mahanist outlook."[16] Ap-
plauding that trend, Lind pointed out that, in his view, it was still no justification for
building more aircraft carriers. Captain R. A. Bowling, U.S. Navy (Ret.), viewed the situation from the opposite side when he declared that Hayward had clearly demonstrated that ". . . debunked Mahanian concepts are being applied in the U.S. Navy
today."[17] But Captain W. J. Ruhe retorted, "Today's reality shows that Mahan is not ob-
solete."[18] Some academic observers, however, found this entire discussion far too simplistic. Dr. Thomas H. Etzold of the Naval War College suggested that much of this
discussion rested on inadequate familiarity with Mahan's writings. "There is also a tendency to discuss the question of Mahan's validity in current naval contexts too much
on its own terms," Etzold wrote, and "to search for direct analogies and mechanical application of concepts from another technological and political era."[19]

Recognizing that Mahan and other classic writings on naval strategy are indispensable
to our own understanding, Etzold concluded, "we need to do better than he did in
thinking through the purpose of any given war as a whole.[20]

Bureaucratic Refinements

While Hayward's strategic concepts were being discussed in various fora, the CNO was
directly concerned with making some organizational changes within the navy that
could assist the navy's leaders in thinking about strategy. First, he wanted to establish a
focal point within the navy staff for discussions on the broad aspects of naval warfare.
In order to do this, in mid-January 1980, Hayward changed OP-095 from the Anti-
Submarine Warfare Directorate to the Directorate of Naval Warfare. The idea behind
this move was to create a directorate that could coordinate the work of the various
platform sponsors, the Deputy CNOs for Air, Submarine, and Surface Warfare, and to
be sympathetic to them while at the same time being the main contact point for the
fleet commanders and their concerns for future war-fighting developments.[21] Much of

the work of OP-095 dealt necessarily with the integration of the various program plans, but under its first director, Vice Admiral Kinnard R. McKee, it developed a direct link to strategic thinking. From his viewpoint, a starting point for assessment in the Program Objective Memorandum (POM) process is a realistic examination of how the navy would be used in a future war. In order to do this, McKee also needed to coordinate his work with the Deputy CNO for Plans, Policy, and Operations (OP-06). Here, Hayward had established the Strategic and Theater Nuclear Warfare Division (OP-65), under Rear Admiral Powell F. Carter, to be the central point of contact for policy and planning for nuclear warfare. More importantly, the Strategic Concepts Branch (OP-603) was soon to become the key office in responding to OP-095's need to coordinate the Navy's Program Planning process with concepts for future plans and policy. The briefing, which OP-603 prepared for OP-095 to use in this process of coordination, was what later became known as *The Maritime Strategy*. This line of development is followed, in further detail, in chapter four of this study.

Hayward saw another need within the navy staff. For many years the navy had undertaken long-range planning, and the various groups which had undertaken this work had varying degrees of success and influence on naval policy.[22] In January 1980, Hayward established the Long Range Planning Group (OP-00X), under Rear Admiral Charles R. Larson on the CNO's personal staff, and this group reported directly to Hayward. The group was designed to be a permanent fixture on the CNO's staff and to have the same administrative status as the CNO Executive Panel of outside experts, which had been established exactly a decade earlier by Admiral Zumwalt. A small group of highly qualified officers, OP-00X, took as its mission the assessment of resource limitations on future naval capabilities and the analysis of alternative strategies for achieving long-range goals.

The Long Range Planning Group had an important area to consider, but Hayward saw that there was still another aspect of strategic thinking that needed to be carefully examined: the interplay between strategy and tactics. In order to deal with this aspect, Hayward wanted to break away from the program planning process that seemed to dominate so much of the navy's thinking and to focus on a realistic and effective strategy for fighting at sea. Hayward wanted to form a group made up of extremely capable and successful naval officers with recent fleet experience, and who themselves would be the future leaders of the navy, to work toward this new strategy. In the area of tactics, Hayward created Tactical Training Groups in the two fleets to train senior officers— flag officers, captains and commanders—en route operational commands in naval tactics and the broad issues of force employment. This initiative was a very important one in raising senior officer sensitivity and professionalism in tactics. Hayward saw the need for a similar approach for strategy.[23]

The CNO Strategic Studies Group Formed

As a leader, Hayward thrived on the interplay of sharply divergent views, and he wanted a variety of sources and viewpoints to assist him. He felt that no one group had a monopoly of wisdom, and for that reason he did not want to replace any group but instead chose to create another to fill a gap in perspective, which he felt was missing in the range of views expressed collectively by the OpNav staff, the CNO Executive Panel, and others. At the same time, Hayward had two parallel interests: to create a core of future naval leaders who were well versed in the role of naval forces in national policy and strategy and to reestablish the Naval War College, in everyone's view, as the pinnacle for education in naval strategic thinking. As Hayward told the Current Strategy Forum at the Naval War College in April 1981, "there is no dearth of strategic thinking going on these days in your navy. What is lacking is a more useful way to capitalize upon that abundant talent with more alacrity."[24] As a step in this direction, Hayward announced the establishment of "a prestigious Center for Naval Warfare Studies" at the Naval War College. Along with this, he announced "the creation of a small but impressive cell . . . a group of the best and brighter of our military officers." Making his point clear, Hayward declared, "Our objective is to make this Naval War College respected around the globe as the residence of the finest maritime strategic logic of our time. A related objective is to provide the Chief of Naval Operations and our senior military officers with stimuli relative to strategy and tactics in order to make certain that regardless of the perception of those less informed, our navy will never, never be found 'sailing backwards.'"[25]

In selecting the first group of officers for the Strategic Studies Group, Hayward received nominations from a wide variety of sources within the navy, and then he personally reviewed the service jackets of candidates, spending hours on them in an attempt to find the men he felt would certainly be the best future choices for flag rank.[26] The first director of the Strategic Studies Group and the first director of the newly established Center for Naval Warfare Studies at the Naval War College was Robert J. Murray, then just leaving office as Under Secretary of the navy. The Strategic Studies Group was designed to be one element of an organization that included elements brought together from several parts of the Naval War College: the Advanced Research Department, the Naval War College Press, and the Naval War Gaming Department. Although the Strategic Studies Group reported directly to the CNO, it was located in Newport in order to take advantage of the academic atmosphere and resources at the Naval War College and to use the distance from Washington as insulation from the bureaucratic traumas of Pentagon life. "In July 1981, nobody knew what the Center for Naval Warfare Studies was to be, including me, . . ." Murray recalled. "There was nothing that we could call all encompassing as to how the navy would operate in war. We didn't even have a system for producing such a concept."[27] In thinking about the problem, Murray saw that a coherent strategy could not be developed in isolation at the Naval War College. What was needed was "kibitzing," talking to responsible admirals and generals, testing ideas, meshing their ideas with others, and "murder boards" for concepts. Through this process, Murray saw that everyone could have a stake in the issues discussed and that, most importantly, the process could spawn broad ideas that could merge narrow concepts together. As the process developed, Murray saw that it was not a question of gaining recognition or glory for one element within the navy, but to eliminate parochialism and to find some consensus, not only about how several parts of the navy would work together in wartime, but how the navy would fit within the broader context of national strategy.[28]

In thinking about how to approach the work that the Strategic Studies Group would do, Murray considered carefully the example of previous groups and examined the process by which a strategy is adopted within the U.S. armed forces. He saw that others had failed for one or more of a number of reasons:[29]

- Poor-quality people.

- Insufficient contacts with influential and responsible people.

- Failure to have an integrated effort.

- Failure to do the legwork in getting the correct input.

- Too involved with the budget process.

- Not being in tune with the concerns of key players.

- Too diverse an effort.

- Parochial in outlook.

- Failure to have a marketing approach.

- Failure to be heard by key people.

- Too much time expended in research.

Murray believed that the Strategic Studies Group could not be all things to all people. One needed to pick one's opportunities and focus, while at the same time using tie-ins with other institutions, such as those with the Center for Naval Analyses, the Naval Postgraduate School, and the Naval War College. At the same time, the Group needed to systemize war-gaming results into a body of analysis. Next, he was convinced that it was essential that the Group produce something concrete, not just roam off working on a nebulous project. Murray clearly saw that writing up the study would help to clarify the group's thinking, focus the effort, and limit the range of subjects dealt with.[30]

From this work, briefings could be developed that reflected the careful in-depth, analytical rigor imposed by a written study.

In choosing a topic, Murray wanted something upon which a general consensus could be developed and which could be used to say something about how the navy could be used. In addition, Murray wanted the Strategic Studies Group to travel and to talk directly with the key military and naval commanders. In order to do this, he needed a topic of importance and of direct interest. Fighting the Soviet Union in the event of a future world war was certainly such a topic, but even that topic was so broad and so complex that it could not be dealt with effectively by a single group in one year of study. From the outset, Murray saw that the issues must be dealt with sequentially and over a period of years.[31]

The first Strategic Studies Group assembled in Newport, R.I. on 31 August 1981. It consisted of Lt. Col. Richard P. Bland, USMC; Cdr. Arthur K. Cebrowski, USN; Capt. Franklin D. Julian, USN; Capt. Stuart D. Landersman, USN; Capt. Rene W. Leeds, USN; Cdr. William A. Owens, USN; Col. Joseph D. Ruane, USMC; and Capt. Daniel J. Wolkensdorfer, USN. Assisting Murray on the staff were Professor Thomas Etzold, Lt. Col. Orville E. Hay, USMC, and Cdr. Kenneth McGruther, USN. Starting with an intense indoctrination schedule, the Group moved quickly through a series of readings, briefings, and lectures from Naval War College faculty, and at the same time, defining in the first ten days the work that they would undertake. In developing this plan, Murray and his staff suggested two key areas for work: A near-term offensive strategy and an offensive strategy of the future. After considering the issues in detail, the Group developed an initial topic and then began a series of discussions in Washington and with the major commanders in chief. Meeting with the CNO on 19 October, Admiral Hayward told the Group that there was a lack of strategic thinking even at the fleet commanders level. Hayward told them that he wanted the Strategic Studies Group to fill the void and to convince the leadership of the armed forces that the navy *is* thinking and that the Naval War College *is* the place for that thinking. In viewing the Washington scene, Hayward believed that there was a need for global perspective in looking at a possible war with the Soviet Union, one that was not oriented toward SIOP. He felt quite strongly that no sensible strategy had been developed. "There was no imagination," he said, "but only reaction." Even OP-603, the Strategic Concepts Branch in the navy staff, was only "crashing for tomorrow." What Hayward wanted was not an instantly created strategy, but a well-framed understanding of the issues with possible resolutions. With these ideas available, Hayward wanted to market them to fleet staffs and through the operational chain of command, in an effort to impact the two-star level and up. In particular, he wanted three and four-star officers themselves to think about strategy and not to be trapped by OP-plans. Hayward believed that flag officers in general had a tendency to wait for Washington to take the initiative, and he believed that they should be operating more independently and innovatively in the area of strategy. This was why he had gone to such lengths earlier to involve the flag community in the preparation of his Strategic Concepts. In conducting his discussion with the Strategic Studies Group, Hayward told them to consider carefully the uncertainties involved in thinking about future strategies and to think in decisive terms, not gradual ones. It was not a question of formulating a strategy to give a signal but to achieve broader strategic aims. "We can afford a war of attrition," he told them. "Don't be timid."[32]

The Ambiance for Strategic Thinking in 1981

The Strategic Studies Group did not operate in a vacuum. Its first mission was to educate itself in the strategic thinking of the day and to move forward, unencumbered by the friction of bureaucracy, to stimulate flag officers who held positions of responsibility for executing strategy in wartime. In the 1970s, one of the characteristic problems of the naval bureaucracy was the way in which it tended to isolate thought within certain communities within the navy, preventing the exchange of views that was a necessary prerequisite to the formation of a generally accepted opinion. Like the Naval Warfare Directorate with the navy staff, the Strategic Studies Group was designed to try to surmount the natural and artificial barriers to a free exchange of thinking that had developed over the years. In many ways, the Strategic Studies Group acted like a small swarm of honeybees, migrating from one flag officer to another, discussing issues, exchanging views, and carrying the pollen of stimulating thought from one widely separated command to another. Charged as they were with thinking, in global terms, about how to win a future conventional war with the Soviet Union, the viewpoints that they carried were so different from what had previously been heard, that they shocked some listeners. As Captain Rene Leeds recounted, "the first reaction was to shoot the messenger."[33] However, once the initial defensive reaction was overcome, a fruitful exchange of opinion developed that was both educational and constructive.

The various viewpoints that were expressed to the Strategic Studies Group were important factors in bringing those ideas directly into the forefront of strategic perceptions within the Navy Department. At Marine Corps Headquarters, for example, the Group was told it would get strong support for its approach and goals. Looking at the issues, Major General Bernard Trainor advised that future naval operations must include use of all appropriate U.S. forces and must integrate the Air Force into naval operations, thereby preventing the Air Force from assuming control of naval tasks. In OpNav, Vice Admiral Gordon Nagler, Director, Command and Control (OP-094), advised that the Soviets were most vulnerable due to centralization of command and control, while the United States was very dependent upon communication and was weak in the area of interconnectivity. In the Office of Naval Warfare, Vice Admiral Kinnard McKee advised the Group that naval strategy could be attempted without national strategy and emphasized his view that there is only one principle of war: concentration of force. Rear Admiral William R. Smedberg IV, the Director of the Force Level Plans Division, pointed out that in reality, we are driven in our strategy by what we can build, due to fiscal constraints, and then we devise how we can best fight with what is provided. But McKee responded that despite that, the navy should press for a naval strategy in isolation from political and fiscal constraints. Vice Admiral Robert Walters, Deputy CNO for Surface Warfare (OP-03) reminded the Group that one year is too short a time to finish the development of a complete strategy. Fully supporting the work of the SSG, Walters thought that its approach to strategy was correct and that it was on the proper course of development. He pointed out that the Reagan administration laid great stress on the necessity to have sustainability in a long war as opposed to the Carter administration's stress on short war. This change, however, had not yet been reflected in a fleet organization that emphasized fighting capabilities. In developing a strategy to go along with this, Walters said that risk acceptance must be weighed.

Some of the most important issues that the SSG faced were brought clearly into focus in discussions with various officers in OP-06. Echoing early advice, one planner asked the Group whether the SSG might "develop strategy in a vacuum" unless it first had a good understanding of national goals, national strategy, vital interests, and so forth, which are "inherently squishy." In response, Vice Admiral Sylvester Foley defended the SSG's position by pointing out that in any war, the role of the U.S. Navy was to first "take care" of the Soviet Navy. Therefore, the goal of the United States is "maritime supremacy" through defeating "the next-best navy." The Strategic Studies Group is right, Foley said. Approaching the issue from another angle, Rear Admiral Ronald Kurth, Director of the Political Military Policy Branch (OP-61) asked the Group whether it would not be more useful to focus on strategy for lesser situations, the ones that we could expect to have to deal with every day rather than for the less likely event of a general war. Kurth's deputy, however, supported the SSG's approach by pointing out that one had to be sure to be able to deal with the Soviet Navy—or the United States would not be able to maintain itself as the best navy and, therefore, could not maintain American maritime superiority.[34]

The various visits and discussions continued throughout the year for the Strategic Studies Group. As they became acquainted with the various segments of American naval thinking, they also learned about the Soviet Navy. As they became aware of the general trend in Soviet naval developments and strategic thought (see pp. 23–36), they were concerned primarily with how they would fare in a war with the Soviets. A key influence on the SSG's thinking in this regard was the work of the Navy Net Assessor. In a briefing to the SSG in Newport, Captain W. H. J. Manthorpe reflected the latest intelligence analysis when he told them:

- Overall the Soviet Navy outnumbers the U.S. Navy 3.5 to 1.

- In open ocean warfare, the Soviets still have an advantage by 1.8 to 1.

- The quality of the two navies appears about equal.

- The Soviet advantage lies in frigates and conventional submarines, while a significant portion of the U.S. Navy open-ocean tonnage is in aircraft carriers, amphibious ships, and supply vessels.

- The U.S. Navy is well poised for dealing with crises without warning, but the Soviet Navy can "outsurge" the U.S. Navy within 4 to 5 days, to a ratio of 1.6 to 1.

- Sheer numbers suggest that if the U.S. Navy is to operate close to Eurasia, it will need the support of NATO's naval force, including France, in order to have the potential for equal strength.

In short, Manthorpe stressed to the Group that the two navies were so equally matched that it was no longer possible for mere brute force to count. The key factors in a war were how the forces would be used, what allies, missions, and force multipliers employed, and who shoots first. The areas of critical importance will be initiative, surprise, and analysis of weakness. In this the SSG had a role in initiating the process of navy-wide thinking on how the U.S. Navy would be used in a war against the Soviets.[35]

In considering naval strategy, the influence of political leaders also played a key role. In office less than six months, Secretary of the Navy John Lehman met with the SSG for a luncheon. During the course of their meeting, Lehman told them that the driving consideration behind development of the 600-ship navy was geographical, not war-time specific. In addition, the basic measure must be of the war-time capabilities of the Soviet Navy with the demand of naval presence and crisis operations as lesser included cases. A key factor in developing the U.S. Navy is to ensure that the rest of the world perceives that the U.S. Navy is capable of coping with the Soviet threat to American interests. In Lehman's view, 600 ships was a minimum to support the 15 carriers that are required for dealing with the geopolitical situation.

In looking at naval strategy in this early period of his administration, Lehman saw that there was too broad a gap between naval operations and the "armchair strategists." He believed that the navy needed coherent and institutionalized thinking about how a 600-ship navy could be used. Those ships and weapons are only tools, he emphasized, the question is "how do you fight with what you are going to get?" The creative thinking that had already been done dealt with peacetime crises, not war, Lehman believed.

We need to raise a generation of warrior admirals, he told the Group, not program managers. We need to focus on the battle of, say, the Norwegian Sea, rather than the battle of the budget. As Lehman himself thought about a maritime strategy for the United States, he believed that any war between the United States and the Soviet Union would be a global one. As he looked at different regions, he thought that the United States should cut back its sights in terms of how much should be invested in the Persian Gulf area during a major U.S.-USSR war. He felt that it would be a great mistake to be overly involved in a ground war in that region, even if the oil resources were closed off without a U.S. presence in southwest Asia. With less than 500 ships, Lehman believed that the United States could not fight a global war, but would have to abandon one or more key areas and allies. In this situation the Soviets would be readily able to block later attempts by the United States to reenter the areas it had abandoned. In summation, Lehman remarked that it was conceivable that the United States could lose the battle for Europe and still not lose the war, but it was inconceivable that the United States could lose at sea and avoid losing the war.[36]

Another important influence on the development of the Strategic Studies Group's thinking came from its early decision to use war gaming as one of its key analytical tools. First, the Strategic Studies Group used the advantage of being at the Naval War College in close contact with the War Gaming Department. Several staff members in the newly formed Center for Naval Warfare Studies, Professor Etzold, Commander McGruther and Lieutenant Colonel Hay, had been closely involved with the Global War Games, which had been started in 1979 through the initiative of Captain Hugh Nott, Commander Jay Hurlburt, and Professor Francis J. West, Jr.

The Global War Games were created to identify issues that required attention in planning a global strategy. Their purpose was to gain a better understanding of those national command authority decisions that were needed early on in a global war. In addition, the games sought to consider the issues involved in escalation, the relationship among regional requirements, constraints created by logistics factors, and the effects of varying strategy during a war. Professor Richmond Lloyd described the Global War Game as "a jellyfish with all its ganglia hanging down for everyone to look at and examine," and Bud Hay suggested further that "it exposes the bad with the good, our weaknesses along with our strengths. The good guys don't always win, the bad guys aren't always ten feet tall and there are a lot more guys who don't like either the good guys or the bad guys."[37] By the time the first Strategic Studies Group assembled in Newport in the summer of 1981, three Global War Games had been played and insights had already been established along the very same perspective that the SSG wished to explore. The war games provide insights along many avenues of thought at the matrix of world events, military capabilities, and technical boundaries. Reflections on the games varied from individual to individual. For Fred Ikle, the experience of the first Global Game in 1979 led him to conclude that:

> Short of a concept for victory, the overarching concept that is needed is some idea about the assets that the United States and the Alliance should protect or secure, so as to terminate the fighting and to prevail in the long drawn-out competition that would follow a cease-fire.[38]

In the following year, another participant concluded, "the game tended to bear out that command of the seas tends after all to be a zero sum matter, and that for a maritime nation such as the U.S., command of the seas is the *sine qua non* for a 'forward strategy' in any type of war."[39] Another participant in the same game concluded that the United States needed a large, high-quality strike capability for an extended campaign. "This is where Navy can play," he concluded, "because submarines, warships, and other vessels can be survivable in general war and can have the firepower and endurance necessary to continue the fight."[40]

By the spring of 1981, the themes that had been developed in the early Global War Games were beginning to be echoed in Washington. The Secretary of Defense's Policy and Capabilities Review concluded in April–June 1981 that planning for a global war required a new pattern of thinking that developed an integrated regional approach, with revised strategy and force priorities. Offensive combinations of force were needed to exploit vulnerabilities and to unbalance Soviet strategy. In this, anti-SSBN operations, anti-LRA/SNA, and ASAT appeared to be promising. In considering a global war, it would be important, however, to deny the Soviets means of escalating the conflict. This would be a key factor in controlling the war to the advantage of the United States, keeping it global, but conventional. Investing in conventional force will in the longer run have a higher payoff than nuclear forces. Prolonging the war by keeping it a conventional war offers the advantage of improving the U.S. industrial defense base. This policy will be long, hard, and expensive, involving many government agencies, but the change to an offensive conventional capability and increased force structure would result in changes to the strategic balance over time, emphasizing American flexibility, mobility, and sustainability, the Review concluded.[41]

In the fall of 1981, the Strategic Studies Group was able to reflect on the major insights that had emerged from the first three Global War Games. The Naval War College staff summarized them as follows:[42]

- Strategic lift and allies' consent are all-essential to U.S. flexibility.

- In a global war, Southwest Asia winds up as a strategic backwater.

- Naval force may offer the sole means of getting at core Soviet vulnerabilities short of intercontinental missiles.

- Need to consider the "value added" of naval forces in getting out of a Central Front syndrome and to think about how to win wars.

- U.S. power plays more heavily in longer wars:
  - but early force employment serves deterrence and helps reassure allies.
  - results in a critical dichotomy in how to use the navy in the early days of a war.
  - initial rules of engagement are critical to survivability.

- Escalation aspects need to be part of all systematic thinking:
  - U.S./NATO "first use" concept is to deny Soviets political advantage.
  - Adverse perceptions of the nuclear balance constrain options at all levels.
  - "Tit-for-tat" escalation usually works to Blue's disadvantage.

The Strategic Studies Group began its own series of seminar war games as a means to develop further insights. During two games in October and November 1981, they examined current war plans cumulatively to determine current naval war-fighting capabilities and vulnerabilities in a global war. These games reinforced the idea that a long-war strategy warranted attention in the overall American strategic approach. In addition to preventing the Soviets from winning by an early move or foreclosing the option for Western rearmament, the games suggested that long-term strategy would compound Soviet calculations for the correlation of forces in the early period of a war and increase the uncertainty for them in taking any dramatic or destabilizing moves that could cause the United States to begin to move toward a major wartime production effort. "However," the Group noted, a long-war strategy is "expensive, politically dangerous on both a domestic and international basis, and has substantial warfighting shortfalls." In the course of the game, the SSG members noted that they had not yet ascertained how the navy could make a strategic difference. At the outset of their work, they could see that the navy provided support to the land battle and secured the sea-lanes of communication over which reinforcements and resupply must pass. "But is that enough?" they asked. It still left the navy in the role of supporting ground forces in an attrition war on a single front. "It still needs to be asked whether there might not be some better way to influence the outcome than merely [by] helping the Army to lose more slowly."[43] In making that observation, they determined that the most important aspect of their work was to seek "a maritime strategy that subsumes the continental strategic approach embodied in the Central Front focus." Viewed regionally, they saw that the development of strategic objectives by which the navy could make a difference might include the ability to operate with relative impunity in the upper reaches of the Norwegian Sea, against Soviet SSBNs, and against the Balkan industrial base from the Eastern Mediterranean.[44] About this same time, SSG staff member Commander Kenneth McGruther reflected on the issues involved in a draft memo entitled, The Essence of Strategic Thinking. "We must continuously reinforce in the Soviet mind the perception that it could not win a war with the United States, both *before* a war, to enhance deterrence, and at all phases of the war should it occur," McGruther wrote. "The key point here is that the desired prospect must be *as perceived and measured in Soviet terms.*"[45] The basic issue, as he had summarized it, was to take the defeat of Soviet strategy as the central frame of reference for American military strategy rather than to derive a strategy from American national interests alone.

As each succeeding group of officers worked within the Strategic Studies Group, it developed and refined a progressively better articulation of the nature of the Soviet threat and a more coherent approach for using naval forces to achieve national aims. Each group found the need to examine the best use of all national resources to understand the role of naval forces, putting the navy in the forefront of thinking about joint and combined strategy. The first Strategic Studies Group established the basic tenets and conceptual feasibility of a forward maritime strategy, focusing on Soviet missions and sensitivities, and using a theater-wide combined arms approach to exploit Western advantages. The first Strategic Studies Group developed a concept for a forward Maritime Strategy, which they explained in the following way:

A U.S. Maritime Strategy of Forward Area Power Projection

Naval forces can contribute to deterring the start of war and, deterrence failing, to terminating war with the Soviet Union on terms favorable to the United States and its allies through a maritime strategy of forward area power projection.[46] Whereas naval forces are currently intended to achieve sea control in the Atlantic and the Pacific in order to protect the sea lines of communication (SLOCs) to Europe and Asia, a naval strategy that projected forces quickly into forward areas on multiple fronts would not only protect those lines of communication but would also upset the Soviets' war-fighting calculations, help break their concentration on the Central Front, and frustrate their ambitions for swift victory.

The purpose of this forward naval strategy is, first, to deter war by convincing the Soviet Union, in political circumstances leading toward war, that a successful combat outcome would be uncertain or unlikely and, therefore, an attempt would be unwarranted; second, in war, to prevent the Soviet Union from achieving its naval objectives, thereby encouraging an early end to hostilities; and, third, to ensure that at fighting's end, whatever the outcome, there remain afloat no significant Soviet naval forces able to threaten the United States and its surviving allies or to protect Soviet shores for years to come.

Although subject to some political constraints, this is a strategy that begins with the rapid placement of forces capable of slowing or halting Soviet expansion inside the Soviet defensive arcs prior to the start of hostilities. The positioning of these forces is supported by intensive surveillance of Soviet force movements to ensure that Soviet actions are consistent with the estimate of Soviet intentions used as the premise for this strategy. Intensive surveillance also demonstrates an intention to assume the initial engagements at the start of war. These actions will cause the Soviet calculations to predict a worse and more uncertain outcome than if the actions were not taken and, therefore, will have a deterrent effect.

Should the USSR continue along the path to war, U.S. and NATO forces would be positioned both to prevent Soviet/Warsaw Pact expansion on the maritime flanks and to destroy promptly the ships and aircraft of the Soviet Navy while they are still close to their home waters and fields. Victories in the initial stages of the war are extremely important for solidifying alliances and for convincing allies that they are on the winning side. The visible loss of major Soviet surface ships early in the war is important not only to NATO but also in the Pacific, where China and Japan may be watching carefully for U.S. successes. In addition, the loss of these major surface ships should impress Soviet allies. Moreover, their loss will be a loss to the Soviets themselves of strategic early warning, command and control, air defense, and antisubmarine defense of strategic forces.

The SSG then went on to discuss, at a higher classification, the stepped up antisubmarine warfare campaign in forward areas that would follow the removal of Soviet surface vessels. This included an option to attack Soviet SSBNs with conventional weapons from U.S. and British nuclear submarines. The SSG believed that losses in Soviet SSBNs would affect the Soviets' calculation of forces required for nuclear war fighting and shake their confidence in the stability of their strategic nuclear forces. While the Soviets seemed to expect to lose some SSBNs, the key issue is the rate at which those losses would occur. Slow attrition would not affect their calculations, but a high attrition before the nuclear threshold was approached would tend to raise that threshold even further as the Soviets calculated that they could not "win" in an exchange of nuclear weapons. It would seem that the Soviets would choose to terminate a war if a significant portion of their SSBNs were sunk—unless they believed that the Communist Party of the Soviet Union was being seriously threatened.

Stripping the surface and anticarrier submarine forces from the Soviets would leave their flanks vulnerable and forestall any sizeable sortie on their part into the Atlantic and Pacific Oceans. Placing U.S. and allied air defense aircraft at bases on the flanks would limit Soviet naval and long-range aviation approaches to carrier battle groups; placing U.S. and allied attack aircraft at the same bases would present a threat that the Soviets could not ignore. This should cause them to divert resources to attack these bases with consequent attrition of their air armies.

At the same time, the SSG pointed out that the anti-SSBN campaign, the U.S., British, and French SSBNs remained a "redundancy of resolve" to use nuclear weapons, giving further doubts to Soviet calculations on their ability to go on the offensive.

Faced with (1) the rapid deployment of forces that are stronger than anticipated, (2) aggressive land and sea defense that slows their expansion on the flanks, (3) stripped naval and air defenses that leave the Soviet homeland threatened, and (4) loss of strategic nuclear systems to conventional forces without any ability to retaliate in kind, it is anticipated that the Soviets would seek war termination prior to increasingly intensive assaults by Marines and CVBGs on the Soviet flanks and not risk nuclear war.

The SSG concluded its statement of the overall strategic concept by noting that this proposed naval strategy did not pretend that war can be deterred or won by naval forces alone. The war will be essentially lost if the Central Front does not hold. Naval achievements, although great in themselves, may well prove insufficient should the Soviet Union be able, or think herself able, to achieve a quick and overwhelming victory on the Central Front. Even though it is likely to continue longer, war games and studies indicate that the war will probably be decided in the first 20 days. The resupply of Europe cannot be conducted within 20 days. A successful national strategy, therefore, will have strong conventional ground and air components that can hold at least long enough for the maritime pressure on the flanks to make a difference.

Looking into the application of the strategy, the SSG concluded that there was one theater in which the major missions of the Soviet Navy in protecting its strategic naval forces (SSBNs) and attacking U.S. and allied strategic naval forces (carriers and SSBNs) are carried out simultaneously. This is in the Norwegian Sea. The northern tier of Europe also is the most sensitive for the Soviets, because it provides direct access to the Soviet heartland. After careful study, the SSG concluded that it was possible for the U.S. and NATO forces to control the sensitive Norwegian Sea area, thereby putting greater pressure on the Soviets, altering their perceptions of risk and of the likelihood to achieve their theater and war objectives. Combined with pressure on the southern and Pacific fronts, U.S. and allied success in the northern tier should influence the Soviets to end the war, even on terms favorable to the United States and NATO.

A U.S. and NATO strategy that included control of the Norwegian Sea would reduce the area in which Soviet naval forces could operate east of the Svalbard Islands–North Cape line. Previously, U.S. and NATO forces seldom ventured beyond the Greenland-

Iceland-Norway line, and waters north of that line were considered, at best, "contested," and at worst, Soviet-dominated. Moving north of the line, U.S. and NATO forces would decrease Soviet ability to defend the homeland, restrict Soviet SSBN operating areas, and complicate Soviet interdiction of the sea lines of communication further south of the Atlantic.

U.S. and NATO success in the northern tier can be achieved through the use of combined arms and forward battle force operations, the SSG concluded. The employment of total capabilities in all U.S. forces would take advantage of mismatches in Soviet capabilities and provide a superior concentration of force.[47]

CINCs Conference in Newport, October 1982

On 28 October 1982, the new Chief of Naval Operations, Admiral James Watkins, convened the first of the annual conferences of navy commanders in chief during his tenure as CNO. He chose Newport, R.I., rather than the traditional locale of Annapolis or Washington, because he wanted to stress the role of the Naval War College as a premier site for strategic thinking within the navy. On 17 August, Admiral Watkins met for the first time, as CNO, with the Strategic Studies Group. The first group had already left Newport for their duty assignments, and the second group had been gathered shortly before to begin its work for the new academic year 1982–1983. In the course of the meeting, Watkins heard the SSG's general approach and its initial plans for the coming year. "I like what I am hearing," he told the Group, "this will be the focal point of naval strategic thinking."[48] Going on, he pointed out that there was a great disparity in the understanding of fleet commanders in the area of naval strategy. Therefore it was important for the strategic concepts to be fully explained. "Let the stuff hang out," Watkins told the Group. "The basic systems of the navy are fundamentally OK, but we need a strategic overlay and confluence of thoughts." Encouraged by what he had heard, he told the SSG II, "You guys make sense." Carrying on from this discussion, Watkins asked Strategic Studies Group Director Robert Murray to prepare a brief memorandum that would outline the framework within which U.S. naval forces could best be utilized toward the objective of defeating Soviet strategy.

The memorandum was drafted by Commander Kenneth McGruther and members of the Strategic Studies Group, then reviewed and approved by the CNO and the Fleet commanders in chief at their Newport conference. As the CINCs listened to the first draft of the briefing by Commander McGruther, they had varying reactions. Admiral William J. Crowe felt that the concepts needed to be fleshed out for the particular problems of the Mediterranean and would be hard to employ there. He felt also that the intelligence estimate overestimated the rigidity of Soviet thinking and practice. Admiral Foley suggested that the concept reflected some intellectual arrogance on the part of the Navy. Admiral Watkins emphasized that it was necessary to deal with the United States as a whole, not just the navy alone. In the absence of a general strategy, it was necessary to create one. He felt that what had been presented was thought provoking, had a great deal of meat to it, and was not far off from the conceptual framework that was wanted. Admiral Small, the vice chief, commented that it is a global strategy to prevent global war. "In most of the world, it is primarily naval. This is a framework for where we are moving." Every one of the commanders in chief had to buy off on it; the concepts of the CINCs must fit within it, Small stressed. "Confidence in ourselves is important; we have to say we'll win. This must become a framework within which we work. We need to build in sufficient flexibility, but also specifically," Small advised.[49]

The final 14-page "Memorandum on Maritime Strategy" that the CINCs agreed to at their Newport meeting, after their initial discussions about it and recommendations concerning its revision, was published in the Center for Naval Warfare Studies, Newport Papers series.[50] The final statement concluded:

> Our first task is to secure access to the battle theater, ensuring needed supplies and reinforcements can arrive *and* helping to keep our lines of communications to our allies open so that they will stay with us. Second, we need to operate aggressively at sea to secure our own flanks and expose those of the enemy. Principally this is the task of sinking the Soviet fleet and securing essential lodgements. Third, our naval forces can help stabilize the front by contributing *directly* to the land battle, *or* do so *indirectly*— and in conjunction with tac air, amphibious, allied forces—by exerting leverage against the enemy's flanks or rear or allies. Finally, the navy can contribute importantly in the time dimension by being able to attack his strategic assets so that the Soviets find what they consider their ultimate strategic leverage being reduced over time. Beyond that, the CINCs agreed that what was necessary was to flesh out the comprehensive approach to strategy by developing a family of regional concepts of operations. These should be tested in war games and amplified with rigorous analysis, being brutally honest in the assumptions used, analyzing the results and applying them. The frame of reference should be implemented, in part, by making better use of the Naval War College. At the same time, the comprehensive approach to strategy must be evolutionary, taking account of evolutions in Soviet strategy as well as changing technologies, vulnerabilities, and force levels.

Strategic Studies Group II

During the academic year 1982–1983, the second Strategic Studies Group adopted the tenets of forward defense and immediate pressure on the Soviets, which had been used in the previous year, but went further to apply them to the southern European and Pacific theaters, continuing the development of a worldwide integrated maritime employment strategy. In its work, the SSG II sought fresh options for initial employment, by examining how, in the critical period of imminent hostilities through the early weeks of combat, we might wrest the initiative from the enemy and score a significant, early Allied victory in the maritime theaters. While its principal task was the development of war-fighting concepts, they took heed of the point Admiral Watkins had made during the October 1982 CINCs conference. Naval forces, Watkins had stressed, must help achieve "deterrence to the last" in a time of rising tensions and potential hostilities. Carrying this concept forward, the SSG II saw that the foundations of deterrence must be laid in peacetime, through forward deployment of forces, national and multinational exercises demonstrating proficiency, and "surge" deployments which demonstrate the U.S. capabilities to reinforce Europe.[51]

In a single theater crisis, naval forces have excelled in rapid deployment to the scene. The global crisis, however, presented a less familiar and less certain situation for deterrence. What one side perceives as a deterrent can as easily be seen as war posturing and provocation by the other. Evaluating that issue carefully, SSG II concluded "that coordinated force deployments in the maritime theater have a potentially synergistic impact which can help deter war, in part because the maritime theaters have the potential for directly threatening the Soviet homeland."[52]

If global deterrence failed and a general war began, the best strategy would be to attack all Soviet forward-deployed forces within hours of the commencement of hostilities. A continuing, coordinated effort to fight forward, SSG II concluded, would significantly reduce the Soviet offensive strategic reserve while reducing homeland defenses. This, they believed, would provide an integrated strategy for all the maritime theaters "that involves a difference."

Examining the Mediterranean theater, SSG II looked at the full range of possibilities, ranging from withdrawal of the carrier battle groups entirely to "a full forward press" into the eastern Mediterranean. They concluded that a full forward posture was preferable, since the United States routinely operates in the eastern Mediterranean in crisis. Such a presence signals both commitment to our allies as well as determination to an enemy. This concept involved risk, and SSG II concluded that earlier studies, which had determined that even a two-carrier battle group could not long survive, were too pessimistic. They went on to develop a tactical concept of carrier havens that could be used to allow carriers to survive in the forward areas and to let them strike at the Soviets from the onset of war. In the Mediterranean this involved an antisurface warfare campaign that rapidly destroyed the Soviet Mediterranean squadron as an anticarrier threat. Then, using deception and target denial as the basis for a campaign against Soviet long-range bombers, these would also be paralleled with early carrier and land-based forces in the southern flank that would slow the Soviets' growing force advance, focus Soviet attention away from the Mediterranean, and tie down Soviet air forces. In achieving these objectives, the defense of both Greece and Turkey would be essential.

This strategic plan envisaged two related and feasible naval campaigns which would contribute greatly to the overall strategic objectives:

(1) The destruction of the Soviet Mediterranean squadron, and possibly its operating bases in Libya and Syria.

(2) The organization of a "gauntlet defense" of the Aegean Sea which, even if the Dardanelles were to fall, would deny entrance to the Mediterranean to all Soviet ships in the Black Sea. This would involve both U.S. and allied air, surface, subsurface, and mining forces.

In looking at the Pacific theater as a third campaign, SSG II identified four objectives:

- Defending U.S. territory.

- Defending the Pacific sea lines of communication.

- Sinking the Soviet Navy.

- Putting direct pressure on the USSR.

To SSG II, all but the last seemed easily scheduled in the Pacific. Beyond participation in a worldwide campaign of attrition against Soviet SSBNs, they saw few targets within reach from the Pacific that could pose a fundamental war-stopping threat to the Soviet Union. However, China was a potential lever to the extent that if U.S. military actions weakened the Soviet position against China, then the United States would put pressure on the Soviets.

In a war in the Pacific, Soviet military forces would be highly dependent on the role of Japan, SSG II concluded. The simultaneous movement of U.S. forces along the Aleutians and north from the Philippines would be designed to force Soviet forces away from the Chinese border or to grant U.S. air superiority over the battle area. The final movement to seize the Kurile Island chain, thereby opening the Sea of Okhotsk, Sakhalin Island, and the northern Belkin coast to further attack would be strongly dependent on Japanese participation, although some options would still remain if Japan chose to stay neutral in a U.S.-Soviet war.

Upon completion of SSG II's work, Robert J. Murray left the Center for Naval Warfare Studies to take up a position at the John F. Kennedy School of Government, Harvard University. Just before leaving Newport in September 1983, Murray wrote to Admiral William N. Small, Commander in Chief, Allied Forces Southern Europe, sending him the first three Newport Papers, consisting of reports of the first two Strategic Studies Group and the memorandum on Maritime Strategy. In his letter, Murray reflected on the work of the previous two years, and concluded that these three documents represented *"an agreed concept"* of naval operations—a maritime strategy—for general war." In short, there was general agreement between the Fleets, OpNav, and Headquarters Marine Corps on the overall approach that they proposed.

Summarizing the outlook that had been developed, Murray wrote,

> The principles espoused here cut across the bow of prevailing opinion in some instances, but the strategy is not radically different from long-held conceptions of the proper employment of naval forces. The principles would not be unfamiliar to Mahan. In particular, our work confirms the value for national strategy of naval forces designed, trained and intended for offensive operations, and rejects as impractical and undesirable the notion, sometimes espoused outside the Navy Department, of a defensively organized and equipped navy. It is clear to us that the best defense remains a *good offense.*[53]

"The concept of forward defense, adopted as NATO strategy and applied to land and air forces already is equally applicable to naval forces," Murray wrote, "it adds much to deterrence and places naval forces in preferred positions if deterrence fails." Going further, Murray noted that the SSG found no instance where it was necessary for U.S. naval forces to employ nuclear weapons to achieve their objection. "While it is necessary to understand how to operate in a nuclear environment," Murray concluded, "it is not necessary to take the initiative in using nuclear weapons for naval purposes; on the contrary, the use of nuclear weapons at sea appears to be to our clear disadvantage."[54]

Strategic Studies Group III

In the summer of 1983, Dr. Robert S. Wood was appointed Dean of the Center for Naval Warfare Studies and Director of the Strategic Studies Group. An academic, Wood had been professor of government and foreign affairs at the University of Virginia and then chairman of the Strategy Department at the Naval War College from 1980 to 1983. When Wood took charge of the SSG, the group was faced with three major issues that it might explore. Since the first two Strategic Studies Groups had examined the issues involved in how to use forces in the early stages of a global war, the strategy that had been developed was a war-fighting strategy. Having established that, one could then examine how such a war-fighting strategy could be used in peacetime as an effective deterrent to war, complementing work being undertaken in OpNav. Alternatively, the SSG could go forward in its examination of global war and examine the issues involved in terminating a war. Or thirdly, quite apart from a global war against the Soviet

Union, which was the focus of *The Maritime Strategy,* one could examine how in crisis the navy might be used so that should a crisis deteriorate into war neither the navy nor the country would be awkwardly placed. When these various choices were presented to Admiral Watkins for his decision as to what direction the Strategic Studies Group should take, he chose the third option.[55]

The third Strategic Studies Group devoted its work during the academic year 1983–1984 to examining strategies for handling outlying Soviet client states during the crisis preceding a NATO–Warsaw Pact war and strategies for employing naval forces in the types of regional crises to which the U.S. Navy must frequently respond. In doing this, they focused on three cases: Cuba, Libya, and Southwest Asia.

The case studies on Libya and the Persian Gulf touched on issues that came to pass later in the U.S. strike against Libya in 1986 and in the Persian Gulf in 1987. Neither of these studies dealt directly with the problem of a regional crisis which would directly affect a global war against the Soviets. The case study on Cuba did do this. In looking at Cuba, SSG III noted that while Atlantic Fleet forces might be deployed in strength against Cuba at the outbreak of a war with the Soviet Union, they could not both do this and "defend forward" in the Norwegian Sea and eastern Mediterranean as postulated by *The Maritime Strategy.* The foreseen problem is one of inopportune positioning or "maldeployment."[56]

The Forward Maritime Strategy requires that virtually all U.S. naval forces be positioned well forward within striking range of the Soviet Union in order to deter the start of a war and to be positioned to seize the initiative should war start. In order to prevent maldeployment in meeting this objective, the United States must rely on economy of force in outlying areas. SSG III concluded that it was not possible to destroy or neutralize outlying Soviet client states. However, sufficient force must be positioned to deter them from participating in the war or to prevent them from affecting the war effort, should they attempt it. The United States would need less force in outlying areas if it confined its objectives to protecting the sea and air lanes of communication in the war against the Soviet Union. Should destruction or neutralization of these client states be required, then the ability to sustain the Forward Maritime Strategy would be reduced, risking failure of that strategy. Conversely, as the Forward Maritime Strategy succeeds, outlying client states would be cut away from the Soviet Union and would be unable, if not unwilling, to support it.

In its final conclusion, SSG III summarized its work into three main points:

1. Crisis responses are not interceptions to our normal business; they are an integral part of it.

2. Crises are primarily political events, not military ones, and naval forces cannot be applied without accommodating political considerations within military operations. The military effort cannot be separated from the political objectives.

3. The Forward Maritime Strategy can be expanded to include suitable responses to crises. If we plan ahead, our strategies for handling those crises can be executed without degrading our ability to carry out that Maritime Strategy.[57]

In addition, SSG III recommended that regional strategies be developed using carefully sized, even modest forces. "The defeat of the Soviets must be the primary objective; we take forces from that objective at our peril," they concluded. At the same time, they warned, "for a CINC to have only one course of action planned may be insufficient . . . no single plan can be expected to fit all enemy actions. A range of alternatives is clearly necessary."[58]

Strategic Studies Group IV

During the 1984–1985 academic year, SSG IV turned to study the issues of deterrence posed by *The Maritime Strategy*. Where SSG I, in particular, had found that the threat posed by naval forces in war might not be enough to terminate a war, SSG IV developed further ideas on what would be required to use naval forces to create the credible prospect of prolonged conventional war. In the era of nuclear parity, conventional forces are a part of the larger issues involved in deterrence. SSG IV carefully studied the instability created by reinforcement of Europe during a crisis. In a discussion with SSG IV members, General Bernard Rogers, Supreme Allied Commander Europe, noted that forward deployed naval forces played an important role and could "prime my NATO pump."[59]

SSG IV recognized that our day-to-day actions shape Soviet calculations to a greater extent than the actions that we might take in a crisis. They concluded that the situations the Soviets fear most are those that they can control least, such as prolonged conventional war. The Soviets recognize that there is no particular territory that they can capture that would allow them to defeat NATO, but that the USSR must destroy the will of the Alliance to fight. To counter this, NATO demonstrations of solidarity and capability create an environment in which the Soviet Union is unlikely to risk direct military confrontation—unless not to do so risks Soviet survival. To support this, SSG IV recommended increased demonstrations of solidarity in the Western alliance, a prepared forward defense with a demonstrated capitalization for sustained interoperability among forces.[60]

Strategic Studies Group V

At the beginning of the 1985–1986 academic year, a new director was appointed for the Strategic Studies Group, Marshall Brement, a career diplomat and former U.S. Ambassador to Iceland, 1981–1985. This division of labor between the two positions of director of the SSG and the Center for Naval Warfare Studies allowed Dr. Robert Wood to focus more closely on the work of the Center as a long-term, stable complement to the transient year-long strategic study groups. Brement, in his turn, was able to focus fully on the work required by the direct personal relationship of the CNO to the Strategic Studies Group. Under Brement's leadership, SSG V focused on the employment of naval forces to support peacetime foreign policy objectives.

The Group concluded that the effective employment of military forces to induce regional stability and respond to acts that threaten national objectives requires great attention, both within the navy and at the National Security Council level. On the national level, they noted that coordinated interagency planning is required to produce regional strategies based on clearly stated policy objectives. SSG V developed a process to deal with events in a crisis and to assist in formulating a reaction without losing focus on the broader objective. They also developed a series of force options to improve response, and a process to account for the difference in criteria in targets for peacetime and in wartime. In the following year, 1986–1987, SSG VI examined Soviet thinking.

Conclusion

In the eight years of evolutionary development between Admiral Hayward's announcement of his strategic concepts in 1978, through the cumulative work of the CNO's Strategic Studies Group in 1986, American naval strategic thinkers had revived classical naval theory and placed it clearly within the context of both the peacetime use of naval force and the context of the nuclear age. In the process, a common approach and view was developing at the highest levels of the navy's leadership, leaving room for future modifications and evolution to take place on a firm, conceptual foundation.

CHAPTER FOUR

The Work of the Strategic Concepts Branch, (OP-603), 1982–1986

The publication entitled *The Maritime Strategy*,[1] prepared in the office of the Chief of Naval Operations, is the official statement of what is sometimes called the "Forward Maritime Strategy" or "The Maritime Component of National Military Strategy." The immediate origins of the CNO/SECNAV-approved *Maritime Strategy* are clearly definable and lead directly from three memoranda written by the Vice Chief of Naval Operations, Admiral William N. Small.

In December 1981, Small wrote a memo to the Director of Navy Program Planning in which he said:

> I think it is high time we take a formal, critical look at how we do the analysis that leads to our appraisals of Navy Programs. Our current methodology is very susceptible to adverse interpretations, not only by those outside the navy who wish to attack navy programs and strategy, but even within the navy where we are professionally misled by both the scenario displayed and the conclusion which may logically be drawn therefrom.[2]

Small objected to the typical thinking within the navy staff in Washington which tended not to consider strategy in discussing programs for ship and weapon construction. The programs often seemed to drive the strategy, he thought, and he wanted to reverse this situation so that serious and responsible thought about the naval part of national strategy would eventually become the basis upon which the United States built its navy for the future.[3]

In Small's view, a major deficiency in naval thinking was a worst-case mentality. "We assign the best capabilities to the enemy and the worst to our own forces," he wrote. In analyzing engagements, we put our forces "into tactical situations which no prudent planner or responsible commander would countenance." Moreover, the U.S. Navy seemed to have adopted a defensive outlook, not an offensive one. "Naval forces are intended to seek out and destroy the enemy," Small declared, "not defend themselves."[4]

Within the Pentagon's Navy staff, Small saw the parochialism of each of the platform sponsors and the failure of the OpNav staff to integrate the analyses, appraisals, requirements, and programs in planning the future navy. "None of the characteristics of a naval engagement are played in isolation from each other in the real world, as they seem to be in our current methods of analysis," Small declared. "If affordability were injected early into analysis, which is itself based on national forces employment against realistic threats, we would have fewer and better supported combat systems."[5] Small believed that the practices which were then current in the Pentagon led to exotic responses to extreme requirements, resulting in insufficient forces for realistic needs.

Almost three months later, Small took up the issue again with another memo to the Director of the Office of Naval Warfare and the Deputy CNO for Plans and Policy. Noting that he had heard little discussion of how naval forces might be employed in wartime, Small said:

> A review of maritime strategy may well change many of the assumptions currently explicit in our systems requirements. I guess the responsibility for this type of thinking lies somewhere between (or among) OP-06 and OP-095, but seems dormant.[6]

At the bottom of the memo, Vice Admiral Sylvester Foley, then Deputy CNO for Plans and Policy (OP-06), wrote a note to his executive assistant asking him to get some of his staff members to discuss the issues. "We can start with the broad maritime strategy script by Lehman," Foley said "and go from there."[7] Rear Admiral W. R. Smedberg IV, Director of the Office of Naval Warfare (OP-095), followed up Small's suggestion with a note to Foley, recommending that OP-06 take the lead in this action. "The Strategic setting and operational concept should be spelled out more explicitly as the backdrop of our POM development," Smedberg wrote.[8]

Concurring completely, Foley reported to Small that OP-06 would take the lead in developing a presentation on maritime strategy and employment options. Foley suggested that the briefing should focus on initial points; among them were:

- The political uses for which maritime forces are to be employed against a potential enemy.

- How we expect U.S. maritime forces to be employed against potential enemies.

- What "ground tactics" are believed to be associated with these employments.

- What forces might reasonably be available.

- Whether the strategy is supported by current programs and whether alternatives should be developed.

Small agreed with Foley's proposal and wrote a note by hand at the bottom of Foley's memo emphasizing the basic problem in strategic thinking. "One of the important findings of our Strategic Studies (Review) Group at NWC [Naval War College] and the OOX [CNO Executive Panel] folks here, during their fleet visits and discussions with navy leadership, is that there is a great deal of confusion about strategies and analysis relating to force *acquisition* and strategy for winning wars. Much of the analysis done is more related to the first than the latter."[9]

Although a general consensus had been formed by Small's first two memos, the document that actually triggered the immediate action to prepare a briefing, which eventually became the CNO/SECNAV-approved *Maritime Strategy*, was a memo written for Small's signature in OP-96, headed by Rear Admiral John A. Baldwin. This memo expressed what was on everyone's mind in the navy staff. Written by Vice Admiral Carlisle Trost on the memo cover sheet that went along the clearance ladder before Small's signature was "We really need this to get the entire OpNav staff moving in the same direction."[10]

The memo was signed on 2 August 1982 by Small and sent to all four flag officers directly concerned with the preparation of the upcoming annual Program Objective Memorandum or POM. The POM is a complete line-by-line list of every appropriation item that the navy requires for the next five years, within fiscal limits. Comparable memoranda are submitted each May by every service to the Department of Defense and are the key inputs in the budget request to Congress. The POM ties the multiple planning functions within the navy together in a single document and serves as the basis upon which a budget can be constructed in support of the defined goals and objectives of the navy. In starting the annual process, which would lead to the submission of the POM in May 1983, Admiral Small repeated his view that a strategy appraisal was needed "at the outset of the POM process with respect to how naval forces will be employed in wartime and their disposition both in the sense of our CINC war plans and in the DG [Defense Guidance] scenario." Action on Admiral Small's memo was passed to the Strategic Concepts Branch (OP-603), then headed by Captain Elizabeth Wylie. Within that office, Captain Wylie selected an action officer, Lieutenant Commander Stanley Weeks, to carry out the required work. Weeks, although the junior officer in that group, had an unusual background, marked by academic depth as an Olmstead scholar in Spain and a Ph.D. in international relations from American University. In addition, he had broad experience at sea, having just spent a year on board British and Dutch ships as the at-sea operations officer for the Commander of NATO's Standing Naval Force, Atlantic (STANAVFORLANT). Weeks eagerly took the assignment because he thought it would be a great challenge to try to pull together and articulate a general statement of U.S. naval strategy. Weeks felt that such a statement could be very valuable, not only in the program appraisal process, but also as a war-fighting frame-work for naval officers and a reply to critics who continued to claim that the United States did not have a strategy. When Weeks was given this task, it seemed only another routine chore in OP-603; neither he nor others realized how quick or extensive would be the success of their project.[11]

As the scope of the work became plain, Commander W. Spencer Johnson was assigned to join Weeks in the project and to produce a draft as soon as possible, focusing his ef-forts on the "front end" connection of national strategy and defense programming.[12] A surface warfare officer with an advanced degree in international relations from the Fletcher School of Law and Diplomacy, Johnson was the key OP-605 officer who coor-dinated the policy work of OP-06 with the offices concerned with programs and the budget process at the Joint Chiefs' and DoD level. Within three weeks, these two offi-cers pieced together a draft briefing, classified secret, which answered Admiral Small's request.[13] As Weeks and Johnson began work on developing a statement of a national maritime strategy, they were aware of the general issues and took note of the informa-tion and problems suggested in the public literature, but sometimes drew quite differ-ent conclusions.[14] Weeks was well aware of Secretary of the Navy John Lehman's views. Weeks had been the action officer in OP-603 for staffing Lehman's annual Posture Statement, which the Secretary had delivered to the House Armed Services Committee on 8 February 1982. Certainly Secretary Lehman's views and proposals to develop a 600-ship navy based on 15 battle groups provided a clear background for the strategy Johnson and Weeks were developing,[15] although they did not explicitly consider his statement as a sole source.

Following Admiral Small's explicit instructions, the strategic discussion for the POM 85 CPAM was based on current forces, rather than projected future forces. In Small's view this was a correction to a basic flow in earlier analyses,[16] and it brought the oppor-tunity for a more realistic discussion of strategy. As Weeks explained,

> The *current-force* nature of strategy CPAM allows OP-06 to "wrap" the CPAM in the cloak of the CINCs' *current* strategy/general war plans, thereby giving greater cre-dence to the *overall* strategy, and leading to greater receptiveness to the strategy than would be the case if it were seen as the whole cloth product of some "06 smart guys."[17]

Indeed, the OP-603 action officers made a great effort to make a consolidated state-ment of the various CINCs' current war plans within the context of basic national pol-icy and strategy. By coincidence, the CINCs were making a series of direct briefings on their current concepts of operations to the Joint Chiefs of Staff in the months of Au-gust and September 1982, and Weeks and Johnson had direct access to these "up-to-the-minute" overviews of war plans as well as the plans themselves. In addition, they wanted to piece together a general and coherent statement of the maritime portions of these briefings that was consistent with national policy and strategy. To do this, they used four basic documents for the general background to the overall strategy consolidating CINCs' maritime plans:

- The Presidential Directive that established national global objectives and priorities: *National Security Decision Directive-32 (NSDD-32)*, issued on 20 May 1982.

- The Secretary of Defense's annual directive to the services, which is reviewed and revised each year, the then most recent being *Defense Guidance for Fiscal Years 1984–88*, issued by Secretary of Defense Caspar Weinberger on 22 March 1982.

- The document that is the principal method by which the Joint Chiefs of Staff recommend changes to the Secretary of Defense's *Defense Guidance: The Joint Strategy and Force Planning Document (JSPD)*. The latter, for the fiscal years 1985–1991, had been approved on 1 September 1982.

- And finally, the latest analysis of actual midterm programmed force capabilities, which identified special areas of strategy and force mismatch and which highlights the risks: *The Joint Program Assessment Memorandum for 1984*. (JPAM-84).

Using these sources, Weeks and Johnson developed a statement of maritime strategy that was focused on the broad aspects of strategy and quite intentionally avoided getting bogged down in specific scenarios, time lines, and tactics. The scenarios in some of the general guidance had already become a source of contention. If *The Maritime Strategy* were tied simply to the illustrative scenario used in *Defense Guidance,* then as Weeks stated, "I was sure the PDRC/CEB [Program Development Review Committee/CNO Executive Board] would spend so much time debating the (debatable) arrival date of this or that CVBG that the big picture would be totally lost."[18]

Piecing together the requirements of national strategy and policy with the regional responsibilities and the perspectives of the various maritime commanders in chief in mind, Weeks and Johnson defined a basic statement: "The essence of our National Strategy is *global forward deterrence,*" they wrote.

> The *global* element here suggests that, . . . our maritime strategy plans should be based on the premise that we will not have the luxury of ceding *any* major region to the Soviets by default . . . the *forward* aspect here means that our maritime strategy plans must keep the SLOCs open to Eurasia, and cooperate fully with the other services and the allies. The third element—deterrence—must be viewed not only in its peacetime or strategic nuclear context, but also in terms of reinforcing deterrence in a crisis or restoring deterrence in wartime.[19]

From the very outset, the purpose of the maritime strategy was to articulate a strategy for deterrence. "In the simplest sense, to deter is to threaten," Weeks and Johnson wrote.[20] The maritime strategy thus had to be able to apply pressure on those places that the Soviet Union valued most highly—its homeland, bases, and both its conventional and nuclear forces. In this way, *The Maritime Strategy* would make a direct contribution to "our military *and* political/psychological strategy objectives."[21] At the same time, it anticipated Congressional critics who would call for more "maneuver warfare" without appreciating that it was inherently part of the nature of war at sea. Maritime forces were to be employed in a "forward pressure" strategy, designed to influence the Soviets to restore a balance of power relationship, even if conflict had already erupted. As Weeks wrote for the first draft strategy presentation, "Our *Maritime Strategy* should help ensure favorable war outcome terms by using our ideally suited (inherently flexible and mobile) battle group and amphibious forces in *maritime maneuver initiatives* to seize territory and strike Soviet vulnerabilities, with the result that we have some negotiating advantages of our own and can preclude the Soviets just "sitting on" their initial territorial gains."[22]

This kind of thinking required appreciation of Soviet naval strategy. At that time, Soviet Naval Strategy was itself a matter of much debate within the navy. The first *Maritime Strategy* briefing dealt with this only subject in a single viewgraph slide, which graphically illustrated Soviet intentions.[23] Behind this brief exposition, however, lay a great deal of the new analytic work on the Soviet Navy. Lieutenant Commander Weeks brought this work into *The Maritime Strategy* through several knowledge sources. His initial source was Captain William Manthorpe, then head of (OP-96N). In addition, he was highly influenced by a report written by Rear Admiral R. Welander, U.S. Navy (Ret.), for the BDM Corporation,[24] the work of Bradford Dismukes at the Center for Naval Analyses, and discussions with Commander Kenneth McGruther on the staff supporting the CNO's Strategic Studies Group located at the Naval War College. Weeks incorporated into his briefing what he considered to be their better insights.

After discussion with McGruther and Manthorpe, Weeks decided to couch the section on the Soviet threat in terms of the new assessment of Soviet intentions, which emphasized the Soviet priority in holding back forces to ensure the survivability and mission readiness of the Soviet SSBN force. Weeks had some misgivings about this and would have liked to have seen more explicit discussion of how the U.S. Navy would counter the Soviet Navy, should it confound our expectations and surge SSN forces into the Atlantic, particularly in a prolonged crisis phase. Privately, he thought that the intelligence community's assessment tended to ignore the possibility that the Soviets might well surge forward with their naval forces for political reasons during an extended, prewar crisis. To deal with this, Weeks wanted to add the concept of what he called

"Maritime Exclusion Areas," but he found little high-level support for this concept. Instead, he positioned on his briefing slides three Carrier Battle Groups in the North Atlantic and Pacific so that they could be "linebackers," moving north or south of the Greenland-Iceland-Norway line in the Atlantic and Japan in the Pacific, depending on the Soviet submarine threat.[25] In short, the strategy was to be a "forward strategy," but the degree of forwardness was seen as a more tactical decision to be made by the maritime commander, based on the political and military situation at the time.

The global perspective of *The Maritime Strategy* demonstrated some serious problems for the navy when the war plans from the various commanders in chief were put together. Each commander in chief's war planners had written their plans on the basis of a "worst case" war starting in their own theater. They assumed full availability and priority in their theater for major force deployments, including aircraft carriers. As a result, when the forces in each plan were added up, they revealed the need for a total of 22 carrier battle groups: 10 in Europe, 3 in Southwest Asia, and 9 in the Pacific. With fewer than 13 carrier battle groups available at that time, "the obvious conclusion as shown here is that our current force maritime strategy for a near-simultaneous global war cannot be the sum of existing CINCs' plans."[26] Looking at the situation from OpNav, the Strategic Concepts Branch wanted to incorporate the best elements of the CINCs' current or preferred general war strategies, but the problem of dealing with current force levels for a "come-as-you-are" global war meant that they had to trim the presumed force requirements written into the current CINCs' plans and the JSCP. The "worst case" presumptions and resulting force mismatch were not new, Weeks noted in the first draft—as Winston Churchill had remarked on the requests of his CINCs on 3 November 1941: "all experience shows that all Commanders in Chief invariably ask for everything they can think of, and always represent their own forces at a minimum."[27]

Despite the need to trim the numbers to match reality, the strategy highlighted a striking symmetry between many of the key elements in Atlantic and Pacific strategies. There was a clear similarity in the way the different plans looked at the Aleutians and Iceland, Japan, and Norway, the Greenland-Iceland-Norway Gap and the northwestern Pacific. "Both CINCs placed fundamental importance on a forward defense pivoted on key northern islands that control access to the U.S. and lie above the vital transoceanic sea-lanes. If these islands are lost, the roof collapses on our links with NATO and the key Pacific Allies," Weeks wrote.[28] In addition, the 1981 concept of maritime operations by the Commander in Chief, U.S. Naval Forces Europe for the Mediterranean was consistent with the basic forward, offensive disposition in the Atlantic and the Pacific CINCs' strategies. Although forward submarine barriers were not as applicable in the Mediterranean area, the strategy there was consistent with the Atlantic and Pacific strategies in emphasizing full cooperation with allies, early coordination with the

Marine Corps and Air Force Tactical Airwings, positioning battle groups to survive initial Soviet strikes, then moving fully augmented naval forces forward to keep pressure
on the Soviets, and if need be, eventually to seize or regain territory to use as leverage
in terminating a war.[29]

In 1982, the first version of the CNO/SECNAV approved statement of *The Maritime
Strategy* began as an internal OpNav effort to state clearly the strategic background
upon which naval force planning and budget decisions should be made informed. But
almost immediately, the Weeks-Johnson *Maritime Strategy* began to develop a wider
significance. By late September 1982, the new Deputy CNO for Plans, Policy and Operations (OP-06), Vice Admiral Arthur Moreau, had reported and immediately approved
the basic Weeks-Johnson *Maritime Strategy* briefing, deleting only the backup "Maritime Exclusion Areas" concept. Then, in early October, the briefing was presented to
the Program Development Review Committee (PDRC), the most junior of the three
oversight committees in the navy programming process. This committee of rear admirals was chaired by the Director of the General Planning and Programming Division
(OP-90) Rear Admiral Joseph Metcalf III, and the PDRC flag officers decided that *The
Maritime Strategy* briefing should be presented "as is" and within a week to the most
senior oversight committee—the CNO Executive Board (CEB), consisting of the CNO
and all his deputy CNOs and principal assistants. This "instant CEB" review was arranged by Rear Admiral Metcalf, and when Weeks and Johnson made their presentation to it, the Chief of Naval Operations, Admiral Watkins and the other senior flag
officers reacted positively. In the discussion following the briefing, Watkins emphasized
the need to keep *The Maritime Strategy* focused on cooperation with allies and with
other services, particularly the U.S. Air Force.

On 7 October, Admiral Watkins issued a message to the Fleet CINCs looking back over
his first 90 days as Chief of Naval Operations and identified the areas in which he
wanted to focus with a new sense of urgency. Among the several areas he identified
were war-fighting readiness, the revitalization of the Naval War College as the crucible
for strategic and tactical thinking, the integrating of the Naval Reserves into our
war-fighting thinking, and improvement of interservice cooperation and greater understanding.[30] The idea behind this was to unify the work of the CINCs and to bring
their collective knowledge and understanding to bear on the broad issues of the navy,
particularly in using naval forces for deterrence. The briefing, which Weeks and
Johnson had developed during August and September 1982 in the Strategic Concepts
Branch for helping decision makers in the budgetary process, played into Watkins's
broader goals.[31] It quickly began to take on a larger significance and to build on a wider
process of thinking within the navy.

At Watkins's request, *The Maritime Strategy* briefing was presented to the Fleet CINCs' conference, which met at the Naval War College on 26–29 October. In order to immediately gain the CINCs' support, the OP-603 team used in their briefing some of the very same viewgraph slides that the CINCs themselves had used in their presentation earlier.[32] At the same meeting, Richard Haver of the Office of Naval Intelligence filled in the detailed background and the basis that substantiated the intelligence analysts' conclusions as to Soviet intentions.[33] With the CINCs' approval, Vice Admiral Arthur Moreau, then Deputy Chief of Naval Operations (Plans, Policy and Operations) (OP-06), was directed to give the briefing to Secretary of the Navy John Lehman with the Chief of Naval Operations, Admiral Watkins, and the Commandant of the Marine Corps, General P. X. Kelley, in attendance.

Vice Admiral Moreau made the presentation on 4 November 1982. At the conclusion of his remarks, Secretary of the Navy Lehman announced, "Bravo, you have just given us a handbook that can be used in our deliberations with the third deck [Office of the Secretary of Defense], with Congress, with OMB, and the joint arena."[34] Admiral Watkins agreed and noted that he planned to use the briefing as a basis to lay the structure for future explorations of strategy. General Kelley was equally impressed and remarked, "it is an aggressive way to do business." It is something people can identify with—"it's fighting wars." What had begun only two short months before as Lieutenant Commander Weeks's and Commander Johnson's briefing was now the Navy's *Maritime Strategy.*

After hearing the briefing, Lehman, Watkins, and Kelley agreed that they would keep the document an internal one for the time being. Admiral Watkins wanted to update NWP-1 in line with the thinking of the CINCs before following up Kelly's suggestion to war-game the strategy with civilian officers at Newport. Secretary Lehman pointed out that this briefing had been the first real session of its kind and was a good avenue to pursue in the POM development. "We can use this as a backdrop for the affordability issues," he said. "We can demonstrate a sound strategy and can readily identify risk areas to many audiences." During the discussion, the three men agreed on some basic points to make in the briefing:

- Use 15 carriers on all force-level issues.
- Incorporate the Surface Action Groups built around battleships.
- Explain the incremental approach to the employment of forces.
- Caveat regional priorities for wartime resource allocation.[35]

Following the Secretary of the Navy's approval of *The Maritime Strategy*, the first concern was to find a means to inform all the people who needed to understand the basic view that it presented. This was no small task given the way the navy staff was spread out bureaucratically in the Pentagon, and because it was so highly structured in its flow of information and concepts. With this in mind, the Vice Chief of Naval Operations, Admiral Small, directed Vice Admiral Moreau to brief *The Maritime Strategy* to the "Captains, etc., who really work the POM and Program Plan during the rest of the year. . . . I doubt it will feed down from the 3-star level otherwise."[36] Moreau responded that he would "solicit wide attendance from OpNav/NAVMAT officers in order to get the information to those who need it," but Small was rather doubtful about merely requesting attendance. "Maybe [it should be] stronger than solicit, I don't know," he wrote to Moreau.[37]

Shortly thereafter, *The Maritime Strategy* briefing was presented to the CNO Executive Panel (CEP) by Rear Admiral Robert E. Kirksey, Director of the Strategy Plans and Policy Division (OP-60). Interestingly, the CEP was the only internal audience that reacted negatively to the briefing. Professor Albert Wohlstetter pointed out that *The Maritime Strategy* presentation was an important departure for the navy in terms of strategic thinking and future force planning. The "current force" limitation, he noted, posed fundamental problems for the navy in terms of identifying and procuring force multipliers that would reduce the present significant risk our country faced when comparing Soviet capabilities with our own. Along the same line, Rear Admiral Eli Reich recalled that several years previously, Admiral Hayward had testified to the effect that we have a one and one-half-ocean navy for a three-ocean commitment. Reich felt that the briefing bore that point out for him.[38]

During the winter and spring of 1982–1983, *The Maritime Strategy* briefing was given widely. In February 1983, it figured largely in Admiral Watkins's posture statement before the House Armed Services Committee. During his testimony, Watkins summarized the basic premises in the strategy briefing, and he stressed in particular the broader institutional interplay within the navy, which the concept of *The Maritime Strategy* implied. In particular, he noted that the strategy relied on the contributions of other U.S. air and land forces and the forces of friends and allies. He mentioned his enthusiastic support for the efforts of General John W. Vessey, Jr. as Chairman of the Joint Chiefs in nurturing interservice measures in an integrated air defense of NATO Europe, a balanced program for nonstrategic nuclear forces, and the continual development of cross-service interoperability in military intelligence resources and the cruise missile program. Complementing this, he noted that he had signed agreements with the Air Force Chief of Staff during the fall of 1982 to increase combined Navy–Air Force effectiveness. In particular he stressed, "We also depend on contributions from our allies, such as their 140-plus diesel submarines which are well versed in their local waters and best employed in executing special missions in those areas."[39]

Watkins's own concept of how strategic and tactical thinking was being improved within the navy was important and reflected the emphasis he placed on certain organizations and their work. He mentioned in his Posture Statement three key elements in his thinking: [40]

- The effort to develop a better understanding of the Soviet thought processes and inherent strengths and weaknesses in order to counter and to exploit them.

- The revitalization of the Naval War College as a crucible for Strategic and Tactical thinking and the parallel effort to expose the finest, tactically proven professionals to strategic thinking as a means of testing professional thought as well as creating a cadre of sound-thinking educated commanders ready for key assignments; the use of combined-arms war games explicitly designed to avoid a parochial, navy-only point of view.

- The use of the semi-annual Navy Commanders in Chief Conference as a forum for discussing national strategy and *The Maritime Strategy* flowing from it, to help establish the basis for organizing fiscal programming considerations related to the CINCs' employment plans.

In Watkins's view, the teachings of Mahan were vital, but they needed modernization and revalidation. An understanding of history is not enough for strategy, it must be dynamic and related to the technological developments that are outrunning us. Strategy cannot be emotion, he said, nor can it be developed alone by a single person or group in a short time. It is an iterative process in which deep thought must be given to each segment of the strategy as it is developed. In order to move ideas and put teeth in them, the strategy needed to supply "the same set of sheet music" for the CINCs, the budget process, the intelligence community, those working on new concepts, and those working out arrangements with other services and allies. In short, *The Maritime Strategy* for Watkins is what "surrounds the employment of Maritime forces." For that reason, Watkins saw *The Maritime Strategy* as his most important contribution to the navy. [41]

For Watkins, the Strategic Studies Group (SSG) at the Naval War College would provide the all-important original thinking on new aspects for the strategy. The officers of the SSG were all senior experienced men who had great potential for the future. Located at the Naval War College, the SSG reported only to the CNO and had direct access to him and the other CINCs. By having this direct link, without the interference of any other chain of command or tasking, and by keeping the group at a distance from the daily brush fires of life in the Pentagon, Watkins tried to ensure that the group focused on the areas that needed in-depth investigation in the gradual evolutionary process of making the strategy. Toward the end of his term as CNO, Watkins reflected that the work of the Strategic Concepts Branch (OP-603) was in some ways an adversarial one. Ultimately, its role was to bring the original, new concepts of the Strategic Studies Groups into the broad general statement of *The Maritime Strategy*, as appropriate, and to reconcile their ideas, pointing out flaws, gaps, and disparities as they worked through what had become an annual strategy review and presentation process. Thus, they modified the strategy as it dealt with new technology, new assessments of threats, and considered CINCs' plans in relation to national policy guidance.[42]

The work of the OpNav Strategic Concepts Branch (OP-603) was no less important. First, it made a key contribution in the initial work by Weeks and Johnson in coalescing and articulating a coherent broad statement of strategy, and secondly, through the subsequent work of later action officers assigned to the Group—who annually refined it, wrote it down, and adapted it to a variety of audiences both inside and outside the navy. The initial work in both the briefing and the written version required a great deal of analytical and creative thought to synthesize the various concepts and ideas of naval strategic thought. Subsequently, as *The Maritime Strategy* was adopted and publicized, the process widened with a spill-off into academic, professional journals and discussions with other services and friendly nations. The challenge of packaging and presentation was added to the need to maintain the strategy as an evolving one, sensitive to changing intelligence assessments and naval capabilities.

By early 1983, Commodore Dudley L. Carlson, Deputy Director of the Strategy, Plans and Policy Division (OP-60B) had become the navy's principal briefing officer for major presentation. Already *The Maritime Strategy* had begun to be used whenever a general statement about naval strategy was required. A milestone in this wider presentation of the strategy came on 24 February 1983, when Commodore Carlson and Lieutenant Commander Weeks gave the briefing to the Subcommittee on Seapower and Strategic and Critical Material of the House Armed Services Committee on *Maritime Strategy*. This was the first time that the full briefing had been given to Congress, and that event happened to be the last briefing in which Lieutenant Commander Weeks served as the primary *Maritime Strategy* action officer. The version given to the House subcommittee was essentially the same as that first prepared five months earlier, but its language and slides had been polished and improved under the guidance of Commodore Carlson. The version given to Congress had one important new element added to it, which remained with the briefing thereafter: a public relations type of tutorial on the basic uses and unique qualities of naval forces.[43]

The new emphasis on a wider role and wider audiences for the strategy briefing, the departure of Weeks for duty as a shipboard executive officer, and the subsequent assignment of Commander Peter Swartz as a replacement for both Weeks and Johnson coincided with the appointment of Captain Roger Barnett as the new Branch Head in

OP-603 and the beginning of the next phase in support of the POM-86 testimony on navy budget and programs. The new key actors were Barnett and Swartz. Captain Roger Barnett was a surface warfare officer with a Ph.D. in international relations from the University of Southern California. He had experience on the U.S. SALT delegation as well as on the 1980–1981 Defense Department Transition Team. He had also been head of the navy staff's Extended Planning Office (OP-965) and Deputy Director of Political Military Planning (OP-61). Swartz was a general unrestricted line officer on his second tour of duty in OP-60. With a master's degree from the Johns Hopkins School of Advanced International Studies, he had just completed three years of additional graduate work at Columbia University.

Vice Admiral Arthur Moreau, The Deputy Chief of Naval Operations (OP-06) took a great personal interest in the plans for the new revision, although he himself would shortly be transferred. In all his twenty-some years in the navy up to 1982, he had not heard the navy articulate a strategy for global warfare. He felt that the navy had not rethought through all the time-tested theories and examined their applicability to the present. Moreau spent a great deal of time with Barnett, working evenings and Saturdays directly with him and also with Swartz. Moreau saw the first version of a *Maritime Strategy* briefing as a categorization of the priorities of naval tasks in global warfare. Through it, the navy had been able to portray the relative importance of tasks and to begin to see that there was a problem in positioning for the navy during a pre-conflict period. "In every scenario, there is always a set of naval tasks to accomplish with competing assets," he said. "Fundamentally, naval tasks are a given. Beyond that it is a question of recognizing Soviet strategy and tactics and dealing with them."[44] The same point was echoed by Captain Roger Barnett when he said "Strategy is not a game of solitaire."[45] For Moreau, however, it was important to take the conceptual underpinnings of the first version and to begin the process of advancing them step by step, prioritizing them, then going on to examine the most probable course of action within this analysis. Moreau saw that there was a danger in this and that it could lead to an absolute vision of strategy unless the concepts were continually open to challenge.[46]

Moreau discussed the substance of the strategy directly with Barnett and Swartz and directed them to build upon the earlier version and to develop an architecture for the strategy that would expand upon it and give it more depth. In essence, the old version, which focused on the carrier battle groups, needed more focus on other naval forces—on allied navies and air forces and on joint U.S. Army and U.S. Air Force strategy. This new version needed to be connected more clearly and in greater depth with our understanding of Soviet naval strategy in both wartime crisis and war. This kind of thinking carried with it the need to look more carefully at Norway, the subject of the Strategic Studies Group's first in-depth work, the whole question of naval support of NATO, and the relation of navies to the Central Front as well as on the sea lines of communication in both the Atlantic and the Pacific. At the same time, less was needed on the "front end" national strategy and programming details of general policy guidance; and the preferences of the commander in chief, which had figured so largely in the first briefings, although a shorter, updated segment was nevertheless retained.[47] As Swartz explained, the difference between the Weeks-Johnson version of *The Maritime Strategy* briefing and his own was "more: more explanation, more forces, more joint, more allied. . . ."[48]

As action officer for *The Maritime Strategy*, Commander Swartz undertook his task with the strong belief that it should not appear to be the product of some brilliant and ethereal strategic thinker, but rather the collective thought of the high command of the entire navy. Influenced in his general approach by Rear Admiral Joseph C. Wylie's book, *Military Strategy*,[49] Swartz tried to employ Wylie's basic thesis that strategy is a form of control that cannot be seen in isolation from other factors. In developing further the Weeks-Johnson statement of the strategy, he tried to use this concept in applying a wide variety of sources including the resources of the Naval War College's Global War Games, the thinking of the Strategic Studies Group, the speeches of Secretary of the Navy Lehman, NATO war plans, and the CINCs' current concepts of operations. As he studied these various sources, he found that they were, for the most part, mutually reinforcing and reflected the "operate well forward" atmosphere in an offensive stance that seemed attractive to naval officers at that time.[50]

Working to establish a broad statement of this approach, he saw clearly that the different and separate branches of thinking within the navy fundamentally complemented one another. Swartz saw his fundamental task as one that would bring these lines of thinking together in a way that would be acceptable to all interest groups within the navy. Having become thoroughly acquainted with strategic thinking throughout the navy, Swartz concluded that the Pacific Command Campaign Plan formulated under Admiral Robert Long, U.S. Navy, as CINCPAC, provided the basic model that could be applied globally. It had also been one of the CINC briefings used by Weeks and Johnson and was compatible without the first version of *The Maritime Strategy*. For Swartz, this was the "main recent antecedent" to his work as the action officer on *The Maritime Strategy*.[51]

Thus, Swartz's task was to fit together the diverse, but fundamentally complementary strategic thinking that had been going on in the navy into the basic concept proposed in the PACOM Campaign Plan. Directly using the script of the briefing used by CINCPAC staff, Swartz laid the groundwork for his own briefing on *The Maritime Strategy*, filling it in from the plans of the other CINCs, while tailoring it to a global perspective. Swartz wanted to co-opt as many key officers on the navy staff as he could, reflecting a wide variety of interests and perspectives. His purpose in this was "to partake of their knowledge and not get knifed later" as well as "to make sure of a baseline that would last."[52] To achieve these goals, he focused at the working-level of captains and commanders rather than flag officers, trying out his ideas and modifying his approach in the Summer and Fall of 1983, through numerous informal, off-the-record, "murder board" sessions. During these sessions, a wide variety of strategically minded officers criticized the ideas and concepts that Swartz synthesized; following the sessions, Swartz's briefing was presented widely, gaining in its concepts and modifying its phraseology as a result of nearly every session.[53]

The first major briefing for the Swartz version of *The Maritime Strategy* came on 13 September 1983 when Rear Admiral Ronald F. Marryott presented the briefing to Admiral Watkins and six former Chiefs of Naval Operations: Admirals Arleigh A. Burke, George W. Anderson, David L. MacDonald, Thomas H. Moorer, James L. Holloway, and Thomas B. Hayward, on board the U.S. Coast Guard cutter *Chase* off Newport. The CNOs, along with Rear Admiral John L. Butts, Director of Naval Intelligence, Commodore David E. Jeremiah, Commodore Clarence E. Armstrong, and Captains William A. Owens and J. S. Hurlburt of the Strategic Studies Group, had embarked in *Chase* to watch the America's Cup race, but since calm weather forced cancellation of the race, the majority of the day was spent in *Chase*'s wardroom discussing strategy. The morning session began with Marryott's briefing, but the format of a discussion instead of a briefing was quickly established as Admiral Watkins amplified Marryott's comments and the former CNOs questioned and commented.[54]

After the briefing on the Coast Guard Cutter *Chase,* the next briefings were for the Program Development Review Committee (PDRC) and the Program Review Committee (PRC) in October 1983. Their response was overwhelmingly positive. Especially noteworthy were the accolades heaped on the strategy at the PRC by Vice Admiral Carlisle Trost (OP-090), Vice Admiral Lee Baggett (OP-095), and Vice Admiral James A. Lyons (OP-06). From Swartz's point of view, *The Maritime Strategy* had done what Admiral William Small had set out to do and did in fact reflect the consensus of the navy's high command. So unanimous was the approval that it was decided that it was unnecessary to present the briefing at the CNO Executive Board (CEB), which is normally the most senior oversight committee for guidance and resource decisions. Following the presentation to the PDRC and PRC, and the comments received there, Swartz and Barnett proceeded to make a significant addition to the strategy. Up to this point, the briefing had only discussed global conventional war with the Soviets. Their new work added a preliminary discussion, which dealt with the role of the navy in peacetime and in crisis leading up to war.[55]

Reactions to the briefing were varied. On 20 October 1983, Rear Admiral Huntington Hardisty, the Assistant Deputy Chief of Naval Operations (OP-06B), presented *The Maritime Strategy* to the CNO Executive Panel. He reported that the briefing was well received and that the CEP considered it a marked improvement on the previous year's brief. There were four general themes in the comments made by panel members:[56]

- Some panel members viewed the purpose of the strategy to be an attempt to predict the strategy rather than what it was actually intended to be—a statement of the navy's preferred strategy.

- Some panel members wanted a precise order of sequence to be stated in the briefing rather than to deliberately avoid doing this and thereby avoid a specific scenario prediction.

- Other members agreed that the preferred strategy should be close-in defense of the sea lines of communication and convoys as the Nation's primary responsibility rather than a strategy of forward defense and offensive operations.

- Finally, some panel members believed that a war at sea with the Soviet Union would probably be a limited war and not inevitably the global war that the briefing suggested.

Among the critics who were uncomfortable with the strategy was Captain Linton Brooks, Deputy Director, Strategy and Nuclear Warfare Division and a veteran of numerous *Maritime Strategy* murder boards. While the strategy was the best of those that the navy wanted to follow, "we might not be able to carry it out," he said. Secondly, he wondered if it might be a strategy that would lead to escalation. Although operations against Soviet SSBNs were not yet explicitly a part of the strategy, there had been discussions about them in relation to the strategy. These and U.S. carrier operations in Soviet-controlled sea areas, and conventional warfare attacks on the Soviet homeland, seemed to Brooks to run a huge risk of preemptive attack. Particularly in looking at that third phase of the strategy, Brooks felt that the policy and strategy goals should be explained and made clear for the full, forward attack concept. Moreover, he said, "if the strategy you describe cannot stand the shift to nuclear use, it is bankrupt and we may as well face up to it."[57] Brooks saw that there was no general agreement about the strategic meaning of submarine operation in the third phase, particularly in regard to war termination and escalation into nuclear war.[58] Rear Admiral Clyde R. Bell, Director Force Level Plans Division, was equally direct. The briefing "waffled," he said. "I believe that our anti-SSBN capability is the highest leverage item in the entire naval strategy for global war against the Soviets. Our ability to conduct offensive ASW/ASUW in Soviet position areas should be a centerpiece. Even if the battle forces don't get into the fight until late in the game, the Arctic campaign gives the navy the opportunity to both sink the Soviet Navy and make a strategic difference."[59] However, Admirals Trost, Baggett, and Lyons had explicitly stated that *The Maritime Strategy* briefing should not discuss anti-SSBN operations explicitly, but at the same time, it should not disavow them either.[60]

On 19 January 1984, Secretary of the Navy Lehman and Chief of Naval Operations Watkins presented the briefing to Secretary of Defense Caspar Weinberger, and on 14 March, the two men presented it to the Seapower Subcommittee of the Senate Armed Services Committee. Finally, on 4 May 1984, Admiral Watkins signed the final version of the Fiscal Year 1984 version of *The Maritime Strategy* for publication in both classi-fied and unclassified forms. An unclassified version of *The Maritime Strategy* was also prepared by OP-603 and approved by Admiral Watkins, but it was not published at the time due to the inability to obtain approval for it through the Joint and OSD clearance process, and to OP-60's preoccupation with institutionalizing the classified version. Nevertheless, a declassified version was released to the public as part of the Congressio-nal Hearings on appropriations for the Fiscal Year 1985.[61]

Between October 1983, when the first full draft briefing was given, and May 1984 when the final version was signed, some 75 briefings were given to audiences ranging from OpNav offices to War College students, allied chiefs of naval strategy, representatives of other services, and members of Congress.[62] Nearly every meeting had produced a nu-ance that led to further polishing and clarification. This very process bothered some observers. As Commander Bruce L. Valley wrote harshly:

> My frank view is that *The Maritime Strategy* brief basically reflects the lowest common denominator approach commonly developed through a committee effort. . . . My reaction to the brief—and the strategy it proposes to develop—is that we genuinely expect the Soviets to do exactly what we want them to do, and that somehow "Right will make Might," enabling us to carry out our plans successfully despite severe under-nourishment in such areas as sustainability, sea-lift, and dare I say it—strategic thought.[63]

Although a rather hostile comment, Valley's remarks touched on an essential aspect of *The Maritime Strategy*: it was a widely held, generally accepted view of strategy in the process of development. As Commander James R. Stark, who followed Roger Barnett as interim Director of the Strategic Concepts Branch (OP-603) commented, "Valley is right that *The Maritime Strategy* has a lowest common denominator problem. But it has to be agreed upon." Moreover, the view the Strategy presented of the Soviet Navy was based on the National Intelligence Estimate, [see Appendix I, pp. 101–183] which at that time was the only view that all agencies within the U.S. Government had agreed upon.[64]

CHAPTER FIVE

Further Developments, 1984–1986

The distribution of *The Maritime Strategy* during the summer of 1984 as a classified document within the navy was a major step in the effort to educate naval officers in the various considerations involved in thinking about a future war with the Soviet Union. At the same time, it opened a new series of developments for the further refinement and examination of the navy's strategic ideas. Most importantly, a larger number of officers were being educated in current strategic concepts. Ideas about strategy were beginning to be widely exchanged, both inside and outside the navy. Using the central focus of *The Maritime Strategy*, officers throughout the naval service were beginning to ask the essential question: What does the navy need to achieve in wartime, and how does it use its forces to achieve those ends?

Through the widespread dissemination of the basic strategic concepts involved in *The Maritime Strategy*, a wide variety of contributions were made to its further development, while the Strategic Studies Group at Newport and The Strategic Concepts Branch in OpNav continued their work. The staffs of the various commanders in chief continued to reexamine and refine their war plans, discussions were held with the other services and with the allied forces, and new campaign concepts were examined at the Center for Naval Warfare Studies at the Naval War College, at the Center for Naval Analyses, and at other institutions. In short, there was a blossoming of maritime and naval thinking in a variety of ways and places. As this is being written, it is too close to the events to know which of the various ideas will become essential elements in the future, as *The Maritime Strategy* continues to be developed. The general trends of development, between 1984 and 1986, however, were quickly reflected in the work of OP-603 and the Strategic Studies Group, while an increasing number of other staffs and individuals became involved in the process.

The Center for Naval Warfare Studies

Complementing the work of the Strategic Studies Group in 1984–1986, the Center for Naval Warfare Studies under Dr. Robert S. Wood was involved in a number of activities related to the development of *The Maritime Strategy*. Particularly important in this respect was the development of various new campaign options within the context of the broad national *Maritime Strategy*. This effort was an attempt to help fill the gap in American naval thinking between the broad issues of maritime strategy and those of fleet tactics, that area which the Soviets term "operational art," but for which no widely accepted term has yet been used in English. Among the projects were amphibious campaign options, and some possible campaigns in Jutland and in the Balkans. In addition, a program of bilateral navy-to-navy strategy discussions were conducted, in cooperation with OpNav, to encourage the development of a shared concept of maritime strategy and joint operational exercises. For these purposes, discussions were held with officers and officials from Japan, Italy, Germany, Turkey, and several Latin American countries.

At the same time, the annual series of Global War Games at the Naval War College interacted with other insights into *The Maritime Strategy*. As the various players worked through a series of plays in a potential future global war against the Soviet Union, several concepts within *The Maritime Strategy* seemed to be proved out, while others were brought into serious question. In the games, the ability of the United States Navy to operate well forward and to seize the initiative when war broke out seemed to have the desired effect of keeping the Soviet Navy in its bastions, thus serving to prevent the enemy from making a massive attack on the Western sea lines of communication. The further phases of the strategy called for the U.S. Navy then to carry the fight to the enemy and proceed to use naval forces as an element in terminating the war. The teams that played in the Global War Game found difficulty, however, in finding ways by which the navy could carry the fight to the enemy in a productive way. In the process, they observed that it was exceedingly difficult for a navy to operate in the narrow seas that border the Soviet Union. Moreover, the attack, which was envisaged against Soviet SSBNs, failed in the games to have the hoped-for result, leading some of the Soviets to terminate a war. What seemed to be more effective to the players was the massing of conventional forces in a carrier battle group in a manner that made the risk too high to attack it without the use of nuclear weapons. Thus, it was suggested through the Global War Games that conventional forces played a key role in deterring nuclear war, even after a war had broken out, and could be used as a lever to persuade the Soviets to terminate a war.[1]

The Strategic Concepts Branch (OP-603)

While the SSG and the Naval War College, along with others, explored various issues in depth during the period 1984–1986, the Strategic Concepts Branch in OpNav continued its work in correlating the new thought and bringing the ideas that had come to be widely accepted into *The Maritime Strategy*. In order to see this parallel, but separate development, one must step back to the summer of 1984 and follow forward from that point the work in that Branch.

By August 1984, following the publication of the first *Maritime Strategy* booklet, a new team of officers had been installed in OP-60; Commodore T. J. Johnson, Captain Larry Seaquist, and Commander T. Wood Parker considered that it was time to begin the cycle of reflection and revision again. With the booklet in hand, Admiral Watkins looked for further, more detailed development of the strategy. He set the Strategic Studies Group the task of looking into developing further insights into peacetime use of navies, emphasizing in particular that *The Maritime Strategy* was primarily designed to be a deterrent strategy whose purpose was to help prevent war. Its effectiveness for such a task, of course, came from the U.S. Navy's ability to be ready for war if deterrence failed and to fight and to help win such a war. With that in mind the Vice Chief of Naval Operations, Admiral Ronald Hays, sent a personal message to the three Navy CINCs saying "the CNO needs to understand fully your views on our present baseline strategy as we gear up to POM-87."[2] Commodore Jerome L. Johnson traveled from OP-06 to each of the CINCs' headquarters for follow-up discussions.

Admiral Wesley L. McDonald, Commander in Chief, Atlantic and Supreme Allied Commander Atlantic, was the first CINC to reply. It was obvious from his reaction that though the CINCs would have differing views on certain aspects of *The Maritime Strategy*, they agreed to it in general. As he read McDonald's message, Watkins wrote a note to his staff along the margin: "make sure we include where we agree and resolve where we disagree. I don't want to have more than one strategy."[3] The effort to resolve these differences and to collate the detailed views of the CINCs in the light of new developments and further thinking became the main continuing task of the action officers as they prepared new versions of the booklet and briefing. These issues were detailed ones that involved primarily the assessment of the Soviet bastion strategy, judgments whether one should emphasize Soviet intentions over Soviet capabilities in assessing an enemy, the risk of forward carrier battle group strikes against the Soviet Union, and the difficulty of dealing with the phasing and the timing of the various operations laid out in the strategy.[4]

In the process of discussing the strategy, it became obvious that some officers questioned the propriety of the CNO's role in creating a strategy. One of the outspoken critics on this point was Admiral William J. Crowe, Jr., the Commander in Chief, Pacific. When Commodore Johnson presented to him the latest version of the strategy, Crowe remarked, "I'm not sure why CNO needs a *Maritime Strategy*. I need one, but he doesn't."[5] For him, and others who shared his views, it was appropriate as a plausible case to present in the procurement process, but not as an actual, operational strategy.

In pointing this out, Crowe was right in the sense that neither the CNO nor the fleet CINCs have responsibility for developing strategy. That is the domain of the President, the Secretary of Defense, The Joint Chiefs, and the Unified Commanders. The recognized instruments were the national strategy, approved by the President, which contains military elements; a national military strategy, prepared by the Chairman of the Joint Chiefs of Staff and approved by the President and the Secretary of Defense. Then there are theater strategies approved by the Unified Commander for accomplishing his assigned mission. *The Maritime Strategy* lay outside this structure and had no formal status in relation to it. Nevertheless, it did influence the strategic thinking of those officers who had responsibility for developing the national military strategy, while attempting to link the procurement process to strategy.

While he was briefing the CINCs, Commodore Johnson also briefed fleet flag officers in operational positions. Many of them had a negative reaction to it, making comments such as "brochuremanship," "PR job—not a strategy," "not executable," "lacking operational insight." Their reaction showed a sophistication about strategy and strategic thinking that had not been present among flag officers a few years earlier, suggesting that they now had much higher expectations and demands in this area.[6]

In OpNav, Commander T. Wood Parker was assigned as action officer for *The Maritime Strategy* in September 1984. He and Captain Larry Seaquist, who had come from the Strategic Studies Group at the Naval War College to be the new head of the Strategic Concepts Branch (OP-603), agreed on three primary objectives: (1) to enhance the substance of the strategy, (2) to get the OpNav and Headquarters Marine Corps staffs to use it as the starting point for all of their efforts in policy, strategy, tactics, budget, and procurement; and (3) to "spread the gospel" throughout the navy by widespread briefings and writings.

While having great respect for Commander Peter Swartz's earlier work in carrying the briefing through and turning it into a widely circulated publication, Parker began his work with the clear impression that Swartz had made compromises in order to get the strategy accepted by all the various interest groups within the navy staff. Now that the strategy had been fully approved by the CNO and accepted by the staffs as well as the CINCs, Parker felt it was time to correct the shortcomings he saw in the strategy. He immediately started working on a new version, which he hoped would enhance the substance of the strategy. To achieve this, Parker tried to accomplish several things:

- Get the CINCs much more involved in the development of the next version by traveling to them as well as meeting with their staffs regularly.

- Explicitly include anti-SSBN operations.

- Describe what is meant by the vague term, "war termination on favorable terms."

- Alter the first part of the briefing and publication by expanding on the parts that deal with peacetime operations, crisis control operations, and transition to war.

- Include the U.S. Navy's SSBN operations as part of the overall concept of strategy.

- Deal with the issues of time phasing and nuclear war which had been omitted earlier.

- Explain, rather than just list, the uncertainties with which the strategy must necessarily deal, and try to explain them in terms of their impact in the case of a war.[7]

In his effort to get the OpNav and Marine Corps Headquarters to use the strategy as the basis for all their work, Parker saw that what was needed was a direct link between the strategic and the POM process. This, of course, had been an objective from the beginning with Admiral Small's memoranda, which had begun the development of the maritime strategy briefing in 1982. However, it was no easy task to place conceptual concerns as the governing factors in a budget and procurement process. For years, the two areas of concern had tended to operate in separate spheres.

In order to try to make this linkage, Vice Admiral J. A. Lyons, the Deputy CNO for Plans and Policy (OP-06), came up with the idea of "Strategy Stoppers." This was a label that Lyons started to apply in the autumn of 1984 to identify those issues and problems in the procurement area which, if not properly funded or supported, could lead to a weakening in the navy's ability to execute the strategy fully. The term "Strategy Stoppers" was criticized by some who thought that it would be misconstrued to mean that the strategy could not be executed at all. For this reason, the term was eventually dropped, but for a time, Vice Admiral Lyons insisted on using it because it was pithy and recognizable.

Although the use of the term had a short history, the concept behind it became established at this point. The purpose of it was to make the strategy identify what must be analyzed, considered, and appraised in the procurement process. At first this was a very difficult process to get across. As Parker described it "every office in the Pentagon and Henderson Hall perceived this as a power grab by the OP-06 organization, and they did not want anyone or anything telling them what must be included in their respective programs." However, after a series of briefings to various officers to convince them that this was a proper use of the strategy and that it would help to provide much needed guidance and cohesiveness to the overall POM process, the idea was presented by Vice Admiral Lyons to the CINCs conference and then to the CNO Executive Board. Admiral Watkins then directed that every program appraisal address the strategy stoppers that had been identified, thus establishing a formal and direct connection between the Strategy and the POM process.

In trying to "spread the gospel," as Parker termed it, his goal was to have *The Maritime Strategy* accepted as a strategic framework.[8] Many people derisively described it as merely a budget document designed to augment naval forces, but Parker and Seaquist concentrated their efforts on combating this view. Doubling their efforts for this purpose, the briefers asked for comments and corrections from all the commanders in chief, not only the Navy CINCs. In particular, they briefed General Bernard Rogers, Supreme Allied Commander Europe, and all his component U.S. commanders; and Admiral W. J. Crowe, Commander in Chief, Pacific, and his component commanders. They also briefed CINC Readiness Command, CINC Southern Command, CINC Central Command, and several former commanders in chief, including Admiral Robert Long, former CINCPAC, and General Alexander Haig, former SACEUR. Through all of these briefings, Parker and Seaquist worked to explain the strategy as the maritime component of a national strategy, which dovetailed naval aspects to those of the other services.

In addition to the series of briefings to the CINCs, Parker briefed the professional staff members of the Senate Armed Services Committee on 7 January 1985. Then, on 30 January 1985, Vice Admiral Lyons and Commander Parker presented the briefings to Senator Barry Goldwater and the members of the Senate Armed Services Committee. This was followed by another briefing to Congress when Lyons and Parker presented the briefing to Congressman Charles E. Bennett and members of the House Subcommittee on Seapower and Strategic and Critical Materials. These briefings to members of Congress were particularly important since, as Parker described it, "we took on some of our most ardent critics head to head."[9] These briefings were very successful. In his report to Congressman Les Aspin later in the year, Congressman Bennett wrote,

> The subcommittee finds that the maritime strategy is, in fact, a proper naval component to national-level military strategy, and that the 600-ship navy as currently described is a reasonable and balanced approach to meeting the force structure requirements of that strategy.[10]

Through widespread emphasis on the concept as that of a strategy rather than just a budgetary argument, Admiral Watkins frequently became personally involved. During the period between January and June 1985, Watkins was most actively involved with the further development and "selling" of the strategy. It was during this period that the idea was developed to publish an unclassified article on *"The Maritime Strategy"* and a first draft was made at that time. However, it was not until January 1986 that it appeared as a special supplement to the U.S. Naval Institute *Proceedings*. The supplement included the lead article by Watkins, "The Amphibious Warfare Strategy" by General P. X. Kelley, "The 600-ship Navy" by John Lehman, and Captain Peter

Swartz's "Contemporary U.S. Naval Strategy: A Bibliography"[11] [see Appendix II, pp. 185–277]. In Parker's view, it was the direct involvement of Watkins in the strategy's development in OP-603 at this point that was the most salient contribution to his work in that office.[12]

By July 1985, the bulk of the creative work for the third version of *The Maritime Strategy* had been completed by Seaquist and Parker. It was at this point that Commander Albert C. Myers was assigned to OP-603 as Parker's relief while Parker went on to the Office of the Secretary of the Navy. What remained to be done was to collate the final recommendations and changes from the various CINCs and Washington offices as well as to shepherd the document through a conference of OpNav and Fleet staff planners in a working-level conference. After this was completed, the draft document had to be submitted up the chain of command for the approval of the Chief of Naval Operations. This was completed on 1 November 1985 when Admiral Watkins formally signed the third version of *The Maritime Strategy.*[13]

The next major phase was begun by Seaquist's successor as Head of the Strategic Concepts Branch, Captain Thomas M. Daly. Daly saw his task as capitalizing on the momentum of his predecessors and broadening familiarity with *The Maritime Strategy* both within and without the navy, while keeping the strategy responsive to the realities of the developing capabilities of the navy and changes in Soviet armed forces. An aggressive briefing schedule was developed, which included expanded contacts and dialogue with civilians at the unclassified level, at both universities and institutions such as Brookings, Georgetown University, CSIS, etc. As this developed, it created significant comment and discussion among academies concerned with strategic issues.

By the end of 1986, there was a large amount of discussion, not only in the *Proceedings* and in the *Naval War College Review* but in newspapers, magazines, and journals. Important comments were made by John J. Mearsheimer in *International Security,* which were paired with an article by Captain Linton Brooks.[14] In addition, in his *Maritime Strategy, Geopolitics and the Defense of the West*[15] Dr. Colin S. Gray made some interesting comments on the criticisms of Ambassador Robert Komer about *The Maritime Strategy.* As the public debate grew wider, it became the basis of discussion in university lecture courses, such as that offered by Professor Paul M. Kennedy at Yale, "Seapower Past and Present,"[16] and even in the works of novelists Tom Clancy and Larry Bond in their best selling book, *Red Storm Rising.*

In January 1987, President Reagan delivered to Congress a public and unclassified statement of *National Security Strategy of the United States.* Rear Admiral W. A. Cockell developed this document while serving as Special Assistant to the President for Defense Policy. It was based on the classified update to the NSDD on National Security completed in the summer of 1986. Sweeping widely across the spectrum of American strategy, a few paragraphs clearly reflected the development of *The Maritime Strategy* that had been the focus of a decade's effort by navy strategists. Most significantly, the report stated:

> Maritime superiority enables us to capitalize on Soviet geographical vulnerabilities and to pose a global threat to the Soviets' interests. It plays a key role in plans for the defense of NATO allies on the European flanks. It also permits the United States to tie down Soviet naval forces in a defensive posture protecting Soviet ballistic missile submarines and the seaward approaches to the Soviet homeland, and thereby to minimize the wartime threat to the reinforcement and resupply of Europe by sea.[17]

By the end of 1986, the public and professional discussion of the issues surrounding *The Maritime Strategy* had taken a sophisticated form. The issues of naval strategy could be, and were, understood and being debated widely. This contrasted starkly with the absence of such discussion a decade earlier, and at the same time, seemed to demonstrate a widespread appreciation of strategy within the officer corps. The formative phase for *The Maritime Strategy* had clearly ended in the years between 1984 and 1986. Its development was closely associated in the mind of the public with the names of Secretary of the Navy John Lehman and Admiral James Watkins who, in the Reagan administration, had been the catalysts who successfully brought the issues and ideas to the fore as the public spokesmen for them. Within the navy, many individuals made claim to having been the "father" of the Strategy. As this study shows, the ideas in *The Maritime Strategy* have long roots that were in fact the cumulative and complementary contributions of many naval officers over many years and several administrations.

Among the many contributions that have resulted in *The Maritime Strategy*, one can point to several key influences beginning with the strategy studies under Admiral Zumwalt's tenure as CNO in the early 1970s, the efforts of the navy staff under Admiral Holloway to come to grips with ways to "size the Navy," the contributions of the analysts at the Center for Naval Analyses in identifying a new area for research on Soviet strategic thinking, and the further development and refinement of that basis in the Office of Naval Intelligence. Admiral Hayward's contributions were widespread and included the Sea Strike Study, which complemented the Navy Department's Sea Plan 2000, and later his Strategic Principles, his organization of the navy staff, an intensified effort to understand Soviet naval strategy, and the creation of the Strategic Studies Group. Then, there was Admiral Small's key effort to rationalize the budget process in terms of strategic purposes, and with this comes the contributions of the Naval Warfare Directorate, OP-603 and the Strategic Studies Group in formulating ideas and breaking down the barriers that hindered discussion of strategy within the navy. These contributions were particularly important in facilitating the cross-fertilization of strategic thought, which was essential in the development of a widely accepted strategic concept based on current assessments of both Soviet capabilities and intentions as well as in terms of U.S. goals for a peacetime strategy of deterrence that could be effective in war, if needed. In this context, Lehman and Watkins clearly deserve credit for their efforts in further coordinating ideas and helping to bring the diverse segments of the navy together, focusing on the basic and continuing strategic issues. The appointments of Admiral Carlisle A. H. Trost as Chief of Naval Operations in 1986, of James Webb as Secretary of the Navy in 1987, and of General Alfred Gray as Commandant of the Marine Corps coincided with the transition to a new phase in the further development of American naval strategic thinking.

As one looks back over this decade, it is apparent that various levels of government worked in the development of strategy. A process of education and the development of a heightened interest in strategic issues within the naval officer corps paralleled the development and application of strategic concepts. One may see here an attempt to apply some of the abstract, theoretical ideas of writers such as Mahan, Eccles, and Wylie. At the same time, one can see the natural stresses between various levels of decision making as they dealt with strategy in terms of the different needs, constraints, and functions that come into play at different levels. For example, one can clearly see this in strategic analysts' examination of the issues in terms of geopolitical studies or in Senators' and Congressmen's reactions in terms of domestic political issues. Within the Department of Defense itself, other issues were raised as broad budgetary constraints were applied to weapons procurement matters in terms of strategy, while at the same time, elements of the bureaucracy took initiative or reacted to one another explaining their positions in terms of strategy, war plans, and exercises in preparation for wartime operations.

Notes

General Preface

1. Wilfried G. Stallmann, "Die maritime Strategie der USA nach 1945: Entwicklung, Einflußgrößen und Auswirkungen auf das atlantische Bündnis." Dissertation zur Erlangung des Doktorgrades der Philosophischen Fakultät der Christian-Albrechts-Universität zu Kiel, 2000. Unpublished.

2. On this subject, see David Alan Rosenberg, "Process: the Realities of Formulating Modern Naval Strategy" in James Goldrick and John B. Hattendorf, eds., *Mahan is Not Enough: The Proceedings of a Conference on the Works of Sir Julian Corbett and Admiral Sir Herbert Richmond.* (Newport: Naval War College Press, 1993), pp. 141–175, with discussion following on pp. 177–209.

Preface to the First Edition

1. This series of classified papers was distributed between 1981 and 1989 and predates the series of unclassified Newport Papers that the Naval War College Press began to distribute in December 1991.

2. The original unclassified article appeared in the Spring 1988 issue on pp. 7–28, but through an error by the printer, two pairs of pages were exchanged inadvertently. An errata notice was issued that pointed out that the text on page 18 should have been on page 17, and that on page 17 should have been on page 18. The text on page 22 should have been on page 21 and that on page 21 should have been on page 22. A fully corrected version was reprinted, with an updated bibliography and small changes in John B. Hattendorf, *Naval History and Maritime Strategy: Collected Essays.* (Malabar, Fla: Krieger Publishing, 2000), pp. 201–228. This corrected version should be used in preference to the first printing.

Introduction

1. Jack Snyder, *The Ideology of the Offensive: Military Decision Making and the Disasters of 1914* (Ithaca, N.Y.: Cornell University Press, 1984), pp. 19–34.

2. Jack Snyder and David Alan Rosenberg, "Reality and Responsibility: Power and Process in the Making of United States Nuclear Strategy, 1945–68," *The Journal of Strategic Studies,* vol. 9, no. 1 (March 1986), pp. 36–38.

Chapter 1

1. Alvin J. Cottrell and Thomas H. Moorer, *U.S. Overseas bases: Problems of Projecting Military Power Abroad* (Beverly Hills and London: SAGE Publications, 1977). Center for Strategic and International Studies, Georgetown University: The Washington Papers, number 47, p. 5.

2. Interview with Robert J. Murray, Naval War College, 6 May 1985.

3. Ibid.

4. Philip D. Zelikow, "The United States and the Use of Force: A Historical Summary," pp. 11–12. Draft. Unpublished.

5. For a more detailed study of these developments, see my essay, "Recent Thinking on the Theory of Naval Strategy," in John B. Hattendorf and Robert S. Jordan, eds., *Maritime Strategy and the Balance of Power: Britain and America in the 20th Century.* (London: The Macmillan Press; New York: St. Martins Press, 1989), pp. 136–161. This is a revised and expanded version of "American Thinking on Naval Strategy, 1945–80" in Geoffrey Till, *Maritime Strategy and the Nuclear Age* (London: Macmillan, 1982), pp. 58–68.

6. A summary of the basic concepts may be found in H. E. Eccles, "Strategy—The Theory and Application," *Naval War College Review,* May–June 1979, pp. 11–21. The key works of Herbert Rosinski and William Reitzel prepared at the Naval War College are reprinted in B. Mitchell Simpson III, ed., *War, Strategy and Maritime Power* (New Brunswick: Rutgers University Press, 1977), pp. 63–110.

7. Eccles, ibid., p. 13.

8. J. C. Wylie, *Military Strategy: A General Theory of Power Control* (New Brunswick: Rutgers University Press, 1967), p. 110.

9. H. E. Eccles, *Military Power in a Free Society* (Newport: Naval War College Press, 1979), p. 205.

10. Hubert Moineville, *Naval Warfare Today and Tomorrow* (Oxford: Basil Blackwell, 1982), pp. 26–27.

11. Richard Smoke, *War: Controlling Escalation* (Cambridge: Harvard University Press, 1977) pp. 301–302.

12. Samuel P. Huntington, "The Defense Policy 1981–1982," in Fred I. Greenstein, *The Reagan Presidency: An Early Assessment* (1983), p. 101.

13. John B. Hattendorf, B. M. Simpson III, J. R. Wadleigh, *Sailors and Scholars: The Centennial History of the Naval War College* (Newport: Naval War College Press, 1984), p. 284.

14. Ibid., p. 285.

15. Hattendorf interview with Rear Admiral William Cockell, U.S. Navy, San Diego, Calif., 5 April 1985.

16. CNO Ltr OP-96/sjg Serial 005 34P96 dated 18 November 1971. Appendix E to *Future Maritime Strategy Study* (FUMAR), volume 1: Report Summary, p. 1-E-2.

17. Ibid., p. E-F.3: Revised Draft Study Plan, 24 January 1972.

18. Ibid., p. 1-2: OP-96 letter serial 090/S276 12 May 1973. Subj: "Future Maritime Strategy (FUMAR) Study Report; promulgation of."

19. J. William Middendorf, Remarks at Sea-Air-Space Exposition Luncheon, Washington, D.C., 4 February 1975.

20. Quoted in Middendorf, Address to the Navy League National Convention Awards Luncheon, Boston, Mass., 20 May 1976.

21. Quoted in Middendorf, Address at Rotary Club Luncheon, Chicago, Ill., 20 July 1976.

22. Sea Control CPAM ser. 96/S59368, 15 May 1975, p. 17; Hattendorf interview with Rear Admiral John A. Baldwin, 8 January 1987.

23. Summary CPAM Briefing Material for CEB. Memorandum. Ser. 96/S58900 dated 4 March 1975, p. 15.

24. Assistant Secretary of Defense (ISA) Report to the Congress on U.S. Strategy and Naval Force Requirements, 15 January 1977.

25. Hattendorf-Cockell interview.

26. Paul Ryan, *First Line of Defense*, pp. 92–95.

27. B. Mitchell Simpson III, ed., *War, Strategy and Maritime Power* (New Brunswick: Rutgers University Press, 1977).

28. Edward N. Luttwak, *Strategy and History: Collected Essays*, vol. 2. (New Brunswick and Oxford: Transaction Books, n.d.), pp. 163–165.

29. W. Graham Claytor, Jr., and R. James Woolsey, Memorandum for the Secretary of Defense, 14 July 1977. Subj: Naval Force Planning After PRM-10. Secret.

30. Ibid.

31. W. Graham Claytor, Jr., Memorandum for the Secretary of Defense, 20 March 1978. Subj: Sea Plan 2000—Information Memorandum. Secret. [Attached to Sea Plan 2000, copy 184, in Naval War College Library.]

32. Ibid.

33. Ibid.

34. Office of the Secretary of the Navy. *Sea Plan 2000: Naval Force Planning Study*. March 1978. Secret. vol. 1, Executive Summary, p. xvii.

35. Ibid., vol. 1, p. 126.

36. Ibid., Executive Summary, p. xli.

37. Ibid., p. xxiv.

38. Ibid., p. xxx.

39. Ibid., p. liii.

40. Letter of Rear Admiral J. A. Sagerholm, Director, Office of Program Appraisal, Navy Department, to D. E. Day, U.S. General Accounting Office, 12 February 1979. Appendix V to Report by the Comptroller General of the United States. *"How Good Are Recent Navy Studies Regarding Future Forces?"* C-PSAD-80-5. 13 February 1980. Secret.

41. Ibid., pp. 11–25.

42. Ibid., p. 25.

43. Ibid., p. 3.

44. Letter from Fred P. Wacker to J. H. Stolarow, Director, Procurement and System Acquisition Division GAO, 6 November 1979. Appendix IV to Ibid., p. 44–45.

45. Ibid., p. xli.

46. Paul Ryan, *First Line of Defense*, p. 91. Hattendorf interviews with Admiral T. B. Hayward, 17 April 1985; with Captain James M. Patton, 13 December 1985; with Rear Admiral William Cockell, 5 April 1985.

47. On this see E. P. Potter, *Nimitz* (Annapolis: Naval Institute Press, 1976), Chapter 15: "CINCPAC and CINCPAC Staff," pp. 221–234.

48. The full original briefing with slides was presented to Hattendorf by Patton in the CNO Briefing Theater at the Pentagon, 13 December 1985.

49. Interview with Hayward, 17 April 1985.

50. Patton Sea Strike Briefing; CINCPACFLT Analysis Memorandum No. 1-85," Analysis Support for Assessment of Wartime Force Employment Strategies. 28 February 1985.

51. Ibid.

52. Ibid.

53. K. McGruther Files: F. J. West Memorandum for the record, 23 December 1977: Atlantic Strategy meeting with CNO and SECNAV in private session and Assistant SECDEF in general meeting.

Chapter 2

1. The bulk of this section is based on Robert B. Pirie, Jr., Director, Naval Strategy Program, CNA, Memorandum for Director, Strategic and Theater Nuclear Warfare Division (OP-60). Subj: Revised "Audit Trail" on Pro-SSBN/Strategic Reserve Missions of the Soviet Navy. (CNA) 82-0762.10–22 June 1983. This is a series of photocopied excerpts from earlier CNA studies gathered on the suggestion of Admiral W. Small, Jr., 20 May 1982. Hereinafter, reference to the excerpts from this document will be made by citing the original document, followed by the note "excerpt in CNA 82-0762."

2. Robert G. Weinland, "SLBM Forces in a War at Sea," CNA 012269.00. December 1968, pp. 1–3. Excerpt in CNA 82-0762.

3. Bradford Dismukes, "Evolving Wartime Missions of the Soviet General Purpose Force Navy," June 1973. CNA 001061-73, p.16. Excerpt in CNA 82-0762.

4. DNI Memorandum for the President, Center for Naval Analyses. Ser 009F/27408, 27 September 1973. Copy in CNA 82-0762.

5. Naval Studies Group, "Estimative Project," p. 16. Excerpt in CNA 82-0762.

6. The points are taken from James M. McConnell, "Gorshkov's Doctrine of Coercive Naval Diplomacy in Both Peace and War," in CNA unclassified study "Admiral Gorshkov on 'Navies in Peace and War,'" September 1974, pp. 71–73. Excerpt in CNA 82-0762.

7. Ibid.

8. Excerpt from "Draft of Study of Grand Soviet Maritime Strategy," Chief of Naval Operations OP-60N, 23 May 1975, p. 3. Excerpt in CNA 82-0762.

9. Ibid.

10. Excerpt from first draft of James M. McConnell, Doctrine, Missions, and Capabilities, (LT) chapter 1, in *Soviet Naval Diplomacy*, pp. I-49, 50. Unclassified, May 1977. Excerpt in CNA 82-0762.

11. James M. McConnell, "Strategy and Missions of the Soviet Navy in the year 2000," in James L. George, ed., *Problems of Sea Power as We Approach the Twenty-first Century* (Washington, D.C.: American Enterprise Institute for Public Policy Research, 1978), pp. 61–62.

12. Ibid., p. 64.

13. Bradford Dismukes, "Implications of Soviet Naval Strategy. CNA 77-0902. Confidential, 16 June 1977.

14. Bradford Dismukes, "The War Termination Mission of the U.S. Navy: A briefing, 31 March 1980. CNA 80-0412.00, p. 1.

15. Ibid., p. 2.

16. Bradford Dismukes, James M. McConnell, Charles S. Peterson, Robert G. Weinland,

"Assessing Options to Counter Soviet Sea-based Strategic Reserves," CNA 81-0437.09, Secret, 23 March 1981.

17. Bradford Dismukes, "The War Termination Mission," p. 7.

18. Interviews with Bradford Dismukes, CNA, 18 April 1985, and comment on first draft, CNA 86-0927, 19 May 1986; William H. J. Manthorpe letter to Hattendorf, 31 December. 1986.

19. This section is based on interviews, except where noted. The author has not had access to compartmentalized information, but when this material is downgraded, future historians will probably find it useful in understanding the impact this data had on strategic thinking in the period 1979–1981.

20. Hattendorf interviews with Commodore William O. Studeman, U.S. Navy, 16 January 1985, and with Mr. Richard Haver and Commodore Studeman, together, 20 March 1985.

21. Capt. W. H. J. Manthorpe, Jr., U.S. Navy (Ret.) letter to Hattendorf 31 December 1986: Section III: "Intelligence Efforts Related to Maritime Strategy."

22. James L. George, op.cit., pp. 39–67.

23. Manthorpe letter to Hattendorf, 31 December 1986. Section III.

24. Ibid., and Rear Admiral Thomas A. Brooks letter to W. H. J. Manthorpe, Jr., 22 October 1986.

25. Manthorpe letter to Hattendorf.

26. Ibid.

27. Ibid., Thomas A. Brooks letter to Hattendorf, 17 September 1986.

28. Manthorpe to Hattendorf, 31 December 1986.

29. Ibid., Hattendorf interview with Studeman, 16 January 1985; Hattendorf interview with Admiral William Small, 11 April 1985.

30. Manthorpe to Hattendorf, 31 December 1986. Quoted from Navy Net Assessment, December 1981, p. 9.

31. CIA Memo: *Recent Soviet Writings on SLOC Interdicting NATO's Sea Lines of Communication* (SOV-M-85-10116, 1 July 1985).

32. Thomas A. Brooks letter to Hattendorf, 17 September 1986.

33. Hattendorf interview with Small, 11 April 1985.

34. Manthorpe to Hattendorf, 31 December 1986.

35. Brooks to Manthorpe, 22 October 1986.

36. Ibid.

37. Hattendorf interview with Haver and Studeman.

38. Ibid.

Chapter 3

1. Hattendorf interview with Admiral Thomas B. Hayward, Pentagon, 17 April 1985.

2. Ibid.

3. Ibid. and Hattendorf interview with Rear Admiral William Cockell, San Diego, 5 April 1985.

4. OP-603 files: "Memo for Distribution: CNO Strategic Concepts dated 8 January 1979" Serial 00/T100113, 26 February 1979.

5. Ibid.

6. Ibid.

7. Hattendorf interview with Cockell; Robert J. Murray files: Flag Officer Seminar on Naval Strategy, 7–11 May 1979.

8. Ibid., Flag Officer Seminar, p. 2.

9. Ibid., p. 12.

10. Ibid., p. 13.

11. Ibid., pp. 13–14 and Flag Officer Seminar on Naval Strategy and Capabilities: The View from the Fleet. 25 October 1979, pp. 8–9

12. Ibid.

13. Comments on draft by Rear Admiral W. A. Cockell, U.S. Navy, 8 July 1988.

14. Thomas B. Hayward, "The Future of U.S. Sea Power," *Naval Review 1979*, U.S. Naval Institute *Proceedings* (May 1979) vol. 105, no. 5, pp. 66–71.

15. Hattendorf interview with Cockell.

16. William S. Lind, "Comment and Discussion," U.S. Naval Institute *Proceedings* (July 1979), vol. 105, no.7 p. 22.

17. Captain R. A. Bowling, U.S. Navy (Ret.), "Comment and Discussion," U.S. Naval Institute *Proceedings* (December 1979), vol. 105, no.12, p. 89.

18. Captain W. J. Ruhe, U.S. Navy (Ret.), "Comment and Discussion," U.S. Naval Institute *Proceedings* (December 1979), vol. 105, no.12, p. 88.

19. Thomas H. Etzold, "Is Mahan Still Valid?" U.S. Naval Institute *Proceedings* (August 1980), vol. 106, no.8, p. 38.

20. Ibid., p. 43.

21. Hattendorf interview with Cockell.

22. For the history of this, see David A. Rosenberg, unpublished draft, *U.S. Navy Long-Range Planning: A Historical Perspective.*

23. Hattendorf interview with Cockell and with Hayward.

24. CNO address to Current Strategy Forum, Newport, Rhode Island, 8 April 1981.

25. Ibid.

26. Hattendorf interview with Cockell and with Hayward.

27. Quoted in Hattendorf et al., *Sailors and Scholars*, p. 313.

28. Hattendorf interview with Robert J. Murray, 6 May 1985.

29. K. R. McGruther Notebook: 11 August–21 September 1981, Meeting with RJM 9/17.

30. McGruther Notebook: 20 January–5 June 1981, SSG Idea (Seed), c. 23 May; Hattendorf interview with Murray.

31. McGruther Notebook: 23 September–5 November 1981, 10/19 CNO Reaction.

32. Memorandum for the Record: Strategic Studies Group Trip to Washington, 20–22 October 1981. 27 October 1981.

33. Captain Rene W. Leeds, U.S. Navy, conversation with Hattendorf, August 1986.

34. Memorandum for the Record, 20–22 October 1981.

35. K. R. McGruther Memorandum for the Record: Visit of Navy Net Assessor (5 November 1981). 10 November 1981.

36. K. R. McGruther Memorandum for the Record: SSG Luncheon 8 December 1981.

37. NWC Archives: Subject file: Advanced Research. Lt. Col. O. E. Hay, USMC, Presentation at Advanced Research Symposium, March 1984.

38. McGruther Files: Fred Charles Ikle, Memo. "The Use of U.S. Naval Power in a Major War" (Reflections on A War Game), Global War Game, August 1979, 19 November 1979.

39. McGruther Files: Memorandum for the Record: Global War Game 80. CO283:05MH Memo 603/S161-80, 14 August 1980.

40. McGruther Files. Henry Young to H.G. Nott, 6 August 1980. Subj: Orange Play in Global War Game, 1980.

41. McGruther Files: OSD Policy and Capabilities Review, April–June 1981.

42. McGruther Files: Vugraph slides: Global War Games 1979–1981.

43. Ibid., p. 8

44. Ibid.

45. McGruther Notebook #14: "The Essence of Strategic Thinking."

46. Strategic Studies Group, *Forward Naval Strategies Employing Combined Arms,* (17 May 1983), pp. 1–6 to 1–9.

47. Ibid., pp. 7–1 to 7–4.

48. McGruther Notebook: 8/17 [82], Meeting with CNO Watkins.

49. McGruther Notebook: 10/28 [82], Comments following brief to CINCs.

50. *"Memorandum on Maritime Strategy,"* October 1982 (Center for Naval Warfare Studies: the Newport Papers, n.d.).

51. Strategic Studies Group, *Fighting Forward and Winning: A Concept for Employing Maritime Forces to Exploit Soviet Weaknesses in a Global Confrontation* (Center for Naval

Warfare Studies: *The Newport Papers,* n.d.), p. iv of xxi in Executive Summary.

52. Ibid.

53. Robert J. Murray letter to Admiral William N. Small, 1 September 1988. Top Secret.

54. Ibid.

55. Discussion with Dr. Robert S. Wood, 12 August 1987.

56. Strategic Studies Group, *The Use of Maritime Forces in Outlying Regions in Crisis and War* (Newport: Center for Naval Warfare Studies, ca.1984.)

57. Ibid., pp. 205–206.

58. Ibid.

59. Comment on draft by John Hanley, August 1987.

60. Strategic Studies Group, *Global Maritime Elements of U.S. National Deterrence Strategy* (Center for Naval Warfare Studies: The Newport Papers, n.d.).

Chapter 4

1. *The Maritime Strategy, OpNav 60 P-1-84, SECRET-NOFORN. Distributed under CNO letter 00-45300236 dated 4 May 1984.*

2. Office Files of The Action Officer for The Maritime Strategy, Strategic Concepts Branch (OP-603). The Pentagon, Room 4E486 [hereinafter, OP-603 Files]. VCNO Memo N-1241 dated 18 December 1981 to Director, Navy Program Planning, Subj.: Program Appraisals and Analysis. This was Small's own initiative. When questioned in interviews, Admiral T. B. Hayward did not recall giving any direction on this subject and Small confirmed that it was his own idea. Interview with Hayward, 17 April 1985, and with Small, 11 April 1985.

3. Interview with Admiral William M. Small, Commander in Chief, Allied Forces Southern Europe, in Naples, Italy, 11 April 1985.

4. OP-603 Files. VCNO Memo N-1241 of 18 December 1981.

5. Ibid.

6. OP-603 Files. VCNO Memo 1 March 1982 to OP-095, OP-06. Subject: Naval Warfare.

7. Ibid.

8. OP-603 Files. OP-095 Memo 095/64-82 of March 1982 to OP-06. Subject: Naval Warfare.

9. Ms. note to Ibid in Small's hand.

10. OP-603 Files: VCNO memo ser 09/300636, 2 August 1982. Memo for Director, Navy Program Planning (OP-090); Director, Office of Naval Warfare (OP-095); DCNO (Manpower, Personnel and Training)/Chief of Naval Personnel (OP-01); DCNO (Plans, Policy and Operation (OP-06). Subject: POM-85 CPAM/Warfare Appraisals. Capt. D. Berkebile, "POM and Long Range Planning" in *U.S. Navy Final Annual Long Range Planner's Conference,* 17–18 September 1985. Conference Summary.

11. Interview with Commander Stanley B. Weeks, USN, 12 December 1985.

12. Ibid. and letter from Captain W. Spencer Johnson to Hattendorf, 5 September 1985.

13. Interview with Commander Weeks, 12 December 1985: Cdr. Weeks's briefing script B06249:05G:MH 3 September 1982.

14. Interview with Commander Weeks, 13 December 1985. See for example, Hugh Luess, "The U.S. Navy and an Escort Shortage," *Maritime Defense,* June 1982.

15. See "Excerpts from the Posture Statement by Secretary of the Navy John Lehman before the House Armed Services Committee, 8 February 1982," *Navy Policy Briefs* May–June 1982, pp. 1–3.

16. Interview with Admiral Small, 11 April 1985.

17. Interview with Cdr. Weeks, 12 December 1985. Lt. Cdr. S. B. Weeks, OP-603 G memo B07263:05G:mh 8 February 1983. "Maritime Strategy CPAM: Observations from the Trenches." Secret.

18. Ibid., p. 2.

19. Cdr. Weeks's briefings script. 3 September 1982, p. 21.

20. Ibid.

21. Ibid.

22. Ibid, p. 22.

23. Ibid, p. 14.

24. BDM Corporation, *The Soviet Navy Declaratory Doctrine for Theatre Nuclear War.* Prepared for the Director Defense Nuclear Agency, 30 September 1977. Contract No. DNA 001-760C-0230. Report DNA 4434T.

25. Weeks, "Observations from the Trenches," p. 3.

26. Briefing script, 3 September 1982, p. 14.

27. Quoted on slide 61 for ibid., p. 23.

28. Ibid., p. 23–34.

29. Ibid., p. 30.

30. CNO Message 071841Z October 82. Personal for Admirals Crowe, Williams, Foley, McDonald, Vice Admiral Hays, Info: Vice Admiral Carroll; Rear Admirals Shugart, Palmer, Horne, Dillingham from Watkins.

31. Interview with Admiral James Watkins, 12 December 1985.

32. Interview with Cdr. Weeks, 12 December 1985.

33. Interview with Vice Admiral Arthur Moreau, 18 April 1985.

34. This entire paragraph is based on OP-603 file "Memo on Maritime Strategy presentation to SECNAV on 4 November."

35. Ibid.

36. OP-603 Files: VCNO Action item N-1642, 7 November 1982 to OP-06.

37. OP-603 Files: OP-06 Memo to VCNO, B06690:05G serial 603/410230 of 26 November 1982, with Small's handwritten response on a copy of the memo.

38. OP-603 Files: Commander W. S. Johnson "Memo for the Record." Maritime Strategy Presentation Briefed on CNO Executive Panel [1000–1200, 17 November 1982 by RAdm. Robert G. Kirksey in CNA Board Room]. OP-605DI/9617-10. Memo 60/S411042.

39. A Report by Admiral James D. Watkins, U.S. Navy, Chief of Naval Operations, on the posture of the U.S. Navy for the Fiscal Year 1984.

40. Ibid.

41. Interview with Admiral James D. Watkins, 12 December 1985.

42. Ibid.

43. Interview with Cdr. Weeks, 12, 13, December 1985. See Statement of Commodore Dudley L. Carlson, U.S. Navy, Deputy Director, Strategic Plans and Policy Division, Office of the Naval Operations before the Subcommittee on Seapower and Strategic and Critical Materials of the House Armed Services Committee on Maritime Strategy, 24 February 1983.

44. Interview with Vice Admiral Arthur Moreau, 18 April 1985.

45. Interview with Captain Roger Barnett, USN (Ret.), 17 January 1985.

46. Interview with VAdm. Moreau; OP-603 files. Critique of POM-85 CPAM.

47. Ibid.

48. Interview with Captain Peter M. Swartz, USN, 25 March 1985.

49. J. C. Wylie, *Military Strategy: A General Theory of Power Control,* (New Brunswick: Rutgers University Press, 1967). See new edition in The Classics of Seapower series by the Naval Institute Press, 1989, edited with an Introduction by John B. Hattendorf.

50. Interview with Swartz, 25 March 1985.

51. Ibid.

52. Ibid.

53. Ibid.

54. Capt. J. S. Hurlburt, "Memorandum for the Record," 21 September 1983. Subj: Former CNOs' Visit; Hattendorf interview with RAdm. Marryott, 18 April 1985.

55. Comments on draft, Swartz to Hattendorf, 9 June 1986.

56. OP-603 files. Assistant Deputy Chief of Naval Operations, (Plans, Policy and Operation) OP-60. Memorandum for the Chief of Operations. Serial 603/3S41024, B09065;051: of 21 October 1983.

57. OP-603 files. OP65B Memo to OP-603, 22 September 1983.

58. Interview with Captain Linton Brooks, 22 March 1985.

59. OP-603 files. OP-950 Memo to OP-60. Serial 950/489-83 of 26 October 1983.

60. Comments on draft, Swartz to Hattendorf, 9 June 1986.

61. U.S. Senate, 98th Cong., 2nd Sess. Senate Hearing 98-724, Part 8: Sea Power and Power Projection. Hearing, March 14, 28, 29, April 5, 11, May 1, 1984.

62. OP-603 files. "The Maritime Strategy Development/Presentation/Publication Schedule," B08447: 06I: HCB. OP-603I, 7 September 1984.

63. OP-603 file. Cdr. Bruce Valley, CSIS Navy Fellow at Georgetown University, to Cdr. Peter Swartz, 4 April 1984.

64. OP-603. Cdr. J. R. Stark, Comments on Valley's Critique. OP-603J. B10282: 05J: bms of 1 May 1984.

Chapter 5

1. Discussion with Dr. Robert S. Wood, 12 August 1987.

2. OP-603 files. VCNO Message 140051Z August 1984 Personal to CINUSNAVEUR, CINCPACFLT, CINCLANTFLT.

3. OP-603 files. Copy of CINCLANTFLT Message to CNO 122042Z September 84.

4. OP-603 files. "CINC Thoughts on Maritime Strategy," Cdr. J. R. Stark, OP-603B Memo B11453: O5B: bms of 13 October 1984.

5. Captain Peter Rice comments on draft, January 1988; Hattendorf interview with CINCPAC Staff, 23 April 1985; Comments by RAdm. William A. Cockell on draft history, 8 July 1988.

6. Ibid.

7. T. Wood Parker Letter to Hattendorf, 14 August 1986.

8. Ibid.

9. Ibid.

10. Bennett to Aspin, 18 November 1985. Letter of transmittal in U.S. House of Representatives, 99th Congress, 1st Session, Committee Print no. 11. 600-Ship Navy: Report of the Sea Power and Strategic and Critical Materials Subcommittee of the Committee on Armed Services, p. iii.

11. *The Maritime Strategy.* Forty-eight-page supplement to U.S. Naval Institute *Proceedings,* January 1986.

12. Parker to Hattendorf, 14 August 1986.

13. Letter Cdr. A. C. Myers to Hattendorf, 11 September 1986.

14. John J. Mearsheimer, "A Strategic Misstep: the Maritime Strategy and Deterrence In Europe," *International Security,* Vol. 11, no. 2 (Fall 1986), pp. 3–7 and Linton F. Brooks, "Naval Power and National Security: The Case for the Maritime Strategy," in ibid., pp. 58–88.

15. Published by National Strategy Information Center, New York, 1986.

16. Professor Kennedy's lecture series ran from September to December 1986, and included guest speakers whose subjects ranged from ancient history to the examples of failed sea powers—Germany, Japan, and Italy in World War II. It concluded with lectures by Michael MccGwire on current Soviet Sea Power and by John Mearsheimer and Secretary Lehman on the Maritime Strategy. Selected papers from the series were published in the *International History Review* (February 1988).

17. The White House, *National Security Strategy of the United States,* January 1987, pp. 29–30.

National Intelligence Estimate on Soviet Programs

15 November 1982

Accession number NN3-263-95-001 31 Jan 1995

NOTE
The following text of NIE 11-15-82/D of March 1983,
copy 393, has been newly typeset but carefully reprints
the declassified version approved for release by the
Central Intelligence Agency. Those portions of the text
deleted during the CIA security review are clearly marked
by square brackets where they occur.

Soviet Naval Strategy and Programs through the 1990s

National Intelligence Estimate

NIE 11-15-82/D

Information available as of 19 October 1982
was used in the preparation of this Estimate.

Note: Leonid Brezhnev died on 10 November 1982, as this Estimate was going to press.
We have not altered the text to take account of his death because our judgments call for
a post-Brezhnev period of maneuvering at various levels in the political and military
hierarchy. We believe that sharp changes in defense efforts would be possible only after
power is consolidated.

THIS ESTIMATE IS ISSUED BY THE DIRECTOR OF CENTRAL INTELLIGENCE.

THE NATIONAL FOREIGN INTELLIGENCE BOARD CONCURS, EXCEPT AS NOTED IN THE TEXT.

The following intelligence organizations participated in the preparation of the Estimate:

The Central Intelligence Agency, the Defense Intelligence Agency, the National Security Agency, and the intelligence organization of the Department of State.

Also Participating:

The Assistant Chief of Staff for Intelligence, Department of the Army

The Director of Naval Intelligence, Department of the Navy

The Assistant Chief of Staff, Intelligence, Department of the Air Force

The Director of Intelligence, Headquarters, Marine Corps

[TEXT DELETED]

Contents

Preface

During the eight years since publication of NIE 11-15-74, the last estimate devoted to the Soviet Navy's strategy and programs, there have been many notable developments in that force, particularly concerning new weapon systems. The Soviets have, for example:

- Deployed long-range, submarine-launched ballistic missiles (SLBMs) with multiple independently targetable reentry vehicles (MIRVs).

- Deployed their first sea-based, fixed-wing tactical aircraft and probably decided to construct their first aircraft carrier capable of handling high-performance aircraft.

- Achieved significant developments in the application of nuclear propulsion to warships.

- Continued the modernization of their fleet through the deployment of a new class of ballistic missile submarine, four new classes of general purpose submarines, and four new classes of principal surface combatants.

- Begun testing a long-range land-attack cruise missile capable of being launched from a variety of submarine, surface, and air platforms.

The substantial allocation of resources for such programs indicates a continued, and probably growing, recognition by Soviet leaders of the value of naval forces in the attainment of wartime and peacetime goals. These programs also raise questions about the future use of such forces and whether their development indicates basic changes in Soviet naval doctrine and strategy.[1]

Many aspects of Soviet naval developments have already been addressed in publications by individual departments and agencies, particularly technical studies and short-term assessments. The subject is also treated as portions of recent estimates (11-14, 11-10, and 11-3/8) and in memorandums (on readiness and on sea lines of communication). In contrast to those studies, the major focus of this Estimate is on the overall significance of current and projected programs for Soviet naval strategy in the late 1980s and the decade of the 1990s, including some of the major options open to the Soviets for performing critical naval tasks. (Nonnaval responses to the maritime threat facing the USSR, such as air defense against sea-launched land-attack missiles, are treated only peripherally in this Estimate.) The groundwork for this assessment is laid by outlining the navy's current status—its major tasks and the forces that would seek to accomplish them. In addition to providing a basis for examining future developments, an understanding of current forces is especially important for naval estimates because of the long time needed to develop naval systems and the long service life of ships and aircraft. Most of the submarine and major surface combatant classes and many of the aircraft that will be in the Soviet Navy of 1995 are already in service today.

The Soviets recognize that their navy is facing severe challenges to the performance of its missions as a result of improvements in Western naval forces, particularly quieter submarines, longer range SLBMs, greater numbers of sea-launched cruise missiles, and improving defensive systems. To meet these challenges, the Soviets support a variety of research and development efforts. Many of these programs have been identified, and we can make some evaluation of their capabilities based on knowledge of past Soviet programs and current technological state of the art. By extrapolating from such information, the general nature of future Soviet naval weapons and sensors can be discussed. Such extrapolations may prove wrong, however, because assessments of evolutionary technical progress may be upset by "breakthroughs" that cannot be predicted on the basis of an understanding of the current state of the art. This is particularly important in those aspects of the Soviet research effort, such as nonacoustic antisubmarine warfare and space-based ocean reconnaissance/targeting, that involve innovative solutions to naval problems. This Estimate considers some of the potential consequences of such breakthroughs in key areas and speculates on how the Soviets might attempt to exploit such successes.

Finally, the development of the Soviet Navy will occur within the broad context of changes in the Soviet system and the international environment. Although a detailed treatment of such subjects is beyond the scope of this Estimate, some of the possible relationships among such factors as the post-Brezhnev succession, economic problems, arms control negotiations, and an increased emphasis on influencing developments in the Third World have been sketched out, especially as they might affect force procurement.

Key Judgments

Over the past decade, the role of the navy within the USSR's national strategy has continued to evolve, supported by additional operational experience and an ambitious naval construction program. This program, emphasizing larger ships with increased endurance and technologically advanced weapon and electronic systems, has enhanced the navy's capability for sustained conventional combat and distant area deployments.

Within the Soviets' overall wartime strategy, however, the primary initial tasks of the navy remain:

• To deploy and provide protection for ballistic missile submarines in preparation for and conduct of strategic and theater nuclear strikes.

• To defend the USSR and its allies from strikes by enemy ballistic missile submarines and aircraft carriers.

Accomplishment of these tasks would entail attempts to control all or portions of the Kara, Barents, and northern Norwegian and Greenland seas, the seas of Japan and Okhotsk, and the Northwest Pacific Basin, and to conduct sea-denial operations beyond those areas to about 2,000 kilometers from Soviet territory. We believe that virtually all of the Northern and Pacific Fleets' available major surface combatants and combat aircraft and some three-quarters of their available attack submarines would be committed initially to operations in these waters. Other initial naval wartime tasks are: support of ground force operations in the land theaters of military operations (including countering naval support to enemy operations in peripheral areas such as Norway), and some interdiction of Western sea lines of communication (SLOCs).

We believe this wartime strategy will remain essentially unchanged over the next 15 to 20 years. Strategic strike—including protection of nuclear-powered ballistic missile submarines (SSBNs)—and strategic defense against enemy SSBNs, aircraft carriers, and other major platforms capable of striking Soviet territory will continue to be the Soviet Navy's primary initial wartime tasks. We expect these requirements—particularly the need to counter Western units armed with the new Tomahawk land-attack cruise missile—will drive the Soviets to expand the area in which their navy would initially deploy the bulk of its Northern and Pacific Fleet forces for sea-control/sea-denial operations—possibly out to 3,000 kilometers from Soviet territory.

A principal portion of the strategic defense task—the destruction of enemy SSBNs before they can launch their missiles (SLBMs)—will pose increasing difficulties for the Soviets. The deployment of hard-target-capable US SLBMs, improved British and French SSBNs, and the first Chinese SSBNs probably will increase the importance of this task. The Soviet Navy's ability to detect and track US SSBNs in the open ocean, however, probably will decline, at least over the next 10 years. This is primarily because we believe that the increased patrol areas of SSBNs carrying Trident SLBMs will more than offset the increased coverage that could be provided by improved Soviet antisubmarine warfare (ASW) platforms. We therefore expect that Soviet naval anti-SSBN operations will continue to be modest, with relatively few attack submarines stationed in choke points or in the approaches to Western or Chinese submarine bases.

We believe that Soviet procurement of naval weapons platforms and systems over the period of this Estimate will be driven primarily by requirements stemming from the strategic offensive and defensive tasks outlined above:

- The size of the modern ballistic missile submarine force will probably remain roughly constant at about 60 units throughout the 1990s. In the absence of new arms control restrictions, the number of SLBM warheads is likely to increase.

- The Soviets will develop long-range nuclear-armed land-attack cruise missiles capable of being launched from a variety of naval platforms. In the absence of arms control restrictions, we believe they will be deployed primarily on newer nuclear-powered attack submarines for use in theater strike roles and possibly for strikes against some targets in the continental United States.

- The first unit of a new class of nuclear-powered aircraft carrier probably will become operational by about 1990.

- The number of principal surface combatants probably will decline somewhat, but the trend toward larger average size, greater weapon loads, and more sophisticated weapon and electronic systems will continue.

- The overall number of general purpose submarines will decline, but the number of nuclear-powered units probably will grow substantially.

- The navy's overall amphibious lift capability will increase gradually. We expect an increase in the size of the naval infantry from some 14,000 to about 18,000 to 20,000 men.

- One or more new classes of underway replenishment ships will be introduced, but construction of such ships probably will continue to receive a relatively low priority.

- The number of fixed-wing naval aircraft probably will increase somewhat, with the major change being the first at-sea deployment of high-performance, conventional takeoff and landing (CTOL) aircraft. The continued production of Backfire bombers and the introduction of a follow-on in the 1990s will be an essential element in the Soviets' attempts to expand their sea-control/sea-denial efforts against Western surface forces in vital areas such as the Norwegian, North, and Mediterranean seas and the Northwest Pacific Basin. Naval aviation bombers will also remain a principal feature of Soviet antisurface capabilities in other areas such as the Arabian Sea.

- Major technical improvements in Soviet fleet air defense are likely. New surface-to-air missiles, guns, and laser weapons will probably be introduced. Fighter aircraft operating from the projected new aircraft carriers will add a new dimension to the navy's air defense resources.

- Expansion of both sea-control and sea-denial operations will be supported by gradual improvements in Soviet capability to surveil Western surface units and provide targeting assistance for antiship missiles. Much of the improvement probably will involve space-based systems.

In addition to its wartime tasks, the Soviet Navy will continue to play important peacetime roles, ranging from routine show-the-flag port visits to support for distant-area client states during crisis situations and limited wars. Given the likelihood of continued instability in the Third World, the use of such naval diplomacy and power projection techniques probably will increase during the 1980s and 1990s.

The most notable change in the Soviet Navy during the period of this Estimate probably will be the introduction of its first aircraft carriers equipped to handle high-performance CTOL aircraft. We believe that the primary mission of such carriers will be to help expand Northern and Pacific Fleet sea-control operations during a general war. The carriers will also give the Soviet Navy for the first time an ability to project power ashore effectively in distant areas in a limited war. Together with other force improvements, they will provide the Soviets the option of using naval force in a number of Third World situations against all but the most well-armed regional powers. We believe that major Soviet Navy task force participation in Third World conflicts would, however, be restricted to limited war situations in which the Soviets judged the risk of escalation to war with the United States or NATO to be small.

Our best estimate on the future of the Soviet Navy reflects our judgment that the trends we have observed in ship construction, naval doctrine, and strategy over the past 20 years will continue. Among the variables that could dictate a different course for the Soviet Navy of the 1990s are:

- A major ASW breakthrough that gives the Soviets the capability to detect and track enemy submarines in the open ocean. Although unlikely throughout the period of this Estimate, such a breakthrough would substantially increase the navy's ability to perform the critically important strategic defensive task of destroying enemy ballistic missile and land-attack cruise missile submarines before they launched their missiles. It would probably lead to major changes in the way the Soviets would deploy their general purpose naval forces before and during general war.

- Arms control negotiations, which could play an important part in determining the role within Soviet strategy and the force composition of the Soviet Navy in the 1990s. For example, severe restrictions on sea-launched cruise missile characteristics and/or deployment would alleviate a serious maritime threat to the USSR and eliminate much of the pressure to conduct sea-denial operations at greater distances from Soviet territory.

- Severe economic problems, which could lead to a reduction of Soviet defense spending in the 1990s. Such a reduction would be likely to result in cuts in the navy's budget, perhaps falling heaviest on major surface ship programs such as the expected new aircraft carrier, projected nuclear-powered cruisers, and large amphibious and

SOVIET NAVAL COMMANDER

One change in the Soviet Navy during the period of this Estimate will be the departure of Sergei Gorshkov, an admiral since 1941, who became commander of the Soviet Navy in 1956.

replenishment ships. The net result of such cuts would be a navy with less capability than the one projected in our best estimate to control waters beyond the range of land-based tactical aircraft and to project power in distant areas. Programs considered essential to the navy's primary strategic offensive and defensive tasks—such as ballistic missile submarines, attack and cruise missile submarines, land-based strike aircraft, and ASW-oriented surface combatants—probably would suffer few, if any, cuts.

Discussion

I. Current Naval Strategy and Programs

A. Introduction

1. By the mid-1970s, when this Estimate was last produced, the Soviet Navy had evolved from a force primarily oriented to close-in defense of maritime frontiers to one designed to undertake a wide variety of naval tasks, ranging from strategic nuclear strikes to worldwide peacetime naval diplomacy. Since then, Soviet naval employment within an overall national strategy has continued to evolve, supported by an ambitious naval construction program and additional operational experience. This chapter describes our understanding of Soviet programs and current naval strategy, particularly how Soviet forces would be employed initially during a general war.

B. Force Composition, Organization, and Readiness

2. The primary forces of the Soviet Navy consist of 85 ballistic missiles and 278 general purpose submarines, 284 large surface combatants, and some 1,200 naval combat aircraft. They are organized into four fleets—the Northern, Baltic, Black Sea, and Pacific Fleets (see figure 1). The Soviet Navy maintains two standing deployed forces, the Mediterranean and Indian Ocean Squadrons, which draw their forces primarily from the Northern and Black Sea Fleets and the Pacific Fleet, respectively.

3. Control of the armed forces of Warsaw Pact countries in wartime would be transferred to a Soviet Supreme High Command (VGK), with the Soviet General Staff as its executive agent. To give this centralized command structure some flexibility, the Soviets have divided areas of anticipated military action into geographical entities called theaters of military operations (TVDs), including probably four ocean TVDs (see figure 2). High commands established in these TVDs probably

FIGURE 1
Major Soviet Naval Forces[a]

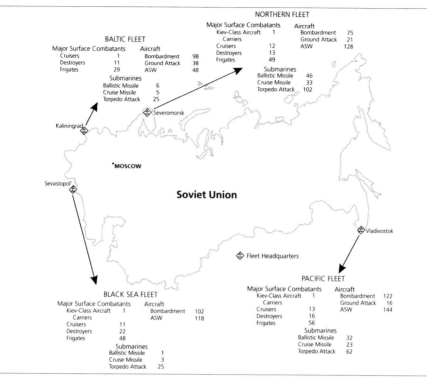

NORTHERN FLEET

Major Surface Combatants		Aircraft	
Kiev-Class Aircraft	1	Bombardment	75
Carriers		Ground Attack	21
Cruisers	12	ASW	128
Destroyers	13		
Frigates	49		

Submarines	
Ballistic Missile	46
Cruise Missile	33
Torpedo Attack	102

BALTIC FLEET

Major Surface Combatants		Aircraft	
Cruisers	1	Bombardment	98
Destroyers	11	Ground Attack	38
Frigates	29	ASW	48

Submarines	
Ballistic Missile	6
Cruise Missile	5
Torpedo Attack	25

Severomorsk

Kaliningrad

*MOSCOW

Sevastopol

Soviet Union

Vladivostok

⊕ Fleet Headquarters

PACIFIC FLEET

Major Surface Combatants		Aircraft	
Kiev-Class Aircraft	1	Bombardment	122
Carriers		Ground Attack	16
Cruisers	13	ASW	144
Destroyers	16		
Frigates	56		

Submarines	
Ballistic Missile	32
Cruise Missile	23
Torpedo Attack	62

BLACK SEA FLEET

Major Surface Combatants		Aircraft	
Kiev-Class Aircraft	1	Bombardment	102
Carriers		ASW	118
Cruisers	11		
Destroyers	22		
Frigates	48		

Submarines	
Ballistic Missile	1
Cruise Missile	3
Torpedo Attack	25

a. Information as of 1 July 1982. These figures do not include units in reserve. Among the other units in the Soviet Navy are some 160 patrol combatants, 85 amphibious warfare ships, 145 mine warfare ships, 80 underway replenishment ships, and 250 other combat aircraft (reconnaissance, refueling, etc.). Black Sea Fleet figures include the units of the Caspian Sea Flotilla. Naval infantry consists of a division in the Pacific Fleet and one brigade in each of the three western fleets.

would directly control those forces within their respective areas, except for those forces, including SSBNs, remaining under the control of the VGK:

• We believe the Northern Fleet commander controls all general purpose military operations in the Arctic and Atlantic TVDs. Some units, such as those involved in amphibious operations, probably would be subordinate to the command of the Northwestern TVD, emphasizing operations against Norway. We believe that, for efficient command and control, a high command would be created for this TVD. We also believe that the bulk of the Northern Fleet's forces would operate within the Arctic Ocean TVD—this TVD would probably encompass all sea areas north of the Greenland-Iceland-United Kingdom (GIUK) gap. Strategic forces, including SSBNs and aircraft on strategic missions, operating in these ocean TVDs would be under the direct control of the VGK.

FIGURE 2
Probable Soviet Ocean Theaters of Military Operations (TVDs)

- The subordination of Pacific Fleet forces and the responsibility of the fleet commander probably are similar to those of the Northern Fleet. We believe that the Pacific Fleet Commander would control all general purpose military operations in the Pacific Ocean TVD. Some units, such as those planned for operations against China and the Japanese islands, probably would be controlled by the high command of the Far East TVD. The Indian Ocean Squadron would be subordinate to the Pacific Fleet—possibly in a separate Indian Ocean TVD—unless a high command were formed in the Southern TVD, in which case, the squadron would be responsive to the high command. As in the Northern Fleet, forces performing strategic missions in the Pacific Ocean TVD would be under the direct control of the VGK.

- The Baltic Fleet, as part of a combined fleet with the Polish and East German navies, would be subordinate to the high command of the Western TVD. This theater would encompass primarily operations against West Germany, Denmark, the Benelux countries, and France, and NATO forces in the Baltic and North Seas.

- The Black Sea Fleet, as part of a combined fleet with the Bulgarian and Romanian navies—as well as the forces of the Mediterranean Squadron—would be subordinate to the high command of the Southwestern TVD, encompassing primarily operations against Turkey, Greece, and Italy, and NATO forces in the Mediterranean.

4. *Readiness Philosophy*. Although Soviet naval presence has expanded globally in the past two decades, only a relatively small portion of the Soviet Navy is still regularly deployed away from home waters. This is due largely to the Soviet approach to readiness, which differs markedly from that of Western navies. Generally speaking, the Soviet readiness philosophy stresses readiness to deploy for combat on relatively short notice rather than routine deployment of large forces. To achieve a maximum force generation capability in times of crisis, the Soviet Navy emphasizes maintenance and in-port/in-area training rather than extended at-sea operations. Even Soviet naval units deployed out-of-area spend much of their time at anchor or in port. To the Soviet mind, it apparently is more important to be ready to go to sea than to be at sea. Under this system, operational experience and some degree of crew proficiency are sacrificed to achieve high material availability. As a result of this readiness philosophy, the Soviets probably would have more than half of their submarines and major surface combatants available for combat within a few days and some 70 percent within two weeks. We estimate that, given several days' warning, Soviet Naval Aviation would have more than 90 percent of its aircraft available, although this percentage could be sustained for only a short time.

C. Key Aspects of Naval Doctrine

5. *Soviet View of General War*. The Soviets' military writings indicate that they believe a war with the West would be decisive, be global in scope, and probably escalate to a nuclear conflict. They probably expect that such a war would begin in Central Europe following a period of rising international tensions and would spread to the Far East, as China enters to take advantage of Soviet involvement in Europe. In the Soviet view, the conflict would probably evolve through four stages:

- A conventional phase in which a NATO offensive is checked by the Warsaw Pact.

- A period of limited theater nuclear war in which the Pact detects NATO preparations to use nuclear weapons and preempts.

- A decisive phase with large-scale use of nuclear weapons, both intercontinentally and within theater.

- A concluding phase in which residual nuclear and conventional forces come into play.

There have been recent indications that the Soviets expect a more protracted conventional war phase than was anticipated in the 1960s and early 1970s.

6. Regardless of the length of the conventional phase, the Soviets probably doubt that a war with the West would be decided at the conventional level. Therefore, initial conventional operations would be conducted with an eye toward escalation. During the initial phase of operations, the Soviets probably would attempt to destroy with conventional munitions as much as possible of the enemy's theater and sea-based nuclear weapons and supporting facilities. We do not believe the Soviets consider that the destruction of potential strategic assets, such as SSBNs, during the conventional phase would by itself trigger an escalation to the use of nuclear weapons.

7. [TEXT DELETED]

8. *Soviet Wartime Tasks.* Our examination of Soviet naval writings, exercises, and construction trends allows us to estimate the Soviet Navy's initial wartime tasks with a good deal of confidence. It also permits an understanding of the Soviets' relative priorities in fighting a war with the West. Since the 1960s, naval exercises and writings have consistently emphasized specific offensive and defensive tasks to be performed concurrently during the first stages of a war with NATO. These tasks are:

- To deploy and provide "combat stability"(that is, protection and support) for ballistic missile submarines in preparation for and conduct of strategic and theater nuclear strikes.

- To defend the USSR and its allies from enemy sea-based strike forces.

- To support ground force operations in the land theaters of military operations, including protecting Pact sea lines of communication and preventing naval support to enemy operations in peripheral areas such as Norway.

- To conduct some interdiction of enemy sea lines of communication.

9. The pattern of implementation of these tasks undoubtedly would vary from fleet to fleet. The Northern and Pacific Fleets would initially be concerned with deploying and protecting their SSBNs. The Baltic and Black Sea Fleets, on the other hand, would initially concentrate on supporting operations in the land theaters. Combating enemy strike groups, especially carrier battle groups, approaching the USSR would also be a major initial concern of all four fleets.

10. The Soviets realize that a conflict may not unfold as they expect. In this case, they would be prepared to reexamine their initial force allocations in these tasks. However, readiness to conduct strategic strikes, including the protection of their SSBN forces, and to attack enemy sea-based nuclear forces would be likely to remain their major concerns, regardless of scenario. The following paragraphs examine

the navy's principal tasks in the context of the standard scenario, as evidenced by their writings and military exercises.

D. Strategic Strike

11. The Soviets regard strategic strike against enemy land targets as the primary naval mission. This priority stems from the Soviet belief that a war with the West would probably escalate to the unlimited use of nuclear weapons and from the capability of SLBMs to strike strategically important targets. According to Fleet Admiral of the Soviet Union Sergei Gorshkov, SLBMs give navies, for the first time in history, the capability to directly affect "the course and even the outcome" of a war. The Soviet Navy's 62 modern SSBNs, over half of which are D-class units capable of striking the continental United States while remaining in home waters, carry a total of 920 SLBMs.

12. The day-to-day disposition of Soviet SSBNs is governed by the wartime requirement to generate maximum force levels on short notice. The Soviet Navy seeks to maintain 75 percent of its SSBNs in an operational status, with the remaining 25 percent in long-term repair. [TEXT DELETED] Every operational SSBN could probably be deployed with three weeks' preparation time. To maintain this high state of readiness, a relatively small portion of the modern SSBN force—typically about 25 percent or 14 units—is kept deployed at sea. However, additional D and Y-class units are probably kept in a high state of readiness in or near home port in order to be ready to fire their missiles on short notice.

13. We believe most SLBMs would be targeted against administrative centers, communications facilities, and industrial and soft military targets, largely because they do not now have the combination of accuracy and yield to destroy hardened military targets. Some SSBNs, particularly the forward-deployed Ys, probably would participate in initial strikes against the continental United States. Many SSBNs, however, probably would be withheld for subsequent strikes or as a residual strategic force. It is feasible that by using the three *Amga*-class missile support ships, the Soviets could reload some SSBNs that had participated in the initial strikes. SLBMs are ideally suited for follow-on strikes, since they are more likely to survive initial nuclear operations than ICBMs in fixed silos, and will remain less vulnerable to subsequent strikes.

14. *Protection and Support for SSBNs.* The Soviets have long been concerned with the vulnerability of their submarines to ASW forces. Soviet authors frequently cite the experience of the two World Wars to reject the notion that submarines can ensure their own survival through concealed operations. Rather, since at least the 1960s,

they have discussed the need to use general purpose forces, including large surface combatants, to protect and support or provide "combat stability" to ballistic missile submarines. Such writings strongly imply that providing combat stability to SSBNs is an integral part of the strategic strike mission and the most important initial wartime task of a significant number of Northern and Pacific Fleet general purpose forces.

15. We believe that the Soviets plan to support and protect their SSBNs through an echeloned defense in-depth. This defense would likely begin while the SSBNs are still in port and continue as they are dispersed and enter assigned operating areas. Surface combatants, mine warfare ships, and ASW aircraft [SIDEBAR DELETED] probably would be used to sanitize SSBN transit routes. General purpose submarines probably would escort transiting SSBNs and, along with aircraft, establish barrier patrols in the approaches to SSBN operating areas. Surface combatant task groups also would probably operate in the vicinity of such areas to assist in combating enemy SSNs and ASW aircraft.

16. Protection of SSBN operating areas entails attempts to control all or large portions of the Kara, Barents, and northern Norwegian and Greenland seas as well as the seas of Japan and Okhotsk and the area off the Kamchatka Peninsula. It also involves sea-denial operations beyond these areas to about 2,000 kilometers from Soviet territory. Some facets of the echeloned defense, such as the operation of attack submarines in proximity to SSBNs and protection of the waters near the ice edge, would serve only one main purpose—the protection of SSBNs—because the only Western units likely to be in such areas would be those attempting to attack the SSBNs. Most of the units involved in the echeloned defense, however, would also contribute to other important tasks, particularly the defense of Soviet territory from attacks by Western forces and the prevention of naval support to Allied operations in peripheral areas such as Norway and Korea. Attack submarines, aircraft, and any surface combatants operating near the GIUK gap, for example, would seek to destroy any Western submarines or major surface combatants detected, thereby protecting both the SSBNs and the Soviet homeland. Forces operating in these waters, therefore, would be accomplishing several important tasks at the same time.

17. We believe that virtually all major surface combatants and combat aircraft available in the Northern and Pacific Fleets and some three-quarters of their attack submarines would be initially committed to conducting "sea-control" and "sea-denial" operations in these waters (see figures 3 and 4 and accompanying text inset), leaving relatively few units available for operations in areas such as the North

FIGURE 3

Current Initial Soviet Operating Areas in the Western TVDs

The outer edge of the initial Northern and Black Sea Fleet sea-denial areas generally conforms to the 2,000-kilometer naval defense thresholds. These initial sea-denial areas undoubtedly would expand or contract to take into account geographic features in each fleet area, such as the GIUK (Greenland-Iceland-United Kingdom) gap and the Strait of Sicily. Initial sea-denial operations by the Baltic Fleet probably would be limited to the North Sea and Baltic approaches.

Atlantic and Central Pacific. Given the likelihood that many SSBNs will be withheld from initial strikes, the requirement to protect SSBNs could tie down substantial assets for an extended period. The Soviets probably would be reluctant to release substantial forces from this task until most missiles had been launched,

FIGURE 4
Current Initial Soviet Operating Areas in the Pacific Ocean

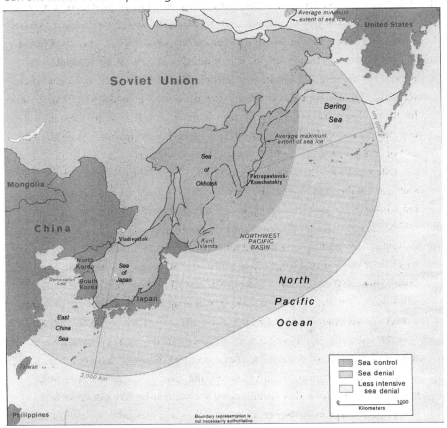

they perceived that the threat had significantly lessened, or the course of the conflict dictated increased emphasis on other tasks.

18. There are indications that suggest that during wartime a fleet's assets not assigned to deployed squadrons or "independent" operations relatively far from the Soviet Union would operate as "mixed force" groups. We do not fully understand how the operations of the general purpose forces, normally under fleet control, will be meshed with those of the SSBNs, a VGK asset. The fleet commander probably would be responsible for coordinating the operations of the separate groups. The Soviets probably intend that this structure would result in simplified transition to a wartime posture, improved responsiveness to rapidly developing situations, and increased flexibility in resource allocations, particularly in the support and protection of SSBNs.

E. Strategic Defense

19. *Anti-SSBN.* The Soviet Navy's most critical defensive task is the destruction of enemy SSBNs before they can launch their missiles. The Soviets probably recognize, however, that there is a wide gap between the importance of this task and the capability of their current forces to carry it out. Soviet writings acknowledge the enormous firepower present in even a single Western SSBN, and we believe they recognize the desirability of attacking such units during the conventional phase of hostilities. They also probably recognize, however, that they do not now have the capability to detect US SSBNs operating in open-ocean areas or to maintain contact or trail if a chance detection occurs. The deployment of the US Trident missile system, whose greater range opens up even larger ocean areas that must be searched, further complicates the Soviets' task. The Soviet Navy, realizing the magnitude of the problem and its shortcomings, probably will concentrate its anti-SSBN efforts on choke points and the approaches to enemy SSBN bases rather than attempting to search larger ocean areas. On occasion, surface combatants, attack submarines, intelligence collectors (AGIs), and aircraft have conducted joint ASW operations off the Rockall Bank, west of the US and British SSBN bases near Holy Loch, Scotland, during major exercises. We have also seen joint AGI-SSN operations off SSBN bases in the United States. We therefore believe that the Soviets would station intelligence collection ships, nuclear attack submarines, and possibly even surface combatants off Western bases in the period preceding hostilities and attempt to detect and trail SSBNs leaving port. Once hostilities commenced, they would attack any submarine they held in contact. Some of their best ASW submarines probably would be used in this effort, although the number would be small relative to the number committed to protect Soviet SSBNs.

SEA-CONTROL AND SEA-DENIAL OPERATIONS

The terms "sea control" and "sea denial" are subject to a variety of interpretations. Generally a state is considered to have "sea control" in an area if it is able to sustain surface combatant and merchant ship operations there with relative security. It is considered to exercise "sea denial" if it prevents such use of the area by its opponent.

The terms "sea control" and "sea denial" are used in this Estimate to indicate the type of naval effort the Soviets probably expect to conduct in various maritime areas at the beginning of a NATO–Warsaw Pact war. Areas labeled "sea control" are those in which the Soviets probably intend to operate surface forces, as well as submarines and naval aircraft, for an indefinite period. Areas labeled "sea denial" are those in which the Soviets probably expect the major share of the combat to be conducted by submarines and land-based strike aircraft. Surface ship operations in these waters will be either nonexistent or of a short duration at the initiation of hostilities. The term "less intensive sea denial" is used to indicate a lower level of effort, primarily by submarines.

The delineation of these areas is heavily influenced by the impact of geography on Soviet naval operations. The Baltic and Black Sea Fleets are separated from open-ocean areas by narrow straits that would be under Western control at the beginning of hostilities. Northern Fleet units would have to transit the GIUK gap if they wished to reach the North Atlantic. Most of the Pacific Fleet units are in a similar situation, with only Petropavlovsk having direct access to the open Pacific.

The Northern Fleet. A major consideration in Northern Fleet operations is NATO control of the passages between Greenland, Iceland, the Faroes, and the United Kingdom. Soviet wartime operations in the region of these waters would be likely to involve primarily submarines, which would attack NATO forces attempting to enter the Norwegian Sea through these passages. Operations in this area would contribute to several tasks, including protecting Soviet SSBNs and territory and countering Western naval support to NATO forces in Norway. This area probably would also be a focus for antiship operations by Backfire bombers, which are much better suited than the older Badgers to deal with the likely air defense environment in this area. Also, Backfire and other bomber attacks can be expected on ASW, early warning, and air defense facilities in the gap area. Operations within the sea-control area are likely to involve surface ships, submarines, and strike aircraft. Farther north the Soviets probably intend to use geographic features such as the ice edge and Soviet islands such as Novaya Zemlya to facilitate the operation of their forces, particularly their SSBNs and supporting general purpose forces.

The Baltic Fleet. Operations of the Baltic Fleet in wartime would be heavily influenced by Western control of the narrow Danish straits and by the proximity of the Baltic to major ground and air operations in Central Europe. It is likely that the major effort of the Fleet and the East German and Polish navies would be directed at controlling the Baltic through the use of surface units, submarines, and a variety of aircraft, including naval fighter-bombers. The Pact would also attempt to deny NATO the use of the North Sea as an operating area for aircraft carriers and a transit area for amphibious groups and logistic units. The principal weapon in such operations probably would be medium bombers, although they would have to overfly NATO territory to reach their targets. Because of its narrow straits and shallow waters, the Baltic is a particularly good area for the employment of mines.

The Black Sea Fleet. The Soviets and their Romanian and Bulgarian allies would employ surface, submarine, and air assets in sea-control operations within the Black Sea. Sea-denial operations by the Soviets in the eastern Mediterranean could involve prehostilities reinforcement of their Mediterranean Squadron. Unless the Pact actually controlled the Turkish straits, however, Soviet attempts to continue sea-denial operations in the eastern Mediterranean would be hampered by the difficulty of reinforcing the Mediterranean Squadron with additional surface ships and submarines once hostilities had begun. Air operations in the Mediterranean would also be constrained by the need for aircraft based in Pact territory to penetrate Western air defenses. Although significant numbers of Soviet surface units would be involved in initial operations in the Mediterranean, the Soviets probably do not expect these would survive more than a few days. The brunt of the subsequent sea denial effort would be carried by submarines and aircraft.

The Pacific Fleet. Soviet control of the Sea of Japan and the Sea of Okhotsk would depend on sealing off several narrow waterways, ranging from the Korea Strait in the south to the Kuril Strait at the tip of the Kamchatka Peninsula. Sea control operations would also be conducted east of the Kamchatka Peninsula to protect the approaches to Petropavlovsk, the only major Soviet naval base with direct access to the open ocean. Sea denial operations would also be conducted in the Yellow Sea and the northwestern Pacific. The outer edge of the sea-denial area is less easily defined than in other fleet areas because such efforts cannot be focused on narrow waterways through which Western units must pass.

20. *Anticarrier.* The Soviets continue to have great respect for the aircraft carrier's importance in US naval strategy. They regard the aircraft carriers not only as the backbone of American general purpose naval forces, but also an important nuclear reserve force that could play a significant role in determining the outcome of the final phases of hostilities. Writings and exercise activity indicate that the Soviets expect US carrier battle groups to undertake vigorous offensive actions in the maritime approaches to the USSR. They believe that carrier battle groups would attempt to use the Norwegian, the North, and the eastern Mediterranean seas and the northwestern Pacific Ocean to attack Warsaw Pact territory, deployed naval forces including SSBNs and their supporting forces, and Pact ground force operations. Destruction of aircraft carriers, therefore, is a critical element of several important Soviet naval tasks.

21. Cruise missile submarines and strike aircraft carrying air-to-surface missiles (ASMs) are the Soviets' primary anticarrier weapons. In addition to more than 300 naval Backfire (see inset, p. 128, and figure 5) and Badger strike aircraft, some elements of the Soviet Air Force (SAF) and Air Armies of the VGK (AAVGK) are also assigned maritime strike tasks (see figure 6). AAVGK Bear B/C aircraft have been involved in simulated strike missions against naval targets during recent Northern and Pacific Fleet exercises. One Bear squadron has been modified to carry the AS-4 ASM—the same missile carried by the Backfire. We believe that all of the 65 to 70 AAVGK Bear B/Cs will be modified for this capability by the mid-1980s. SAF Badgers and Blinders have also been involved in antiship exercises.

22. In wartime, these forces would attack carrier battle groups crossing fleet defensive thresholds, generally some 2,000 kilometers from Soviet territory. Antiship-missile-equipped surface combatants would also be used in areas where they are in proximity to US carrier battle groups at the outset of hostilities or as carrier battle groups approach Soviet sea-control areas. Soviet doctrine emphasizes

FIGURE 5
TU-22M Backfire Bomber with AS-4 Antiship Missile

preemptive or "first salvo" strikes against carriers before they can launch air strikes. The Soviets would attempt to use tactical surprise and coordinated multiple missile strikes on different threat axes to overwhelm battle group defenses.

F. Support for Land Theaters of Military Operations (TVDs)

23. Although the Soviet Navy has acquired increasingly important strategic offensive and defensive tasks, support for combined-arms operations in the continental TVDs remains a major responsibility of the Baltic and Black Sea Fleets and a secondary responsibility of the Northern and Pacific Fleets. In wartime, the Baltic and Black Sea Fleets would join with navies of other Warsaw Pact nations to form the Combined Baltic and Combined Black Sea Fleets, respectively. The broad objectives of these combined fleets would be to gain control of the Baltic and Black seas and to help secure access to the North and Mediterranean seas. In the Baltic, initial naval operations would focus on destruction of NATO submarines, missile-armed patrol combatants, and naval aviation forces. Western carrier battle groups would become primary targets as they moved into the North Sea. Amphibious landings in support of ground and airborne attacks on West Germany and Denmark also are likely. In the Black Sea, initial naval operations would focus on supporting the movement of ground forces along the western littoral and assisting in seizing the Turkish straits. Romanian and Bulgarian naval forces would be primarily responsible for patrol duties along their own coasts. The Soviet Black Sea Fleet would assist Mediterranean Squadron operations against Western carrier battle groups and amphibious forces. The Northern Fleet would also conduct amphibious operations in support of ground forces operations against northern Norway. The wartime role of the Pacific Fleet's amphibious forces is less well understood. These forces could be used for the seizure of key straits such as La Perouse or could be retained to defend Soviet coastal regions.

THE BACKFIRE

The introduction of the Backfire bomber in 1974 into the navy significantly improved Soviet strike capability against NATO surface forces. Because of the modern, higher speed air-to-surface missile it carries, its variable flight profiles, its maneuverability, and its high-speed capabilities and electronic countermeasures (ECM) equipment, the Backfire has a greater probability of penetrating or avoiding NATO naval air defenses and attacking targets in the open ocean than does the Badger. Some 90 aircraft are in service with Soviet Naval Aviation (SNA), and additional aircraft are being introduced at the rate of about 15 per year. SNA Backfires are currently organized into four complete regiments (two in the Baltic Fleet, one in the Black Sea, and one in the Pacific). A fifth regiment is being formed in the Pacific Fleet. For wartime operations the Soviets probably would deploy aircraft from their peacetime locations to those areas from which they could best operate against Western surface units, especially US carrier battle groups. The Soviets often deploy Backfires from one fleet area to another for exercises; in particular, Baltic Fleet aircraft annually deploy to Northern Fleet bases.

Although the Backfire is capable of carrying a variety of ordnance—including bombs and mines—its principal antiship weapon is the AS-4 missile. The AS-4 can be armed with either a conventional or nuclear warhead, has a speed of Mach 3 plus, and has a maximum range of some 400 kilometers. In wartime each SNA Backfire probably would carry one or two of these missiles. To concentrate their firepower, the Soviets probably would attack carrier battle groups with at least one regiment (20 aircraft) and preferably two. Although Backfire operations over ocean areas have been rare, the aircraft has participated in some antiship exercises against Soviet units. In September 1982 the first use of the Backfire in a simulated strike against a US carrier battle group occurred when Pacific Fleet units operated against two US carriers east of the Kuril Islands.

The Soviets undoubtedly view the Backfire as a vital part of their strategic defense forces to keep Western carrier battle groups from striking important targets within the Soviet landmass. The Backfire will continue to be an essential feature of Soviet antisurface capabilities in areas such as the Norwegian, Mediterranean, and Arabian seas and the northwest Pacific Ocean.

G. Interdiction of Sea Lines of Communication (SLOCs)

24. The Soviets view SLOC interdiction as a less urgent task than providing combat stability for their SSBNs and defeating the West's nuclear-capable naval strike forces. They believe that Warsaw Pact forces would defeat the main grouping of NATO forces in Central Europe or the war would escalate to theater nuclear conflict before NATO's seaborne reinforcement and resupply of Europe or US forces in the Far East became a critical factor. Only a few forces—primarily diesel submarines—would therefore be allocated to open-ocean SLOC interdiction from the outset of hostilities. The Soviets probably plan to use such units for attacks on shipping primarily to disperse and tie down NATO naval forces and to reduce the efficiency of NATO military shipping. Some mining against European ports,

primarily by aircraft, also is likely. Such actions probably would be intended to complicate NATO naval operations and facilitate performance of the Pact's more critical initial tasks. The Soviets could increase their emphasis on SLOC interdiction before or during a war with the United States and its allies in response to their perception of a changing strategic situation. One circumstance that would motivate the Soviets to widen their emphasis on SLOC interdiction would be the lengthening of a war into a protracted conventional conflict. Another circumstance might be a conflict that began after a prolonged period of mobilization during which NATO began the reinforcement and resupply of Europe by sea. In such a case, the Soviets might see interdiction as an urgent task at the beginning of hostilities, but an increased interdiction effort would be at the expense of SSBN protection and the defense of the Soviet homeland.

H. Naval Diplomacy in Peacetime and Limited War

25. In addition to its wartime tasks, the Soviet Navy is assigned the important peacetime role of serving as an instrument of state policy or, in more traditional terms, conducting naval diplomacy. Today, Soviet naval forces maintain a continuous presence in the Mediterranean Sea, the Indian Ocean, the Atlantic off West Africa, and the South China Sea. They also conduct deployments to the Caribbean (see figure 7). Although the level of presence has fluctuated within and between geographic areas (growing in the Indian Ocean and Pacific and declining in the Mediterranean), the overall level of Soviet surface ship and submarine presence in distant areas has remained relatively stable since 1974. Operations by Soviet naval aircraft have increased considerably since 1979 (see figure 8). The out-of-area operations of the navy continue to reflect the Soviets' interest in strengthening their position in the Third World (especially in areas of potential Western vulnerability), balancing Western presence, and countering potential strategic threats. Although strategic military concerns remain prominent in Soviet distant operations, particularly in the Mediterranean, the navy is performing increasingly important tasks related to the projection of Soviet power and influence in the Third World.

26. In addition to routine show-the-flag deployments and port visits, Soviet naval forces have demonstrated support for friendly nations and sought to inhibit the use of hostile naval forces against Soviet allies. During recent Third World crises, the Soviets have augmented their naval presence in the areas of conflict: the Angolan civil war in 1975; the Ethiopian-Somali conflict in 1977–1978, the Sino-Vietnamese conflict in 1979; and the Iranian hostage crisis in 1979–1980. Such use of Soviet naval forces is likely to continue in future distant-area crises. We do

FIGURE 6
Selected Soviet ASM-Carrying Strike Aircraft

		Deployment	Fuselage Length (meters)	Maximum Speed at Optimum Altitude (knots)
TU-22M Backfire 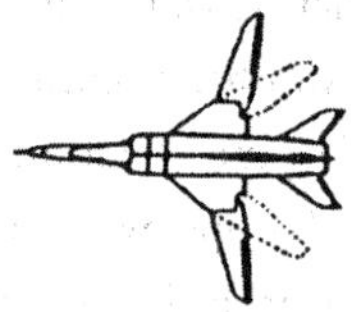	CIA Assessment	Naval Aviation and VGK Air Armies	39	1,050
	DIA/Army/Air Force Assessment	Naval Aviation and VGK Air Armies	39	1,150
TU-16 Badger 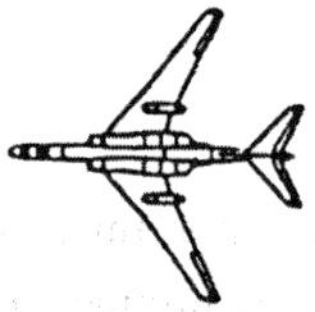	C	Naval Aviation	37	535
	C (Modified)	Naval Aviation	37	510
	G	Naval Aviation and VGK Air Armies	35	510
TU-95 Bear 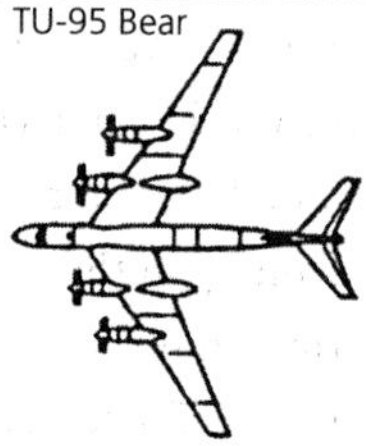	B/C	VGK Air Armies	43.9	500
TU-22 Blinder 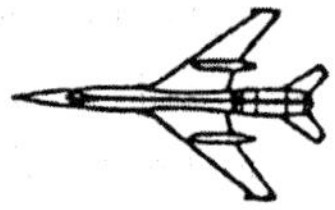	B	VGK Air Armies	39	790

a. These radii are achievable only under optimum conditions and they would be unrealistic in most wartime situations. They allow for only a minimum fuel reserve, and they do not allow for such variables as loitering, high-speed flight, indirect routing, low-altitude flight, or combat maneuvering. Allowances for such variables reduce combat radius, usually substantially. Realistic maximum radii for theater missions under wartime conditions probably would be some 30 to 50 percent lower.

b. Assumes that aircraft are refueled by a Bison A tanker at the optimum point for maximum distance.

c. Backfires technically could carry three AS-4s. With three missiles, however, Backfire performance—including range—would be substantially degraded, and we do not consider such a payload likely in wartime.

not believe, however, that the Soviets would deploy major naval forces in response to a Third World crisis in an area other than the Mediterranean and possibly the Indian Ocean, if they judged the crisis involved a high risk of escalation to general war with the West. The Soviets would probably fear that, if war broke out, such forces would be out of position to perform the initial wartime tasks of protecting SSBNs and the sea approaches to the USSR.

FIGURE 6 (CONTINUED)
Selected Soviet ASM-Carrying Strike Aircraft

Normal Payload	Maximum Unrefueled Radius (nm) [a]	Maximum Radius With Prestrike Refueling (nm) [a] [b]
1 AS-4 or 2 AS-4s or bombs or mines [c]	1,825–2,150 with bombs [d] 1,750–2,075 with 1 AS-4 [d] 1,400–1,650 with 2 AS-4s [d]	2,825–3,200 with bombs [d] 2,700–3,100 with 1 AS-4 [d] 2,500–2,800 with 2 AS-4s [d]
1 AS-4 or 2 AS-4s or bombs or mines [c]	2,900 with bombs [e] 2,800 with 1 AS-4 [e] 2,550 with 2 AS-4s [e]	4,000 with bombs [e] 3,850 with 1 AS-4 [e] 3,650 with 2 AS-4s [e]
1 AS-2	1,540	2,150
2 AS-6s [f]	1,170	1,780
2 AS-5s or 2 AS-6s or bombs or mines	1,220 with 2 AS-5s	1,850 with 2 AS-5s
1 AS-3 or 2 AS-4s	3,950	5,050
1 AS-4	1,370	2,460

d. The longer radius values in the assessment of the Backfire by the Central Intelligence Agency are based on an assumed aerodynamic design which is optimized for subsonic performance, while the shorter radius values are based on an assumed compromised design. CIA has considered both designs because they represent reasonable upper and lower bounds of the Backfire's subsonic cruise efficiency. [TEXT DELETED]

e. [DELETED]

f. Probably more that 80 percent of the Badger Cs have been modified to carry two AS-6s. The Badger C (Modified), however, retains the capability to carry a single AS-2, and it may carry AS-5s in place of the AS-6s.

27. *Power Projection.* Although Soviet amphibious forces were developed to conduct assault landings on the maritime flanks of the USSR in support of ground theater operations, they could undertake assault operations against limited opposition in many areas of the Third World. The amphibious exercises conducted on Socotra Island in May 1980 and in cooperation with the Syrians in July 1981 demonstrate an interest in and a modest capability for distant-area projection. The Soviet Navy

FIGURE 7
Soviet Ship-Days in Distant Waters, by Region, 1974–81

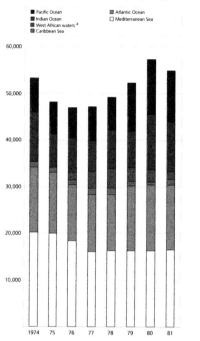

a. West African ship-days are not available for 1974–1975 and are included in Atlantic Ocean data.

has never conducted large-scale amphibious landings away from the periphery of the USSR. Exercise ZAPAD-81 in the Baltic, however, included a large-scale amphibious exercise that for the first time used ships drawn from all four Soviet fleets. Units involved included the aircraft carrier *Kiev*, the helicopter carrier *Leningrad*, and the amphibious assault ship *Ivan Rogov*. We believe one of the purposes of this unusual gathering of forces was to test planning concepts for amphibious operations in distant areas. It is still doubtful that a Soviet amphibious task force could carry out a successful landing abroad against substantial opposition, in large part because of the lack of adequate tactical air support, either land or sea-based.

I. Trends in Naval Programs

28. The Navy's share of the growing Soviet defense budget has remained basically unchanged in recent years—about 20 percent. Much of this share has been devoted to ship construction programs, including a variety of surface platforms ranging from small patrol craft to large cruisers. The lion's share of the construction budget, however, continues to be devoted to submarines (see figures 9–11).

FIGURE 8
Overseas Deployment of Soviet Naval Aviation, 1976–81

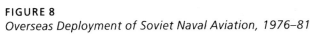

TU-16 Badger, Syria	TU-142 Bear F, Vietnam
IL-38 May, Syria	TU-95 Bear D, Vietnam
IL-38 May, Libya	TU-95 Bear D, Angola
IL-38 May, Ethiopia	TU-95 Bear D, Cuba
IL-38 May, South Yemen	

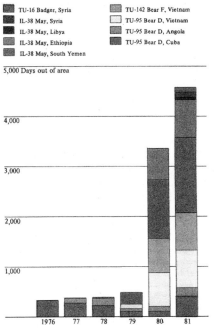

29. The most notable trend over the decade has been an evolution toward what Admiral Gorshkov calls a "balanced fleet"—that is, a navy capable of fighting at both the nuclear and conventional levels as well as protecting state interests in peacetime. As late as the mid-1970s, the Soviet Navy could be described as a fleet with capabilities maximized for a short, intense war that rapidly escalates to the use of nuclear weapons. The small weapons loads and limited endurance of most surface combatants severely limited the Soviet Navy's ability for sustained combat. In the 1970s, however, new classes of generally larger, more sophisticated ships incorporating greater endurance, larger weapon loads, and extensive communication and electronic warfare systems began to enter service, resulting in enhanced capabilities for sustained conventional combat and distant-area deployments.

30. *SSBNs.* Beginning in the mid-1960s and continuing through the late 1970s, the Soviets allocated considerable resources to the construction of SSBNs. During this period, the construction rate of Y and D-class SSBNs averaged about five per year and accounted for more than half of Soviet nuclear submarine construction. Although construction rates have tapered off and SSBN force levels have stabilized to accommodate the level agreed to in the SALT I Protocol of 62 units and 950 launch tubes, the SSBN force still receives significant emphasis, as

FIGURE 9
Soviet Naval Spending

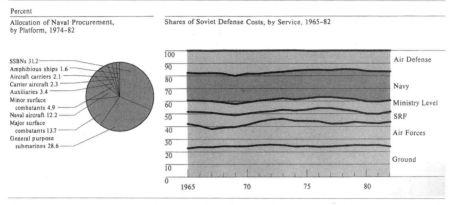

a. These graphics are based on estimated Soviet defense costs in rubles prepared by the Econometric Division of CIA's Office of Soviet Analysis, using the methodology customarily employed in calculating the costs of Soviet defense activities.

evidenced by the continued construction of the D-III and the new Typhoon-class (see figure 12).

31. The D-class series (the D-III being the latest modification) is basically an extension of Y-class SSBN technology. Fourteen D-IIIs have entered the fleet, and an additional two to three are expected. The Typhoon, on the other hand, is the USSR's first entirely new SSBN design since the Y-class was introduced in 1966. It is probably somewhat quieter than earlier SSBNs and incorporates features that indicate an intention to conduct underice operations, including surfaced launches from within the ice pack. The Typhoon is designed to carry 20 SS-NX-20 SLBMs. The SS-NX-20 is a three-stage, solid-propellant missile with multiple independently targetable reentry vehicles (MIRVs) [TEXT DELETED] that will probably give it improved accuracy over other Soviet SLBMs. The first Typhoon is on sea trials and probably will achieve initial operational capability (IOC) when its missile finishes its test program, probably in 1983, but certainly by 1984. The second Typhoon was launched in September 1982, and another two or three units are under construction. As many as 12 units could be operational by the early 1990s.

32. To maintain the number of launch tubes permitted under the terms of the SALT Interim Agreement, as new SSBNs have begun sea trials, the Soviets have dismantled nine Y-I-class SSBNs by removing the entire missile compartment. One unit has been reconfigured by the insertion of a new midsection, and another is undergoing probable conversion/modification. There is insufficient evidence at this time to indicate the purpose of this conversion/modification or the plans for the other Ys. Reconfiguration of some as SSNs is one option; conversion as

FIGURE 10
Major Soviet Surface Combatants in Production [a]

	Major Armament	Propulsion	Full-Load Displacement (metric tons)	Year Operational	Units in Operation
Kiev Class Aircraft Carrier 	26–30 ASW helicopters and VSTOL fighters SS-N-12 antiship cruise missile SA-N-3, SA-N-4 SAMs SUW-N-1 ASW rocket (Unit 4 extensively modified; new SAMs, radar)	Steam	37,000	1976	3
Kirov Class Guided-missile cruiser 	SS-N-14 ASW missile SA-N-6 SAM SS-N-19 antiship cruise missile 4 helicopters (Unit 2 extensively modified)	Combined nuclear and steam	About 28,000	1980	1
Sovremennyy Class Guided-missile destroyer 	SA-NX-7 SAM 130-mm guns SS-NX-22 antiship missile 1 helicopter	Steam	About 8,000	1981	2
Udaloy Class Guided-missile destroyer 	SS-N-14 Possible SAM 2 ASW helicopters	Gas turbine	About 8,000	1981	2
BLK-COM-1 Guided-missile cruiser 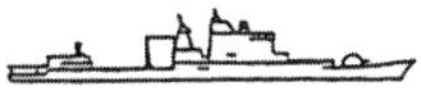	SS-N-12 SA-N-4 SA-N-6 130-mm guns	Gas turbine	About 12,500	1982	1
Krivak Class Guided-missile frigate 	SA-N-4 SS-N-14	Gas turbine	3,900	1970	32

a. Major surface combatants of more than 3,000 metric tons displacement.

sea-launched cruise missile (SLCM) carriers is another. Additional Ys will be dismantled if the Soviets decide to continue adherence to the SALT I accords.

33. *Attack Submarines.* The Soviets are currently producing two classes of SSNs, the V-III and the A-class. The V-III, an extensive modification of the earlier V-I/II design, first became operational in 1979. It may become the first Soviet submarine class with a towed passive sonar array, greatly increasing its passive detection range over that of existing hull-mounted sonar arrays. V-III construction may continue through 1984 for a total of as many as 18 units.

34. The A-class SSN is the world's fastest submarine and probably the deepest diving [TEXT DELETED]. The first unit was launched in early 1969 in Leningrad but was subsequently dismantled because of initial technical difficulties. By mid-1982, six units had become operational in the Soviet Northern Fleet. In addition to the

FIGURE 11
Soviet Submarines in Production

	Armament	Propulsion	Submerged Displacement (metric tons)	Year Operational	Units in Operation
D-III Class SSBN 	16 SS-N-18s	Nuclear	13,250	1978	14
Typhoon Class SSBN 	20 SS-NX-20s	Nuclear	27,000–29,000	1983 or 1984	0[a]
O Class SSGN 	Torpedoes SS-N-19 antiship cruise missile	Nuclear	12,000–14,000	1981	1
V-III Class SSN 	Torpedoes Probable SS-NX-16 ASW missile Possible SS-NX-21 SLCM	Nuclear	6,250	1979	13
A Class SSN 	Torpedoes ASW missile	Nuclear	3,680	1978	6
New Class of SSN No drawing available	Torpedoes Probable ASW missile Possible SS-NX-21 SLCM	Nuclear	Est. 7,000	1984	0
Tango Class SS 	Torpedoes Probable ASW missile[b]	Diesel	3,900	1973	17
K Class SS 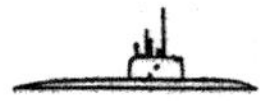	Torpedoes	Diesel	3,000	1981	2

a. Typhoon unit 1 has joined the fleet, but its missile probably will not be operational until 1983, certainly by 1984.

b. The Deputy Director for Intelligence, Central Intelligence Agency, believes the Tango SS is not equipped with ASW missiles. These submarines have been operational since 1973, and in these nine years there has been no evidence to suggest that Tango submarines are equipped with such missiles. These submarines have been observed in ASW exercises and weapon firings on numerous occasions, and they have never used ASW missiles.

use of titanium alloy for A-class pressure hulls, an improved reactor and improved propulsion system have been installed. The energy required to drive the A at a speed of 42 to 43 knots suggests a machinery power density on the order of twice that of earlier Soviet SSN designs. A-class production is continuing at two shipyards, and a total of 10 or 11 units is expected.

35. A submarine under construction at the United Admiralty Shipyard in Leningrad is estimated to be the lead unit of a new SSN class that could reach IOC in 1984. This new submarine probably represents a production follow-on to the present V-class SSN series; it is likely to have a steel hull and a submerged displacement greater than that of the V-III.

FIGURE 12
Typhoon SSBN Firing SS-NX-20 SLBM

36. Series production of the Tango SS and introduction of the new K-class SS are in-
dicative of the Soviets' intention to retain diesel-powered submarines while phasing out the W and Z-classes of the 1950s. The Tango (18 produced to date) is the
largest new-construction class of Soviet diesel-electric-powered attack submarine
and is a production follow-on to the F-class SS. Tango has approximately 70 percent more pressure hull volume than the F-class, permitting increased submerged
endurance and improved sensors and weapons. The first K-class was launched in
1980 and became operational in 1981. At 3,000 tons' submerged displacement, the
K is 20 percent larger than the F, but considerably smaller than the Tango. We estimate the K-class SS will fill Soviet requirements for a medium-range diesel submarine replacing the W and R-classes and may also be produced for export.

37. *SSGNs.* In April 1980, the Soviets launched a new nuclear-powered cruise missile
submarine (SSGN), the O-class (see figure 13), that is twice as large as any of their
previous SSGNs. It has 24 missile launchers (three times the number carried by
the E-II or C-class) for the SS-N-19, a new antiship supersonic cruise missile with
a range of about 270 to 300 nautical miles (500 to 550 kilometers). The O-class is
quieter than earlier Soviet SSN/SSGNs. A total of 10 units is expected to be completed by the mid-1990s.

38. *Principal Surface Combatants.* The Soviets currently have active building programs for at least seven classes of major surface combatants. The fourth and
probably last unit of the *Kiev*-class aircraft carrier is in the final stage of construction. It differs significantly from earlier units of the class in the improved arma-
ment and early warning radar suits to be installed. The second and probably last
unit of the *Kirov*-class guided-missile cruiser is also fitting out. Unlike the first

FIGURE 13
O-Class SSGN Launching SS-N-19s

unit, it is equipped with an as-yet-unidentified vertically launched weapon system, probably a surface-to-air missile (SAM). Three units of the BLK-COM-1 guided-missile cruiser are under construction. Like the *Kirov* and *Kiev* classes, the BLK-COM-1 ships are multipurpose platforms armed with a mix of antisubmarine, antiship, and air defense weapons. Two classes of guided-missile destroyer, the *Sovremennyy* and the *Udaloy*, are also in series production. The *Sovremennyy* is best suited for antisurface warfare. It is equipped with the SS-NX-22, a high-performance antiship cruise missile nearing the end of its test program, the SA-NX-7 SAM system, and a new 130-mm gun possibly capable of firing guided munitions (see photograph on figure 14). The *Udaloy* is best suited for antisubmarine warfare using its SS-N-14 missiles and two Helix helicopters. Production of BLK-COM-1, *Sovremennyy*, and *Udaloy* ships will probably continue through the decade. Construction of the *Krivak*-class guided-missile frigate and the *Grisha*-class light frigate is drawing to a close.

39. *Amphibious Forces.* Amphibious forces in the Soviet Navy have a lower priority than the submarine, air, and surface combatant programs. Nevertheless, the Soviets continue to make gradual improvements in these forces. Construction of the *Ivan Rogov* class, the Soviets' largest amphibious ship, proceeded at a very slow pace and probably ended after the recently launched second unit. The *Ivan Rogov* has several unique features, however, that may indicate the direction of future improvements in Soviet amphibious capabilities. These include the ability to carry helicopters and air-cushion vehicle landing craft. The Soviets have an active program for the development and production of air-cushion vehicles. Construction of *Ropucha*-class amphibious ships for Soviet use has resumed in Poland. In addition, the two KASP B wing-in-ground vehicles being developed in the Caspian Sea

FIGURE 14
Major Soviet Surface Combatants

Kirov CGN

are probably naval subordinated. While such units could have a wide range of maritime applications because of their high speed and load capabilities, use in amphibious warfare is among the more likely intended missions. A development in recent years has been the use of commercial roll-on/roll-off (Ro-Ro) cargo ships during amphibious exercises. There has also been a reorganization in the Soviet Naval Infantry (SNI), primarily to improve firepower, which has resulted in a moderate increase in personnel strength and the upgrading of the three western fleets' SNI regiments into brigades. The Soviet Navy does not have enough amphibious ships to lift all of the SNI. If, however, amphibious ships were combined

FIGURE 14 (CONTINUED)
Major Soviet Surface Combatants

Udaloy DDG

Sovremennyy DDG

130-mm gun on *Sovremennyy*

BLK-COM-1 CG

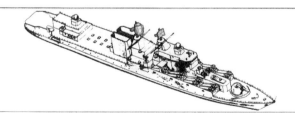

with merchant Ro-Ro's and barge carriers, all of the naval infantry and nearly three motorized rifle divisions could theoretically be carried. Some ground force units routinely train either for amphibious assault landings or, more usually, as follow-up forces.

40. *Replenishment Ships.* Construction of logistic support ships is sporadic and also has a lower priority than that of surface combatants and submarines. The most important unit built in recent years is the *Berezina*, a 40,000-ton multipurpose replenishment ship, completed in 1977. No further units of this class have been built, nor are any other underway replenishment ships known to be under

FIGURE 15
Tarantul *Patrol Combatant*

construction. The number of logistic support ships capable of transferring strategic and tactical missiles to combatants remains small. The generally low priority accorded replenishment ships probably is linked with several aspects of Soviet naval practice and doctrine, including a heavy reliance on merchant tankers to support naval operations, the intention to operate many naval units relatively close to Soviet territory, and a belief that the war is unlikely to be so prolonged that replenishment at sea would affect its outcome. The Soviets probably also prefer to improve the sustainability of their naval combatants by changes in the units themselves rather than by emphasizing the construction of auxiliary vessels. Thus new-construction surface combatants such as the *Kirov* and BLK-COM-1 include features such as nuclear power (*Kirov*) and larger missile loads.

41. *Small Combatants and Mine Warfare Units.* The Soviets continue to regard small surface combatants and mine warfare units as important elements of their navy. These units are particularly useful in the confined waters of the Baltic and Black seas, but they are also assigned important roles in the echeloned defense of Soviet territory and SSBN operating areas in the Northern and Pacific Fleet areas. Small surface combatants now in series production include the *Nanuchka, Matka,* and *Tarantul* (see figure 15) guided-missile patrol combatants, equipped primarily for antiship operations, and the *Pauk* and *Muravey* boats, whose major role is ASW. Mine warfare units in production include the *Natya* and *Sonya*-class minesweepers, and the Soviets are also continuing to develop a helicopter mine countermeasures capability. A large number of naval units are also capable of minelaying.

42. *Naval Aviation.* The most significant recent development was the beginning in 1977 of construction of a catapult and arresting gear test facility at the Saki naval base in the Crimea. This project probably will be completed in 1983, with the first aircraft launches occurring in mid-1984. It is a major indicator of Soviet intentions to

FIGURE 16

Comparison of Selected US and Soviet Carrier Flight Deck Configurations

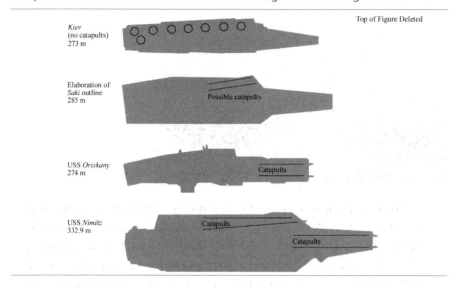

construct an aircraft carrier capable of operating conventional takeoff and landing
(CTOL) high-performance aircraft (see figure 16). Construction of such a ship
may soon begin at Nikolayev on the Black Sea. Another facility at Saki, begun in
1979, has recently been identified as an aircraft ski jump. A ski jump, such as that
on the British carrier *Hermes,* is used to increase the payload and/or combat radius of vertical/short takeoff and landing (VSTOL) aircraft. The ski jump facility
may be related to the development of an improved VSTOL aircraft, primarily for
use on *Kiev*-class aircraft carriers.

43. The Soviets are also continuing the gradual introduction of Backfire medium
bombers and Bear F long-range ASW aircraft into their land-based naval aviation.
Forger fighter-bombers are being built for service on *Kiev*-class ships, and deployment of a new shipborne helicopter, the Helix, has begun (see figure 17). Although most of the Helix helicopters probably will be used for ASW, some will be
configured to provide targeting data for antiship missiles, and others will be amphibious assault and transport versions.

J. Command, Control, and Communications

44. The Soviet Navy, subject to the same centralization of authority that characterizes
most Soviet military operations, depends on a smoothly functioning command,
control, and communications system. The Soviets nonetheless recognize the potential weakness in such a highly centralized system. Consequently, Soviet naval

FIGURE 17
Selected Soviet Shipborne Aircraft

Helix helicopter

Forger fighter-bomber

commanders of general purpose forces at the fleet and group levels probably enjoy some greater latitude in tactical command and control to accomplish their warfare tasks. Naval forces are integrated into a theater concept, but the control of strategic elements of the navy remains centralized. Soviet doctrine stresses the need for reliable, flexible, redundant, and survivable control of naval forces. Thus, the Soviet Navy's command, control, and communications structure includes features such as the hardening of command posts and communications facilities and the use of mobile command posts and communications units. Recent efforts to further improve this structure have included:

- The continued construction of bunkered command posts at echelons ranging from the Main Naval Staff to flotillas.

- The availability of large numbers of communications vans at the national and fleet levels to augment communications and support field-deployed command posts.

- Equipping major naval ships with communications capabilities that provide for flexible seaborne command and control.

- The modification of submarines for communications relay. Three former G-class ballistic missile submarines (SSBs) [TEXT DELETED] have been modified for such use. Further, we believe that the Soviets are interested in development of submarine command posts.

- The development of probable airborne naval command posts. The first such platform, a modified IL-22 Coot, was identified in 1978.

- Testing of a modified TU-142 Bear F as an airborne maritime communications relay platform.

- Development and use of new and sophisticated communications that offer increased efficiency, reliability, and security.

- Increased use of automation to improve the efficiency of command and control.

45. One major problem area in the command, control, and communications system is the lack of continuous communications with deployed submarines, especially SSBNs. To deal with this problem, the Soviets are probably developing an ELF system that will act as an ideal altering system enabling Soviet submarines to remain at safer patrol depths during a crisis.

46. *Automated Battle Management.* Soviet doctrine stresses the commander's responsibility to achieve the maximum possible combat effectiveness from his limited resources. Soviet naval commanders at all echelons are expected to achieve this by the detailed management of forces in battle. For this battle management, the Soviet Navy seems to be relying increasingly on computer-aided mathematical combat models as decision aids. Such models were probably first used at the Moscow level during the OKEAN-70 exercise. By 1978, they were in use at lower echelon, short-based command posts, and their cautious introduction into operational use at sea was probably beginning. Potentially, they offer significant improvement in the quality and timeliness of naval command and control, although there are numerous practical problems in their implementation. The future availability of small, high-speed large-memory computers and of sophisticated computer communications networks is likely to alleviate some of these problems.

K. Soviet Ocean Surveillance

47. The Soviet ocean surveillance system (SOSS) is designed to provide information on the location, identity, and movements of foreign naval forces, especially those posing a threat to the Soviet homeland or forces. The most important elements in the system are land-based SIGINT stations, space-based ELINT and radar satellites,

AGIs, and reconnaissance aircraft. Ships of the merchant and fishing fleets can also be tasked to conduct surveillance. Among the recent improvements in the system are:

- The addition of land-based SIGINT stations in Vietnam and South Yemen.

- The construction of the Soviet Navy's largest and most capable AGI, the *Balzam*. Two units of this class are in service, and a third is being built.

- An increase in the number of naval units capable of receiving targeting data directly from satellites.

- Growing access to and use of foreign facilities—in Cuba, Angola, Ethiopia, South Yemen, Vietnam and Libya—for Soviet naval air reconnaissance operations.

Such improvements have reinforced the major strength of the SOSS, its ability to detect and identify surface ships, especially aircraft carriers, operating in or approaching waters from which they could strike the Soviet Union. Its value against surface ships can still be reduced by Western cover and deception techniques such as emission control (EMCON) against SIGINT collection. Radar satellites are also limited by weather and by the difficulty of identifying contacts. The major weakness of the SOSS, however, remains its lack of any significant capability to detect deployed submarines, especially in open-ocean areas such as the central Atlantic and Pacific.

L. Radio-Electronic Combat

48. The operations of Soviet naval forces and the design of their electronic equipment are deeply influenced by the Soviet concept of radio-electronic combat (REC). This concept emphasizes the importance of both denying the enemy the use of his electronic systems and of protecting Soviet systems from disruption. The REC concept applies equally to sensors and to command, control, and communications systems. This concept has broader application than the Western notion of electronic warfare (EW) and includes widespread, integrated use of:

- Attacks on enemy electronic emitters.

- EMCON.

- Surprise.

- Multisensor integration.

- Redundancy of command, control, and communications.

- Active electronic countermeasures (jamming).

- Passive electronic countermeasures (chaff).

- Deception, to include decoys.

The prime focus of this concept is to ensure that Soviet forces can operate more effectively than their opponents in a common EW environment. Ideally this would be accomplished by ensuring the reliability of Soviet command, control, and communications systems exposed to hostile EW through jam proofing and redundancy of the Soviets' own equipment, together with offensive EW and co-vert tactics to degrade enemy electronic systems. Although the Soviets have en-countered problems with both REC equipment and training, they regard REC as a fundamental principle of modern electronically dependent warfare and vital to the success of naval operations.

II. Factors Bearing on the Future of the Soviet Navy

A. Political and Economic Changes

49. As Soviet leaders formulate their naval plans for the period of the late 1980s and 1990s, they face major political and economic uncertainties. They view the fluid international situation as requiring a strong naval posture, both to protect estab-lished Soviet interests and to exploit situations in which the use of naval forces can increase Soviet influence. Soviet perceptions of Western and Chinese naval improvements and of opportunities for the use of naval forces in the Third World are likely to be among the arguments for continued qualitative improvement in Soviet maritime power. On the other hand, problems in the Soviet economy prob-ably will increase the opportunity costs associated with defense. To maintain even a modest rate of economic growth the Soviets must allocate more resources to capital investment and improve labor productivity. The competing demands for economic resources could be reflected in domestic political tension, particularly during a period of leadership transition.

50. *International Environment.* The Soviets view the international arena as a shifting combination of threats and opportunities likely to last indefinitely. They will con-tinue to be concerned about the prospect that the United States will augment its defense efforts, including major improvements in both strategic and general pur-pose naval forces. They probably do not anticipate any substantial improvement in relations with China and believe that instability is likely to persist in border areas such as Iran and Poland. They probably will continue to view the Third World as fertile ground for the expansion of Soviet influence and will align themselves selectively with states and insurgent movements in that area. On the whole, the

Soviets' expectations regarding international developments probably will support their traditional belief in the value of military power as a cornerstone of foreign policy. Such expectations probably will favor the continued development of Soviet naval power, for both its nuclear and conventional wartime value and for its peacetime role in promoting the image of the Soviet Union as a global power and projecting power and influence in distant areas.

51. *Economic Environment.* Soviet leaders in the late 1980s and 1990s will probably be operating in an environment characterized by severe economic resource constraints. Poor agricultural performance, a slower increase in labor productivity, a low rate of GNP growth, labor shortages, and shortfalls in energy production will require tougher choices among defense, investment, and consumption. If defense spending continues to grow at its historical rate (4 percent annually since 1965), the defense share of GNP could increase from about 14 percent to approach 20 percent by 1990. Such growth would drastically reduce the extent to which additional resources could be allocated to investment and consumption and would also erode future increments to GNP. Such increments have been important in the past in easing political tensions that arise from the competition for resources. While there is insufficient evidence as yet to predict a change in the current rate of growth in defense spending, economic pressures could result in a slower rate of growth. While less likely, a zero growth rate or even a net reduction is possible. In any case, within the amount allocated to defense, any competition among the services for resource allocation would be likely to increase.

52. The Soviet Navy's case for justifying its share of resource allocation is likely to include arguments based primarily on its evolving role in a NATO–Warsaw Pact war—the need to counter a growing Western naval threat to Pact territory and forces and to improve the Soviet Navy's capability to strike the United States and its allies. Naval programs will also be supported in terms of their contribution to the USSR's capability to defend and expand Soviet influence in the Third World during peacetime and limited war situations, but any programs that cannot be solidly defended as essential to the NATO-Pact scenario are likely to be more susceptible to pruning.

53. *Domestic Political Environment.* It is unlikely that Leonid Brezhnev will be in office during the period of greatest interest to this Estimate. His departure probably will result in a struggle for power that could be reflected in defense policies. It is not possible to predict the nature and timing of changes in military policy that might result from changes in national leadership, particularly because Brezhnev's immediate successor is likely to be himself succeeded by a new generation of

leaders in the late 1980s to early 1990s. Information is sparse concerning the attitude toward defense of leading contenders in the succession. Insofar as such information exists, it suggests that they would continue to place a strong emphasis
on military spending. We have no specific information on the attitude of leading
contenders concerning naval issues. During any succession period, variations in
policy could occur. It would, however, be difficult to change basic priorities until a
new leader could consolidate power. During the jockeying for power the defense
effort probably would not be significantly redirected. Few aspirants for leadership
would risk antagonizing the military or placing themselves in a position to be ac-
cused of selling defense short. Once power is consolidated, however, severe economic pressures could contribute to sharp changes in the direction of the Soviet
defense effort such as those that took place under [Nikita] Khrushchev.

54. During the same period of transition in the Soviet political hierarchy, there will
also be changes in the leadership of the Soviet Navy. Whoever succeeds Admiral
Gorshkov is unlikely to acquire immediately the high degree of authority that
stems from Gorshkov's continuity as commander of the Soviet Navy since 1956.
The views of a new leader, moreover, are likely to have been affected by a different
operational background. Although any officer succeeding Gorshkov probably will
have had experience as a fleet commander and will thereby have become familiar
with all types of naval platforms and operations, it is possible that he will favor
some shifts in emphasis in Soviet naval programs and policies. It is unlikely, however, that the personalities or individual backgrounds of a new Soviet naval leadership would cause major near-term changes in the strategy and programs
underlying the navy's role in Soviet military strategy.

B. Key Issues Facing Soviet Naval Planners (1982–2000)

55. *Protection and Use of the SSBN Force.* The ability to conduct strategic strike operations will continue to be the single most important mission of the Soviet Navy
throughout the period of this Estimate. Although sea-launched cruise missiles
will expand the number of potential naval strategic platforms, the bulk of the Soviet Navy's strategic capabilities will remain in the SSBN force. We expect this
force to be further modernized and upgraded through the continued production
of Typhoon-class units and the introduction of a new class in the 1990s. By the
late 1990s, Typhoon and follow-on SSBNs will have largely replaced the Y-class
force, resulting in:

- A substantial increase in the number of sea-based strategic warheads because
  the Y-class SSBN typically carries only 16 warheads while one Typhoon carries

20 SS-NX-20 missiles, which could have as many as 280 warheads by the late 1980s.

- A less vulnerable SSBN force because almost all units could strike targets in the continental United States from within the Arctic icecap and/or from home waters.

56. The size of the SSBN force in the 1990s will be governed largely by the status of East-West arms limitation agreements and developments in strategic offensive and defensive technology. If the SALT I limit of 950 modern submarine launch tubes remains in effect, the number of SSBNs would decline somewhat in the 1990s because Y-class units would have to be retired on a more than one-for-one basis to compensate for the greater number of tubes carried by new classes of SSBNs. In the absence of arms limitation restrictions, we believe the Soviets would increase the size of the SSBN force along with increases in the rest of their strategic arsenal. Moreover, the Soviets may increase the proportion of the overall strategic arsenal assigned to SSBNs if:

- Improvements in the accuracy of Western ICBM/SLBMs lead the Soviets to judge that their SLBMs are increasingly more survivable than ICBMs.

- Soviet SLBMs obtain a hard-target kill capability.

57. On the other hand, the Soviets probably would reduce the number of SLBM launchers if arms control negotiations resulted in a treaty requiring substantial cuts in the overall strategic arsenal. SLBM reductions probably would be proportionate to cuts in the ICBM force, but could be more severe if:

- The Soviets perceive that the West has achieved an ASW breakthrough that increases the vulnerability of Soviet SSBNs.

- Soviet SLBMs do not achieve sufficient hard-target kill capability.

- The survivability of the land-based element of Soviet strategic forces is enhanced through the introduction of mobile ICBMs and/or ABM protection.

58. We believe that the Soviets will continue to regard their SSBN force as vulnerable to enemy ASW forces through the 1990s. In this time frame, the SSBN force will consist primarily of older D and Y-class units—in the 1990s, Y and D units will compose over three-quarters of the force; in 2000, D-class units will still constitute well over half of the force. The perceived requirement to protect and support these SSBNs is unlikely to change. Typhoon and follow-on SSBNs will be quieter than Ys and Ds and thus less vulnerable to acoustic detection. Nevertheless, it is unlikely that the Soviets will regard them as capable of ensuring their own survivability. The Soviets probably foresee no slackening in Western interest in ASW

and expect that the positive effects of their quieting programs will be at least partially negated by improvements in Western ASW capabilities. Moreover, the Soviets' concept of SSBN protection is based on their apparent judgment that all submarines are inherently vulnerable to ASW prosecution, particularly as they exit and enter port, if they are not protected by friendly forces. The Soviets, therefore, do not regard SSBN vulnerability as a short-term problem that will disappear as new, quieter classes are introduced. The requirement to protect and support SSBNs will thus remain an integral part of the strategic strike mission and the most important initial wartime task of a large portion of Northern and Pacific Fleet general purpose forces through the remainder of the century.

59. We expect that Typhoon and follow-on SSBNs would be deployed in wartime in much the same fashion as D-class SSBNs—primarily in "havens" close to Soviet territory. Other measures to decrease the vulnerability of Soviet SSBNs probably would include:

- More extensive use of patrols under the icecap.

- Introduction of an ELF communications system (perhaps in 1983), making it possible for units to receive communications while remaining at patrol depth or under ice.

60. Although such a move is unlikely, the Soviets might choose to deploy a few Typhoons to open-ocean areas in more southerly latitudes. The Soviets might use such open-ocean deployments to complicate the US defensive problem by requiring ASW forces to conduct open-ocean search in vast areas where sound surveillance system (SOSUS) coverage is limited. This could increase the survivability of SSBNs in havens by dispersing enemy ASW forces. Notwithstanding this potential benefit, the disadvantages of deploying SSBNs to distant areas would make this an unlikely option for wartime deployment. In particular, the transit through potentially enemy-controlled waters argues against SSBN deployments to southern latitudes.

61. We do not believe that likely changes in Soviet SLBM capabilities or in the Soviet perception of NATO's ASW capability will lead to significant changes in the way Soviet SLBMs would be employed in wartime. A substantial number of SLBMs probably would still be withheld from the initial strategic nuclear exchange for subsequent strikes and as a residual force. One consequence of such a withholding policy is a need to sustain SSBN protection operations during the nuclear as well as the conventional phase of the war. The greater endurance features that we believe the Soviets will continue to build into their general purpose units will be useful in this task. Such improved endurance is likely to stem from factors integral to the combat units themselves—such as nuclear power for surface ships, larger

FIGURE 18
V-III-Class SSN

magazine capability, and improved damage control—rather than from a major increase in the size of the naval auxiliary force.

62. The Soviets will probably continue to allocate SLBMs for initial strike operations against the United States for targets such as soft command, control, and communications facilities and bomber bases. SS-N-8 and SS-N-18 SLBMs launched from D-class units and possibly SLCMs from forward-deployed attack submarines would assume more of the Soviet Navy's initial strike role as Y-class SSBNs are retired or converted. The Soviet Navy's ability to participate in counterforce strikes would be enhanced considerably if the accuracy of SLBMs could be improved to the point where they would be effective against hardened targets such as ICBM silos. All agencies agree that the Soviets place a high priority on achieving improved accuracy for the SLBMs planned for testing in the middle and late 1980s. There are different interpretations as to whether and when the Soviets would opt to deploy SLBMs with a hard-target capability. One view holds that this capability probably will be achieved in the late 1980s.[1] Another view holds that such a capability could not be achieved before the early 1990s and that it would require major efforts, which the Soviets may not be willing to undertake because of costs in system reliability and the number of deliverable reentry vehicles (RVs).[2] All agencies believe that, despite the increased utility for initial nuclear strikes that a hard-target capability could provide, many such SLBMs, if deployed, would probably still be withheld from the initial exchanges for use in subsequent strikes or as a residual force.

63. *Soviet Naval Land-Attack Cruise Missile.* The Soviet Navy is developing a sea-launched, land-attack cruise missile similar to the US Tomahawk. This missile, designated the SS-NX-21, is expected to become operational by 1983 or 1984. It is

estimated to be compatible with the torpedo tubes of all Soviet submarines and possibly for employment on a variety of surface combatants. We believe it is designed to carry a nuclear warhead, probably has a terrain contour matching position update system (TERCOM), and is probably capable of 2,700 km at subsonic speeds.[3]

64. We believe that the primary application of the SS-NX-21 will be as a submarine-launched weapon for nuclear strikes against theater targets, but it might be used during a first strike against targets in the continental United States, such as command, control, and communications facilities and naval and bomber bases, despite its range and speed limitations. We believe the Soviets will choose to concentrate nuclear-armed SS-NX-21s in a few of their newest SSNs. The best candidate for such a role is the projected new class of SSN, which we believe will be quieter and larger than current Soviet SSNs and have the command, control, and communications and fire control capabilities necessary for employing SLCMs. V-IIIs (see figure 18) would also be suitable. Another possible candidate would be those few dismantled Y-class SSBNs, which presumably will retain their sophisticated ship's internal navigation system and require the least modification of existing classes to carry SLCMs. If the Soviets opt for a dedicated SLCM submarine, they may initiate periodic peacetime SLCM patrols off the US east and west coasts. Patrols by SLCM submarines could eventually replace Y-class SSBN patrols in the western Atlantic and eastern Pacific. In Soviet eyes, such SLCM patrols could offer the dividend of forcing the United States to invest in an expanded early warning/air defense system to counter the new threat.

65. Concentration of the missiles on a few units, however, would place them in the same category as the early SSBNs—platforms that were high-value targets for Western ASW and which, because of their missile range, had to operate relatively close to Western territory. The Soviets therefore could deploy the SS-NX-21 as part of the weapons load of a large number of submarines. Assuming that the missile is compatible with the standard Soviet 53-cm torpedo tubes, the SS-NX-21 could be employed in modified SSNs/SSGNs such as the V-I, V-II, A, and O-classes or even possibly in diesel-electric units. We believe this use of a larger number of submarines would be less likely because these submarines are required for important ASW and antisurface warfare (ASUW) tasks, and some of them—particularly the diesel-electric units—may not have sufficient command, control, and communications capabilities or space for necessary additional fire control and navigation systems.

66. We do not know whether the Soviets are developing a version of the SS-NX-21 with a nonnuclear warhead. [TEXT DELETED] SLCMs armed with nonnuclear

warheads would be useful against theater targets (such as US SOSUS facilities) and for concentrated attacks on Iceland, the United Kingdom, Spain, the Philippines, Guam, and other important targets that would be difficult to reach and costly to attack with Soviet land-based aircraft. Nonnuclear-armed SLCMs could be employed on current attack submarines with fire control system modification. Such deployment, however, would involve some trade-offs for general purpose submarines, reducing their capability to perform their traditional antiship and antisubmarine tasks because:

- Each SS-NX-21 carried will reduce the number of torpedoes carried by one or two.

- In some instances the operating areas required for land-attack cruise missile launches would differ considerably from those required for optimum ASW and antiship operations.

The Soviets probably recognize that proliferation of SLCMs could also represent a significant impediment to future arms control agreements since it would be virtually impossible to verify which submarines were strategic arms carriers.

67. The Soviets may also be considering placing SS-NX-21s on some of their principal surface combatants. [TEXT DELETED] Surface-launched SS-NX-21s probably would be limited to strikes against theater targets, although occasional peacetime deployments of SLCM-armed surface combatants off the US coasts (for example, to Cuba) might be viewed by the Soviets as having significant political value.

68. The successful development and deployment of the SS-NX-21 is undoubtedly an item of high interest to the Soviet national leadership as well as the naval command. If, as we expect, it is to be deployed primarily as a nuclear weapon aboard dedicated submarines, the Soviet Navy's strike capability, particularly against theater targets, will be enhanced considerably with minimal impact on its other missions and capabilities. By giving the Soviet Navy yet another nuclear-capable land-attack system, the SS-NX-21 could increase the stature and utility of the navy within the Soviet military/political establishment and conceivably result in the provision of additional assets to protect the SS-NX-21–carrying units. At the same time, the SS-NX-21 is a weapon system with significant potential political value to the Soviet leadership in future arms limitation negotiations. In fact, it is conceivable that the Soviet SLCM has been developed partly as a bargaining chip for US nuclear land-attack cruise missiles. If it is deployed, the SS-NX-21 would add a new dimension to Soviet Navy capabilities and would complicate the defensive tasks of Western forces.

69. *Strategic ASW against Ballistic and Land-Attack Cruise Missile Submarines.* The Soviets recognize that their strategic ASW task will become not only more important but increasingly difficult during the 1980s and 1990s. During this period they almost certainly expect:

- Longer range SLBMs to enter service in the US, French, and British navies. The US/UK Trident II D-5 (6,000-nm range), for example, will greatly increase the ocean areas from which such missiles can strike Soviet territory (see figure 19).

- Western SLBMs such as the US Trident II D-5 to achieve sufficient accuracy for use against hard targets.

- Western general purpose submarines to be armed with long-range, nuclear land-attack cruise missiles such as the US Tomahawk.

- Western programs to improve SSBN survivability through noise reduction, more reliable communications, and better sensors.

- China's first SSBNs to enter service.

70. We expect that the Soviets will seek to improve the ASW capability of their submarines, surface ships, and aircraft in several ways, especially:

- Improved sonar systems, most notably the deployment of towed passive arrays, low-frequency sonobuoy systems, and associated signal processing equipment.

- Increased emphasis on quieting of attack submarines.

- Development of nonacoustic sensors.

Such efforts probably will significantly improve Soviet capability to conduct ASW in relatively small areas. They could, therefore, be vitally important for the protection of Soviet SSBN havens against intrusion by Western SSNs. Such improvements also could enhance the capability of Soviet SSNs to detect Western SSBNs as they exit their bases or pass through choke points. We do not believe, however, that such efforts will substantially improve the Soviet capability to counter Western SSBNs effectively, because none of them are likely to solve the Soviet Navy's major problem—the inability to detect SSBNs in open-ocean areas.

71. We believe the Soviets will continue to seek such a detection capability through the development of sensors whose range or search rate can cover broad ocean areas. Approaches that the Soviets may explore in developing such a capability include:

- A system of fixed passive sonar arrays installed in Western SSBN operating areas, comparable to the US SOSUS system. A major problem in creating such a system probably would be the large number of arrays needed to have a

FIGURE 19
Soviet Navy's View of Potential Search Areas for Its ASW Operations

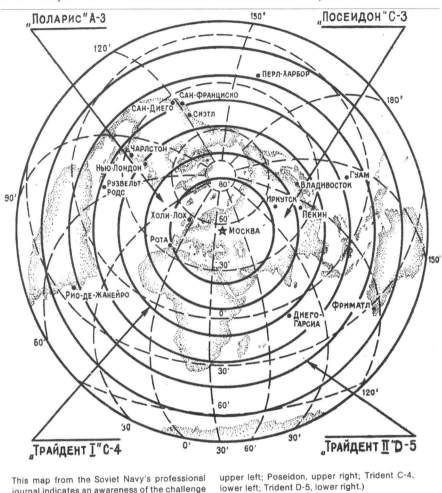

This map from the Soviet Navy's professional journal indicates an awareness of the challenge to Soviet ASW caused by the introduction of Western SLBMs with longer ranges. (Polaris, upper left; Poseidon, upper right; Trident C-4, lower left; Trident D-5, lower right.)

Morskoy Sbornik (Naval Digest)
No. 6, 1981
"The U.S. Navy by the Year 2000"

reasonable chance of detecting SSBNs, which will be even quieter in the 1990s. Another problem would be the probable requirement for several shore facilities in Third World countries to serve as initial processing points for the data. The Soviets' use of fixed sensors has thus far been limited to equipment installed near their own territory. We have no evidence that they are planning a worldwide system, which would take several years to install.

- Aircraft or a space-based system relying on nonacoustic sensors. To be effective, such a system would have to be able to cover broad ocean areas rapidly and to relay detection data both to shore facilities and ASW platforms. The development of such a system would be a logical evolution of current Soviet use of satellites in monitoring the activity of Western surface units. It would, however, require a breakthrough in nonacoustic sensor development that cannot be predicted. The Soviets are continuing their research into the use of nonacoustic sensors, despite a long history of apparent failure. Our limited knowledge of their program's precise nature [TEXT DELETED] makes it impossible to predict with confidence their chances of success.

- The development of towed passive acoustic arrays with increased performance due to array and signal-processing improvements. Such arrays could be developed by the 1990s. If deployed in large numbers, such as on hundreds of research ships and intelligence collectors, these arrays could theoretically provide initial detection of older Western SSBNs. The arrays, however, probably would not be effective against the quieter *Ohio*-class SSBNs, and their capability against even the older Western SSBNs while patrolling would be very limited. In addition, tactical and technical countermeasures could further reduce the vulnerability of older units.

72. We do not believe the Soviets will be able to solve the initial detection problem during the period of this Estimate. For this reason, we expect that the Soviet Navy will continue to focus its anti-SSBN efforts on attempting to detect and attack Western SSBNs as they exit their bases or pass through choke points. If, however, through some technological breakthrough the Soviets were able to detect Western SSBNs in the open ocean, they would then have a new problem of how to attack them. Such attacks might be conducted by the traditional technique of deploying surface, submarine, and/or air units to the datum. This approach would require that the Soviets deploy larger numbers of general purpose naval units at greater distances from Soviet territory than is currently anticipated. In addition to attack submarines, these operations might involve surface combatants, including carrier battle groups. ASW aircraft operating from Third World airfields could cover at least some SSBN operating areas if access rights were granted and the host country were willing to risk becoming a belligerent. Unless there were a substantial increase in the size of the Soviet Navy or the detection breakthrough enabled the Soviets to provide SSBNs protection with fewer general purpose units, such a change in naval wartime deployments would require sacrificing some of the capability to protect the SSBN havens.

73. The Soviet Navy's strategic ASW problem will be further complicated by the United States' plan to arm its newest classes of attack submarines—potentially over 70 units—with the land-attack version of the Tomahawk SLCM. Although there are plans for a conventional variant, the Soviets are undoubtedly most concerned with the strategic implications of nuclear-tipped SLCMs. The employment of such SLCMs will complicate the Soviet ASW problem in two ways:

- The number of US strategic-missile-firing submarines will triple.

- The range of the nuclear Tomahawk will allow SLCM-armed submarines to strike Soviet territory from areas where it will be difficult for the Soviets to concentrate ASW forces.

74. Much of the defensive requirement against Tomahawk-armed submarines would coincide with and overlap other ASW efforts against Western units within Soviet sea-control/sea-denial areas. To reach targets deep within the USSR from the Norwegian Sea or Northwest Pacific, for example, Tomahawk-armed submarines would have to approach Soviet territory. In doing so they would pass through at least some of the echeloned ASW defenses the Soviets would establish to protect their SSBNs. Some targets near the Soviet coast, on the other hand, could be reached by SLCMs fired from the outer edges of the Northern and Pacific Fleets' defensive thresholds. SLCM-armed submarines operating in these areas would be able to avoid the bulk of the Soviet ASW defenses in the Norwegian Sea and Pacific Ocean.

75. One option available to the Soviets to counter this threat could be to extend the area of sea-denial operations, possibly out to about 3,000 kilometers. The Soviets probably believe that a capability to conduct more extended sea denial will largely depend on their ability to contest the air superiority and ASW capability afforded NATO by carrier and land-based aircraft in areas such as the GIUK gap. They probably also believe that their ability to contest such airspace will necessitate operations by future surface combatant task groups, including CTOL aircraft carriers, at greater range from Soviet territory than currently planned. Any extension of the area for sea-denial operations therefore will probably be accompanied by a corresponding extension of initial sea-control areas—possibly as far as 2,000 kilometers. This would be more feasible for the Northern Fleet than for the Pacific Fleet. Given improved air cover from carrier-based aircraft in the 1990s and/or from captured airfields in Norway, the Northern Fleet could shift the focus of its ASW efforts away from the SSBN havens in Arctic waters southward to the GIUK gap. Control of the gap would both significantly increase Soviet capabilities to contest Western use of the Norwegian Sea as an SLCM launch area and help

protect Northern Fleet SSBNs from enemy ASW forces. Access to the Northwest Pacific Basin, on the other hand, is not restricted by any choke points that would facilitate a more forward-oriented ASW strategy. The Soviets, however, probably do not believe that the threat from SLCMs would be as great in the Pacific as in the Norwegian Sea. They probably expect that the majority of US SLCM-armed submarines would be deployed in European waters from which the more numerous military and economic targets located in the western USSR could be engaged.

76. The Soviets believe submarine-launched cruise missiles can also reach targets in the western USSR when fired from the central Mediterranean and North seas, areas where the Soviets plan sea-denial operations against carrier battle groups but probably only limited ASW efforts (see figure 20). Countering SLCM submarines in these areas could pose some tough choices for the Soviets. Any additional submarines deployed to these areas would lessen force allocations for other missions such as SSBN protection, prosecution of Western SSBNs, and interdiction of Western sea lines of communication. If the Soviets do opt for increased ASW efforts in the North and Mediterranean seas, they probably would allocate more diesel submarines for barrier patrols in the northern entrance to the North Sea and in Mediterranean choke points such as the Straits of Gibraltar and Sicily.

77. The Soviets could ultimately decide that the required allocation of resources and the opportunity costs involved in countering SLCM-armed submarines in their patrol areas were too costly. Given their limited ASW detection capabilities, moreover, the Soviets probably would be pessimistic about their ability to counter SLCM-armed submarines in areas such as the central Mediterranean and the North Sea, even if substantial forces were deployed there. An alternate strategy might limit efforts specifically aimed at the cruise missile submarine to deploying a few attack submarines in the approaches to Western attack submarine bases— efforts similar to the Soviets' anti-SSBN tactics. Major emphasis would then be placed on countering the missiles themselves through a combination of improved land-based air defense systems.

78. *Antisurface Warfare (ASUW).* Although the Soviets view Western submarines as the major naval threat to their territory and SSBN havens, their perception of the threat from Western surface forces and the importance they attach to ASUW are likely to increase during the next two decades. Carrier battle groups will continue to be perceived as major threats to Soviet and Warsaw Pact territory, SSBN havens, and operations in the land TVDs. Concern with carrier battle groups will remain high because of:

- Soviet expectations that the number of carriers in NATO will at least remain constant and probably increase as the result of US plans to expand to a 15-battle-group navy, the reemergence of sea-based, fixed-wing aviation in the Royal Navy, and French and Spanish plans for new carrier construction.

- Expected improvements in the offensive capability of carriers by equipping their aircraft with cruise missiles such as Tomahawk.

- Improvements in the ability of carrier battle groups to defend themselves against attack through such programs as the AEGIS air defense system.

79. Further, the Soviets will no longer be able to concentrate on aircraft carriers as the only Western surface units posing a significant threat to their territory. The Soviets are fully aware of US plans to equip battleships, cruisers, and destroyers with the land-attack version of the Tomahawk missile. They realize that this would result in a substantial increase in the number of Western surface combatants capable of striking the USSR with nuclear weapons. This would greatly complicate their strategic defensive task because any surface combatant would have to be considered a potential nuclear threat.

80. To meet this threat the Soviet Navy will continue efforts to improve its ASUW capabilities. Of particular importance will be:

- Construction of general purpose submarines equipped with advanced antiship torpedoes and cruise missiles. Construction of the O-class SSGN, with its 24 SS-N-19 missiles, is likely to continue into the 1990s, as will that of torpedo-equipped SSNs and SSs. The tactical distinction between cruise-missile-equipped submarines (SSGN, SSG) and torpedo attack units (SSN, SS) would become less clear if the Soviets introduced antiship cruise missiles that can be fired from torpedo tubes.

- Construction of surface combatants equipped with antiship missiles. The number of major surface combatants armed with such missiles is likely to increase substantially as a result of current construction programs (*Kirov*, *Kiev*, BLK-COM-1, *Sovremennyy*) and their projected follow-ons. There is evidence, moreover, that the SS-N-14 ASW cruise missile may have a secondary antiship capability.

- Continued production of Backfire bombers for Soviet Naval Aviation and a probable new bomber in the late 1980s to early 1990s to replace the Badgers and Blinders, as well as a possible increase in the number of SNA missile regiments. In addition, aircraft introduced in the 1990s may incorporate Stealth technology to make them less susceptible to detection.

FIGURE 20
Soviet View of Tomahawk

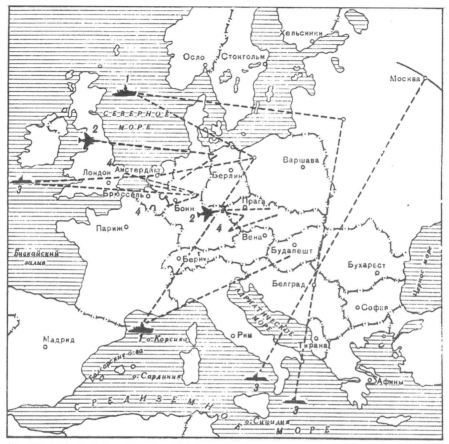

We believe this illustration, although published in an unclassified Soviet naval journal, accurately reflects Soviet concern regarding potential use and employment areas for the Tomahawk. Soviet caption: "This is how NATO strategists propose using Toma-hawk: from surface ships (1), aircraft (2), submarines (3), and ground launchers (4).

Morskoy Sbornik (Naval Digest)
No. 5, 1980
"Attention: Tomahawk!"
Capt. First Rank B. Rodionov

- Deployment of more capable sea-based fighter-bombers, both VSTOL aircraft operating from *Kiev*-class ships and CTOL aircraft operating from a new class of carrier.

The introduction of these new platforms will greatly increase the number of missiles available for attack and will coincide with other efforts to improve ASUW capability. In particular:

- Improvements are likely in antiship missiles, especially in target discrimination capability, survivability, and reaction times. The SS-NX-22, for example, is much faster (Mach 2+) and can approach the target at lower altitudes [TEXT DELETED] than such currently operational missiles as the SS-N-2 and SS-N-9. We believe the SS-NX-22 will be operational on *Sovremennyy* and *Tarantul*-class units in 1983.

- The capability of the radar ocean reconnaissance satellite (RORSAT) to detect ships and distinguish target size probably will be enhanced.

- Evolutionary improvements are likely in the electronic-intelligence ocean reconnaissance satellite (EORSAT) directed toward increased longevity, enhanced probability of detection, and continuous targeting capability through higher orbits, better sensors, and a wider field of view. We expect the Soviets will continue to convert older submarines and equip new surface and submarine units with the capability to use real time EORSAT (and RORSAT) data to support antiship cruise missile systems.

- The development of a synthetic aperture radar oceanographic satellite to provide improved all-weather, worldwide naval surveillance is possible during the latter period of this Estimate.

- Some new AAVGK bombers, possibly including a version of the Blackjack, could be configured for a maritime strike role. With an estimated radius of some 3,200 to 4,000 nautical miles, the Blackjack could attack Western surface targets in the central Atlantic from Soviet territory.

81. The execution of the ASUW task probably will continue to be primarily concentrated in areas such as the Norwegian and North seas, the eastern Mediterranean, and the northwestern Pacific—the principal areas from which carrier aircraft and sea-based cruise missiles could be launched against Soviet territory. Coordination of Soviet submarine and surface ship operations with those of land-based medium bombers is improved by concentrating ASUW in these areas. Soviet ASUW doctrine is likely to continue its emphasis on "first salvo" attacks—tracking Western surface units during the prewar period of tensions and attacking the most important of them with maximum force at the outset of hostilities. The Soviets undoubtedly recognize that this goal will become more difficult to achieve as the number of important targets grows through the introduction of the nuclear Tomahawk and increases in the number of NATO surface battle groups and improved missile defensive systems such as AEGIS. The proliferation of high-value targets is likely to contribute to a greater emphasis on ASUW operations of extended duration (days and weeks rather than minutes and hours).

Indications of such emphasis are already visible in exercises and in weapons-loading features of new units.

82. Although most ASUW operations will be concentrated relatively close to Soviet territory, the Soviets probably will seek by the mid-1980s to extend the outer edge of the Northern and Pacific Fleet sea-denial area somewhat beyond the current threshold of roughly 2,000 kilometers to counter the long range of Western SLCMs. Some attacks at much greater distances from Soviet territory are possible. Among the options they might find attractive for such operations are the deployment of missile-equipped aircraft to bases outside the USSR—if the host country were willing to risk becoming a belligerent—and equipping SNA with long-range bombers such as the Blackjack A now under development. A less likely possibility is the use of ballistic missiles against surface ships at sea. [TEXT DELETED] Although the Soviets probably do not consider the ASUW problem to be as difficult as ASW, they apparently expect it to remain a major and growing challenge through the 1990s.

83. *Antiair Warfare at Sea.* The Soviets recognize that the ability of their surface ships to conduct ASW and ASUW operations and project power beyond the range of land-based air cover is heavily dependent on their capability to defend themselves against air attack. The successful use of sea-skimming antiship missiles in the Falklands crisis probably has increased the already evident Soviet concern over the proliferation of these weapons in Western navies. The Soviets also realize that Western use of radar-cross-section reduction techniques will further complicate defense efforts against cruise missiles. In the past, the Soviets' air defense efforts concentrated primarily on point defense and self-protection weapons. Recent Gatling and dual-purpose gun systems, the new SA-NX-7 SAM, and the probable *Udaloy* SAM system continue this philosophy.

84. The SA-N-6 SAM being deployed on cruisers of the *Kirov* and BLK-COM-1 classes, however, is a long-range system that could provide the Soviets their first genuine area air defense capability against aircraft. There is disagreement within the US Intelligence Community on the capability of the SA-N-6 to engage low-altitude, low-radar-cross-section antiship cruise missiles. Some[4] believe the SA-N-6 has such a capability. Others[5] believe that the SA-N-6 may encounter severe guidance and fusing problems when used against cruise missiles, such as the Harpoon, which have a small radar cross section [TEXT DELETED]. We expect that the SA-N-6 or follow-on area air defense weapons will be deployed on all future cruisers.

85. The Soviets also probably will improve their defensive systems' signal processing capability and will continue to improve radar performance. Other likely

developments in naval air defense will include improvements in handling multiple targets, better low-altitude fusing and target detection in a sea clutter environment, and additional electronic countermeasures (ECM) and electronic counter-countermeasures (ECCM).

86. In addition to continued work in gun and missile technology, the Soviets are exploring the potential value of laser air defense weapons. It is likely that the Soviet Navy now has an R&D facility test area for high-energy lasers to explore shipborne air defense applications. It is possible that a prototype laser weapon, perhaps a low-energy system designed to counter electro-optical systems, will be installed on some new ship classes in the mid-to-late 1980s. We also believe a naval high-energy laser weapon may be operational by 1990. If laser weapons prove practical in a naval environment, we expect them to be deployed on many Soviet principal surface combatants by the year 2000, particularly for close-in and low-level defense against cruise missiles.

87. Soviet fleet air defense capability will be further enhanced by the introduction of high-performance fighter aircraft on the projected new class of aircraft carrier (see next paragraph). The overall effectiveness of the Soviets' efforts to protect their surface fleet, however, will depend on their ability to integrate the operations of carrier and land-based aircraft with shipborne SAM, gun, and laser systems. We believe the Soviets are working on a system to coordinate their air defense assets through the use of airborne warning and control system (AWACS) and possibly carrier-based airborne early warning (AEW) aircraft in conjunction with shipborne air warfare control centers to provide a communications/navigation/identification net (CNI). This will allow exchange of command and control and reliable IFF data (a system to differentiate between friendly and hostile units) and provide a common navigation baseline for participants in a more integrated and effective air warfare system. During the period of this Estimate, however, we believe Soviet efforts will evolve slowly, primarily because of lack of experience in the complex management of fleet air defense operations involving both aircraft and ships.

88. *Air Power at Sea.* The most notable change in the Soviet Navy in the next 10 to 20 years probably will be the introduction of its first Western-style aircraft carriers—that is, ships equipped with catapults and arresting gear and thereby capable of handling CTOL high-performance aircraft. We expect that the first of these ships, probably a 60,000-ton unit with nuclear propulsion, will become operational by about 1990 and that three or four could be in service by the end of the century. Each ship probably could carry an air group of some 60 aircraft.

89. Although aircraft carriers will enhance Soviet capabilities to project power and influence in distant areas, we believe their primary mission will be to help expand the area of Northern and Pacific Fleet wartime sea-control operations. During a general war, Soviet aircraft carrier operations probably will focus initially on providing air defense for surface groups supporting Soviet SSBNs and defending the sea approaches to the USSR in the Norwegian Sea and Northwest Pacific Basin. The air cover provided by carrier-based fighter aircraft probably will allow the Soviets to operate surface units at greater distances from Pact territory than currently envisioned. Other tasks of Soviet carrier aircraft could include:

- Conducting ASW with embarked helicopters.

- Attacking Western surface units.

- Escorting land-based reconnaissance, strike, and ASW aircraft during part of their operations.

- Attacking Western land bases and facilities.

- Attacking Western aerial resupply efforts.

In conducting such operations, Soviet carriers will operate with other surface units and possibly submarines and land-based aircraft. Their lack of experience in such complex operations, however, suggests that it will be at least the mid-1990s before a reasonable standard of operational proficiency can be attained.

90. Although the construction of a new class of aircraft carrier is apparently the policy of the present Soviet political and naval leadership, it is the type of program that could suffer from changes in such leadership and from economic problems. The enormous costs involved, not only for the ships themselves but for the air group, supporting vessels, and shore-based infrastructure, could make the program vulnerable to cancellation or delay if the Politburo seeks to reduce the burden of defense expenditures.

91. Regardless of Soviet decisions concerning CTOL aircraft carriers, the Soviet Navy probably will introduce improvements in its VSTOL aircraft units aboard the four *Kiev*-class ships. Such improvements are likely to involve a replacement for the Forger that has greater endurance, speed, payload, and air defense capability.

92. *Protection of State Interests in Peacetime and Limited War.* Although the primary emphasis in Soviet naval developments will continue to be on improving capabilities in a war with NATO, Soviet writings, construction programs, and exercises indicate a growing recognition of the value of naval forces in situations short of general war. Programs currently identified or projected by the US Intelligence

Community will result by the mid-to-late 1990s in substantial improvements in the Soviet Navy's capability to project power and influence in distant areas.

93. The most important improvement will stem from the construction of aircraft carriers capable of handling high-performance aircraft. The lack of adequate air support has been the major operational weakness of Soviet naval forces in distant areas. A force of two carriers with a total of some 120 aircraft would eliminate much of this weakness. Although much smaller than the US carrier force, it would provide the basis for establishing air superiority in many Third World situations in which the West did not become involved. Soviet writings concerning the use of carriers emphasize their value in show-the-flag and limited-war situations.

94. Projected improvements in Soviet amphibious forces will also contribute to an improved capability to project power in distant areas. We expect continued gradual construction of naval amphibious ships, including additional LPDs (Landing Ship, Personnel Dock) as well as smaller units. The Soviets also will continue exploring the use of advanced cargo ships such as roll-on/roll-off and ocean-going barge carrier (LASH) ships in amphibious landings. The Soviet naval infantry (now at a strength of about 14,000) will grow, perhaps to some 18,000 to 20,000 men. Additional amphibious assault forces will be available from ground forces units trained in such operations.

95. We do not believe that these estimated improvements will be sufficient to enable the Soviets to conduct amphibious operations in distant areas during a war with NATO. Such wartime operations will continue to emphasize areas on the Soviet periphery. Nor will such improvements make it practical to conduct landings in situations in which Western forces would be in opposition. These improvements, however, will provide Soviet leaders with a much-improved capability to overcome the opposition that could be offered by most Third World countries, especially those that were intrinsically weak or beset by internal divisions. Such improvements could also be used to support client states involved in military operations against other states or internal opponents. We believe that certain aspects of the recent exercise ZAPAD-81 suggest an interest in testing planning concepts for amphibious operations in the Third World.

96. The amount of time spent by Soviet general purpose units outside home waters is likely to increase only slightly in the 1980s and 1990s. Constraints on a major increase in regular out-of-area deployments probably will continue to include:

- The need to retain most naval forces close to Soviet home waters and in a readiness condition for rapid deployment to major wartime operating areas such as the Norwegian Sea.

- The fuel, maintenance, and personnel costs of out-of-area deployments, even at the low levels of activity typical of Soviet units.

- A possible recognition by the Soviets that the usefulness of deployed naval forces is not necessarily a direct correlation of size, but also involves capability and the value of any naval presence as a signal of Soviet interest in an area.

Changes in out-of-area deployments are likely to be most significant in terms of the capabilities of the units involved (new aircraft carriers, *Ivan Rogovs*, *Kirovs*, and so forth) and the areas in which they will operate. The areas in which the Soviets maintain a permanent naval presence (Mediterranean, Indian Ocean, South China Sea, West Africa) are likely to undergo further gradual expansion in response to political imperatives, primarily a desire to support the maintenance of established "socialist" regimes and the creation of new ones. Among the most likely candidate areas for such permanent naval presence are the Caribbean and the Philippine Sea. To support such operations, the Soviets will continue their attempts to achieve increased access to foreign facilities.

97. In addition to supporting peacetime naval operations, the Soviets probably would seek to use facilities in Third World countries in both a war against NATO and other lesser conflicts. The most likely role of such facilities in wartime would be as positions from which Western force movements can be monitored during the period of tension before the outbreak of war. We therefore expect to see continued efforts to obtain the use of airfields to support reconnaissance flights, as well as the establishment of SIGINT, communications, and possibly submarine-tracking facilities. The Soviets probably will continue to regard the use, especially the sustained use, of facilities in Third World countries in wartime as questionable because of their vulnerability and the possible unwillingness of host governments to risk becoming belligerents. The advantages to the Soviet Navy, however, of using such facilities are potentially substantial, particularly in operations against SSBNs and carrier battle groups. We think it likely, therefore, that efforts will be made to develop relations with Third World countries that will make wartime use of facilities, especially by aircraft, a more realistic possibility.

III. Prospects for the Soviet Navy

98. We believe that an examination of the current role of the Navy in Soviet military strategy, naval R&D, and construction programs, and the key issues facing Soviet planners enables us to make a judgment as to the most likely course of development for the Navy over the remainder of this century. We recognize, however, that an estimate covering such a long period of political, economic, and technological

changes must be viewed with caution. An examination of some less likely but still feasible courses of development is therefore included as well. These alternative courses of development are not meant to be exhaustive but rather to indicate some of the types of variables that could change our baseline estimate.

A. Baseline Estimate

99. We believe that the wartime strategy of the Soviet Navy will remain essentially unchanged over the next 15 to 20 years in terms of major tasks and the composition of forces to carry out those tasks. The requirement to counter advances in Western naval offensive capabilities, however, probably will cause the Soviets gradually to expand the areas in which their forces would be deployed for sea-control/sea-denial operations. They will introduce new weapon platforms and systems into the Navy and will seek an improved capability to use those weapons. We believe, however, that these changes will occur within the framework of the Soviets' present strategy because they probably will continue to view it as offering the best chance of accomplishing their vital wartime tasks.

100. The single most important mission of the Navy will continue to be strategic strike, primarily using SLBMs and possibly SLCMs. The importance of sea-based nuclear strike assets within the USSR's overall military strategy could grow because:

- The percentage of Soviet strategic nuclear warheads assigned to SSBNs will increase as Typhoons with MIRVed SLBMs enter service.

- New Soviet SLBMs could be sufficiently accurate to be used effectively against hardened targets.

- Soviet silo-based strategic systems may become more vulnerable.

The combination of increased SLBM accuracy and fixed intercontinental ballistic missile (ICBM) vulnerability could provide powerful incentives for the Soviet Union to move an even larger portion of its strategic strike capability to sea. Although such a shift probably would be resisted by other elements within the Soviet armed forces, especially the Strategic Rocket Forces, it will continue to be advocated by the Soviet naval leadership and has a reasonable chance of gaining political endorsement.

101. We nonetheless believe the Soviets will continue to regard their SSBNs as vulnerable to enemy ASW forces throughout the period of this Estimate. Protection and support for Soviet SSBNs, therefore, is likely to remain the most important consideration in the initial wartime deployment of a large portion of general purpose

naval forces of the Northern and Pacific Fleets. Pacific Fleet forces would be concentrated in the Northwest Pacific Basin, the Sea of Japan, and the Sea of Okhotsk area. The Northern Fleet would deploy the bulk of its forces to the Barents, Greenland, and northern Norwegian seas, although the outer edge of what we describe as the Northern Fleet sea-control area probably will expand gradually to include the southern Norwegian Sea, primarily to facilitate an extension of sea-denial operations beyond the GIUK gap. This would be intended principally to counter Western SLCM-armed ships and submarines, but would also support other operations in the Atlantic (see figure 21). Pacific Fleet sea-control operations would also expand somewhat (see figure 22). The major mission of Soviet CTOL aircraft carriers will probably be to assist in expanding these areas. Concentrating forces there will continue to appeal to the Soviets because it will enhance integration of their submarine and surface units with the land-based air support which, even after the introduction of a few aircraft carriers, will continue to constitute the bulk of the forces of SNA.

102. The Soviets probably will continue to view Western SSNs as the primary threat to their SSBN force and will conclude that the best chance of detecting such SSNs lies in waiting for them to enter relatively confined areas where the Soviets will have a concentration of forces and where their short-range sensors can be used to best advantage. Expected improvements in Soviet ASW platforms, tactics, and fixed-sensor technology, such as Cluster Lance, and increased use of under-ice patrols probably will improve—perhaps substantially—the Soviet Navy's ability to protect its SSBNs. We doubt, however, that the Soviets will view such improvements as sufficient to allow a lessened initial commitment of forces for SSBN protection.

103. Northern and Pacific Fleet operations for the protection of SSBNs will coincide with those for a portion of a second important task, strategic defense. Such operations, together with some of those of the Black Sea and Baltic Fleets, will seek to destroy Western aircraft carriers and strategic cruise missile platforms as they cross Soviet defense thresholds, now generally some 2,000 kilometers from Soviet territory. We expect such operations to be of growing importance to the Soviets because of their expectations concerning the proliferation of Western strategic cruise missiles. To counter Western cruise missiles launched from surface ships and submarines and the added range these missiles afford carrier-based strike aircraft, the Soviets probably will seek to extend the outer edge of the sea-denial areas of the Northern and Pacific Fleets to approximately 3,000 kilometers.

FIGURE 21
Future Initial Soviet Operating Areas in the Western TVDs

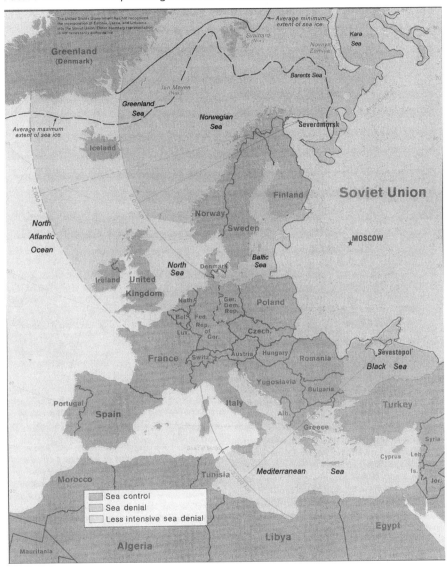

104. Another portion of the strategic defense task—the destruction of enemy SSBNs before they can launch their missiles—will pose an increasing dilemma for the Soviets. The deployment of hard-target-capable US SLBMs, improved British and French SSBNs, and the first Chinese SSBNs probably will increase the importance of achieving such destruction. The Soviet Navy's ability to detect and track US

FIGURE 22
Future Initial Sovet Operating Areas in the Pacific Ocean

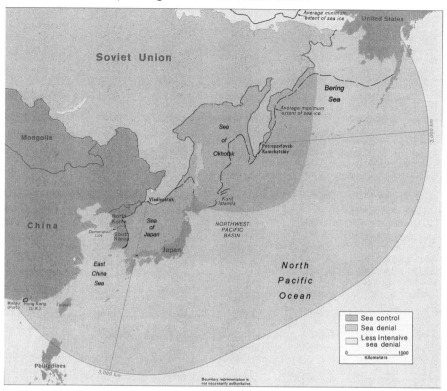

SSBNs in the open ocean, however, probably will decline, at least over the next 10 years. This assessment is based on our belief that:

- The increased patrol areas of SSBNs carrying Trident SLBMs will more than offset the increased coverage that could be provided by improved Soviet conventional ASW platforms.

- The Soviets probably will be unable to deploy a broad-ocean acoustic or nonacoustic sensor.

- Soviet SSNs will not be sufficiently quiet—at least throughout the next decade—to engage in covert trail, and Soviet ASW aircraft will not be deployed in sufficient numbers or have adequate range to maintain contact in US SSBN patrol areas.

- Overt trail will continue to be technically feasible—particularly in choke points and relatively confined areas—but the Soviets will not have sufficient platforms to threaten the US SSBN force. A decision to use a substantial number of SSNs in this manner, moreover, would divert them from other missions, such as protecting Soviet SSBNs.

We therefore expect that Soviet naval anti-SSBN operations will continue to be modest, with only a relatively few attack submarines stationed in choke points or in the approaches to Western or Chinese submarine bases.

105. We believe that Soviet procurement of naval weapon platforms and systems over the period of this Estimate will be driven primarily by requirements stemming from the strategic offensive and defensive tasks outlined above. The importance of these tasks should provide a solid basis for the navy to continue receiving at least the same share of the defense budget that it has received since the 1960s. Such an allocation of resources means that the Soviet Navy will continue to receive new platforms, including new classes of large surface combatants, attack submarines, and aircraft. The production rate will not completely offset the retirement of older units. The accelerating cost per ton of new combatants would make ship-for-ship replacement prohibitively expensive. Indeed, considering manpower/maintenance constraints, this may not be feasible. The force in the year 2000 will therefore be somewhat smaller than that of today. Newer units, however, will generally be larger than those being replaced and will be equipped with more sophisticated weapon systems:

- The size of the modern ballistic missile submarine force will probably remain roughly constant at about 60 units throughout the 1990s. The size of the overall force (now 85 units) will decline by approximately 30 percent as older units (G-class SSBs and H-class and older Y-class SSBNs) are converted or retired. The new units will be larger and will carry more missile tubes than most or all of those units retired. In the absence of an arms control or reduction treaty, the number of SLBM launch tubes as well as the number of warheads carried by the SSBN force is likely to increase.

- The first unit of the new class of 60,000-ton nuclear-powered aircraft carriers probably will become operational by about 1990. A total of three or four is expected by the year 2000.

- The number of principal surface combatants probably will decline somewhat—to about 260 units. New construction programs are likely to include two or three new classes of nuclear-powered guided-missile cruisers (CGNs); two new classes of guided-missile destroyers (DDGs); and three or four new classes of frigates. As a result of these programs, the trend toward larger average unit size, greater weapons loads, and more sophisticated air defense and antisurface weapons, sensors, and electronic warfare systems will continue, thereby improving the Soviet Navy's capability for sustained operations.

- The overall number of general purpose submarines probably will decline to about 260 units, but the number of nuclear-powered units probably will grow substantially. New classes will include follow-ons to the C-class and possibly to the O-class SSGN and A-class SSN, as well as the V-class SSN follow-on we expect to reach IOC in 1984. These units should continue the trend toward quieter platforms with improved sensors and increased command and control capability. Construction of improved diesel submarines with greater submerged endurance will also continue.

- The Soviet Navy's overall amphibious assault lift capability will increase gradually. A follow-on to the *Ivan Rogov*–class assault ship (LPD) and two new classes of tank landing ships (LSTs) are likely to be introduced. Construction of smaller units, including air-cushion vehicles (ACVs), will also continue. Emphasis on amphibious utility in merchant ship construction—especially for Ro-Ro and similar ships—will remain unchanged. Soviet interest in the use of helicopters in amphibious assault may lead to construction of a helicopter assault ship (LPH or LHA) in the 1990s. We expect an increase in the size of the naval infantry from about 14,000 to about 18,000 to 20,000 men.

- The Soviet Navy's underway replenishment capabilities should be enhanced by the introduction of one or more new classes of multipurpose replenishment ships. Construction of such ships, however, is likely to continue receiving a lower priority than the construction of the ships they are intended to support.

- The number of fixed-wing naval aircraft probably will increase somewhat, with the major changes being the first deployment to sea of high-performance CTOL aircraft as part of the air group on the first aircraft carriers and the introduction to Soviet Naval Aviation (SNA) of the Blackjack A bomber or, more likely, a Backfire follow-on. SNA will be an essential element in the Soviets' attempts to expand their sea-control/sea-denial efforts against Western surface forces in vital areas such as the Norwegian, North, and Mediterranean seas and the Northwest Pacific Basin. SNA bombers will also remain a principal feature of Soviet antisurface capabilities in other areas such as the Arabian Sea.

This projected Soviet naval construction program was subjected to econometric analysis, which determined that it would be consistent with current Soviet budgetary trends in ship and aircraft construction.

106. We believe that major technical improvements in Soviet fleet air defense are likely during the period of this Estimate. New SAMs, guns, and laser weapons will

probably be introduced and radio-electronic combat measures will continue to receive a high priority. Fighter aircraft operating from the projected CTOL carriers of the Northern and Pacific Fleets, probably in cooperation with AWACs and possibly AEW aircraft, will add a new dimension to the Navy's air defense resources. We cannot confidently assess the net effect of these changes on the ability of Soviet surface forces to defend themselves against air attack during a war with NATO. Such an assessment is highly dependent on tactical variables. The performance characteristics of key systems, such as the SA-N-6, are not yet fully understood. Changes in the Soviet Navy's air defense systems will be occurring simultaneously with those in Western antiship capability, including the introduction of large numbers of cruise missiles. Despite these uncertainties, the major Soviet commitment to the construction of large surface combatants persuades us that the naval leadership probably judges the overall result of changes in air defense capability as sufficient to support the wartime deployment of surface units farther from Soviet territory in a gradual expansion of their intended sea-control areas.

107. Expansion of both sea-control and sea-denial operations would be supported by gradual improvements in Soviet capability to surveil Western surface units and provide targeting assistance for antiship missile attacks. Improved over-the-horizon targeting would allow individual Soviet units to make better use of the range of their missiles, thereby covering a broader ocean area. Much of the improvement we expect in surveillance and targeting will involve satellite systems. We believe that the Soviets will introduce by the early 1990s an improved EORSAT with the capability to detect and identify additional types of radars. By the late 1990s, further improvements in the EORSAT are likely to result in near-continuous targeting capability by use of higher orbits, better sensors, and expanded fields of view. Probably a new RORSAT will also be introduced with improvements in probability of detection and a wider field of view. It is also possible the Soviets will produce a synthetic aperture radar satellite for improved all-weather surveillance. We expect that the improved EORSAT and RORSAT may be used in cooperation with a new satellite data relay system to provide real-time battle management information to command authorities ashore. In addition, during the period of this Estimate, advances in maritime surveillance from manned space vehicles can be expected. The use of satellites, however, cannot be considered exclusively in the context of Soviet naval operations. Such use will continue to provide one of the many linkages between naval operations and overall Soviet military strategy. The Navy's ability to use satellite systems in wartime would depend on such nonnaval factors as the extent to which antisatellite warfare would be conducted at the outset of war and the ability of satellites to survive Western attack.

Recognizing the danger of being dependent on any single system, the Soviet Navy will continue to integrate surveillance and targeting support from satellites with that from traditional platforms such as manned aircraft and possibly from new systems such as reconnaissance drones.

108. The Soviets probably recognize that future operations in areas such as the southern Norwegian Sea will place greater demands on the navy's command, control, and communications system because of factors such as larger operating areas, more emphasis on the integration of diverse platforms, and the need to counter a greater number of high-value targets. We expect the Soviets to respond to this challenge by improving their capabilities in technical areas such as satellite communications, very-low-frequency communications support to submarines, and low-probability-of-intercept systems, and by striving for greater automated data system compatibility. Another major trend will include increased automation to support battle management at all levels of the command structure. We believe that the major emphasis in the command, control, and communications system will continue to be on highly centralized control of wartime operations, but there are indications of an intention by the fleet staffs to delegate a larger portion of their battle management responsibilities to the flotilla and squadron-level commands.

109. In addition to its primary wartime tasks, the Soviet Navy also will continue to be responsible for supporting ground forces in the land TVDs and for interdicting sea lines of communication. Antiship and ASW operations by the Baltic Fleet in the North Sea and the Black Sea Fleet in the Mediterranean probably will receive increased emphasis to counter the growing capability of Western naval forces to strike targets in the land TVDs from increased ranges. The relatively low priority of open-ocean SLOC interdiction in Soviet naval strategy probably will not change radically unless the Soviets foresee a protracted conventional war with NATO or are responding to major changes in NATO's force structure or strategy for the reinforcement and resupply of Europe. Despite increased capabilities for power projection in distant areas, Soviet amphibious forces will continue to be structured primarily for landings close to Warsaw Pact territory during a war with NATO.

110. Soviet naval out-of-area operations in peacetime will continue to focus on maintaining permanent presence in areas such as the Mediterranean, the Arabian Sea, the South China Sea, and off the west coast of Africa. We expect the Soviets will attempt to expand their level of naval activity in areas such as the Caribbean Sea, the Philippine Sea, and the southwest Indian Ocean islands. They also are likely to step up efforts to acquire access to foreign naval support facilities. The new ships

entering service undoubtedly will be used in the traditional techniques of Soviet naval diplomacy ranging from routine show-the-flag port visits to demonstrations of support for client states during crisis situations and limited wars. Given the likelihood of continued instability in the Third World, the use of such naval diplomacy and power projection techniques probably will increase during the 1980s and 1990s.

111. We believe, however, that the most significant change in the Soviet Navy during the period of this Estimate will be the achievement for the first time of an ability to project power ashore effectively in distant areas in a limited war environment—that is, one that does not involve a confrontation between the USSR and NATO. Although we believe that Soviet naval programs are motivated primarily by requirements for a general war with the West, new platforms and weapon systems will help to close some of the current gaps in Soviet capability to conduct such distant area operations. In particular, the ability to form a task force around two or three CTOL aircraft carriers will give the Soviet Navy its first significant capability to provide tactical air support for ground force operations and amphibious landings by Soviet or client forces in distant areas. The new medium-caliber gun and air defense systems on new classes of surface ships and the probable acquisition of additional large amphibious ships and a seaborne assault helicopter (perhaps Helix B) will also improve the Soviet Navy's capability to conduct opposed landings.

112. These enhanced capabilities will give the Soviets the option to use naval force in a number of Third World situations against all but the most well-armed regional powers. Because the Soviets probably will have, at most, four CTOL carriers by the year 2000, they would have to draw heavily on the assets of more than one fleet—as they did during the large amphibious portion of exercise ZAPAD-81—to assemble a force sufficient to conduct an opposed distant-area landing. The assembly of such a force at a great distance from the USSR would seriously undermine the Soviet Navy's ability to perform its priority strategic offensive and defensive missions in the event of escalation to general war. We believe, therefore, that major Soviet naval task force participation in Third World conflicts will be restricted to limited war situations in which the Soviets judged the risk of escalation to a war with the United States or NATO to be small.

113. Perhaps the most compelling argument against a more ambitious power projection strategy during the period of this Estimate is our judgment that programs directly supporting the Navy's strategic offensive and defensive missions—nuclear-powered ballistic missile, cruise missile, and attack submarines, land-based

strike aircraft, and ASW-oriented surface combatants—will continue to receive top priority in the allocation of the Soviet Navy's budget. Other factors that cast doubt on a significantly increased power projection commitment in the near term include the following:

- The naval infantry's growth has been modest. Since its reestablishment in 1963 it has grown to a current strength of about 14,000.

- The pace of LPD construction has been slow.

- Only one *Berezina* AOR has been built and no other large replenishment units are known to be under construction.

114. The likelihood of an ambitious naval power projection strategy during the period of this Estimate is further reduced by the practical difficulties involved in rapidly constructing a large number of CTOL aircraft carriers, the most important instruments of such a mission. We estimate that the Soviets will construct such carriers at the same Nikolayev shipyard on the Black Sea at which *Kiev*-class aircraft carriers are built. This facility has been specially configured at great expense (including the installation of the USSR's largest overhead gantry cranes) for the construction of such large warships. We estimate that this yard, if operating at a normal construction pace, will be able to produce one large CTOL aircraft carrier every four years, with the first unit being delivered about 1990. It is possible for the Soviets to construct carriers at a faster rate, by using additional, less suitable shipyards or by placing construction at Nikolayev on a crash basis. Such practices would, however, be inconsistent with past Soviet practice when constructing new types of large combatants. (The construction of the first unit of the *Kirov*-class CGN, for example, began in 1973 but was not completed until 1980.) We believe that the Soviets recognize the complexity of building and operating CTOL carriers and are likely to develop this capability at a slow-but-sure pace. For these reasons, we reject the concept of a Soviet Navy in which power projection by major naval task forces plays a dominant role.

B. Alternate Courses of Development

115. Our best estimate on the future of the Soviet Navy reflects our judgment that the trends we have observed in ship construction, naval doctrine, and strategy over the past 20 years will continue. The following paragraphs discuss three variables that could precipitate major changes in the Soviet Navy of the 1990s: a major Soviet ASW breakthrough, a strategic arms reduction treaty, and a severe economic crisis that forces a cut in military spending.

116. *An ASW Breakthrough.* The development that would result in the most profound change in Soviet wartime strategy from that outlined above would be an ASW breakthrough that gives the Soviets the capability to detect and track enemy submarines in the open ocean—a breakthrough derived from one of the many research efforts they are conducting on acoustic and nonacoustic sensors. Although unlikely throughout the period of this Estimate, such a breakthrough would substantially increase the Soviet Navy's ability to perform the critically important strategic defensive tasks of destroying enemy ballistic missile and land-attack cruise missile submarines before they launched their missiles. It would also increase the Soviets' ability to protect their SSBNs, because enemy attack submarines could be identified and attacked long before they closed Soviet SSBN havens.

117. We believe an ASW breakthrough would lead to major changes in the way the Soviets would deploy their general purpose forces, particularly attack submarines, before and during a general war. During the prehostilities phase, the Soviets probably would opt to deploy substantial numbers of SSNs to suspected enemy SSBN operating areas, in choke points, and in likely transit lanes near enemy submarine bases. These nuclear-powered attack submarines would attempt to gain contact and maintain trail on detected Western submarines. As a consequence, fewer submarines would be available for SSBN protection, unless the Soviet SSN order of battle were increased. Surface and air units probably would also be deployed farther forward. Planning for these operations probably would lead to a greater effort to acquire foreign facilities, particularly to support ASW aircraft.

118. The development of a reasonable capability to detect and trail Western SSBNs in the open ocean would provide the Soviet Navy with a powerful argument for increased budgetary allocations. The Navy could argue persuasively that it could not effectively counter enemy strategic submarines and ensure the survivability of its own SSBNs without a substantial increase in forces, especially in SSN production rates. Given this choice, the Soviet leadership could grant the Navy increased funds for a greater SSN construction effort, perhaps twice as many units per year as the five to six we currently expect.

119. If there were an initial detection breakthrough, we cannot rule out the possibility that the Soviets would explore techniques for destroying submarines, especially SSBNs, by means other than the traditional reliance on general purpose naval platforms. There have, for example, been vague references in Soviet writings to the possible use of land-based ballistic missiles against submarines in the open ocean. Exploring such a technique would be consistent with past Soviet interest in

innovative solutions to naval problems [TEXT DELETED]. It would also be consistent with Soviet doctrinal emphasis on a multiservice approach to the accomplishment of wartime tasks. The Soviets are probably aware of the myriad technical problems likely to be encountered in any such use of land-based ballistic missiles including:

- The need to develop a remote sensor that could precisely locate SSBNs patrolling in the open ocean and constantly update that position.

- The need to develop a system that could rapidly update the trajectory of a ballistic missile in flight to compensate for target movement.

- The need to solve fusing problems associated with a warhead surviving water impact from high altitude.

We are skeptical that such problems could be overcome, at least during the period of this Estimate, and believe the Soviets would be unlikely to pursue seriously such a course unless they had high confidence that the initial detection problem would soon be solved. This example is mentioned, however, to illustrate that a breakthrough in ASW detection could lead to radical changes, not only in the Navy, but in overall Soviet military strategy.

120. *Strategic Arms Control.* Arms control negotiations, such as the ongoing strategic arms reduction talks (START), could play an important part in determining the role within Soviet strategy and the force composition of the Soviet Navy in the 1990s. For example, severe restrictions on SLCM characteristics/deployment, or a ban, would alleviate a serious maritime threat to the USSR and eliminate much of the pressure to conduct sea-denial operations at greater distances from Soviet territory. Provisions governing strategic ballistic missile force levels could have a significant impact upon general purpose force programs because a substantial portion of those forces will remain dedicated to protecting Soviet SSBNs. A START provision simply limiting or freezing SSBN/SLBM levels probably would have little impact upon Soviet general purpose programs, although SSGN/SSN construction could increase slightly as facilities dedicated to SSBNs shifted to general purpose programs. Plans to protect Soviet SSBNs probably would not be affected by such a freeze/reduction. On the other hand, a START provision calling for a sharp reduction in land-based ballistic missile systems, which would be likely to encourage both the United States and the Soviet Union to move a greater percentage of their strategic arsenals to sea, could provide strong justification for increased production of ASW-capable general purpose forces to protect the increased number of Soviet SSBNs. If a treaty encouraging a "move to sea" were signed, we would expect increases in the production of SSNs, Bear F, or follow-on

ASW aircraft, and ASW-oriented surface ships such as the *Udaloy*. Although a US move to sea could also justify an increased Soviet anti-SSBN effort, we do not believe the Soviets would allocate increased forces against Western SSBNs unless they had first achieved a significant ASW breakthrough allowing them to detect and trail enemy submarines in the open ocean.

121. *Severe Economic Stringencies.* The Soviets' ability to sustain the ambitious naval program we project in our baseline estimate may ultimately depend upon the health of the Soviet economy and the willingness of future leaders to continue the Brezhnev policy of favoring guns over butter. We have no evidence of a Khrushchevian inclination within the next generation of Soviet leaders to bolster the economy by cutting military spending. Indeed, we believe such a cut would be unlikely, at least through the 1980s. It nonetheless is conceivable that the post-Brezhnev elite would be more willing to curb military spending, especially if agricultural performance and the economic growth rate continue to falter through the 1980s and/or arms control agreements allow significant economies.

122. With the possible exception of the Strategic Rocket Forces, budgetary cuts driven primarily by economic stringencies probably would fall on all branches of the Soviet armed forces. Within the Navy, programs considered fundamental to its primary strategic offensive and defensive tasks, such as SSBNs, attack and cruise missile submarines, and land-based strike aircraft, probably would suffer few, if any, cuts. Rather, some cutbacks or slowdowns in programs relating more to distant-area power projection and sea-control capabilities—such as large surface combatants, amphibious ships, and naval auxiliaries—could be expected. It is conceivable, however, that through a combination of factors, budget cuts could fall more heavily on the Soviet Navy, resulting in substantial cuts in surface ship programs. These factors include:

- A new political leadership that lacks Brezhnev's apparent commitment to building a large balanced navy and/or is less inclined to use naval forces as instruments of foreign policy to project Soviet power and influence in distant areas.

- A new chief of the Soviet Navy who lacks Admiral Gorshkov's influence within the political and military hierarchies and/or does not fully share his vision of a blue-water navy in which large surface combatants play a prominent role. Gorshkov's successor, for example, could be a submariner and could be more inclined to push for the construction of additional attack submarines.

- Technical advances in antiship weaponry and targeting convince the Soviets that large surface ships are too costly and vulnerable, and that ASW and

ASUW tasks assigned to large surface combatants can be done more effectively by smaller combatants, submarines, and land-based aircraft.

123. It is doubtful that the interim collective leadership we expect to follow Brezhnev will be inclined to make major policy departures such as cutting defense spending. A decision to make significant reductions in military spending probably would be impossible until the next generation of Soviet leaders is firmly in place and one man has emerged as first among equals. Since this process is likely to take several years, a decision to cut naval programs could not be made until the late 1980s. By that time, most of the major surface combatant programs currently under way—the BLK-COM-1 cruisers and the *Udaloy* and *Sovremennyy* guided-missile destroyers—should be nearing completion. Any reductions then probably would come in Soviet programs we project for the late 1980s and 1990s. Programs that probably would be deleted or sharply reduced in order to comply with a significant cut in naval spending include:

- The 60,000-ton nuclear-powered aircraft carriers. The first unit of this class, and possibly the second, may be too near completion to be affected by a budgetary decision made in the late 1980s. The projected third and fourth units, however, probably would be deleted, and any plans for a follow-on class canceled.

- New class(es) of nuclear-powered cruisers.

- New classes of large amphibious ships (LPDs and LPHs) and underway replenishment ships.

In addition, the Soviets may opt for early retirement of some older destroyers and frigates and construct fewer units than originally programed of new classes to follow the *Sovremennyy* and *Udaloy* DDGs. Programs clearly identified with coastal ASW and SSBN protection, such as the projected follow-on classes for the *Krivak* and *Grisha* frigates, probably would be least affected by a sharp budgetary cutback.

124. The net result of cuts in surface ship programs such as those outlined above would be a navy with much less capability than the one projected in our baseline estimate to control waters beyond the range of land-based tactical aircraft and to project power in distant areas. By the mid-1990s, such cuts could reduce the overall size of the surface navy by as much as 20 percent, lessening Soviet capabilities to sustain current peacetime deployment levels in areas such as the Mediterranean, the Indian Ocean, and off West Africa. The Soviets probably would attempt to compensate for any reduction in naval capabilities to perform key strategic defensive tasks by relying even more on advances in antiship missiles that could be

launched from aircraft, submarines, and land and receive targeting information from satellites. In addition, they might stress nonnaval solutions to maritime threats, such as land-based antiballistic missile and air defense systems—to counter SLBMs and SLCMs, respectively—and an increased maritime role for the Soviet Air Force.

Dissemination Notice

1. This document was disseminated by the Directorate of Intelligence. This copy is for the information and use of the recipient and of persons under his or her jurisdiction on a need-to-know basis. Additional essential dissemination may be authorized by the following officials within their respective departments:

   a. Director, Bureau of Intelligence and Research, for the Department of State

   b. Director, Defense Intelligence Agency, for the Office of the Secretary of Defense and the organization of the Joint Chiefs of Staff

   c. Assistant Chief of Staff for Intelligence, for the Department of the Army

   d. Director of Naval Intelligence, for the Department of the Navy

   e. Assistant Chief of Staff, Intelligence, for the Department of the Air Force

   f. Director of Intelligence, for Headquarters, Marine Corps

   g. Deputy Assistant Secretary for International Intelligence Analysis, for the Department of Energy

   h. Assistant Director, FBI, for the Federal Bureau of Investigation

   i. Director of NSA, for the National Security Agency

   j. Special Assistant to the Secretary for National Security, for the Department of the Treasury

   k. The Deputy Director for Intelligence for any other Department or Agency

2. This document may be retained, or destroyed in accordance with applicable security regulations, or returned to the Directorate of Intelligence.

3. When this document is disseminated overseas, the overseas recipients may retain it for a period not in excess of one year. At the end of this period, the document should be destroyed or returned to the forwarding agency, or permission should be requested of the forwarding agency to retain it in accordance with IAC-D-69/2, 22 June 1953.

4. ~~The title of this document when used separately from this text is unclassified.~~

Notes

Preface

1. The terms "naval strategy" and "naval doctrine" are used in this Estimate in the general sense of principles by which forces are guided in their actions. In Soviet usage, "military doctrine" and "military strategy" have very specific meanings. Neither term is applied to an individual service. Military doctrine comprises the views of the leadership of the Soviet state on the nature of future war and the tasks of the state and the armed forces in preparing for and conducting such a war. Military doctrine is a starting point for military strategy, which directs the armed forces as a whole in a complex system of interdependent large-scale strategic operations. Individual services execute strategic missions but always do so under the overall unified military strategy. The Soviet Navy's missions are firmly defined by this overall military strategy and cannot be properly understood outside that context.

Discussion

1. The holders of this view are the Director, Defense Intelligence Agency, and the Director of Naval Intelligence, Department of the Navy.

2. The holders of this view are the Deputy Director for Intelligence, Central Intelligence Agency, and the Director, Bureau of Intelligence and Research, Department of State.

3. Other land-attack cruise missiles under development may be for naval use. Evidence available as this Estimate went to press suggests that the reconfigured Y-class submarine launched in October 1982 may be intended as a test platform or as the lead unit in a class of submarines retrofitted to employ SLCMs.

4. The holders of this view are the Director, Defense Intelligence Agency, and the Director of Naval Intelligence, Department of the Navy.

5. The holders of this view are the Deputy Director for Intelligence, Central Intelligence Agency, and the Director, Bureau of Intelligence and Research, Department of State.

The Maritime Strategy
Debates

A Bibliographic Guide to the Renaissance of
U.S. Naval Strategic Thinking in the 1980s

Captain Peter M. Swartz,
U.S. Navy (Retired)

Compiler's Preface

This is the fifth published edition of the annotated bibliography on *The Maritime Strategy*. Drafting and circulation of annotated bibliographies have been a feature of *The Maritime Strategy* process within the U.S. Navy since the early 1980s. The earliest editions were internal documents generated within the Strategic Concepts Branch (OP-603) of the Office of the Chief of Naval Operations (OPNAV). They were designed both to aid the leadership of the Navy to keep track of the policy debates over *The Maritime Strategy* as they progressed, and to stimulate further internal Navy research and analysis of issues related to the strategy by publicizing relevant source materials.[1]

At the suggestion of the leadership of the U.S. Naval Institute, the first publicly released edition was published in *The Maritime Strategy*, a supplement to the January 1986 *Proceedings*.[2] The second edition was published in 1987 by the Naval Institute.[3] The third edition was published in 1988 by the Naval Postgraduate School.[4] All three editions adhered to the same chronological format, to enable users to follow the progress of the debates. A fourth edition was published by the Naval Postgraduate School in 1989, this time with an alphabetical format.[5]

This fifth edition returns to the format and text of the earlier editions. Essentially, as necessary to retain its authenticity as a product of 1980s U.S. naval thinking, it is only a slightly updated version of the third edition. The differences are the addition of this Preface and an Epilogue and the deletion of some entries in section III, "The Debate Continues: 1987 and Beyond." The entries deleted from section III are those describing works planned but as yet unpublished when the third edition went to press. Those works that were subsequently completed and published are included in the Epilogue.

It is fitting that the various editions of the annotated bibliography on *The Maritime Strategy* have been published by the U.S. Naval Institute, the Naval Postgraduate School, and now the Naval War College. All three institutions were instrumental during the 1980s in ensuring that the debates on *The Maritime Strategy*—both within the U.S. Navy and beyond—were unvarnished, well informed, sophisticated, and spirited. Those debates accounted for much of the power, vitality, and influence of *The Maritime Strategy* during the last decade of the Cold War and beyond.

Notes

1. Responsibility for drafting and keeping up the annotated bibliographies was assigned to the present author, then Cdr. Peter M. Swartz, in 1983. Commander Swartz served in the Strategic Concepts Branch (OP-603) on the staff of Chief of Naval Operations Admiral James Watkins from 1982 through 1984. From 1984 through 1986, he served in the Office of Program Appraisal (OPA) on the staff of Secretary of the Navy John F. Lehman, Jr. He was promoted to captain during this tour. In 1986 and 1987 he was the Navy Fellow at the Center for Strategic and International Studies (CSIS) in Washington, D.C. From 1987 through 1990, he was the Director of Defense Operations at the U.S. Mission to NATO in Brussels, Belgium. During this period, he was assisted in keeping the bibliography current and useful by Dr. Jan Breemer and Dr. James Tritten of the Naval Postgraduate School. At the time of publication of this fifth edition, he was a senior analyst at the Center for Strategic Studies (CSS) of the CNA Corporation.

2. Capt. Peter M. Swartz, U.S. Navy, "Contemporary U.S. Naval Strategy: A Bibliography," *The Maritime Strategy* Supplement, U.S. Naval Institute *Proceedings* 112 (January 1986), pp. 41–47.

3. Capt. Peter M. Swartz, U.S. Navy, *Addendum to "Contemporary U.S. Naval Strategy: A Bibliography"* (Annapolis, Md.: U.S. Naval Institute, April 1987). This edition was summarized in Capt. Peter M. Swartz, U.S. Navy, "*The Maritime Strategy* in Review," U.S. Naval Institute *Proceedings* 113 (February 1987), pp. 113–116.

4. Capt. Peter M. Swartz, U.S. Navy, *The Maritime Strategy Debates: A Guide to the Renaissance of U.S. Naval Strategic Thinking in the 1980s* (Monterey, Calif.: Naval Postgraduate School, 24 February 1988).

5. Capt. Peter M. Swartz, U.S. Navy, and Jan S. Breemer, with James J. Tritten, *The Maritime Strategy Debates: A Guide to the Renaissance of U.S. Naval Strategic Thinking in the 1980s* (Monterey, Calif.: Naval Postgraduate School, 30 September 1989).

Contents

Introduction

This is a bibliography with a point of view. It takes as a departure point the U.S. Navy–Marine Corps Maritime Strategy of the 1980s, as enunciated by the civilian and military leaders of the U.S. Government, especially the Department of the Navy. It includes criticisms of and commentaries on that strategy, as well as items relating *The Maritime Strategy* to overall national and allied military strategy, and to historical precedents. In addition, it covers both how the strategy was developed and who developed it, and the important role of war gaming.

The Maritime Strategy has generated enormous debate. All sides and aspects of the debate are presented here. The focus, however, is on that strategy. Absent are discussions of naval affairs that do not have as their points of departure—explicitly or implicitly—the contemporary *Maritime Strategy* debate.

In order to trace the ebb and flow of ideas and events over time, items are listed chronologically, by occurrence or publication date, rather than merely alphabetically. Authoritative official statements of *The Maritime Strategy* are indicated by an asterisk (*). Explicit direct commentaries on *The Maritime Strategy* are indicated by a double asterisk (**). The other items listed deal implicitly with various issues or aspects of *The Maritime Strategy* or with its immediate antecedents.

Publications on sister-service and allied contributions to *The Maritime Strategy* are listed separately, to aid the reader/researcher. (Admittedly, this and other artificial typological devices run against a central theme of *The Maritime Strategy*: its global, "seamless web" character). Also, only cursory attention is paid to pre-1981 Navy strategic thinking on global war, a structural shortcoming that cannot legitimately be cited as evidence that such thinking was lacking.

I. Maritime Strategy Debates: 1979–1985

American military strategy and its maritime component have been debated since the foundation of the republic. Following World War II, maritime strategy concerns centered around peacetime presence, antisubmarine warfare (ASW), and the Navy's role in nuclear strike warfare against the Soviet Union. During the late 1950s and 1960s the focus shifted to limited war and deterrence through nuclear-powered ballistic missile submarine (SSBN) operations. In the early 1970s, the debate centered on then Chief of Naval Operations Elmo R. Zumwalt's formulation of the "Four Missions of the Navy"—strategic deterrence, sea control, power projection, and peacetime presence. (A major body of literature on presence began to be created at that time.) In the mid-1970s, sea control seemed to dominate discussions.

In 1978, Admiral Thomas B. Hayward became Chief of Naval Operations. His views on strategy had been heavily influenced by his experience as Seventh Fleet commander and Pacific Fleet commander in chief in the post-Vietnam environment. Admiral Hayward's focus was on flexible offensive forward power projection, conducted globally and in conjunction with allies and sister services, especially against the Soviet Union and its attacking forces. Much of this was a return to concepts familiar to U.S. naval officers of the first post–World War II decade. That era's focus on nuclear strikes, however, now broadened to encompass a much wider range of options, primarily conventional.

Admiral Hayward outlined his views publicly in his initial 1979 testimony before Congress, and subsequently in the pages of the *Proceedings*. The naval strategic renaissance and the resultant debate he and others sparked continues to this day, fueled by the statements and policies of the Reagan administration, especially its first Secretary of the Navy, John F. Lehman, Jr., who served from February 1981 to April 1987.

The initial public Maritime Strategy discussion of the early 1980s had largely taken the form of a debate on the pages of American public and foreign affairs and national security periodicals. This debate had focused on two themes: the general forward strategic principles (and certain highly publicized Norwegian Sea examples) enunciated repeatedly by Secretary of the Navy John F. Lehman, Jr., and a perceived "Maritime Strategy versus Coalition Warfare" dichotomy incessantly alleged by former Under Secretary of Defense Robert Komer and others.

At the same time, however, the staffs of the Chief of Naval Operations and the Commandant of the Marine Corps—in conjunction with officers of their sister services and allies—had been tasked to develop for internal use a detailed description of *The Maritime Strategy* component of U.S. national military strategy. This Maritime Strategy rigorously integrated into one clear, consistent document a number of long-held views of Navy and Marine Corps senior officers, certain newly refined concepts developed in the fleet and at the Naval War College, agreed national intelligence estimates, the strategic principles articulated by Secretary Lehman and other Reagan administration officials, and a thoughtful discussion of the variety and range of uncertainties inherent in the strategy.

Concepts developed by the Navy's warfare communities and fleets, as well as by Army, Air Force, joint, and allied commanders, were examined and incorporated as appropriate. Where inconsistencies appeared, hard choices were made. Uncertainties and limitations were identified. Properly, the job was spearheaded by the Strategic Concepts Group on the staff of the Chief of Naval Operations (OP-603).

The U.S. Navy–Marine Corps Maritime Strategy was codified initially in 1982 to focus Navy program development efforts more tightly. Its basic premises already had been underlying Navy planning, gaming, and exercises. Subsequently, congressional testimony in 1983 released an initial edition of *The Maritime Strategy* to the public. A classified revision to the strategy statement was approved by the Navy's Program Review Committee (chaired by then Vice Adm. Carlisle Trost) in October 1983 and signed and distributed Navywide by Admiral James D. Watkins, then Chief of Naval Operations, in 1984.

Various unclassified elements of the strategy began to find their way into naval-affairs journals, especially the *Proceedings*. Writings on naval strategy that did not take *The Maritime Strategy* as a starting point began to fade. By 1985, enough authoritative congressional testimony, speeches, op-ed pieces, journal articles, and letters to the editor— penned by senior naval officers and well-placed civilian commentators—had appeared for the essential elements of *The Maritime Strategy* to be accessible to the public. Public commentary gradually shifted from exegeses on the press conferences, speeches, and articles of Secretary Lehman and Ambassador Robert W. Komer to discussions on aspects of the actual Maritime Strategy developed largely by military officers from national and alliance guidance and approved by civilian leadership.

Promulgation of *The Maritime Strategy* fostered increasing public and government discourse. Within the Navy, the interplay among *The Maritime Strategy*, force-level planning, fleet plans and operations, and professional education and training became a governing dynamic. In the open literature, the number of writings on the strategy rose from a handful of newspaper and journal articles in 1981 to an avalanche of government documents, books, and articles in 1986, including over 145,000 copies distributed of the *Proceedings'* watershed *The Maritime Strategy* January 1986 supplement alone. This quantitative leap was accompanied by qualitative changes in both the background of the commentators and the sophistication of their arguments.

Contrary to much uninformed external criticism of the early 1980s, *The Maritime Strategy* was presented by the Navy as only one—albeit a vital—component of the national military strategy. It was not presented as a recommended dominant theme of that national strategy. Also contrary to earlier uninformed criticism, the strategy embodied the views of unified and fleet commanders as well as Washington military and civilian planners and Newport thinkers. The Navy Department and the fleet were now speaking with one sophisticated voice to—and increasingly for—the nation and its allies.

Hayward, Adm. Thomas B. "The Future of U.S. Sea Power." Naval Institute *Proceedings* [hereafter *Proceedings*]/*Naval Review* (May 1979): 66–71; see also Zumwalt, Adm. Elmo R., Jr. "Total Force": 103–106; and "Comment and Discussion" (July 1979): 23–24; (August 1979): 87–89; (September 1979): 89–91; (October 1979): 21; (December 1979): 88; (January 1980): 82–86. Public debate on the new era of U.S. Navy strategy begins. Hayward, Zumwalt, Bill Lind, Norman Friedman, et al. See also Hayward "Posture Statement" testimony before Congress, 1979–1982.

Moorer, Adm. Thomas H., USN (Ret.), and Cottrell, Alvin J. "Sea Power and NATO Strategy." In *NATO: The Next Thirty Years,* edited by Kenneth A. Myers. Boulder, Colo.: Westview, 1980, 223–236. (Detailed arguments on the necessarily global nature of any major future war with the Soviets and the need for forward carrier operations off the Kola Peninsula, Vladivostok, and Petropavlovsk, by the 1970–1974 Chairman of the Joint Chiefs of Staff and 1967–1970 Chief of Naval Operations.) Arguments against a "swing" strategy from the Pacific are also echoed in "For Want of a Nail: The Logistics of the Alliance" by Adm. Isaac Kidd, USN (Ret.), former U.S. Navy and NATO commander in both the Mediterranean and the Atlantic, in the same volume (pages 189–205).

Turner, Adm. Stansfield, USN (Ret.). "Thinking About the Future of the Navy." *Proceedings* (August 1980): 66–69. Also "Comment and Discussion" (October 1980): 101; (November 1980): 124–127; (January 1981): 77. (Admiral Turner questions role of power projection in general war strategy.)

U.S. Senate. Committee on Armed Services. Nomination of John F. Lehman, Jr., to be Secretary of the Navy. 97th Cong., 1st sess., 28 January 1981. ("I think the major need of the Navy today is the establishment by the President and the Congress of a clearly articulated naval strategy, first and foremost.")

Prina, L. Edgar. "Budget Increases Reflect 'A Major Change in Naval Strategy.'" *Sea Power* (April 1981): 13–22. (Best coverage of Secretary Lehman's press conference of 3 March 1981, when he unveiled his "major change.") See also page 1 of the *Wall Street Journal*, *New York Times*, *Washington Post*, and *Baltimore Sun*, 4 March 1981, and George, James L. "U.S. Carriers—Bold New Strategy." *Navy International* (June 1981): 330–335. (Compare with Hayward and Moorer/Cottrell pieces above.)

Hart, Senator Gary. "Can Congress Come to Order?" In *The Tethered Presidency*, edited by Thomas Franck. New York: New York University Press, 1981, 242–243. (A call for a national maritime-only strategy and "obvious and indisputable naval superiority." The U.S. Navy certainly shares the second goal, but not the first.)

Betts, Richard K. *Cruise Missiles: Technology, Strategy, Politics.* Washington, D.C.: Brookings Institution, 1981, 537–540. (Sees discussion of carrier penetration of Soviet waters as "peacetime deterrent rhetoric" about risky "missions that could turn into a naval Charge of the Light Brigade.")

Carnegie Panel on U.S. Security and the Future of Arms Control. *Challenges for U.S. National Security: Assessing the Balance: Defense Spending and Conventional Forces: A Preliminary Report, Part II.* Washington, D.C.: Carnegie Endowment for International Peace, 1981. (Chapter 3: 99–148, assesses the naval balance and identifies key issues. No policy recommendations. Comprehensive and evenhanded. Unlike *The Maritime Strategy*, purely budget oriented.)

Lehman, John F., Jr. "Rebirth of a U.S. Naval Strategy." *Strategic Review* (Summer 1981): 9–15. (For more than two years, the basic Navy public statement on Maritime Strategy. See also Lehman "Posture statement" testimony before Congress, 1981–1987, especially regarding linkages among operations, strategy, and programs.)

Zumwalt, Adm. Elmo R., Jr., USN (Ret.). "Naval Battles We Could Lose." *International Security Review* (Summer 1961): 139–155. (By the 1970–1974 U.S. Navy CNO. Argues for more stress on the U.S. Navy as "geopolitical cavalry" for low-to-middle-level conflict, and for a "distributed force" building program as optimum for the full spectrum of naval warfare requirements, including nuclear war at sea.)

Stockman, David. *The Triumph of Politics: How the Reagan Revolution Failed.* New York: Harper and Row, 1986, 280–281. (Anonymous "experts" ridicule "the theory of 'getting in harm's way'" in mid-1981 to President Reagan's gullible budget director.)

Caldwell, Hamlin. "The Empty Silo: Strategic ASW." *Naval War College Review* (September–October 1981): 4–14. (Call for anti-SSBN operations in Soviet home water bastions.)

Koburger, Capt. C. W., USCGR. "Pitts' Choice: An Alternative NATO Strategy for the USA." *Navy International* (December 1981): 730–731. (Like that of Senator Hart, one of the very few real examples of a call for a "pure" national maritime strategy, a position often falsely attributed to proponents of the U.S. Navy Maritime Strategy.)

Ikle, Fred Charles. "The Reagan Defense Program: A Focus on the Strategic Imperatives." *Strategic Review* (Spring 1982): 11–18. (By the Under Secretary of Defense for Policy. Especially good on administration requirements for naval forces to provide options to fight on a variety of fronts.)

Kennedy, Col. William V., USAR (Ret.). "Tailor Military Strategy to the Economy." *Philadelphia Inquirer* (26 May 1982): 25. (Sees the Reagan administration as building a new maritime strategy on top of an old continental strategy. Considers the Soviet Far East as the key Soviet vulnerability for naval forces to exploit.)

Record, Jeffrey, and Rear Adm. Robert J. Hanks, USN (Ret.). *U.S. Strategy at the Crossroads.* Washington, D.C.: Institute for Foreign Policy Analysis, July 1982. (Two different arguments for a shift to a national maritime strategy, including one by a prominent U.S. Navy strategist of the mid-1970s.)

Komer, Robert. "Maritime Strategy vs. Coalition Defense." *Foreign Affairs* (Summer 1982): 1, 124–131, 144. Also Adm. Stansfield Turner and Capt. George Thibault. "Preparing for the Unexpected: The Need for a New Military Strategy" (Fall 1982): 125–135; "Comments and Correspondence: Maritime Strategies" (Winter 1982–1983): 453–457. (The debate jumps to a wider arena: Komer vs. Turner vs. Lehman. Ambassador Komer had been a leading Carter administration Defense Department official from 1977 to 1981.)

Vlahos, Michael. "U.S. Naval Strategy: Geopolitical Needs and the Soviet Maritime Challenge." In *Strategic Responses to Conflict in the 1980s,* edited by William J. Taylor, Jr., et al. Lexington, Mass.: D.C. Heath, 1984, 427–432. (1982 views of a former Naval War College faculty member. Especially good on late-1970s internal U.S. Navy strategy debates and as critique of tying U.S. naval strategy too closely to the Soviet naval threat. See approach taken by McGruther, cited in section XI below. This volume also contains some of Ambassador Komer's early—and retrospectively, most lucid—arguments, at 196–199.)

Vlahos, Michael. "Maritime Strategy versus Continental Commitment." *Orbis* (Fall 1982): 583–589. (Argues that the two approaches are not mutually exclusive.)

Posen, Barry A. "Inadvertent Nuclear War? Escalation and NATO's Northern Flank." *International Security* (Fall 1982): 28–54. (Claims forward U.S. Navy operations in the Norwegian Sea and elsewhere are a bad thing.)

Zakheim, Dov. "The Unforeseen Contingency: Reflections on Strategy." *Washington Quarterly* (Autumn 1982): 158–166. (Reagan administration maritime strategy in overall military context, by a Deputy Under Secretary of Defense.)

Lehman, John. "Support for Defense Is Still Strong." *Washington Post* (16 December 1982): 23. ("The Navy is working to do its part in a team effort of forward-based air, land, and naval power. Navy strategy is part and parcel of the national strategy of deterrence, not a substitute for it.")

Cohen, Eliot A. "The Long-Term Crisis of the Alliance." *Foreign Affairs* (Winter 1982–1983): 325–343. (A Naval War College faculty member argues for strengthening the U.S. Navy, creation of a "Fifth Fleet," global U.S. military focus, and increased European military responsibilities in NATO. Seeks to bridge the "Atlanticist vs. navalist" debate.)

Huntington, Samuel P. "The Defense Policy, 1981–1982." In *The Reagan Presidency, An Early Assessment*, edited by Fred I. Greenstein. Baltimore: Johns Hopkins University Press, 1983, 82–116. (Initial Reagan overall defense policies and strategy, the context of *The Maritime Strategy*.)

Glenn, Senator John, Barry E. Carter, and Robert W. Komer. *Rethinking Defense and Conventional Forces*. Washington, D.C.: Center for National Policy, 1983. (Two ex-Army officers, Carter: 33–35, and Komer: 46–48, attack *The Maritime Strategy* and the 600-ship Navy.)

Posen, Barry, and Stephen Van Evera. "Reagan Administration Defense Policy: Departure from Containment." In *Eagle Defiant: United States Foreign Policy in the 1980s*, edited by Kenneth A. Oye, Robert J. Lieber, and Donald Rothchild. Boston: Little, Brown, 1983, 67–104. (Critical of all aspects of Reagan defense policy and strategy, including offensive conventional warfighting, especially with naval forces. "Overall, a counteroffensive strategy is a bottomless pit, since it generates very demanding missions that cannot be achieved without huge expenses, if they can be achieved at all . . . a counteroffensive strategy defeats the basic purpose of American conventional forces—the control of escalation." Advocates a ten-carrier force.)

Brown, Harold. *Thinking about National Security: Defense and Foreign Policy in a Dangerous World*. Boulder, Colo.: Westview, 1983. (By the 1977–1981 Secretary of Defense. Mildly critical of forward carrier operations; more strongly critical of the 600-ship Navy buildup. See especially 100–101, 121–123, 171–187.)

Miller, Steven. "The Northern Seas in Soviet and U.S. Strategy." In *Nuclear Disengagement in Europe*, edited by Sverre Lodgaard and Marek Thee. London: Taylor and

Francis, 1983, 117–137. (Comprehensive analysis, especially of tie-in between U.S. naval strategy and Reagan administration policy.)

Staudenmaier, Col. William, USA. "One if by Land—Two if by Sea: The Continental-Maritime Debate." *Army* (January 1983): 30–37. (Opening salvo of the "Carlisle School." A leading Army War College faculty member contributes to the misperceptions that the central U.S. naval strategy debate is about Maritime Strategy vs. Continental Strategy and that it is driven solely by budgetary considerations.)

* U.S. House Armed Services Committee. *Hearings on the Department of Defense Authorization for FY84*; Part 4. 98th Cong., 1st sess., 24 February 1983, 47–51. (Commodore Dudley Carlson publicly unveils a version of the U.S. Navy's "first cut" Maritime Strategy, February 1983, published later that year.)

Tritten, Cdr. James J. "It's Not Either Or." *Wings of Gold* (Spring 1983): 49–52. (Argues Mahanian concept of U.S. seapower is necessary to support U.S. forward defense continental strategy.)

Nunn, Senator Sam. *The Need to Reshape Military Strategy.* Washington, D.C.: Georgetown University CSIS (18 March 1983), 7. (Advocates choke point defense, vice carrier-based airpower, vs. the Soviet homeland.)

Caldwell, Hamlin. "Arctic Submarine Warfare." *Submarine Review* (July 1983): 4–13. (Develops further the arguments in his 1981 article.)

Dunn, Keith A., and Col. William O. Staudenmaier, USA. "Strategy for Survival." *Foreign Policy* (Fall 1983): 22–41. Also Komer and Dunn and Staudenmaier letters (Winter 1983–1984): 176–178. (The "Carlisle School" again. Seeks to synthesize all points in the maritime-continental debate.)

Arkin, William M. "Nuclear Weapons at Sea." *Bulletin of the Atomic Scientists* (October 1983): 66–81. (Sees U.S. Navy theater nuclear weapons under development as destabilizing, despite Soviet theater nuclear naval programs.)

** Murray, Robert J., "A War-Fighting Perspective." *Proceedings* (October 1983): 66–81. (By a former Under Secretary of the Navy and the first Director of the Naval War College's Center for Naval Warfare Studies. See especially pages 70 and 74 on *The Maritime Strategy* and the role of the Naval War College. "You have to discard the term 'naval strategy,' and even the slightly more modern variant, 'maritime strategy' and talk instead about the naval contribution to national strategy. . . . Newport is not, of course, the planning center for the Navy. It is, however, one place where naval officers get together and try to produce better ideas.")

Epstein, Joshua M. "Horizontal Escalation: Sour Notes of a Recurrent Theme." *International Security* (Winter 1983–1984): 19–31 and especially 23–25. Also reprinted in *The Use of Force*, 2nd ed., edited by Raymond Art and Kenneth Waltz. Lanham, Md.: University Press of America, 1983. Updated as chapter 3 of Epstein's *Strategy and Force Planning: The Case of the Persian Gulf*, Washington, D.C.: Brookings Institution, 1987. (Critique of "Horizontal Escalation," not only as a counter to a Soviet invasion of Iran but also apparently as a function of maritime forces in a global war with the Soviets. Sees Soviet-Chinese wartime relationship as unaffected by naval considerations, and regards Soviet ground force numbers as virtually limitless. No discussion of possible Soviet air force redeployment, however.)

Record, Jeffrey. "Jousting with Unreality: Reagan's Military Strategy." *International Security* (Winter 1983–1984): 3–18. Also "Correspondence." (Summer 1984): 217–221. (Echoes Komer's and Turner's stated positions.)

Kaufmann, William W. *The 1985 Defense Budget.* Washington, D.C.: Brookings Institution, 1984, 29–34. (A snide critique of U.S. Navy strategy and force level requests. Naval power projection forces seen as needed only in Third World areas during a global war with the Soviets. Unlike *The Maritime Strategy*, a purely budget-oriented document.) See also Kaufmann chapters in earlier 1982 and 1983 Brookings annuals edited by Joseph Pechman, *Setting National Priorities: 1983* and *1984*, and his 1981 *Defense in the 1980s.*

Record, Jeffrey. *Revising U.S. Military Strategy: Tailoring Means to Ends.* Washington, D.C.: Pergamon-Brassey's, 1984. (An argument for a national maritime strategy, but without the offensive forward operations characteristic of the U.S. Navy Maritime Strategy. See especially 83–86.)

Ullman, Cdr. Harlan, USN (Ret.). *Crisis or Opportunity? U.S. Maritime Industries and National Security.* Washington, D.C.: Georgetown CSIS, 1984. (Pages 4–7 give a good quick summary of the basic opposing viewpoint on U.S. naval strategy, eschewing the extraneous elements usually dragged in by unknowledgeable would-be analysts.)

Kennedy, Floyd D., Jr. "From SLOC Protection to a National Maritime Strategy: The U.S. Navy under Carter and Reagan, 1977–1984." In *In Peace and War*, 2nd ed., edited by Kenneth J. Hagan. Westport, Conn.: Greenwood, 1984, 304–326. (Mostly on operations and shipbuilding. Sees Secretary Lehman's contribution as a reorientation of national strategy rather than simply an enhancement of its maritime elements.)

Dunn, Keith A., and Col. William O. Staudenmaier, USA. *Strategic Implications of the Continental-Maritime Debate.* Washington Paper 107. Washington, D.C.: CSIS, 1984. (Expands arguments made in their *Foreign Policy* article.)

Tritten, Cdr. James J. "Strategic ASW: A Good Idea?" *Proceedings* (January 1984): 90, 92. (Argues for procuring anti-SSBN systems without declaring an anti-SSBN policy. See also his "Strategic ASW." *Submarine Review* (January 1984): 52–55, and "The Concept of Strategic ASW." *Navy International* (June 1984): 348–350.)

Lehman, John F., Jr. "Nine Principles for the Future of American Maritime Power." *Proceedings* (February 1984): 47–51. (Refinement of Secretary Lehman's thought after three years in office.)

Zakheim, Dov S. "The Role of Amphibious Operations in National Military Strategy." *Marine Corps Gazette* (March 1984): 35–39. (Deputy Under Secretary of Defense explains Marine missions and programs in context of overall administration strategy.)

*   Senate Armed Services Committee. *Hearings on the Department of Defense Authorization for FY85; Part 8.* 98th Cong., 2nd sess., 14 March 1984. (Secretary of the Navy and CNO jointly describe Maritime Strategy as a component of national military strategy, March 1984. Further exposure of the Maritime Strategy presented by Commodore Carlson a year earlier.)

Rivkin, D. B. "No Bastions for the Bear." *Proceedings* (April 1984): 36–43. Also "Comment and Discussion" (June 1984): 14–15; (July 1984): 14–20; (August 1974): 101; (September 1984): 164; (October 1984): 97–100; (January 1985): 129. (The anti-SSBN mission debate.)

Turner, Adm. Stansfield, USN (Ret.). "A Strategy for the 90s." *New York Times Magazine* (6 May 1984): 30–40, etc. (Argues for focus on USN Third World intervention role, amphibious warfare, and more/smaller ships.)

Hamm, Manfred. "Ten Steps to Counter Moscow's Threat to Northern Europe." *Backgrounder.* Heritage Foundation, no. 1356, 30 May 1984. (Calls for rather modest U.S. and allied maritime counters to a greatly increased Soviet threat.)

Perry, Robert, Mark A. Lorell, and Kevin Lewis. *Second-Area Operations: A Strategy Option.* Publication R-2992-USDP. Santa Monica, Calif.: RAND, May 1984. (Pros, cons, risks, and uncertainties associated with multitheater war and "horizontal escalation." Historical and analytical survey.)

Bond, Larry, and Tomas Ries. "Controversy: A New Strategy for the North-East Atlantic?" *International Defense Review* (December 1984): 1803–1804. (USN and NATO naval strategy.)

*   Watkins, Adm. James D. "Current Strategy of U.S. Navy." *Los Angeles Times* (21 June 1984): 22. (USN rebuttal to Robert Komer. "Carrier Heavy Navy Is Waste-Heavy." *Los Angeles Times* [16 May 1984], especially to alleged maritime vs. continental and

Navy vs. Europe dichotomies. See also Watkins "Posture Statement" testimony before Congress, 1983–1986.)

Komer, Robert. *Maritime Strategy or Coalition Defense.* Cambridge, Mass.: Abt Books, 1984. Also review by Dr. Dov Zakheim. *Political Science Quarterly* (Winter 1984–1985): 721–722. (Ambassador Komer's last salvo before November 1984 elections, with administration retort.)

** Brooks, Capt. Linton F. "Escalation and Naval Strategy." *Proceedings* (August 1984): 33–37. Also "Comment and Discussion" (October 1984): 28–29; (November 1984): 18, 24; (December 1984): 174. (On Maritime Strategy and nuclear weapons by an important and articulate contributor to development of the strategy. Focus of public debate begins to shift to the strategy as it actually is, rather than as it is alleged to be.)

* "Navy Maritime Strategy Moving on Offensive." *Navy Times* (20 August 1984): 25–26. (Commodore William Fogarty outlines *The Maritime Strategy.*)

Stewart, Maj. Richard A., USMC. "Ships That Can Deliver." *Proceedings* (November 1984): 37–43. (Amphibious versus prepositioning issues.)

** George, James L., ed. *The U.S. Navy: The View from the Mid-1980s.* Boulder, Colo.: Westview, 1985. (Papers delivered at a Center for Naval Analyses conference, Fall 1984. See chapters by Dov Zakheim on "Land Based Aviation and Maritime Warfare," Robert S. Wood and John T. Hanley, Jr., on "The Maritime Role in the North Atlantic," and "Commentaries" by retired admirals Robert Long and Harry Train. Admiral Long's Pacific Command "Concept of Operations" and his Pacific Command Campaign Plan were important building blocks for *The Maritime Strategy.*)

Jampoler, Capt. Andrew. "A Central Role for Naval Forces? . . . to Support the Land Battle." *Naval War College Review* (November–December 1984): 4–12. Also "In My View" (March–April 1985): 96–97; (July–August 1985): 83. (Mainstream U.S. Navy thinking.)

Nagler, Vice Adm. Gordon, USN (Ret.), ed. *Naval Tactical Command and Control.* Washington, D.C.: AFCEA International Press, 1985. (See the articles in chapter III: "Tactical Space Assets" and chapter IV: "EW: A Force Multiplier," on how the U.S. Navy uses space and electronic warfare systems to resolve a variety of operational problems inherent in implementing *The Maritime Strategy.*)

Kaufmann, William W. *The 1986 Defense Budget.* Washington, D.C.: Brookings Institution, 1985, especially 32–35. (Another sarcastic Kaufmann budget-oriented critique, including an unduly sanguine view of allied naval capabilities.)

Jenkins, Ronald Wayne. "Coalition Defense versus Maritime Strategy: A Critical Examination Illustrating a New Approach to Geopolitical Analysis." PhD diss., Pennsylvania State University, 1985. (A political geographer's take. Buys into categorization of "Schools" popularized by Komer, Dunn, and Staudenmaier. Recognizes irrelevance of much of the pre-1984 literature to "real-world" USN planning and programming problems. Includes a study of the views of Naval War College officers on geography and Maritime Strategy.)

Thomas, Cdr. Raymond E. "Maritime Theater Nuclear Warfare: Matching Strategy and Capability." In *Essays on Strategy*, Washington, D.C.: National Defense University Press, 1985, 39–51, especially 50. (Criticizes U.S. naval strategy for not addressing theater nuclear warfare adequately; disagrees with forward carrier operations in high threat areas.)

Collins, Col. John M., USA (Ret.). *U.S.-Soviet Military Balance 1980–1985.* Washington, D.C.: Pergamon-Brassey's, 1985. (Compares strategy and policy as well as force levels. See especially chapter 11. Also chapters 9, 12, and 16.)

Zimm, Lt. Cdr. Alan D. "The First Salvo." *Proceedings* (February 1985): 55–60. Also "Comment and Discussion" (April 1985): 16; (June 1985): 132; (July 1985): 106. (See especially for timing of forward carrier battle group moves and for Soviet strategy issues.)

Klare, Michael T. "Securing the Fire Break." *World Policy Journal* (Spring 1985): 229–247. (Sees forward offensive operations of ships with both nuclear and conventional capabilities as eroding the firebreak between nuclear and nonnuclear combat and raising the likelihood of nuclear war.)

Breemer, Jan S. "The Soviet Navy's SSBN Bastions: Evidence, Inference, and Alternative Scenarios." *RUSI Journal* (March 1985): 18–26. (Includes useful review of literature.)

Ackley, R. T. "No Bastions for the Bear: Round 2." *Proceedings* (April 1985): 42–47. Also "Comment and Discussion" (May 1985): 14–17; (July 1985): 112. (More on the anti-SSBN mission.)

* Watkins, Adm. James D. "Maritime Strategy: Global and Forward." *Baltimore Sun* (16 April 1985): 15. (USN rejoinder to a variety of critics, especially Jeffrey Record, "Sanctuary Warfare." *Baltimore Sun* [26 March 1985]: 7.)

** Ullman, Harlan K., and Thomas H. Etzold. *Future Imperative: National Security and the U.S. Navy in the Late 1980s.* Washington, D.C.: CSIS, 1985. (See especially Ullman's critique of Maritime Strategy: 20–21, 67. Contrast with Ullman riposte to Turner, *Proceedings* [January 1988]: 77.)

Dunn, Keith A., and Col. William O. Staudenmaier, USA. "The Retaliatory Offensive and Operational Realities in NATO." *Survival* (May–June 1985): 108–118. (Shows Maritime Strategy similarities to Samuel Huntington proposals to adopt retaliatory offensive strategy on the ground and in the air in Europe. Argues against both.)

Arkin, William M., and David Chappell. "Forward Offensive Strategy: Raising the Stakes in the Pacific." *World Policy Journal* (Summer 1985): 481–500. (Forward operations in the Northeast Pacific seen as "provocative and destabilizing." Similar in tone and political coloration to Barry Posen 1982 critique of Norwegian Sea operations.)

"The Defense Budget: A Conservative Debate." *Policy Review* (Summer 1985): 12–27, especially 20–21. (Prominent conservatives line up, pro or con, on the 600-ship Navy and *The Maritime Strategy*, as they understand it.)

*/** U.S. House of Representatives. Committee on Armed Services, Subcommittee on Seapower and Strategic and Critical Materials. *Hearings: The 600-Ship Navy and The Maritime Strategy.* 98th Cong., 1st sess., Washington, D.C.: U.S. Government Printing Office, 1986. (June and September 1985 graphics-laden testimony by the Secretary of the Navy, the Chief of Naval Operations, the Commandant of the Marine Corps, and several critics and commentators, notably retired admirals Turner and Carroll. With the *Proceedings* January 1986 Supplement and related "Comment and Discussion" letters, the most comprehensive public statement and discussion of the Navy's official views on *The Maritime Strategy*, although lacking in the in-depth discussion of uncertainties that characterized internal Navy Maritime Strategy documents.)

Martin, Laurence. *NATO and the Defense of the West.* New York: Holt, Rinehart and Winston, 1985, especially 30–35 ("Flanks"), 51–56 ("Warning, Mobilization and Reinforcement"), and 57–67 ("The Maritime Battle"). (Features graphics rivaling those in the official U.S. Navy Maritime Strategy testimony in their explanatory power and—often—their complexity.)

Holloway, Adm. James L., III, USN (Ret.). "The U.S. Navy: A Functional Appraisal." *Oceanus* (Summer 1985): 3–11. (Reformulation of pre–Maritime Strategy USN positions by Admiral Hayward's predecessor as CNO. Similar to the Navy's *1978 Strategic Concept of the U.S. Navy* [NWP-1.] Focus on sea control and on Soviet Navy as anti-SLOC force.)

** Friedman, Norman. "U.S. Maritime Strategy." *International Defense Review,* no. 7 (1985): 1071–1075. (A prominent civilian naval affairs commentator analyzes rationale for USN Maritime Strategy.)

*   Foley, Adm. Sylvester R., Jr. "Strategic Factors in the Pacific." *Proceedings* (August 1985): 34–38. (Retiring PacFlt commander in chief discusses his task in context of overall Maritime Strategy. Shows one component commander's view of the strategy.)

Turner, Adm. Stansfield, USN (Ret.). "U.S. Naval Policy." *Naval Forces,* no. 3 (1985): 15–25. (Update of Turner's thought, emphasizing amphibious interventions and North Atlantic SLOC protection.)

** O'Donnell, Maj. Hugh K., USMC. "Northern Flank Maritime Offensive." *Proceedings* (September 1985): 42–57. (USN/USMC global Maritime Strategy as applied to one region; comprehensive commentary on *The Maritime Strategy* debate.) Also "Comment and Discussion" (October 1985): 16, 20; (December 1985): 20–23. See especially January 1986 (p. 19) letter discussing complementary Norwegian Navy operations; and February 1986 (pp. 19–25) letter by Dr. Norman Friedman elaborating on and endorsing *The Maritime Strategy* and placing it in historical context.

*   "NATO Forces Flex Muscles in Norwegian Sea." *Virginian-Pilot* (9 September 1985): 1ff. (Another fleet view of the strategy. Vice Adm. Henry C. Mustin, Commander U.S. Second Fleet and NATO Striking Fleet Atlantic, on exercising and implementing Maritime Strategy in his theater.) See also "Protection of Convoy Routes a Key Objective for OCEAN SAFARI '85." *Jane's Defense Weekly* (5 October 1985): 749–753.

** U.S. Navy. *First Annual Long Range Planners' Conference: 17–18 September 1985.* Washington, D.C.: Office of the Chief of Naval Operations (OP-00K), 1986. (On relationships among *The Maritime Strategy* and U.S. Navy long-range planning, program development, and research.)

Gordon, Michael R. "Lehman's Navy Riding High, But Critics Question Its Strategy and Rapid Growth." *National Journal* (21 September 1985): 2120ff. (Wide-ranging review of many aspects of the debate.)

*   Lehman, John F., Jr. "Talking Surface with SecNav." *Surface Warfare* (September–October 1985): 2–10. (Secretary of the Navy ties the strategy, surface warfare, and procurement issues together.)

** West, F. J. "Bing," Jr. "Maritime Strategy and NATO Deterrence." *Naval War College Review* (September–October 1985): 5–19. (By a former Reagan administration Assistant Secretary of Defense, naval strategic thinker, and principal author of "SEAPLAN 2000," a 1978 progenitor of *The Maritime Strategy*. Excellent discussion of conventional protracted war and deterrence concepts underlying the strategy.)

*   McDonald, Adm. Wesley. "Mine Warfare: A Pillar of Maritime Strategy." *Proceedings* (October 1985): 46–53. (By the NATO Supreme Allied Commander, Atlantic and Commander in Chief, U.S. Atlantic Command and U.S. Atlantic Fleet. Actually on relationship of Maritime Strategy to NATO fleet strategy in the Atlantic, with emphasis on mine warfare.)

** Harris, Cdr. R. Robinson, and Lt. Cdr. Joseph Benkert. "Is That All There Is?" *Proceedings* (October 1985): 32–37. (Surface combatants and *The Maritime Strategy.*)

** Powers, Capt. Robert Carney. "Commanding the Offense." *Proceedings* (October 1985): especially 62–63. (Central strike warfare theme of the strategy is criticized, along with the tactical organization evolved thus far for its implementation.)

** Watkins, Adm. James D. "The Greatest Potential Problem: Our National Willpower." *Sea Power* (October 1985): 71. (CNO describes utility and development process of *The Maritime Strategy.*)

Friedman, Norman. "A Survey of Western ASW in 1985." *International Defense Review*, no. 10 (1985): 1587–97. (Maritime Strategy and the North Atlantic ASW campaign: Open ocean vs. close-in vs. convoy campaigns.)

** "Phoenix." "The SSN-21 and U.S. Maritime Strategy." *Submarine Review* (October 1985): 27–31. (Discusses linkages between threat, strategy, and ship design. See also letter by Capt. D. M. Ulmer [April 1986]: 58–60, questioning using estimated Soviet intentions, vice capabilities, to drive strategy and programs. Cf. McGruther article cited in section XI below.)

* Norton, Capt. Douglas M. "Responding to the Soviet Presence in Northern Waters: An American Naval View." In *The Soviet Union and Northern Waters*, edited by Clive Archer. London: Croom, Helm, 1987, 179–204. (A paper presented in October 1985 at Aberdeen, Scotland, as part of the dialogue between U.S. Navy strategists and allied civilian and military leaders and defense specialists.)

** Wood, Robert S., and John T. Hanley, Jr. "The Maritime Role in the North Atlantic." *Naval War College Review* (November–December 1985): 5–18. (The Naval War College faculty begins to weigh in heavily in the public debate.)

** Ullman, Cdr. Harlan K., USN (Ret.). "The Pacific and U.S. Naval Policy." *Naval Forces*, no. 6 (1985): 36–48. (Sees U.S. Navy Pacific experience as primary driver of *The Maritime Strategy.* Especially good as the role of Adm. Thomas Hayward as Pacific Fleet commander, originator of the "Sea Strike" study, and Chief of Naval Operations.)

** U.S. House of Representatives. Committee on Armed Services. *Report of the Seapower and Strategic and Critical Materials Subcommittee on the 600-Ship Navy.* 98th Cong., 1st sess., 18 November 1985. (The House Seapower Subcommittee endorses *The Maritime Strategy.* Essentially the same report is in Rep. Charles E. Bennett, "The 600-Ship Fleet: Is It Necessary?" *Naval Forces*, no. 21 [1986]: 26–38.)

*   Watkins, Adm. James D. "Reforming the Navy from Within." *Defense 85* (November
      1985): 18–20. (The CNO on the role of *The Maritime Strategy* within the Navy and its
      basic characteristics. "We lean heavily on our unified commanders-in-chief and Navy
      fleet commanders to help strengthen, modernize, and then put into practice our naval
      strategy. This plurality of perspective and the resulting competition of ideas have
      made for a robust dynamic strategy that recognizes and reflects the complexity of
      strategic issues as viewed by all key U.S. military leaders worldwide, not as viewed by a
      parochial naval bureaucracy in Washington.")

Bowling, Capt. R. A., USN (Ret.). "Keeping Open the Sea-Lanes." *Proceedings* (December
      1985): 92–98. (Argues for a return to SLOC protection focus for the U.S. Navy.)

Ball, Desmond. "Nuclear War at Sea." *International Security* (Winter 1985–1986): 3–31.
      (Argues against anti-SSBN operations and for more U.S. Navy focus on the escalatory
      dangers of theater nuclear war at sea. Not particularly accurate.)

Owens, Lt. Col. Mackubin Thomas, USMCR. "The Hollow Promise of JCS Reform." *In-
      ternational Security* (Winter 1985–1986): 98–111, especially 106–109. (Links the strat-
      egy debate to the contemporaneous debate on JCS "reform": "The JCS reorganization
      debate is really a debate about strategic doctrine." Cf. Best and Donatelli February
      1987 articles, cited below.)

Martin, Ben L. "Has There Been a Reagan Revaluation in Defense Policy?" *World Affairs*
      (Winter 1985–1986): 173–182, especially 175–176. (Sees Maritime Strategy as the ba-
      sis for horizontal escalation doctrine, and both important only as U.S. Navy budget
      rationales. "The idea of horizontal escalation itself is too inherently implausible to
      find an enduring place in American strategic doctrine.")

II. The Maritime Strategy Debate: 1986, the Watershed Year

In late 1985, Secretary of the Navy John F. Lehman, Adm. James D. Watkins, and Gen. P.
X. Kelley—having ensured that *The Maritime Strategy* met their requirements and represented both their thinking and that of their superiors—submitted manuscripts containing the strategy's basic tenets, less its uncertainties and limitations, to the Naval
Institute. Following the publication of *The Maritime Strategy,* a special supplement to
the January 1986 *Proceedings,* public discussion of the strategy took on a new, sophisticated tone, more relevant to the actual requirements of U.S. national security decision
making. Subsequent statements by President Ronald Reagan, Secretary of Defense
Caspar Weinberger, and others confirmed for the public that the strategy was consistent with higher civilian and military defense guidance.

In the United States and abroad, discussions ranging from global warfare with the Soviets to naval history, fleet balance, and peacetime and crisis operations became

suffused with the vocabulary and concepts of *The Maritime Strategy*. Much of the writing was now done by senior military officers. Most notably, a spate of broad-gauged articles by naval aviation, surface, and submarine warfare specialists appeared, transcending narrow "unionism." Knowledgeable civilian strategic thinkers and historians also offered their cogent commentary on the strategy.

Proceedings now served as the primary forum, along with the *Naval War College Review, Sea Power*, and *Naval Forces*. The arena, however, also broadened to include more newspapers and popular magazines. The public affairs and national security journals rediscovered *The Maritime Strategy*, but now in a manner that brought together not only academics, pundits, and military retirees but also serving naval professionals. By 1987, the uniformed naval officer corps once again—as in the days of Alfred Thayer Mahan or the pre–World War II War Plan Orange—had captured the high ground and catalyzed thinking about the Navy's role in national and alliance strategy.

*/** Watkins, Adm. James D. "*The Maritime Strategy*"; Gen. P. X. Kelley and Maj. Hugh O'Donnell. "Amphibious Warfare Strategy"; and John P. Lehman, Jr. "The 600-Ship Navy." *Proceedings, The Maritime Strategy* supplement (January 1986). Also Col. John Collins, USA (Ret.), in "Comment and Discussion" (February 1986): 26–28; (March 1986): 18–21, raises twenty questions; (May 1986): 25; (June 1986): 83, questions nuclear aspects of the strategy; and Rear Adm. William Pendley: 84–89, answers Collins's questions and elaborates on the strategy; (July 1986): 24–27, posits significant Soviet forward submarine operations; (August 1986): 10, still more questions from the insatiable Col. Collins; (January 1987): 25–30, argues for new role for PHMs in *The Maritime Strategy*; and (April 1987): 22–27, another response to Colonel Collins by the indefatigable Rear Admiral Pendley.

** Gordon, Michael R. "Officials Say Navy Might Attack Soviet A-Arms in Nonnuclear War." *New York Times* (7 January 1986): 1. See also (*New York) Daily News* (8 January 1986): C-10; *Oregonian* (9 January 1986): C10; *Los Angeles Times* (10 January 1986): 4; *Boston Globe* (11 January 1986); *New York Times* (12 January 1986): E-1; and *The Times* (London) (26 February 1986). (Initial press comment on publication of "*The Maritime Strategy*" by the Naval Institute. Ignores all strategy issues except the anti-SSBN operations debate.)

*/** Jervell, Sverre, and Kare Nyblom, eds. *The Military Buildup in the High North: American and Nordic Perspectives*. Lanham, Md.: University Press of America, 1986. (1985 Harvard conference. Eliot Cohen, Robert Weinland, Barry Posen, Vice Adm. Henry Mustin, and a number of distinguished British and Nordic officials, military officers, and thinkers debate *The Maritime Strategy* and much else.)

**   Train, Adm. Harry, USN (Ret.). "Seapower and Projection Forces." In *American Defense Annual 1986–1987*. Lexington, Mass.: Lexington Books, 1986, 128–129. (This former Sixth Fleet and Atlantic theater commander updates his views on *The Maritime Strategy*. Book also contains routine arguments by Ambassador Komer. More detailed— and controversial—views by Admiral Train can be found in James L. George, ed. *The Soviet and Other Communist Navies: The View from the Mid-1980s.* Annapolis, Md.: Naval Institute Press, 1986, 283–287.)

Hughes, Capt. Wayne P., Jr., USN (Ret.). *Fleet Tactics: Theory and Practice.* Annapolis, Md.: Naval Institute Press, 1986. (By a Naval Postgraduate School faculty member. Shot through with important insights on naval strategy and its relationship to tactics. See especially chapter 1 on the relationship between war at sea and war ashore, and chapter 9 on the relationship between peacetime and wartime naval missions.)

Connell, John. *The New Maginot Line.* New York: Arbor House, 1986, 71–81. (Another journalist—this time British—for whom the strategy debate is largely between Secretary Lehman and Ambassador Komer, and solely driven by budgetary considerations. Arguments totally derivative from other journalists. It would have been news four years earlier.)

Archer, Clive, and David Scrivener, eds. *Northern Waters: Security and Resource Issues.* Totowa, N.J.: Barnes and Noble, 1986. (A series of survey papers focusing on the Norwegian Sea. See especially Geoffrey Till on strategy, David Hobbs on military technology, and Steven Miller on Reagan administration strategy. The Miller piece is essentially an update of his 1983 paper cited in section I above.)

Oliver, James K., and James A. Nathan. "Concepts, Continuity, and Change." In *The Reagan Defense Program: An Interim Assessment*, edited by Stephen Cimbala. Wilmington, Del: Scholarly Resources, 1986, 1–22. (Sees Reagan administration naval strategy and force planning as derived essentially from concepts and goals developed by the Navy in the late 1970s.)

Brzezinski, Zbigniew. *Game Plan: The Geostrategic Framework for the Conduct of the U.S.–Soviet Contest.* Boston: Atlantic Monthly Press, 1986. (Views role of the Navy as one of "Sea Control" and projecting American power into "distant local conflicts," rather than carrier strikes on "Soviet home ports" or "strategic nuclear warfare." See 183–184, 191–192.)

Clancy, Tom. *Red Storm Rising.* New York: Putnam, 1986. (Fiction. Wartime Maritime Strategy implemented under drastically changed assumptions, some plausible and some fanciful, to suit the storyteller's needs. Soviet fear of global forward pressure leads to preemptive seizure of Iceland, SSN surge to the Atlantic, but operations are somehow limited to Central and Northern Europe. Inherent flexibility and lethality enables NATO navies to adapt rapidly and successfully, but with heavy losses. In this vein, see reviews by Capt. David G. Clark in *Naval War College Review* [Winter 1987]: 139–141, and Adm. Thomas B. Hayward, USN [Ret.] in *Proceedings* [March 1987]: 164. Cf. Hackett and McGeoch et al., *The Third World War: The Untold Story,* cited in section V below; and Hayes et al., *American Lake,* below, chapter 19, which addresses the Pacific in a hypothetical global war, although probably not in a manner with which Captain Clark or Admiral Hayward would agree.)

** Hayes, Peter, Lyuba Zarsky, and Walden Bello. *American Lake: Nuclear Peril in the Pacific.* New York: Penguin, 1986. (Thorough and extensive analysis of *The Maritime Strategy* and much else, but in a shrill, leftist, Australian context. See especially chapters 8 and 16, and chapter 19, a fictional scenario. They understand that "what appeared a mere budget battle was in fact a conflict over military strategy.")

Daniel, Donald C. *Anti-Submarine Warfare and Superpower Strategic Stability.* Champagne: University of Illinois Press, 1986. (An excellent survey by a Naval War College faculty member, concludes that "it seem[s] implausible the U.S. could so reduce the number of Soviet SSBNs that the USSR might be pushed into using the remainder." See especially 151–157.)

** West, Francis J., Jr., et al. *Naval Forces and Western Security.* Washington, D.C.: Pergamon-Brassey's, 1986. (Contains two essays: "U.S. Naval Forces and NATO Planning," by West: 1–9; and "NATO's Maritime Defenses," by Jacquelyn K. Davis, James E. Dougherty, Rear Adm. Robert J. Hanks, USN [Ret.], and Charles M. Perry: 10–53. West restates his 1985 *Proceedings* article assertion that there is a profound divergence between U.S. and West European perspectives on the purpose and potential contribution of naval forces in NATO contingency planning, although it is sometimes difficult to understand which Americans and Europeans he is talking about. The other essay offers an overview of current issues regarding the role of naval forces in NATO strategy.)

Kaufmann, William W. *A Reasonable Defense.* Washington, D.C.: Brookings Institution, 1986, especially 72–92. (Kaufmann's annual attack on his own highly personal interpretation of *The Maritime Strategy,* ceding the Mediterranean totally to indigenous allied naval forces but sailing a major fleet into the Indian Ocean. Unlike *The Maritime Strategy,* solely aimed at influencing legislative budgetary decisions.)

Cohen, Eliot A. "Do We Still Need Europe?" *Commentary* (January 1986): 28–35. (A Naval War College faculty member views NATO flanks and the Far East as of increasing importance; sees little utility in discussions of stark strategic alternatives, e.g., "Europe vs. the Pacific, going it alone vs. having allies, keeping resolutely to the sea vs. preparing to engage the Red Army on the continent.")

** "OCEAN SAFARI '85: Meeting the Threat in the North Atlantic." *All Hands* (January 1986): 20–29. (Publicizes close-in convoy defense, coastal defense, and mine countermeasures aspects of the strategy, as well as strike warfare and tactical innovations.)

** Gray, Colin. "Maritime Strategy." *Proceedings* (February 1986): 34–42. (Supportive commentary by a top-ranking civilian geopolitician and strategist. Especially helpful in untangling arguments regarding "horizontal escalation.")

* "Message to Moscow: 'Be My Guest'—The Navy." *Newsweek* (3 February 1986): 16–17. (Vice Adm. Henry C. Mustin on U.S. Second Fleet implementation of *The Maritime Strategy*.)

* U.S. Senate. Committee on Armed Services. *Hearings on the Department of Defense Authorization for Appropriations for Fiscal Year 1987: Part 1.* 99th Cong., 2nd sess., 5 February 1986, 82–83. (The Secretary of Defense and the Chairman of the Joint Chiefs of Staff testify on the budget and in response to questioning from Senator Nunn on anti-SSBN operations. A key Maritime Strategy element enunciated by the highest Defense Department officials. See also George C. Wilson and Michael Weisskopf, "Pentagon Plan Coldly Received." *Washington Post* [6 February 1986]: A14; Caspar Weinberger, "U.S. Defense Strategy." *Foreign Affairs* [Spring 1986]: 695; and Walter Andrews, "Weinberger Warns of 'Hollow Strategy.'" *Washington Times* [30 July 1986]: 4.)

* Lehman, John F. "The U.S. Secretary of the Navy: Towards the 600-Ship Fleet." *Naval Forces,* no. 1 (1986): 14–23. (Update of Lehman's thought.)

* "Surface Warfare: What Does the Future Hold?" Annapolis, Md.: U.S. Naval Institute Professional Seminar Series Transcript (12 February 1986): 19–20. (Rear Adm. Dennis Brooks, ComCarGru 7, on *The Maritime Strategy*. Another admiral whom Stansfield Turner never met.)

* U.S. House of Representatives. Committee on Appropriations. *Hearings on the Department of Defense Appropriations for 1987: Part 1.* 99th Cong., 2nd sess., 26 February 1986, 500–504 and 547–550. (Admiral Watkins and Secretary Lehman respond to congressional questioning by Rep. Les AuCoin on *The Maritime Strategy*. "The decision to go after an SSBN in time of conflict would be a Presidential decision.")

* Watkins, Adm. James D. "Power Projection—Maritime Forces Making a Strategic Difference." *NATO's Sixteen Nations* (February–March 1986): 102–106. (CNO discusses Maritime Strategy within a NATO context. N.B; this annual special issue contains articles signed by most of NATO's naval chiefs.)

**   Lapham, Lewis H. "Notebook: Pictures at an Exhibition." *Harper's* (March 1986): 8–9. (A bizarre, overwritten exposition on *The Maritime Strategy* as propaganda and the U.S. Navy as incompetent.)

**   Ausland, John. "The Silence on Naval Nuclear Arms Should Be Broken." *International Herald Tribune* (12 March 1986): 25. (A critical look at naval theater nuclear weapons and warfare and *The Maritime Strategy*.)

**   Reed, Fred. "Soldiering: Navy's Sensitivity Works against It." *Washington Times* (27 March 1986): 2. (Criticizes U.S. Navy explanations of the strategy as lacking in "strategic substance," a rather ironic criticism given the author's own arguments.)

*   Mustin, Vice Adm. Henry C. "The Role of the Navy and Marines in the Norwegian Sea." *Naval War College Review* (March–April 1986): 2–6. (The NATO Striking Fleet Atlantic commander on U.S. and NATO Maritime Strategy in the Norwegian Sea. See also "In My View," *Naval War College Review* [Autumn 1986]: 101–102.)

         Landersman, Capt. S. D., USN (Ret.). "Naval Protection of Shipping: A Lost Art?" *Naval War College Review* (March–April 1986): 23–34. (By a member of the initial U.S. Navy Strategic Studies Group at Newport. Excellent critique of U.S. Navy attitudes and practices regarding Naval Control of Shipping [NCS] as well as Naval Protection of Shipping [NPS], essential but too-little-discussed aspects of *The Maritime Strategy* that are often overshadowed by discussion of concomitant forward operations. See also his "I am a . . . Convoy Commodore," *Proceedings* [June 1986]: 56–63.)

         Kennedy, Col. William V., USAR (Ret.). "New NE Asian Geography?" *Naval War College Review* (March–April 1986): 91–92. (An extreme view of the role of Pacific operations. Calls for North Pacific Maritime Strategy to split the Soviet Far East from the rest of the country at the Urals.)

**   Doerr, Capt. P. J. "CWC Revisited." *Proceedings* (April 1986): 39–43. (Organizing the battle force to implement *The Maritime Strategy*. Contrast with Captain Powers's October 1985 *Proceedings* views.)

**   Watkins, Adm. James D. "Laurels, Accomplishments, and Violent Peace." *Sea Power* (April 1986): 6–20, especially 9–10 on the rationale for publishing *The Maritime Strategy*.

*   Kelley, Gen. P. X. "The United States Marine Corps Today." *Sea Power* (April 1986): 82–97. (See especially 83–86 for an overview of *The Maritime Strategy* from the Commandant of the Marine Corps perspective.)

         Bagley, Adm. Worth H., USN (Ret.). "U.S. Military Power in the Pacific: Problems and Prospects." In *National Security in Northeast Asia,* edited by International Security

Council. New York: CAUSA, April 13–15, 1986. (Reverses the usual argument by treating NATO as a "second front threat" diverting the Soviets from the Far East.)

Liska, George. "From Containment to Concert." *Foreign Policy* (Spring 1986): 3–23 and "Concert through Decompression" (Summer 1986): 108–129. (U.S.-Soviet rivalry seen as "fed primarily by its own momentum and, at bottom, by the timeless asymmetry between land and sea powers." Argues, however, for a "land-sea power concert" by the two. "The salience of sea-over land-based power has diminished as the principal maritime power finds it increasingly difficult to maintain clear naval superiority.")

**   "The United States Navy: On the Crest of the Wave." *The Economist* (19 April 1986): 49–65. (Strategy and programs.)

**   Hart, Senator Gary, with William S. Lind. *America Can Win: The Case for Military Reform.* Bethesda, Md.: Adler and Adler, 1986, 77–81. (Criticizes *The Maritime Strategy* for its linkages to the land war in Europe, its early forward focus, and its relationship to current force structure. Major concern, however, seems to be with the semantics of the term "Maritime Strategy.")

**   Ausland, John C. *Nordic Security and the Great Powers.* Boulder, Colo.: Westview, 1986. (Comprehensive and detailed treatment of *The Maritime Strategy* in peace and war within the overall context of Nordic military security. See especially chapter 20, "The Battle for the Norwegian Sea," the author's "climax.")

*   Hughes, Vice Adm. Thomas J., Jr. "Logistics Became Legitimate." *Sea Power* (May 1986): 17–24, especially 22. (By the Deputy Chief of Naval Operations for Logistics. "The logistics of the Navy are matched to our maritime strategy.")

**   Ullman, Cdr. Harlan K., USN (Ret.). "Precept for Tomorrow: A Busy Agenda Awaits the Next CNO." *Sea Power* (May 1986): 48–51. (Sees a need for the new Chief of Naval Operations to examine the future maritime environment as well as the reactions of U.S. and foreign political and military leaders to *The Maritime Strategy*.)

**   Wettern, Desmond. "Maritime Strategy: Change or Decay." *Navy International* (May 1986): 304–308. (Endorsement of *The Maritime Strategy* by a prominent British naval affairs writer. Questions, however, whether SLOC interdiction remains as low a Soviet priority under Admiral Chernavin as it did under Admiral Gorshkov.)

**   "Bridge over Troubled Waters." *Defense and Foreign Affairs* (May 1986): 38–39. (On the U.S. Navy's efforts to link technology and weapons acquisition to *The Maritime Strategy*.)

"Sailing the Cold Seas." *Surface Warfare* (May–June 1986): 6–8. (On the steps being examined and taken to increase U.S. Navy ability to operate in northern latitudes as required by *The Maritime Strategy*.)

Williams, Cdr. E. Cameron, USNR. "The Four 'Iron Laws' of Naval Protection of Merchant Shipping." *Naval War College Review* (May–June 1986): 35–42. (An argument for convoying. Sees SLOC protection debate as between conveying and "sanitized lanes." Oblivious, however, to the debate between either or both of these options and forward defense, the more topical issue.) See also "In My View," *Naval War College Review* (Autumn 1986): 108–109 and (Spring 1987): 91–92.

* Pendley, Rear Adm. William. "Comment and Discussion: *The Maritime Strategy*." *Proceedings* (June 1986): 84–89. (This ostensible response to an earlier "Comment and Discussion" item is actually an important official amplification of *The Maritime Strategy* by the 1985–1986 Director of Strategy, Plans, and Policy [OP-60], the Navy's principal global strategist.)

** Mather, Ian. "NATO Row over Boundary Shift." *Sunday London Observer,* 16 June 1986. (Sees Secretary of Defense Weinberger's call for an expanded NATO reach beyond Europe as derived from *The Maritime Strategy*.)

*/** Samuel, Peter. "State Dept., Navy Agree on Opening Pacific Front in Case of War in Europe." *New York City Tribune* (23 June 1986): 1. (State Department's Director of Policy Planning espouses views congruent with *The Maritime Strategy,* especially regarding global nature of war with the Soviet Union and early antisubmarine operations.) For an updated version of these views, see Solomon 1987 article cited below. See also Paul Bedard, "Pacific Waters Boil with American and Soviet Warships." *Defense Week* (23 June 1986): 1; and Frank Elliott, "U.S. Looks to Pacific Fleet to Help Europe" and "Soviet Power Grows." *Navy Times* (7 July 1986): 29 and 32.

** Epstein, Joshua M. *The 1987 Defense Budget.* Washington, D.C.: Brookings Institution, 1986. (Brookings's annual attack on *The Maritime Strategy*. Pages 13, 41–45, and 55–58 reject *The Maritime Strategy* as "inefficient and potentially escalatory" and recommend U.S. Navy force posture cuts accordingly. Sees defense of Norway as not requiring significant U.S. naval forces. Arguments derived from Kaufmann, Komer, Posen, and the Congressional Budget Office. Unlike *The Maritime Strategy*, a purely budget-driven document.)

** Gray, Colin S. "Keeping the Soviets Landlocked: Geostrategy for a Maritime America." *The National Interest* (Summer 1986): 24–36. (Masterful discussion of the relationships between geopolitics and *The Maritime Strategy*.)

**   Wood, Robert S., and John T. Hanley, Jr. "The Maritime Role in the North Atlantic." *Atlantic Community Quarterly* (Summer 1986): 133–144. (Latest incarnation of this oft-reprinted article by two Naval War College faculty members.)

**   Polmar, Norman. "The Soviet Navy: Nuclear War at Sea." *Proceedings* (July 1966): 111–113. See also "Comment and Discussion," *Proceedings* (September 1986): 90. ("*The Maritime Strategy* must be challenged for its lack of definition in how we are to deter nuclear war at sea.")

**   *Defense Choices: Greater Security with Fewer Dollars.* Washington, D.C.: Committee for National Security, 1986. (The committee's annual attack on *The Maritime Strategy* and the 600-ship Navy. "There is no need to ask the U.S. Fleet to take on high risk missions close to Soviet shores." Advocates a "return to a more sensible naval strategy." Unlike *The Maritime Strategy*, a purely budget-driven document. This study achieved a certain notoriety due to its endorsement by Dr. Larry Korb, a former Reagan administration defense official and earlier advocate of a 600-ship Navy.)

**   Stefanick, Tom. "Attacking the Soviet Sea Based Deterrent: Clever Feint or Foolhardy Maneuver?" *F.A.S. Public Interest Report* (June–July 1986): 1–10. (The author seems to lean more to the "foolhardy maneuver" persuasion. "The U.S. must reduce the current emphasis on submarine operations in waters heavily defended by the Soviet Union." But cf. his December article, below.)

**   Truver, Scott C. "Can We Afford the 15-Carrier Battle Group Navy?" *Armed Forces Journal International* (July 1986): 74–81. (On the relationship between *The Maritime Strategy* and carrier force levels.)

O'Rourke, Ronald. "Tomahawk: The U.S. Navy's New Option." *Navy International* (July 1986): 394–398. (Good coverage of the benefits and problems associated with integrating sea-launched cruise missiles into *The Maritime Strategy*.)

Ryan, Capt. T. D. "SubDevRon Twelve: In the Global War Games." *Submarine Review* (July 1986): 39–40. (Good examples of uses of Naval War College Global War Games to test *The Maritime Strategy* and to identify problems needing new technological and tactical solutions.)

**   Winkler, Philippa. "A Dangerous Shift in Naval Strategy." *Oakland Tribune* (7 July 1986). (Decries the Navy's "forward offensive strategy" for going "beyond legitimate defense purposes.")

Canby, Steven L. "South Korea's Defense Requires U.S. Air Power, Not Troops." *Wall Street Journal* (17 July 1986): 24. (Sees limited utility of Pacific Fleet carriers in a war with the Soviets. Advocates naval force level cuts.)

**   O'Shea, James. "U.S. to Sink Billions into New Attack Sub." *Chicago Tribune* (20 July 1986): 1. (On the role of the SSN-21 Seawolf in the future Maritime Strategy.)

Smith, Lee. "How the Pentagon Can Live on Less." *Fortune* (21 July 1986): 78–85. (See especially page 87. *Fortune* and ex–Reagan administration official Richard DeLauer oppose as misguided the "Lehman developed" "forward strategy," construed as carrier strikes on Murmansk, Vladivostok, and Petropavlovsk. For more on DeLauer's negative views, see "Interview: Richard DeLauer on Defense," *Technology Review* [July 1986]: 58–67.)

*/**   "Maritime Strategy Seminar." *Proceedings* (August 1986): 8–10. (Former SacLant/ CincLant Adm. Wesley McDonald, former Undersecretary of Defense Robert Komer, former Assistant Secretary of Defense Bing West, and then–U.S. Second Fleet/NATO Striking Fleet Atlantic commander Vice Adm. Henry Mustin debate *The Maritime Strategy*. For more details, see the excellent *Maritime Strategy Seminar Transcript*. Annapolis, Md.: U.S. Naval Institute, 1986.)

**   Polmar, Norman. "600 Ships: Plus or Minus?" *Proceedings* (August 1986): 107–108. (The author's views on the relationship between the strategy and the 600-ship Navy force level goals. "While some would argue with specific components of both the strategy and the ships that Lehman seeks, it is a coherent and long-term plan . . . one that Congress has long demanded from the Navy and the other services.")

**   Parry, Dan. "U.S. Navy's Role in Space." *Navy International* (August 1986): 477. (Quotes Deputy Assistant Secretary of the Navy for C3 and Space Ann Berman on the role of space in *The Maritime Strategy*.)

**   Hinge, Lt. A., RAN. "The Strategic Balance in the Asia-Pacific Region: Naval Aspects." *Journal of the Australian Naval Institute* (August 1986): 31–50. (Poses important questions regarding USN force posture requirements in each oceanic theater and potential naval roles of Pacific allies, China and ASEAN. Very sanguine regarding Western maritime superiority in the Pacific.)

"Rust to Riches: The Navy Is Back." *U.S. News and World Report* (4 August 1986): 28-37. (Secretary of the Navy John Lehman's influence on naval strategy seen as paramount.)

Isherwood, Julien. "Russia Warns Oslo on U.S. Base." *Daily Telegraph* (13 August 1986). (Cites major Soviet propaganda offensive against forward battle group operations in the Norwegian Sea, "the so-called Lehman Doctrine.")

"Aircraft Carriers Use Technology"; "Speed to Stage Vanishing Acts on High Seas." *Baltimore Sun* (17 August 1986): 16. (Discusses U.S. Navy countermeasures to Soviet intelligence and targeting at sea, a key element in carrying out *The Maritime Strategy*.)

Bunting, Glenn F. "Navy Warms Up to Idea of Presence in Cold Bering Sea." *Los Angeles Times* (31 August 1986): 3. (Maritime Strategy as reflected in increased U.S. Navy peacetime North Pacific presence.)

* Demars, Vice Adm. Bruce. "The U.S. Submarine Force." *Naval Forces,* no. 4 (1986): 18–30; and "Speech at the Submarine Symposium, Lima, Peru." *Submarine Review* (January 1987): 5–12. (By the Deputy Chief of Naval Operations for Submarine Warfare. See especially 20–21 of the former and 8–11 of the latter on the role of U.S. and allied submarines in *The Maritime Strategy*: "We dare not go it alone.")

** Drury, F. "Naval Strike Warfare and the Outer Air Battle." *Naval Forces,* no. 4 (1986): 46–52. (Sees *The Maritime Strategy* as merging the two concepts, which he feels had grown apart, into one coherent plan to defeat the Soviet air threat.)

** Tellis, Ashley J. "The Soviet Navy, Central America and the Atlantic Alliance." *Naval Forces,* no. 4 (1986): 54–60. (Endorses *The Maritime Strategy* for its geopolitical logic, especially regarding forward operations.)

* Cropsey, Seth. "Forward Defense or Maginot Line? The Maritime Strategy and Its Alternatives." *Policy Review* (Fall 1986): 40–46. (An excellent restatement of the Navy's arguments by the Deputy Under Secretary of the Navy for Policy. Particularly useful on the historical background of *The Maritime Strategy*.)

* Mustin, Vice Adm. Henry C. "Maritime Strategy from the Deckplates." *Proceedings* (September 1986): 33–37. (U.S. Navy Second Fleet/NATO Striking Fleet Atlantic commander's positive views on the utility of *The Maritime Strategy* to an operational commander. See also "Comment and Discussion" [November 1986]: 14.)

Hampton, Lt. Cdr. J. P. "Integrated Air Defense for NATO." *Proceedings* (September 1986): 114–116. (On integrating U.S. Navy carrier battle groups with U.S. and allied air force aircraft to counter the Soviet air threat on the NATO Southern Front: an essential component of *The Maritime Strategy* too often overshadowed in the public debate by discussion of the Northwest Pacific and especially the Norwegian Sea.)

** Wood, Robert S. "Maritime Strategy for War in the North." *Journal of Defense and Diplomacy* (September 1986): 17–20. (Development of this Naval War College faculty member/strategist's thought. Stress on combined arms.)

** Fouquet, David. "NATO Soldiers March into Autumn, Testing Tactics, Equipment, Systems." *Defense News* (15 September 1986): 14. (The Allies test *The Maritime Strategy* on the Northern Front.)

* Lehman, Hon. John F., Jr. *Maritime Strategy in the Defense of NATO.* Washington, D.C.: CSIS, 25 September 1986. (His 1986 views: "No maritime strategy can be a successful strategy without an effective land deterrent on the continent of Europe." "The forward strategy, articulated by the Reagan administration, is in fact orthodoxy of the oldest sort, conforming precisely to NATO alliance doctrine." "In summary we have a maritime strategy in the defense of NATO that is universally accepted by the maritime forces of Europe and the United States.")

** Gray, Colin S. *Maritime Strategy, Geopolitics, and the Defense of the West.* New York: National Strategy Information Center, 1986. (An extension of his classic 1977 work on geopolitics, focusing on implications for U.S. national military strategy. The footnotes include some excellent rebuttals to the arguments of Ambassador Komer. A new classic.)

Mearsheimer, John. "A Strategic Misstep: *The Maritime Strategy* and Deterrence in Europe." *International Security* (Fall 1986): 3–57. (Despite its biases, distortions, and misleading discussions of the development of *The Maritime Strategy* over time, probably the most important piece of writing critical of the strategy to date. Faults *The Maritime Strategy* for its too "elastic quality," actually regarded by U.S. naval officers as one of its great deterrent and warfighting strengths. This West Point graduate and former U.S. Air Force officer's bottom line: "The key to deterrence is not the Navy, but the forces that will be fighting on the Central Front. Those forces should be given first priority when deciding how to allocate defense budgets.")

** Brooks, Capt. Linton. "Naval Power and National Security: The Case for *The Maritime Strategy.*" *International Security* (Fall 1986): 58–87. (One of the strategy's contributors definitively expands on its basic elements and on its rationale. Especially useful in discussing the rationale for anti-SSBN operations and the strategy's inherent uncertainties, integral aspects of *The Maritime Strategy* often slighted in public official U.S. Navy discussions.)

* Schoultz, Vice Adm. Robert F. "Strikefleet: Cost-Effective Power." *Armed Forces* (October 1986): 446–448. (Deputy Commander in Chief, U.S. Naval Forces Europe and former Deputy Chief of Naval Operations for Air Warfare on the role of the Carrier Battle Group in *The Maritime Strategy.*)

** Winnefeld, Lt. James A., Jr. "Topgun: Getting It Right." *Proceedings* (October 1986): 141–146. (The Navy Fighter Weapons School seen as a key contributor to *The Maritime Strategy*'s execution, by the school's training officer, one of the new generation of naval officers for whom *The Maritime Strategy* was truly the cornerstone of the profession.)

* Weinberger, Caspar. "The Spirit and Meaning of the USS *Theodore Roosevelt.*" *Defense Issues* 1, no. 76 (24 November 1986). (*The Maritime Strategy* as a component of

national military strategy, by the Secretary of Defense. "The greatest value of President Reagan's maritime strategy is that it focuses on the crucial issue of how we can best use our maritime forces and those of our allies to achieve the basic goal of deterrence—and deny the adversary his preferred warfighting strategy.") Summarized in George Wilson. "USS *Theodore Roosevelt* Joins Active Service as 15th Carrier." *Washington Post* (26 October 1986): A21; and William Matthews, "Carrier *Theodore Roosevelt* 'Charges' to Life." *Navy Times* (10 November 1986): 33, 37.

** "U.S. Maritime Strategy for the 1980s." *Security Digest* (November 1986), published by the Wilson Center. (Capt. Linton Brooks and Prof. John Mearsheimer debate *The Maritime Strategy*.)

** Morring, Frank, Jr. "Navy Chief: 'Forward Defense' Doesn't Mean Kamakazi Missions." *Nashua (N.H.) Telegraph,* 26 November 1986. (First reported public discussion of *The Maritime Strategy* by the new CNO, Adm. Carlisle Trost, with a critique by Brookings Institution researcher Joshua Epstein.)

** Friedman, Norman. "U.S. Strategy and ASW." *Jane's Defense Weekly* (29 November 1986): 1269–1277. (An update of Dr. Friedman's thought on *The Maritime Strategy*, ASW, and the SSN-21.)

*/** "The Future Mix of Subs and Strategy." *Proceedings* (December 1986): 11–12. (The director of U.S. Navy Attack Submarine Programs, the Naval War College Professor of Submarine Warfare, and two noted civilian naval analysts debate the role of the U.S. submarine force in *The Maritime Strategy*. For more than this brief summary, see "The Future Mix of Subs and Strategy." Annapolis, Md.: U.S. Naval Institute Professional Seminar Series, 25 September 1986.)

** O'Neil, Capt. W. D., USNR. "Executing *The Maritime Strategy*." *Proceedings* (December 1986): 39–41. (Recommends measures that the U.S. Navy must take to ensure the continued executability of *The Maritime Strategy* by keeping the Soviets on the defensive and improving defense penetration and strike effectiveness.)

** Stefanick, Tom A. "America's Maritime Strategy—The Arms Control Implications." *Arms Control Today* (December 1986): 10–17. (Appears to favor *The Maritime Strategy* more than he did in July. "The implicit threat to Soviet ballistic missile submarines during a conventional naval conflict would be likely to yield an advantage to the U.S. Navy in the conventional balance at sea. . . . The likelihood of widespread escalation of the use of nuclear weapons as a direct result of threats or even attacks on Soviet SSBNs in their home waters appears to be low.")

** "Dossier: U.S. Report." *Naval Forces,* no. 6 (1986): 132. (Alleges there is current "indecision about what a U.S. maritime strategy should comprise." A remarkable piece of reportage for October 1986. There's always 10 percent who do not get the word.)

* Matthews, William. "Marines Would Storm by Air, Not Sea if NATO Attacked." *Navy Times* (1 December 1986). (Despite the misleading headline, a generally accurate rendering of the views of the principal Marine Corps global strategist, Brig. Gen. Michael Sheridan, on the role of the Marines in North Norway, as part of *The Maritime Strategy.*)

** Halloran, Richard. "A Silent Battle Surfaces." *New York Times Magazine* (7 December 1986): 60, 94–97. (On the antisubmarine warfare component of *The Maritime Strategy.*)

** Elliott, Frank. "Exon Says Maritime Plan Could Trigger War." *Defense Week* (8 December 1986): 16. (Senator Exon opposes the anti-SSBN aspects of *The Maritime Strategy.* "There are good elements in that strategy, but much of it concerns me.")

Greeley, Brendan M., Jr. "Third Fleet Increases North Pacific Operations to Counter Soviet Activity." *Aviation Week and Space Technology* (22 December 1986): 28–29. (On Vice Adm. Diego Hernandez and the Third Fleet North Pacific buildup, especially joint and allied coordination.)

* "U.S. Navy Appears to Expand Operation in Pacific Ocean." *Jane's Defense Weekly* (27 December 1986): 1474–1475. (Interview with Vice Admiral Hernandez on new peacetime measures to more successfully deter war or—should deterrence fail—conduct wartime operations in the North Pacific in accordance with *The Maritime Strategy.*)

III. The Debate Continues: 1987 and Beyond

The first half of 1987 saw *The Maritime Strategy* firmly in place as an acknowledged vital element of U.S. and allied military strategy. President Reagan, Defense Secretary Weinberger, Deputy Defense Secretary Taft, and Chairman of the Joint Chiefs of Staff William Crowe all publicly cited its importance and utility. Likewise, James H. Webb, Jr. (John Lehman's successor as Secretary of the Navy), Adm. Carlisle Trost (Admiral Watkins's successor as CNO), and a number of other top flag officers provided numerous examples of the extent to which it had become the common strategic framework of the naval leadership. Perhaps the best illustration of this phenomenon was, however, the July 1987 issue of the *Proceedings.* Therein, *The Maritime Strategy* formed the baseline for a wide range of discussions of specific U.S. and allied peacekeeping and warfighting issues: by active duty U.S. Navy junior officers, senior officers, and admirals; by naval aviators, surface warfare officers, submariners, and a Marine; and by officers concerned with inter-allied relations, regional strategic objectives, fleet operations, and weapons system employment and development.

The second half of 1987 and 1988 promise to add yet another dimension to the discussions: a number of book-length treatments of *The Maritime Strategy* and related subjects are scheduled for publication. That the 1980s saw a long-needed burgeoning of naval strategic thought, both in the United States and abroad, has become indisputable. What remained to be seen was what use future generations of planners, policy makers, and thinkers would make of this outpouring.

* Reagan, President Ronald. *National Security Strategy of the United States.* Washington, D.C.: The White House, January 1987. (The framework within which *The Maritime Strategy* operated. Clear focus on global, forward, coalition approach, especially vs. the Soviets. See especially 19: "U.S. military forces must possess the capability, should deterrence fail, to expand the scope and intensity of combat operations, as necessary"; and 27–30: "Maritime superiority is vital. [It] enables us to capitalize on Soviet geographic vulnerabilities and to pose a global threat to the Soviets' interests. It plays a key role in plans for the defense of NATO allies on the European flanks. It also permits the United States to tie down Soviet naval forces in a defensive posture protecting Soviet ballistic missile submarines and the seaward approaches to the Soviet homeland.")

* Weinberger, Caspar W. *Report of the Secretary of Defense to the Congress on the FY 1988/ FY 1989 Budget and FY 1988–92 Defense Programs.* Washington, D.C.: U.S. Government Printing Office, 1987, 165. (Reconfirms *The Maritime Strategy* as a component of declared U.S. national military strategy.) See also Ed Offley and S. L. Sanger, "Backing at Top for Home Port." *Seattle Post-Intelligencer* (28 April 1987): 1. (SecDef, in Seattle, "agrees with the Navy's controversial wartime strategy." SecDef direction and endorsement is no flash in the pan.)

* Crowe, Adm. William J. "Statement on National Security Strategy." U.S. Senate. Committee on Armed Services. *Hearings on National Security Strategy.* 100th Cong., 1st sess., 21 January 1987. (Solid concurrence in *The Maritime Strategy* by the Chairman of the Joint Chiefs of Staff: "In recent years we have benefited from some excellent conceptual thinking by the Navy about global maritime strategy—how to phase operations in a transition from peace to war, clear the way of submarines opposing military resupply or reinforcement shipping, and use our carrier battle groups for either offensive strikes or in direct support of such allies as Japan, Norway, Greece, and Turkey. It is imperative, of course, to fold these concepts into our larger military strategy and that is exactly what we are doing.")

*   Trost, Adm. Carlisle. "Looking beyond *The Maritime Strategy.*" *Proceedings* (January 1987): 13–16. Also "Comment and Discussion" (July 1987): 19–20. (Admiral Watkins's successor as CNO briefly reaffirms *The Maritime Strategy*'s fundamentals: deterrence, forward defense, alliance solidarity, the global view, coexistence with other vital components of our national military strategy, and—most important—flexibility. Highlights antisubmarine warfare in particular.)

*   U.S. Senate. Committee on Armed Services. *Hearings on the Department of Defense Authorization for Appropriations for Fiscal Years 1988 and 1989.* 100th Cong. 1st sess. (Prepared annual "posture" statement by SecDef, CJCS, Secretary of the Navy, CNO, and other officials. Also hearing repartee, and responses to questions for the record. Maritime Strategy permeates the entire Navy budget legislative process. In addition to those just cited, see especially statements by Assistant Secretary of the Navy Melvyn Paisley, CincLantFlt Adm. Frank Kelso, and Deputy Chiefs of Naval Operations for Surface and Air Warfare, Vice Admirals Joseph Metcalf and Robert Dunn.)

*/** U.S. Senate. Committee on Armed Services. *Hearings on National Security Strategy.* 101th Cong., 1st sess., January–April 1987. (Testimony by administration civilian and military officials and by government and nongovernment defense specialists. Includes much discussion of *The Maritime Strategy.* See especially testimony by Adm. Lee Baggett, NATO Supreme Allied Commander Atlantic and Commander in Chief, U.S. Atlantic Command.)

Hendrickson, David C. T*he Future of American Strategy.* New York: Holmes and Meier, 1987. (A new and different perspective. Advocates a scaled-back mix of continental and maritime strategies and forces. Sees some U.S. naval forces particularly useful in Third World contingencies, especially carriers, but he would cut back on naval—and air and ground—forces he sees as only useful for highly unlikely forward global operations against the Soviets. Wrongly believes this includes Aegis cruisers and destroyers.)

**   Brooks, Capt. Linton. "Conflict Termination through Maritime Leverage." In *Conflict Termination and Military Strategy: Coercion, Persuasion, and War,* edited by Steven Cimbala and Keith Dunn. Boulder, Colo.: Westview, 1987, 161–172. (Actually written a year before his 1986 *International Security* article for a 1985 Naval War College conference on war termination.)

**   Kaufmann, William W. *A Thoroughly Efficient Navy.* Washington, D.C.: Brookings Institution, 1987. (The annual Kaufmann broadside, this time designed to influence the congressional votes on carrier construction. See especially chapter 2, "*The Maritime Strategy.*")

** Stefanick, Tom A. *Strategic Anti-Submarine Warfare and Naval Strategy*. Lexington, Mass.: Lexington Books, 1987.

** Luttwak, Edward N. *Strategy*. Cambridge, Mass.: Harvard University Press, 1987, 156–164, and 268. (Cursory discussion of *The Maritime Strategy* as "nonstrategy.")

** Van Cleave, William R. "Horizontal Escalation and NATO Strategy: A Conceptual Overview." In *NATO's Maritime Strategy: Issues and Developments*, edited by E. F Gueritz et al. Washington, D.C.: Pergamon-Brassey's, 1987. (A leading conservative defense thinker argues that "the Navy's version of Horizontal Escalation"—*The Maritime Strategy*—"fails because it does not come to grips with the nuclear factor—indeed, it seems to attempt ignoring it.")

** West, F. J. ("Bing"), Jr. "*The Maritime Strategy*: The Next Step." *Proceedings* (January 1987): 40–49. (By a former Assistant Secretary of Defense, Naval War College faculty member, lead author of *Seaplan 2000*, and U.S. Marine Corps officer. One of the most important analyses of *The Maritime Strategy* by an outside observer to date. Develops further his 1985 and 1986 views, cited in "Contemporary Naval Strategy" and section II above, on the relationships between the strategy and U.S./NATO doctrine. Cf., however, actual statements by allied military leaders in section V below.) See also "Comment and Discussion" (March 1987): 14–15; (July 1987): 19–20; and (August 1987): 31–32.

** Gray, Colin S. "Maritime Strategy and the Pacific: The Implications for NATO." *Naval War College Review* (Winter 1987): 8–19. (A thoughtful, wide-ranging, and often provocative article examining linkages, especially between continental and maritime power, between the European and Pacific theaters, and between strategic and conventional deterrence. The article is notable also for the contributions of Capt. Roger W. Barnett, USN [Ret.], one of the foremost original architects of *The Maritime Strategy*.)

** Solomon, Richard H. "The Pacific Basin: Dilemmas and Choices for American Security." *Naval War College Review* (Winter 1987): 36–43, especially 38–39. (The director of the State Department Policy Planning Staff updates his June 1986 Naval War College Current Strategy Forum lecture: "We must be prepared to open a second front in Asia.")

"From the Editor." *Submarine Review* (January 1987): 3–5. (Challenges some of the basic strategic concepts of *The Maritime Strategy* regarding the employment of SSNs.)

* Connors, Lt. Cdr. Tracy. "Northern Wedding '86." *All Hands* (January 1987): 18–26. See also "Cape Wrath Feels *Iowa*'s Fury"; "Nimitz and Northern Wedding"; and "Alaska" in same issue. (Vice Adm. Charles R. Larson, Commander Striking Fleet Atlantic:

"We went north to test tactics designed to support NATO's maritime strategy of forward defense. I am proud to report those tactics worked.")

** Thomas, Capt. Walter "R," USN (Ret.). "Deterrence, Defense, Two Different Animals." *Navy Times* (26 January 1987): 23. (Critique of John Mearsheimer's Fall 1986 *International Security* article.)

** Keller, Lt. Kenneth C. "The Surface Ship in ASW." *Surface Warfare* (January/February 1997): 2–3. ("Any future ASW conflict, by necessity, will be fought in accordance with *The Maritime Strategy*." Another of the new generation of naval officers gets—and passes—the word.)

** Doerr, Capt. Peter J., USN (Ret.). "Comment and Discussion: Large Carriers: A Matter of Time." *Proceedings* (February 1987): 78. (On the "defense within an offense within a defense" nature of the putative Battle of the Norwegian Sea and, by implication, other potential wartime operations implementing *The Maritime Strategy* globally.)

Tritten, Cdr. James J. "(Non) Nuclear Warfare." *Proceedings* (February 1987): 64–70. (By the chairman of the National Security Affairs Department at the Naval Postgraduate School. On the symbiotic nature of nonnuclear and nuclear warfare, at sea and ashore, under conditions of crisis response, intra-war deterrence, and warfighting.)

** Best, Richard. "Will JCS Reform Endanger *The Maritime Strategy*?" *National Defense* (February 1987): 26–30. ("The passage of JCS reform will provide a future administration with a handle on defense policy that will allow it to override previous strategic conceptions, including the Navy's maritime strategy, [which] will come under heavy criticism by those using arguments derived from the approach of the systems analysts." Best decries this since "only the Navy has thought through the implications of the continuum of operations in a way which will not cause civilian populations to shrink in horror.")

** O'Rourke, Ronald. "U.S. Forward Maritime Strategy." *Navy International* (February 1987): 118–122. (Especially good on the "complex, interactive relationship" between *The Maritime Strategy* and the 600-ship Navy, and on "the issues." Less useful—because occasionally inaccurate—in tracing the prehistory and history of the strategy, probably because of deficiencies in the public record.)

** Donatelli, Thomas. "Go Navy." *The American Spectator* (February 1987): 31–33. (On the linkages between defense reorganization and the maritime elements of the national military strategy. Supports *The Maritime Strategy* and fears for its future under the new Defense Department setup.)

Matthews, William. "U.S. Navy's Exercises in Aleutians Underscore Pacific Interest Concern." *Defense News* (9 February 1987): 25. Reprinted as "Marines, Navy Test

Amphibious Skills in Aleutians." *Navy Times* (16 February 1987): 27. (The Navy and Marine Corps practice cold-weather operations to implement *The Maritime Strategy* in the North Pacific.)

** Lynch, David J. "Maritime Plan a 'Prescription for Disaster' Educator Says." *Defense Week* (23 February 1987). (Professor Mearsheimer again, this time at the American Association for the Advancement of Science.)

** O'Rourke, Ronald. "Nuclear Escalation, Strategic Anti-Submarine Warfare and the Navy's Forward Maritime Strategy." Washington, D.C.: Library of Congress Congressional Research Service, 27 February 1987. (Especially useful for Navy staff officer views.)

Wood, Robert S. "The Conceptual Framework for Strategic Development at the Naval War College." *Naval War College Review* (Spring 1987): 4–16. (Further development of the views of this Naval War College strategist/faculty member. His focus was now on integrated national military strategy and its teaching and gaming. See also commentary by Rear Adm. J. A. Baldwin, President of the Naval War College, 2–3.)

Piotti, Rear Adm. Walter T., Jr. "Interview." *Journal of Defense and Diplomacy* 5, no. 2 (1987): 14–16. (The commander of the U.S. Military Sealift Command on global wartime planning for sealift.)

** Pocalyko, Lt. Cdr. Michael. "Neutral Sweden Toughens NATO's Northern Tier." *Proceedings* (March 1987): 128–130. (By a 1985–1986 member of the Strategic Concepts Group (OP–603.) On the interrelationships among Swedish, Soviet, and NATO strategies and *The Maritime Strategy*.)

** Daskal, Steven E. "Added Sealift Protection in Time of War." *National Defense* (March 1987): 38–41. (Recommends a variety of merchant ship self-protection measures for wartime, given the realities of *The Maritime Strategy* and U.S./allied force levels.)

** "Analysis: U.S. Carriers." *RUSI* (March 1987): 1ff. (Drags out yet again the false choice between a continental or maritime strategy as an issue. Claims West Germany "would object strongly if moves were made to convert *The Maritime Strategy* into the U.S.'s general war strategy." It is, in part, and they have not, at all. Cf. Bonn's actual *White Paper 1985*, cited in section V below.)

** Grove, Eric. "The Future of Sea Power." *Naval Forces,* no. 2 (1987): 12–28. (Excellent *tour d'horizon*, showing where *The Maritime Strategy* fits in the context of total world sea power issues.)

* Dunn, Vice Adm. Robert F. "NANiews Interview." *Naval Aviation News* (March–April 1987): 4. (The Deputy Chief of Naval Operations for Air Warfare comments on

"today's maritime strategy in terms of its effects on Naval Aviation": "Tactical commanders must deal with the strategy on a day-to-day basis. From that derives a new tactical awareness.")

Taylor, Rear Adm. R. A. K. "BBBG Power: Validated!" *Surface Warfare* (March–April 1987): 2–5. (Testing Battleship Battle Group warfighting concepts at sea, an important element of *The Maritime Strategy*.) See also William Matthews. "Navy Leans to Battleships with More Cruise Missiles." *Navy Times* (13 April 1987): 37–38; and *Defense News* (13 April 1987): 35; and Richard Halloran. "Warship Cleared for Duty off Iran." *New York Times* (12 April 1987): 32.

** "Push Anti-Mine Work, Navy Urged." *Defense Week* (2 March 1987): 5. (Rear Adm. J. S. Tichelman, RNLN, argues that emphasis on minesweeping "should go hand in hand with the forward strategy" at a U.S. Naval Institute Seminar on Mine Warfare.)

** Daggett, Stephen, and Jo L. Husbands. *Achieving an Affordable Defense: A Military Strategy to Guide Military Spending.* Washington, D.C.: Committee for National Security, 10 March 1987. (The annual CNS attack, using the usual W. W. Kaufmann "data" and arguments. Unlike *The Maritime Strategy,* solely designed to influence the U.S. legislative budget process.) A summary is in Lawrence J. Korb and Stephen Daggett, "A 15-Carrier Navy: Is it Really Necessary?" *Defense News* (30 March 1987): 27, reprinted as "15 Carrier Navy Leaves Forces out of Balance." *Navy Times* (6 April 1987): 32, and criticized by R. C. Mandeville in "Experts Only." *Navy Times* (27 April 1987): 22.

** Wilson, George C. "600-Ship Navy Is Sailing toward Rough Fiscal Seas." *Washington Post* (16 March 1987): A1, A6. (Sees forward anti-SSBN operations as a "Watkins scenario" and forward carrier battle group operations as a "Lehman scenario," with little backing in the officer corps. Cites a number of [unnamed] Navy officers as predicting that the latter "aspect of the forward strategy will start fading as soon as Lehman leaves the Navy Department." This seemed doubtful, given the primary role of the officer corps in drafting *The Maritime Strategy;* time would tell. See also retort by Rep. Charles E. Bennett, "A 600 Ship Fleet Is What's Needed." *Washington Post* [22 April 1987]: 19.)

** Cushman, John H., Jr. "Navy Warns of Crisis in Anti-Submarine Warfare." *New York Times* (19 March 1987): 19. (Outgoing Assistant Secretary of the Navy for Research, Engineering and Systems Melvyn Paisley on need for increased Navy ASW research: "We are faced with a crisis in our antisubmarine warfare capability which undermines our ability to execute maritime strategy." For context, however, see actual Paisley statements before congressional committees, 1987.)

**   Trainor, Lt. Gen. Bernard E., USMC (Ret.). "Lehman's Sea-War Strategy Is Alive, but for How Long?" *New York Times* (23 March 1987): 16. (Another article in the "Will-the-Strategy-survive-John-Lehman?" vein. General Trainor's understanding of the uniformed Navy, joint, and allied aspects of the strategy does not appear to be on a par with his understanding of the Marine Corps aspects.)

*   Dorsey, Jack. "NATO Navy Called 'A Constant Source of Pride.'" *Virginian Pilot* (28 March 1987): 133. (Deputy Secretary of Defense William H. Taft IV: It is "naive and dangerous" to believe that strong naval forces are merely expensive competitors to ground forces in Europe, an argument that has become fashionable in recent years for critics of naval programs and maritime strategy.)

**   Trainor, Lt. Gen. Bernard E., USMC (Ret.). "NATO Nations Conducting Winter Maneuvers in Northern Norway." *New York Times* (29 March 1987): 14. (Practicing the reinforcement of North Norway. Brig. Gen. Matthew Caulfield, USMC: "Marine reinforcement is part of our maritime strategy." Gen. Fredrik Bull-Hansen, RNA: With or without American carriers, northern Norway will be defended.)

**   Lessner, Richard. "Quick Strike: Navy Secretary's Wartime Strategy Is Contested Legacy." *Arizona Republic* (29 March 1987): C1ff. (Comprehensive discussion of the issues, including a lengthy interview with Secretary Lehman, on the eve of his departure from office, on his Maritime Strategy opinions. Contributes, however, to the erroneous view—running throughout America journalism—that the strategy was solely his creation.)

*   Goodman, Glenn W. Jr., and Benjamin F. Schemmer. "An Exclusive AFJ Interview with Admiral Carlisle A. H. Trost." *Armed Forces Journal International* (April 1987): 76–84, especially 79. (The Chief of Naval Operations discusses his views on *The Maritime Strategy*, including forward pressure, anti-SSBN operations, and relations with the NATO allies. "Our intent is to hold Soviet maritime forces at risk in the event of war. That includes anything that is out there.")

     Liebman, Marc. "Soviet Naval Initiatives in the Pacific: 1942 Revisited?" *Armed Forces Journal International* (April 1987): 58–64. (On Pacific maritime operations during a global war with the Soviets.)

     Truver, Scott C., and Jonathan S. Thompson. "Navy Mine Countermeasures: Quo Vadis?" *Armed Forces Journal International* (April 1987): 70–74. (An adequate survey of the problems and prospects. No discussion, however, of the primary U.S. mine countermeasures concept of operations embedded in *The Maritime Strategy*—killing minelayers far forward, in transit, and offshore, before they sow their mines.

Illustrative of the dangers of discussing any one warfare area in isolation from the total strategy.)

** Brooks, Capt. Linton. "The Nuclear Maritime Strategy." *Proceedings* (April 1987): 33–39. (A major contributor to *The Maritime Strategy* thinks it through under the highly unlikely conditions of nuclear war at sea. An important and prize-winning essay.) See also "Comment and Discussion" (May 1987): 14, 17 and (August 1987): 27–28.

** Cross, Lt. Col. Michael J., USMC. "No More Carrier Debates, Please." *Proceedings* (April 1987): 79–81. (Relates *The Maritime Strategy*'s requirements to the CVS-CVV debate.)

* "Individual Human Beings and the Responsibilities of Leadership." *Sea Power* (April 1987): 81–96. (Valedictory interview with Secretary Lehman. See page 85 for his parting views on *The Maritime Strategy*.)

Bliss, Elsie. "Fleet Hardening: Responding to the Nuclear Threat." *All Hands* (April 1987): 30–31. (On USN efforts to "harden" its ships, aircraft, and equipment against nuclear attack.)

** "Naval Strategy: America Rules the Waves?" *Science* (3 April 1987): 24. (Another journalistic attempt to summarize the debate. A little better than most.)

"Sea-War Plan All Wet?" *Columbus Dispatch* (7 April 1987): 10A. (A call for a "vigorous review" by the Pentagon of "Lehman's plan," including "aircraft carrier battle groups . . . sent to the . . . Barents, [a plan] never . . . formally approved by the Joint Chiefs of Staff, Defense Secretary Caspar Weinberger, or NATO." As has often been the case with public journalistic commentary on *The Maritime Strategy*, no mention was made of the extent to which the strategy *reflects* longstanding JCS, SecDef, or NATO policy and strategy, or of its roots in the naval officer corps.)

* Smith, Lt. Gen. Keith A. "The Posture of Marine Aviation in FY 88–FY 89." *Marine Corps Gazette* (May 1987): 46ff. (U.S. Marine Corps Deputy Chief of Staff for Aviation on Marine aviation requirements to support the national, maritime, and amphibious strategies. A reprint of earlier congressional testimony.)

** Beatty, Jack. "In Harm's Way." *The Atlantic* (May 1987): 37–53. (Having listened to naval leaders and to college professors, Beatty sides with the college professors. His criticisms, however, pale beside Theo Rudnak's sensationalist artwork.) See also (August 1987): 6–10, for retorts by Norman Friedman, Richard Best, Mark Jordan, Bing West, and Colin Gray, and a final rejoinder by Beatty, who apparently believes *The Maritime Strategy* calls for carrier operations in the Black Sea.

Matthews, William. "Webb Downplays 'Forward Strategy' Issue." *Navy Times* (4 May 1987): 33. (A new Reagan administration Secretary of the Navy takes over. His first publicly reported statements on *The Maritime Strategy*.)

** Korb, Lawrence J. "A Blueprint for Defense Spending." *Wall Street Journal* (20 May 1987): 34. ("The Navy's proper wartime job is . . . to secure the sea lanes necessary to support a ground campaign and to take the Soviet Navy out of the war, not primarily by seeking it out and destroying it, but by bottling it up. For this, a 12-carrier Navy should suffice.")

*/** Cushman, John H., Jr. "A Dialogue: What Kind of Navy Does the U.S. Need?" *New York Times* (31 May 1987): 4-3. (Vice Adm. Joseph Metcalf III vs. Dr. William W. Kaufmann on *The Maritime Strategy* and other naval issues.)

* Webb, James H., Jr., "The Aircraft Carrier: Centerpiece of Maritime Strategy." *Wings of Gold* (Summer 1987): S-2, S-3. (The new Secretary of the Navy on the national military strategy, *The Maritime Strategy*, and the role of the carrier. Continuity of the Reagan-Weinberger-Lehman view of maritime strategy confirmed.)

** Barnett, Capt. Roger W., USN (Ret.). "The Maritime Continental Debate Isn't Over." *Proceedings* (June 1987): 28–34. (Still more on the two famous alleged "mindsets," by one of the most prominent crafters of *The Maritime Strategy*.) Also, see "Comment and Discussion" [August 1987]: 30.)

** George, Lt. James L., USN (Ret.). "INNF." *Proceedings* (June 1987): 35–39. (A Center for Naval Analyses staffer on the effect on the Navy and its Maritime Strategy should European intermediate nuclear force arms control be achieved.)

** Stefanick, Tom. "The U.S. Navy: Directions for the Future." *F.A.S. Public Interest Report* (1 June 1987): 1ff. (Mostly about the budget, but some discussion of *The Maritime Strategy*, most elements of which the author opposes.)

** "The Navy Sails on Rough Seas." *Newsweek* (1 June 1987): 23–26. (A summary of the arguments, pro and con, as influenced by reactions to the Iraqi attack on the USS *Stark* in the Persian Gulf.)

* "Lehman on Sea Power." *U.S. News and World Report* (15 June 1987): 28. ("*The Maritime Strategy* I've promoted is not new; it is NATO strategy that was never taken seriously—a formula for holding Norway and the Eastern Mediterranean, two high-threat areas.") See also related articles on pages 36–43.

* "Trost Wants Flexibility in U.S. Thinking, Assessment of Soviets." *Aerospace Daily* (22 June 1987): 462; and "Naval Strategy Must Change says Adm. Trost." *Jane's Defence*

Weekly (27 June 1987): 1345. (The Chief of Naval Operations warns against rigid assumptions about Soviet naval options.)

Rostow, Eugene V. "For the Record." *Washington Post* (30 June 1987): A18. (Extract from a Naval War College lecture by a former high Reagan administration arms control official: "I can imagine no better antidote for the frustration and irritability which now characterize allied relationships than allied cooperation in mounting successful applications of counter-force at outposts of the Soviet empire and shifting geographical points around its periphery. The Soviet empire is extremely vulnerable to such a peninsular strategy.")

*   "Interview: James A. Lyons, Jr. Admiral, U.S. Navy." *Proceedings* (July 1987): 67. (CincPacFlt on the importance of the Pacific in *The Maritime Strategy*, despite media focus on Euro-Central Atlantic theater considerations.)

*   Hernandez, Vice Adm. D. E. "The New Third Fleet." *Proceedings* (July 1987): 73–76. (Commander Third Fleet on the revitalization of his organization to implement its share of carrying out *The Maritime Strategy*.)

**   Nelson, Cdr. William H. "Peacekeeper at Risk." *Proceedings* (July 1987): 90–97. (On applying *The Maritime Strategy* to the Persian Gulf region.)

**   Peppe, Lt. P. Kevin. "Acoustic Showdown for the SSNs." *Proceedings* (July 1987): 33–37. (On the effects of "acoustic parity" on *The Maritime Strategy*. He makes similar points in the July 1987 *Submarine Review*.)

**   Winnefeld, Lt. James A., Jr. "Fresh Claws for the Tomcat." *Proceedings* (July 1987): 103–107. (On the relationship between *The Maritime Strategy*, CVBG operations, and hardware requirements. "The F-14D is not just another nice fighter; it offers a significant enhancement of the CVBG's ability to execute *The Maritime Strategy*. The aircraft's true worth is apparent only in this light.")

**   Newell, Lt. C. Clayton R. USA. "Structuring Our Forces for the Big Battle." *Armed Forces Journal International* (July 1987): 6. (Takes on both the U.S. Navy's "vaunted maritime strategy" and the U.S. Army's "large complex corps designed to fight the Soviets in Western Europe." Prefers force structures and strategies enabling the United States to "apply its military power sparingly in small well-focused engagements in unexpected parts of the world.")

**   Prisley, Jack. "Submarine Aggressor Squadron: Its Time Has Come." *Submarine Review* (July 1987): 83–86. (A call for a "Top Fish" program to enable submariners to practice better what they must do to implement *The Maritime Strategy*.)

**   Wilson, George. "Soviets Score Silent Success in Undersea Race with U.S." *Washington Post* (17 July 1987): A20. (Claims Admiral Crowe, Chairman of the Joint Chiefs of Staff, "has never been enamored of the forward strategy" and that "other Defense Department officials said the forward strategy started to sink as soon as Lehman left the Pentagon." On the former, see Crowe testimony earlier in 1987, cited above. On the latter, see Mark Twain's cable from London to the Associated Press, 1897.)

**   Truver, Scott. "Phibstrike 95—Fact or Fiction?" A*rmed Forces Journal International* (August 1987): 102–108. (A case study of how *The Maritime Strategy* has been used as a framework by the Marine Corps to develop an amphibious warfare concept of future.)

IV. Sister Service Contributions to, and Views on, *The Maritime Strategy*

The Maritime Strategy fully incorporated U.S. Navy, Marine Corps, Coast Guard, Air Force, and Army contributions to the global maritime campaign. In fact, the case can be made that more thought was given to actual joint combat operations (as opposed to problems of command relationships or lift) by the Navy and Marine Corps in codifying *The Maritime Strategy* than by either the Air Force or the Army in developing their own "cornerstone" publications. The open literature on potential Army contributions to maritime warfare—such as air defense batteries based in islands and littoral areas—was particularly weak.

U.S. Joint Chiefs of Staff, *Unified Action Armed Forces,* JCS Pub. 2. Washington, D.C.: Joint Chiefs of Staff, December 1986. (Reflecting the National Security Act of 1947, as amended, The Goldwater-Nichols Department of Defense Reorganization Act of 1986, Title 10 and Title 32 U.S. Code, as amended, and DOD Directive 5100.1 [The "Functions Paper"], JCS Pub. 2. governs the joint activities of the U.S. armed forces. See especially chapter 11, sections 1 and 2–3, charging each military department, including the Navy, to "prepare forces . . . for the effective prosecution of war and military operations short of war." This responsibility [and not—as some critics charge—a desire to usurp somehow the authority of the JCS or the unified and specified commanders] was the primary impetus and justification for Navy and Marine Corps development, promulgation, and discussion of *The Maritime Strategy*. It is the Navy Department's framework for discharging its responsibilities to "organize, train, equip and provide Navy and Marine Corps forces for the conduct of prompt and sustained combat incident to operations at sea.")

U.S. Army. *Operations,* FM 100-5. Washington, D.C.: Department of the Army, 20 August 1982. (The Army's "keystone warfighting manual" and therefore a building block of *The Maritime Strategy*. Almost no discussion of Army-Navy mutual support, however, e.g.: air defense and island/littoral reinforcement. On page 17-7 is a useful discussion of the importance and essentially maritime nature of the NATO northern and southern European regions. Superseded in May 1986; distribution restricted to U.S. government agencies.)

U.S. Air Force. *Basic Aerospace Doctrine of the United States Air Force,* AFM 1-1. Washington, D.C.: Department of the Air Force, 16 March 1984. (The "cornerstone" Air Force doctrinal manual and therefore a building block of *The Maritime Strategy.* Takes a somewhat narrower view of potential areas of mutual support than does the Navy. See especially the discussion of objectives of naval forces on page 1-3, neglecting projection operations, e.g., strike or amphibious warfare; and pages 2-15, 3-1, and 3-5/3-6, covering possible Air Force actions to enhance naval operations, virtually all of them incorporated in *The Maritime Strategy.* Note, however, the lack of mention of any concomitant naval role in enhancing "aerospace" operations, and the lack of discussion of Air Force AAW contributions to maritime warfare, a key element of *The Maritime Strategy.*)

Cooper, Bert H. *Maritime Roles for Land-Based Aviation.* Report 83-151F. Washington, D.C.: Library of Congress Congressional Research Service, 1 August 1983. (Analyzes recent classified studies, identifies problems and issues, and discusses recent USN-USAF initiatives.)

Wilkerson, Lt. Col. Thomas, USMC. "Two if by Sea." *Proceedings* (November 1983): 34–39. (On important role of the U.S. Air Force in Maritime Strategy by the principal Marine Corps contributor to the strategy.)

Lewis, Kevin N. *Combined Operations in Modern Naval Warfare: Maritime Strategy and Interservice Cooperation.* RAND Paper 6999. Santa Monica, Calif.: RAND, April 1984. (See especially for arguments on alleged unique "Navy Planning Style," many of which are belied by *The Maritime Strategy.*)

Killebrew, Lt. Col. Robert B., USA. *Conventional Defense and Total Deterrence: Assessing NATO's Strategic Options.* Wilmington, Del.: Scholarly Resources, 1986. (Unique among studies of NATO defense in its attempt at an integrated discussion of U.S. and allied land, sea, and air forces. Argues NATO conventional defense is possible. Advocates early employment of naval forces as a defensive barrier "guarding" force. Sees a potential role for carrier air on the Central Front in a protracted war.)

Atkeson, Maj. Gen. Edward, USA (Ret.). "Arctic Could Be a Hot Spot in Future Conflicts." *Army* (January 1986): 13–14. (Fanciful proposal for expanded U.S. Army role in helping implement *The Maritime Strategy*: "An Army air cavalry force, properly tailored for the mission, should be able to locate submarine activity under the ice as well as, if not better than, another submarine.")

Alberts, Col. D. J., USAF. "U.S. Naval Air and Deep Strike." *Naval Forces,* no. 1 (1986): 62–75. (The strike warfare elements of *The Maritime Strategy* from an Air Force officer's point of view.)

** Harned, Maj. Glenn, USA. "Comment and Discussion: *The Maritime Strategy.*" *Proceedings* (February 1986): 26–28. (Argues that the U.S. Army suffers from lack of a Maritime Strategy equivalent and from Navy reticence in explaining its operational and tactical doctrines.)

* Pendley, Rear Adm. William. "The U.S. Navy, Forward Defense, and the Air-Land Battle." In *Emerging Doctrines and Technologies*, edited by Robert Pfaltzgraff, Jr., et al. Lexington, Mass.: Lexington Books, 1987. (Official views of the Navy's Director of Strategy, Plans, and Policy [OP-60] as of April 1986. Argues that Maritime Strategy and Air-Land Battle doctrine are similar and complementary. Sees both as essential parts—along with nuclear deterrence—of an "essential triad" of U.S. defense strategy. A short summary is on pages 15–16 of *Emerging Doctrines and Technologies: Implications for Global and Regional Political Military Balance: A Conference Report: April 16–18, 1986.* Cambridge, Mass.: Institute for Foreign Policy Analysis, 1986. Cf. Dunn and Staudenmaier May–June 1985 *Survival* article; March–April 1986 views of Vice Admiral Mustin on linkage between *The Maritime Strategy* and "Deep Strike," cited above; and West German government official views on *lack* of linkage, cited in section V below.)

** Kennedy, Col. William V, USAR (Ret.). "There Goes the U.S. Navy: Steaming the Wrong Way." *Christian Science Monitor* (23 June 1986): 14. (Calls for the Navy to refocus on Asia, crediting a U.S. Army "counterattack" with having turned *The Maritime Strategy* from an alleged early Pacific orientation to a current European one. Attempts to drive a wedge between the Navy and Marine Corps, and alleges "only nominal mention of the Army and the Air Force in the *Proceedings*' "Maritime Strategy" Supplement, charges belied by actually reading the supplement.)

** Grace, Lt. Cdr. James A. "JTC3A and *The Maritime Strategy.*" *Surface Warfare* (July–August 1986): 22–24. (On the role of the Joint Tactical C3 agency in fielding joint and allied programs and procedures to ensure implementation of *The Maritime Strategy.*)

Yost, Adm. Paul, USCG. "The Bright Slash of Liberty: Today's Coast Guard: Buffeted but Unbowed." *Sea Power* (August 1986): 8–24. (See especially pages 11–12 and 21–22 on the Maritime Defense Zones, an important Navy–Coast Guard element of *The Maritime Strategy*, by the Commandant of the Coast Guard.)

**   Builder, Carl H. *The Army in the Strategic Planning Process: Who Shall Bell the Cat?*
     Bethesda, Md.: U.S. Army Concepts Analysis Agency, October 1986. (A study done
     for the U.S. Army to "try to find out why the Army doesn't seem to do very well in the
     strategic planning process." Analyzes Army, Navy, and Air Force strategic planning,
     especially *The Maritime Strategy*. Looks for—and therefore "finds"—differences
     rather than similarities. Revised and reissued as a RAND Corporation publication
     in 1987. Revised and reissued yet again as the influential *The Masks of War: American
     Military Styles in Strategy and Analysis*. Baltimore, Md.: Johns Hopkins University
     Press, 1989.)

     Prina, L. Edgar. "The Tripartite Ocean: The Air Force and Coast Guard Give the Navy a
     Helping Hand." *Sea Power* (October 1986): 32–45. (Good update on tri-service con-
     tributions to implementing *The Maritime Strategy*.)

**   Fraser, Ronald. "MD . . . Z Mission Defines Coast Guard Wartime Role." *Navy Times* (20
     October 1986): 27. (On the role of the maritime defense zones.)

**   Breemer, Jan S., and Todd Hoover, SSG, USAF. "SAC Goes to Sea with Harpoon." *Na-
     tional Defence* (February 1987): 41–45. (A history and an update.) Cf. Chipman and
     Lay article cited in section XI below.

     Ley, Capt. Michael USA. "Navy Badly Needs to Beef Up Land Operations Fire Support."
     Army (May 1987): 12ff. (Argues for more large-caliber naval guns to support Army
     operations ashore.)

**   Chipman, Dr. Donald D. "Rethinking Forward Strategy and the Distant Blockade."
     Armed Forces Journal International (August 1987): 82–88. (Argues for joint integrated
     USN-USAF wartime operations in NATO's Northern Region, the GIUK gap, and the
     Norwegian Sea. Well in keeping with *The Maritime Strategy*.)

**   Estep, Col. James L., USA. "Army's Role in Joint Global Military Strategy." *Army* (August
     1987): 11ff. (Decries "lack of a more global, jointly oriented strategy" by the U.S.
     Army and applauds the Navy's development of same.)

V. Allied Contributions to, and Views on, *The Maritime Strategy*

The Maritime Strategy as developed by the U.S. Navy of the 1980s was heavily oriented
toward combined (and joint) operations, and this was reflected in the *Proceedings* January 1986 Supplement, *"The Maritime Strategy."* The postwar U.S. Navy had never been
"unilateralist." Allied contributions to the global campaign were worked out years before and then had been continually updated in the drafting of allied war plans, memoranda of agreement, and other documents. They were routinely discussed at annual
navy-to-navy staff policy talks and CNO-to-CNO visits, held between the U.S. Navy

and each of its most important allied associates. Thus, most of the hard bargaining and tradeoffs had already been done, and integrating allied efforts with the U.S. Navy component of *The Maritime Strategy* was not particularly difficult. Once *The Maritime Strategy* was drafted, it was briefed to key allied CNOs and planning staffs and to NATO commanders. Allied feedback was considered and utilized in updating revisions to the strategy, and the process continued after its issuance.

Allied naval strategy—and its relationship to *The Maritime Strategy*—is well enough documented. The NATO Information Service was prolific, and NATO commanders wrote relevant articles frequently. Most allied defense ministries published occasional or annual "Defense Reports" or "White Papers" that sometimes touch on naval strategy as well as policy and procurement issues. As is evident from these and other writings, U.S. Navy and allied military thought was generally congruent.

The North Atlantic Treaty Organization: Facts and Figures (10th and subsequent editions.) Brussels: NATO Information Service, 1981 and subsequently. (The basic official public document on NATO policy and strategy. See especially the 1984 edition, pages 108–111, 143–144, and 380. "The primary task in wartime of the Allied Command Atlantic would be to ensure security in the whole Atlantic area by guarding the sea-lanes and denying their use to an enemy, to conduct conventional and nuclear operations against enemy naval bases and airfields and to support operations carried out by SACEUR." "NATO's forces [have] roles of neutralizing Soviet strategic nuclear submarines, safeguarding transatlantic sea lines, and in general preventing the Warsaw Pact from gaining maritime supremacy in the North Atlantic.")

Train, Adm. Harry. "U.S. Maritime Power." In *U.S. Military Power in the 1980s,* edited by Christopher Coker. London: Macmillan, 1983, 107–114. (SacLant provides details on the 1981 NATO *Maritime Concept of Operations* [ConMarOps], one of the building blocks of *The Maritime Strategy.*)

Wemyss, Rear Adm. Martin LaT., RN. "Naval Exercises 1980–81." *Jane's Naval Annual* (1981): 151–158. (Highlights problems in interallied naval cooperation resulting from U.S. Navy communication and intelligence systems advances.)

Wemyss, Rear Adm. Martin LaT., RN. "Submarines and Anti-submarine Operations for the Uninitiated." *RUSI Journal* (September 1981): 22–27. (Restatement of classic Royal Navy arguments for focusing allied ASW efforts around expected afloat targets instead of U.S. Navy–spearheaded forward operations.)

The North Atlantic Assembly. *NATO Anti Submarine Warfare: Strategy Requirements and the Need for Cooperation.* Brussels: 1982. (Good survey of the issues, with a call for resolution of the debate over mission priorities.)

Hackett, Gen. Sir John, BA (Ret.), Vice Adm. Sir Ian McGeoch, RN (Ret.), et al. *The Third World War: The Untold Story.* New York: Macmillan, 1982. (Fiction. Sequel to *The Third World War: August 1985* [1978]. A British vision, stressing the war at sea and on the northern front, and all but ignoring the Mediterranean and Pacific. "Swing" and carrier strikes on the Kola understood—as in 1978—as normal NATO modus operandi. Cf. Clancy's 1986 *Red Storm Rising* and Hayes et al.'s *American Lake,* chapter 19, cited in section II above.)

Tonge, David. "Exposure Troubles NATO's Northern Commanders." *Financial Times* (27 October 1982): 3. (Reports NATO Northern Region ground commanders' concerns that carrier battle groups may not arrive in the Norwegian Sea early enough.)

Eberle, Adm. Sir James, RN. "Defending the Atlantic Connection." In *The Future of British Sea Power,* edited by Geoffrey Till. Annapolis, Md.: Naval Institute Press, 1984, 146–150. (See especially for frank overview of four Royal Navy tasks in the Atlantic.)

British Atlantic Committee. *Diminishing the Nuclear Threat: NATO's Defense and New Technology.* London: February 1984. (A group of retired British generals and others rail against the "practicality" and "very purpose" of the NATO reinforcement mission, given their assumptions of a short conventional war phase in Europe and overwhelming surface ship vulnerability. See also Mitchell, Lt. I. G., RN, "Atlantic Reinforcement: A Re-emerging Debate." *Armed Forces* [September 1986]: 399–400.)

Hunter, Robert, ed. *NATO—The Next Generation.* Boulder, Colo.: Westview, 1984. (See especially—and unexpectedly—for Japanese Maritime Self-Defense Force role in closing off Far Eastern straits and protecting the western Pacific sea lines of communication, in chapters by Jun Tsunoda and Shunji Taoka.)

Bouchard, Lt. Joseph, and Lt. Douglas Hess. "The Japanese Navy and Sea-Lanes Defense." *Proceedings* (March 1984): 88–97. (On the concurrent Japanese maritime strategy debate. See also Lt. Col. Otto Lehrack, "Search for a New Consensus." In the same issue: 96–99.)

Toyka, Cdr. Viktor, FGN. "A Submerged Forward Defense." *Proceedings* (March 1984): 145–147. (Complementary German maritime strategy for the Baltic.)

King-Harman, Col. Anthony, BA. "NATO Strategy—A New Look." *RUSI* (March 1984): 26–29. (By a former longtime member of the International NATO Staff. Alleges and decries a NATO "lack of political direction in the maritime sphere." "It has been largely left to SacLant himself to develop and implement a maritime strategy for deterrence. . . . There is also a Tri-MNC concept of operations again carrying no political endorsement." Calls for a new NATO "strategic review," one result of which he anticipates would be a finding that "reinforcements . . . would only need the mini-mum of a maritime protection.")

Mabesoone, Capt. W. C., RNLN, and Cdr. N. W. G. Buis, RNLN. "Maritime Strategic Aspects of the North Sea." *RUSI* (September 1984): 12–17. (Dutch navy view of North Sea operations. Complements *The Maritime Strategy*. Stresses need for land-based air forces in air defense and possibility of SSN TLAM-C support of Central Front operations. Emphasis on barrier vice close-support naval protection of shipping operations.)

Federal Minister of Defence (Federal Republic of Germany.) *White Paper 1985: The Situation and the Development of the Federal Armed Forces.* (Includes latest official West German defense policy and strategy views. See especially pages 27–29, 76–77, 111, and 211–216. Declares unequivocal German support for "forward defense at sea" in accordance with the NATO commanders' maritime concept of operations, which "calls for countering the threat far from friendly sea routes and shores. Interdiction of enemy naval forces should be affected immediately in front of their own bases." Differentiates clearly, however, between such use of naval [and air] forces and "aggressive forward defense by ground operations in the opponent's territory," which "NATO strategy rules out.")

Holst, Johan Jorgen, et al., eds. *Deterrence and Defense in the North.* Oslo: Norwegian University Press, 1985. (See especially authoritative chapters by high Norwegian government officials and Kenneth Hunt. "The Security of the Center and the North." "The Stronger the North, the Stronger the Center.")

Caufriez, Chaplain G. "Comment and Discussion: Plan Orange Revisited." *Proceedings* (March 1985): 73 and 79. (From Home Forces Headquarters, Belgium, a plea for Norwegian Sea vice GIUK Gap defense, lest "at one go, the northern flank would have crumbled.")

Stavridis, Cdr. James. "The Global Maritime Coalition." *Proceedings* (April 1965): 58–74. Also "Comment and Discussion" (October 1985): 177. (On role of allies in *The Maritime Strategy*, by a former OP-603 staffer.)

Grove, Eric J., "The Convoy Debate." *Naval Forces*, no. 3 (1985): 38–46. (Update of classic postwar Royal Navy pro-convoy/anti–forward ops arguments, by a leading British civilian naval analyst.)

"Royal Navy Edges Closer to Kola." *Defence Attache*, no. 4 (1985): 9–10. (On actual complementary contemporary Royal Navy northern Norwegian Sea strategy.)

Shadwick, Martin. "Canada's Commitments to NATO: The Need for Rationalization." *Canadian Defense Quarterly* (Summer 1985): 22–27. (The range of options for future Canadian deployment strategies, any of which would affect *The Maritime Strategy*.)

Crickard, Rear Adm. F. W., CN. "Three Oceans—Three Challenges: The Future of Canada's Maritime Forces." *Naval Forces*, no. 5 (1985): 13–27. (On complementary Canadian strategy, especially area ASW in the North Atlantic SLOC.)

** Heginbotham, Stanley. "The Forward Maritime Strategy and Nordic Europe." *Naval War College Review* (November–December 1985): 19–27.

Dunn, Michael Collins. "Canada Rethinks Its Defense Posture." *Defense and Foreign Affairs* (November 1985): 12–19. (Discusses Canadian ground and air contributions to NATO's Northern Front and naval contribution to Atlantic ASW and Arctic defense.)

Sokolsky, Joel J. "Canada's Maritime Forces: Strategic Assumptions, Commitments, Priorities." *Canadian Defence Quarterly* (Winter 1985–86): 24–30. (By a leading Canadian civilian defense and naval specialist. See especially 28–29 regarding similarities between *The Maritime Strategy* of the 1980s and NATO naval strategy of the 1950s. Also see David R. Francis, "Canada Ponders Major Shift in Defense Policy." *Christian Science Monitor* [4 February 1987]: 9, for update of Sokolsky's views.)

Cole, Paul M., and Douglas M. Hart, eds. *Northern Europe: Security Issues for the 1990s.* Boulder, Colo.: Westview, 1986. (See especially Col. Jonathan Alford, BA [Ret.], "The Soviet Naval Challenge": 43–56; and Lt. Gen. Heinz von zur Gathen, FRGA [Ret.], "The Federal Republic of Germany's Contribution to the Defense of Northern Europe": 57–82. The former sees forward U.S. operations in the Norwegian Sea as unlikely and argues that the Royal Navy should therefore concentrate on the Channel, the North Sea, and the Norwegian Sea, rather than either "unspecific flexibility" or "keeping open the sea lines of communication to the United States," options that parallel those discussed in the concurrent U.S. Maritime Strategy debates. The latter discusses the increasing West German role in Baltic, North, and Norwegian Sea defense. Both authors base their arguments for enhanced European naval power on the premise that the U.S. Navy would not be available, at least not in strength, in the Norwegian Sea early in a war.)

Dibb, Paul. *Review of Australia's Defense Capabilities.* Canberra: Australian Government Publishing Service, 1986. (Against Australian involvement with United States and other allied contingency planning for global war. Claims that Radford-Collins Agreement "convoying and escort connotations which extend more than 2000 nautical miles west of Australia to the mid-Indian Ocean suggest a disproportionate commitment of scarce resources to activities which may be only marginally related to our national interest and capabilities." An input to the March 1987 government white paper on defense.)

Riste, Olav, and Rolf Tamnes. *The Soviet Naval Threat and Norway.* Oslo: Research Center for Defense History (FHFS), National Defense College Norway, 1986. (See especially 18–22. Two Norwegian defense specialists see recent U.S. naval and other efforts as providing "from the Norwegian point of view . . . a considerably improved probability that the supply lines to Norway will be kept open.") See also Tamnes's "Integration and Screening" (also FHFS 1986) on Norwegian attitudes in the 1970s and 1980s.

Richey, George. *Britain's Strategic Role in NATO.* London: Macmillan, 1986. (Argues for Britain's return to a *classic* maritime strategy, as Ambassador Robert Komer, Senator Gary Hart, and William Lind—but not the U.S. Navy—use the term.)

Price, Alfred. *Air Battle Central Europe.* New York: Free Press, 1986. (See chapter 14, "Guardians of the Baltic Shore," on Federal German Naval Aviation forward air-to-surface warfare concepts in the Baltic, and chapter 15, "Protecting the Lifeline," on air defense of the seas surrounding the United Kingdom.)

Okazuki, Hisahiko. *Japan's National Security Strategy.* Cambridge, Mass.: Abt Books, 1986. (Ambassador Okazuki presents persuasive arguments why Japan could not stay out of large or small conflicts involving its interests.)

Small, Adm. William N. "The Southern Region: The Key to Europe's Defense." *Armed Forces* (January 1986): 12–13. (By the NATO commander in chief, Allied Forces Southern Europe/Commander in Chief, U.S. Naval Forces Europe. NATO's plans for defense of its Southern Region, including allied and U.S. Navy Sixth Fleet/StrikeForSouth Mediterranean operations and Turkish Black Sea operations.)

Bjarnason, Bjorn. "Iceland and NATO." *NATO Review* (February 1986): 7–12. (By one of Iceland's leading journalists. "It is crucial that in any defence of sea routes between North America and Western Europe, . . . the Soviet fleet is confined as far north towards its home base at the Kola Peninsula as possible. . . . [T]he Greenland-Iceland-UK gap . . . is not an adequate barrier; instead, NATO envisages a forward defence in the Norwegian Sea." Includes update on the defense debate in Iceland.)

Stryker, Russell F. "Civil Shipping Support for NATO." *NATO Review* (February 1986): 29–33. (By a U.S. Maritime Administration official and member of the NATO Planning Board for Ocean Shipping. On the shipping that is to use the North Atlantic SLOC.)

Margolis, Eric. "Will Canadian Waters Become the Next Maginot Line?" *Wall Street Journal* (21 February 1986): 23. (A Canadian call for increased U.S.-Canadian ASW capabilities in the Arctic.)

Schlim, Vice Adm. A. J. P., BN. "Mine Warfare in European Waters." *NATO's Sixteen Nations* (February–March 1986): 20–28. (By the Belgian CNO. How NATO plans to use mines and mining against the Soviets. Excellent complementarity with *The Maritime Strategy.*)

Leenhardt, Adm. Yves, FM. "France: The Need for a Balanced Navy." *NATO's Sixteen Nations* (February–March 1986): 41–46. (Rowing to the beat of a different drum. Authoritative statement by the French CNO. Heavy emphasis on nuclear deterrence, crisis prevention and control, and allied cooperation. Minimal discussion relating to global or regional forward conventional operations against the Soviets, however, in contrast to U.S. Maritime Strategy and other allied writers.)

Young, Thomas-Durell. "Australia Bites Off More than the RAN Can Chew." *Pacific Defence Reporter* (March 1986): 15–17. See also his "'Self-Reliance' and Force Development in the RAN." *Proceedings* (March 1986): 157–161, and "Don't Abandon Radford-Collins." *Pacific Defence Reporter* (September 1986): 16. (On Australian and New Zealand ASW and naval control/protection of shipping roles in the Indian and southwest Pacific oceans.)

Kampe, Vice Adm. Helmut, FGN. "Defending the Baltic Approaches." *Proceedings* (1 March 1986): 88–93. (By the NATO Commander, Allied Naval Forces, Baltic Approaches. Complementary German and Danish naval strategies: "In the Baltic Sea, forward defense begins at the Warsaw Pact ports.")

Grove, Eric J. "After the Falklands." *Proceedings* (March 1986): 121–129. (Questions the wisdom of the Royal Navy functioning primarily in conjunction with Striking Fleet Atlantic and U.S. Navy SSNs in the Norwegian Sea. Would prefer RN focus to return to naval control and protection of shipping in the eastern Atlantic and the Channel.)

Grimstvedt, Rear Adm. Bjarne, RNN. "Norwegian Maritime Operations." *Proceedings* (March 1986): 144–149. (By the Norwegian CNO. Stresses Norwegian Navy intent and capabilities to defend North Norway, including same Vestfjorden area that focused ComSecondFlt/ComStrikFltLant's attention in 1985 and 1986.)

Secretary of State for Defence (UK). *Statement on the Defence Estimates 1986: 1.* London: HMSO, 1986; see especially pages 29, 34, and 60–61. ("Enemy attack submarines are successfully to be held at arm's length from the critical Atlantic routes. Defence against these submarines would begin when they sailed"; "The availability of U.S. ships in the Eastern Atlantic at the outbreak of hostilities cannot be assumed"; "U.S. and European navies are continuing to ensure the preservation of an essential margin of allied maritime superiority in key ocean areas.")

Defense Agency (Japan). *Defense of Japan: 1986.* (Includes latest official Japanese defense policy and strategy views. See especially 99 and 154. Outlines agreed division of labor between the Maritime Self-Defense Force and the U.S. Navy in the event of an attack on Japan, as understood by the Japanese government. *The Maritime Strategy* was developed in full accordance with these concepts.)

Greenwood, David. "Towards Role Specialization in NATO." *NATO's Sixteen Nations* (July 1986): 44–49. (Argues against a significant eastern Atlantic naval role for Belgium, the Netherlands, West Germany, and Denmark. This amounts largely to an attack on the existence of the Dutch Navy, one of the world's best.)

Armitage, Richard. "The U.S.-Japan Alliance." *Defense/86* (July–August 1986): 23–27. (Reagan administration defense policy vis-à-vis Japan by the Assistant Secretary of Defense for International Security Affairs. The context of *The Maritime Strategy* in Northeast Asia and the Northwest Pacific. See also his "Japan's Defense Program: 'No Cause for Alarm.'" *Washington Post* [18 February 1987]: A18.)

** Eberle, Adm. Sir James, RN. "Editorial." *Naval Forces,* no. 4 (1986): 7. (By a former top Royal Navy and NATO commander in chief. "The New Maritime Strategy is to be welcomed as a brave effort to bring some much-needed clarity into the field of maritime strategic thinking. But it is more likely to be welcomed in Europe by naval officers than it is by political leaders.")

Tokinoya, Atsushi. *The Japan-U.S. Alliance: A Japanese Perspective,* Adelphi Paper 212. London: IISS (Autumn 1986).

** Huitfeldt, Lt. Gen. Tonne, RNA. *NATO's Northern Security.* London: Institute for the Study of Conflict, September 1976. (By the retired director of the NATO International Military Staff. "United States maritime strategy is in harmony with the agreed NATO strategy." Good coverage of the 1981 NATO Concept of Maritime Operations, a major building block of *The Maritime Strategy.*)

Howlett, Gen. Geoffrey, BA. "Interview." *Journal of Defense and Diplomacy* (September 1986): 13–16. (NATO Commander in Chief, Allied Forces Northern Europe rejects a GIUK Gap maritime defense line. Advocates a forward defense on land and sea in North Norway and the Baltic, and containment of the Soviet Northern and Baltic Fleets in their home waters.)

** Grove, Eric. "*The Maritime Strategy.*" *Bulletin of the Council for Arms Control* (UK) (September 1986): 5–6. (Regards the strategy as "self-consciously offensive" and "self-consciously coalition-minded," as "yet another example of the growing difference in mood between the two sides of the Atlantic." Challenges fellow Europeans to inject amendments reflecting their own "interests and fears." The "difference in mood" he sees, however, may well be more between military leaders and some political writers on both sides of the ocean than between Americans and Europeans.)

** Ausland, John C. "The Heavy Traffic in Northern Seas." *International Herald Tribune,* 16 September 1986. (On some effects of *The Maritime Strategy* in Norway.)

** Huitfeldt, Lt. Gen. Tonne, RNA. "The Threat from the North: Defense of Scandinavia." *NATO's Sixteen Nations* (October 1986): 26–32. (The former NATO International Military Staff director's endorsement of *The Maritime Strategy* as "making a more effective contribution to deterring the Soviet Northern Fleet from any adventurism in the Norwegian Sea, and Soviet aggression in general," with the caution that it "not go beyond what is essential for deterrence and defense.")

Boerresen, Capt. Jacob, RSN. "Norway and the U.S. Maritime Strategy." *Naval Forces,* no. 6 (1986): 14–15. (By the military secretary to the Norwegian minister of defense. ("During the 1970s, NATO and the USA expressly limited their carrier operations . . . to the waters in and south of the GIUK gap[;] Norway . . . found this situation rather uncomfortable. . . . The official Norwegian reaction [to forward deployment of CVBGs] has been positive, [but] Norway is . . . sensitive to all developments that it fears may threaten the low level of tension.")

"Japan, U.S. Map Out Sea Defenses." *Washington Times* (1 December 1986): 6. (On the wartime division of labor between the U.S. Navy and the Japanese Maritime Self-Defense Force.)

Cremasco, Maurizia. "Italy: A New Definition of Security?" In *Evolving European Defense Policies,* edited by Catherine M. Kelleher and Gale A. Mattox. Lexington, Mass.: Lexington Books, 1987, 257–272. (On the Italian military policy debate and Italian Navy views on strategy.)

Gann, L. H., ed. *The Defense of Western Europe.* London: Croom Helm, 1987. (Surveys all the defense forces of all the Western European nations. Particularly useful is Nigel de Lee's "The Danish and Norwegian Armed Forces," 58–94, which examines in some detail their wartime sea and air concepts of operations in the Norwegian Sea, the Baltic approaches, the Baltic itself and inshore waters. These concepts are well integrated into *The Maritime Strategy.* As regards Denmark, de Lee notes: "Plans for naval action are based on aggressive tactics in depth, and this entails a forward defence." Particularly useless is the highly parochial chapter by Col. Harry Summers, USA [Ret.], allegedly on "United States Armed Forces in Europe," which should have been styled "The U.S. Army in Germany.")

Secretary of State for Defence (UK). *Statement on the Defence Estimates 1987: 1.* London: HMSO, 1987. (See especially 25 for reaffirmation of previous year's policy statements and commitment to Royal Navy "forward deployment operations in the Norwegian Sea.")

** Nakanishi, Terumasa, "U.S. Nuclear Policy and Japan." *Washington Quarterly* (Winter 1987): 81–97, especially 84–85 and 90. (*The Maritime Strategy* in the context of the overall military situation in Northeast Asia. "The new 'Full-Forward' strategy of the U.S. Pacific Fleet . . . is certainly in the interest of Japan's conventional security." He is less sanguine regarding Japan's nuclear security.)

Newman, Peter C. "Business Watch: About-Face in Defense Strategy." *Maclean's* (12 January 1987): 28. (Naval aspects of the defense debate in Canada on the eve of publication of the 1987 white paper.)

Ebata, Kensuke. "Ocean Air Defense Japanese Style." *Proceedings* (March 1987): 98–101. (On Japanese AAW concepts and programs, essential elements of *The Maritime Strategy* in the Pacific.)

** Till, Geoffrey. "Maritime Power: The European Dimension." *Naval Forces,* no. 11 (1987): 83–104. (Excellent and comprehensive survey by a European of how European naval power complements *The Maritime Strategy* in supporting overall NATO Maritime Strategy. A partial antidote to Bing West's concerns.)

Auer, Cdr. James, USN (Ret.), and Cdr. Sadao Seno, JMSDF (Ret.). "Japan's Maritime Self-Defence Force." *Naval Forces,* no. 11 (1987): 178–190. (Stress on the division of labor between the U.S. Navy and the Japanese Maritime Self-Defense Force in the Northwest Pacific and on the deterrent value of same.)

** Crickard, Rear Adm. Frederick. "The Canadian Navy: New Directions." *Naval Forces,* no. 11 (1987): 78–87. (Sees *The Maritime Strategy* as forcing hard choices on Canadian naval planners. Cf. his views of a year earlier, cited above.)

Longbottom, Squadron Leader S. P., RNAF. "Maritime Strike Strategy for the Royal Australian Air Force." *Defense Force Journal* (March–April 1987): 5ff. (Argues for increased RAAF attention to mine warfare.)

Department of Defence (Australia). *The Defence of Australia: 1987.* Canberra: Australian Government Publishing Service, 19 March 1987. (The first official Australian Defense "White Paper" since 1976 ensures continued RAN cooperation within *The Maritime Strategy.* "In the remote contingency of global conflict. . . . [O]ur responsibilities would include those associated with the Radford-Collins Agreement for the protection and control of shipping. Subject to priority requirements in our own area, the Australian Government would then consider contributions further afield. . . . [F]or example, our FFGs . . . are capable of effective participation in a U.S. carrier battle group well distant from Australia's shores.")

** Sokolsky, Joel. "The U.S. Navy and Canadian Security: Trends in American Maritime Strategy." *Peace and Security* (Spring 1987): 10ff. (Sees *The Maritime Strategy* as creating problems for Canada. Advocates a Canadian naval buildup.)

** Mackay, Cdr. S. V., RN. "An Allied Reaction." *Proceedings* (April 1987): 82–89. (Concludes that a peacetime USN Norwegian Sea CVBG presence is required with concomitant "greater commitment from Norway," and "a firm and agreed-upon line . . . on ROEs." "There are clear indications from recent exercises that this Maritime Strategy is the way ahead for U.S. maritime forces and not solely to support the cause for a 600-ship Navy. . . . [T]he supporting maritime nations in NATO must follow the lead. [But] We in Europe must be sure that *The Maritime Strategy* is a genuine U.S. policy for the future and not just a product of the current administration.") See also "Comment and Discussion" (July 1987): 19–20.

** Urban, Mark. "New Navy Plan to Attack Soviet Subs near Bases." *Independent* (London), 14 April 1987. (Commander in chief of the British Fleet, Admiral Hunt, on forward Royal Navy and NATO submarine—including anti-SSBN—operations.)

Challenge and Commitment: A Defence Policy for Canada. Ottawa: Minister of Supply and Services Canada, 1987. (June 1987 official Canadian Ministry of Defense white paper, the first since 1971. Current Canadian contributions to allied Maritime Strategy and future plans. See especially maps on pages 13, 52, 64, and discussion of proposed changes in Canadian policy, which will increase the requirements for USN and USMC forces in the Norwegian Sea and elsewhere but should help improve other elements needed to carry out the strategy.)

Nishihara, Masashi. "Maritime Cooperation in the Pacific: The United States and Its Partners." *Naval War College Review* (Summer 1987): 37–41. ("The U.S. strategy of horizontal escalation by which the United States would open up armed tensions in different parts of the world in order to force the Soviets to disperse their forces may not meet Japanese interests.")

Arkin, William M., and Steve Shallhorn. "Canada Even More under U.S. Thumb in Sub Plan." *Globe and Mail* (Toronto) (17 July 1987): 7. (Decries *The Maritime Strategy*, the new Canadian defense policy, and the linkage between the two.)

VI. Soviet Strategy and Views

U.S. and allied Maritime Strategy was not a game of solitaire. The Soviet threat—along with U.S. national and allied interests and geopolitical realities—was one of the fundamental ingredients of that strategy. No attempt can be made here, however, to recount the considerable literature on Soviet naval affairs. The focus in the relatively few works listed below is how the Soviets viewed their own maritime strategy as well as ours, and how correctly we divined their views. A critical issue is which missions they saw as primary and which they saw as secondary for their navy and for those of the West, and whether these priorities would change soon. Much material on the Soviets also can be found in other entries in this bibliography.

Gorshkov, Rear Adm. Sergei G. *The Sea Power of the State.* Annapolis, Md.: Naval Institute Press, 1979. See especially 290 and 329. ("The employment of naval forces against the sea-based strategic systems of the enemy has become most important in order to disrupt or blunt to the maximum degree their strikes against targets ashore.")

Yashin, Rear Adm. B. "The Navy in U.S. Military-Political Strategy." *International Affairs* (Moscow), no. 2 (1982). (Sees "new U.S. Naval Strategy" of Secretary Lehman as deriving from the "ocean strategy" of Admirals Zumwalt and Turner.)

Rumyantsev, Rear Adm. A. "The Navy in the Plans of the Pentagon's 'New Military Strategy.'" *Zarubezhnoye voyennoye obozreniye* (June 1982): 59–64. (Soviet public interpretation of Reagan administration naval policy, including Norwegian Sea battle group operations and Arctic SSN anti-SSBN operations. Soviets fully expected a USN anti-SSBN campaign.)

Sturua, G. M. "The United States: Reliance on Ocean Strategy." *USA: Economics, Politics and Ideology* (November 1982). (A prominent Soviet civilian defense analyst's views on the U.S. Navy's Maritime Strategy. He sees it as primarily a nuclear counterforce strategy, employing submarine and carrier-launched nuclear weapons.)

U.S. Senate Armed Services Committee. *Hearings on the Department of Defense Authorization for FY84: Part 6.* 98th Cong. 1st sess. Washington, D.C.: U.S. Government Printing Office, 1983, 2935 and 2939. (Rear Adm. John Butts, new Director of Naval Intelligence, gives authoritative U.S. Navy view of Soviet navy strategy, April 1983. See also updates in Butts testimony of 1984 and 1985.)

McConnell, James M. *The Soviet Shift in Emphasis from Nuclear to Conventional.* CRC 490. 2 vols. Alexandria, Va.: Center for Naval Analyses, June 1983. (Includes alternative views of Soviet naval strategy.)

Strelkov, Capt. First Rank V. "Naval Forces in U.S. 'Direct Confrontation' Strategy." *Morskoy sbornik* no. 5 (1983): 78–82. (Highlights maritime roles of allies and sister services as well as USN.)

Stalbo, Vice Adm. K. "U.S. Ocean Strategy." *Morskoy sbornik,* no. 10 (1983): 29–36. (The Soviet Navy's leading theoretician writes in its official journal. Reaction to the *Proceedings* October 1982 issue on the Soviet Navy and to statements by the Secretary of the Navy. Criticizes the "new U.S. Naval Strategy" for its geopolitical roots, its global scope, and its aims of "isolating countries of the Socialist community from the rest of the world.")

Leighton, Marian. "Soviet Strategy towards Northern Europe and Japan." *Survey* (Autumn–Winter 1983): 112–151. (Sees "striking and disquieting similarities" between recent "patterns of Soviet coercion against northern Europe and Japan.")

Office of the Chief of Naval Operations. *Understanding Soviet Naval Developments.* 5th ed. Washington, D.C.: U.S. Government Printing Office, 1985. (Latest in a series of official U.S. Navy handbooks on the Soviet fleet. See also critique by Norman Friedman in *Proceedings* [November 1985]: 88–89.)

Sturua, G. "Strategic Anti-Submarine Warfare." *USA: Economics, Politics, and Ideology* (February 1985). (Strategic ASW viewed as a primary USN mission.)

"Soviet Naval Activities: 1977–1984." *NATO Review* (February 1985): 17–20. (A series of charts reflecting recent Soviet exercise activity in the North Atlantic.)

Bystrov, Rear Adm. Yu. "U.S. Games in the World Ocean." *Literaturnaya gazeta* (4 September 1985): 14. (Soviet public reaction to exercise OCEAN SAFARI '85 and other forward exercises.)

Tritten, Cdr. James J. *Soviet Naval Forces and Nuclear Warfare: Weapons, Employment and Policy.* Boulder, Colo.: Westview, 1986. (By the acting chairman of the National Security Affairs Department at the U.S. Naval Postgraduate School. Examination of Soviet naval missions, including implications for U.S. naval strategy. Anticipates Soviet navy wartime bastion defense, anticarrier warfare, strategic antisubmarine warfare, and—controversially—anti-SLOC operations. See also his "Defense Strategy and Offensive Bastion." *Sea Power* [November 1986]: 64–70.)

Watson, Cdr. Bruce W., and Susan M. Watson, eds. *The Soviet Navy: Strengths and Liabilities.* Boulder, Colo.: Westview, 1986. (See especially chapters by Richard Fisher, "Soviet SLOC Interdiction," and Keith Allen, "The Northern Fleet and North Atlantic Naval Operations," which see SLOC interdiction as more likely than most other knowledgeable experts expect, since they see Soviet thinking as evolving toward greater consideration of protracted conventional conflict.)

** George, James L., ed. *The Soviet and Other Communist Navies: The View from the Mid-1980s.* Annapolis, Md.: Naval Institute Press, 1986. (An outstanding collection of papers from a 1985 CNA-sponsored conference of top experts in the field, including several references to *The Maritime Strategy.* See especially Brad Dismukes's discussion of the contending views on Soviet Navy missions; the authoritative judgments of Rear Adm. William Studeman, Rear Adm. Thomas Brooks, and Mr. Richard Haver, the nation's top naval intelligence professionals; and the contrasting views of Adm.

Sylvester Foley and Adm. Harry Train, two former "operators." Wayne Wright's "Soviet Operations in the Mediterranean" is especially good on the interplay of Soviet and U.S. Maritime Strategy. The excellent paper by Alvin Bernstein of the Naval War College and the paper by Anthony Wells have also been reprinted elsewhere: the former in *National Interest* [Spring 1986]: 17–29; the latter in *National Defense* [February 1986]: 38–44.)

Trofimenko, Ginrikh. *The U.S. Military Doctrine.* Moscow: Progress, 1986. (See especially 34–36 on Mahan, geopolitics, and restraining Russia; and 193–201 on the alleged "Blue Water Strategy" of the day.)

Fitzgerald, Capt. T. A. "Blitzkrieg at Sea." *Proceedings* (January 1986): 12–16. (Argues Soviets may use their navy as a risk fleet for a "Blitzkrieg" and not for sea denial. A view shared by many U.S. Navy operators.)

** Falin, Valentin. "Back to the Stone Age." *Izvestia* (23/24 January 1986): 5/5. (A top Kremlin spokesman takes *The Maritime Strategy* to task as "remarkably odious": "It is hardly possible to imagine anything worse." Highlights opposing arguments by Barry Posen.) See also commentary by Capt. William Manthorpe, USN (Ret.). "The Soviet View: The Soviet Union Reacts." *Proceedings* (April 1986): 111.

Petersen, Charles C. "Strategic Lessons of the Recent Soviet Naval Exercise." *National Defense* (February 1986): 32–36. (A leading strategy analyst at the Center for Naval Analyses sees Soviets' strategy as threatening U.S. ports and SLOCs in addition to defending SSBNs close to their homeland. Urges USN strategic homeporting, mine warfare, and shallow-water ASW initiatives, in addition to "carrying the fight to the enemy.")

** Friedman, Norman. "Soviet Naval Aviation." *Naval Forces,* no. 1 (1986): 92–97. (Sees Soviet naval aviation as perhaps the greatest threat to NATO navies.)

** Balev, B. "The Military-Political Strategy of Imperialism on the World Ocean." *World Economics and International Relations* (April 1936): 24–31. (A Soviet perspective on *The Maritime Strategy*—the "*novaya morskaya strategiya.*" The three notional phases restyled as "Keeping Oneself on the Verge of War," "Seizing the Initiative," and "Carrying Combat Operations into Enemy Territory.")

** Komenskiy, Capt. First Rank V. "The NATO Strategic Command in the Atlantic" and "Combat Exercises of the Combined NATO Forces in 1985." *Zarubezhnoiye voyennoiye obozreniye* (April 1986): 47–53; and (August 1986): 45–51. (Includes discussion of roles and missions of NATO naval forces in the context of *The Maritime Strategy.*) See also Colonel V. Rodin, "The Military Doctrines of Japan" (August 1986): 3–9.

Ries, Tomas, and Johnny Skorve. *Investigating Kola: A Study of Military Bases Using Satellite Photos.* Oslo: Norsk Utenrikspolitisk Institutt, 1986. (See especially 21–49 on the place of Fenno-Scandia and adjacent waters in the context of overall Soviet strategy.)

MccGwire, Cdr. Michael, RN (Ret.). "Soviet Military Objectives." *World Policy Journal* (Fall 1986): 667–695. (Adapted from his book, cited below. Much that goes against the grain of contemporary informed conventional wisdom regarding Soviet intentions, including the naval threat. Mediterranean seen as particularly important. See especially 676–680.)

**   Manthorpe, Capt. William, USN (Ret). "The Soviet View: RimPac-86." *Proceedings* (October 1986): 191. (The Soviets see linkages between *The Maritime Strategy* and allied exercises.)

van Tol, Robert. "Soviet Naval Exercises 1983–1985." *Naval Forces,* no. 6 (1986): 18–34. (Most useful in its discussion of the interactions between NATO and Soviet strategies and between NATO and Soviet exercises.)

MccGwire, Cdr. Michael, RN (Ret.). *Military Objectives in Soviet Foreign Policy.* Washington, D.C.: Brookings Institution, 1987. (Individualistic, iconoclastic, and debatable.)

Schandler, Herbert Y. "Arms Control in Northeast Asia." *Washington Quarterly* (Winter 1987): 69–79. (Wide-ranging article that gives the context within which *The Maritime Strategy* operates in the Pacific. Highlights "the ever-looming nightmare of a two-front war" as gaining in credibility for the Soviet Union. "This two-front threat is enormously important to Soviet psychology and provides the United States with a major pressure point on Soviet leaders.")

**   Mozgovoy, Aleksandr. "For Security on Sea Routes." *International Affairs* (Moscow), no. 1 (1987): 77–84, 103. (See especially 83 on *The Maritime Strategy* as "an unprecedentedly impudent document, even given the militaristic hysteria reigning in Washington today.")

**   Manthorpe, Capt. William, USN (Ret.). "The Soviet View: More than Meets the Eye." *Proceedings* (February 1987): 117–118. (Sophisticated analysis of 3–4 October 1986 *Red Star* article on potential changes in Soviet doctrine, strategic thinking, and planning that, if adopted, would have important implications for Soviet response to *The Maritime Strategy.*)

*   Weinberger, Caspar. *Soviet Military Power 1987.* Washington, D.C.: U.S. Government Printing Office, March 1987. (More extensive analysis of Soviet strategy and operational concepts than in previous five editions.)

*   U.S. Navy. Office of Naval Intelligence. *Current Intelligence Issues.* Washington, D.C.: Department of the Navy Office of Information, March 1987. (See especially 1–4 on the anticipated employment of Soviet naval forces in wartime.)

**   Breemer, Jan. "U.S. Maritime Strategy: A Re-Appraisal." *Naval Forces,* no. 2 (1987): 4–76. (Discusses the background behind and the issues surrounding current U.S. Navy thinking on Soviet naval strategy.)

**   Elliott, Frank. "Soviets Knew of Maritime Strategy before Lehman, Watkins Publicized It." *Defense Week* (4 May 1987): 5. (Reports on important seminar on Soviet views of *The Maritime Strategy.* See also seminar transcript, Annapolis, Md.: U.S. Naval Institute, 1987.)

**   Daniel, Donald C. F. "The Soviet Navy and Tactical Nuclear War at Sea." *Survival* (July/August 1987): 138ff. (The then director of the Naval War College's Strategy and Campaign Department concludes, inter alia, that Soviet decision makers would use nuclear weapons at sea only if they had already been used ashore or if NATO used them at sea first.)

VII. Peacetime, Crises, and Third World Contingencies

Most of the above works deal principally with use of the Navy in general war. What follows are books and articles of the 1970s and 1980s discussing the uses of the U.S. Navy in peacetime, crises, and "small wars" (the "violent peace" of *The Maritime Strategy*). Many of these derive from the increased discussion of peacetime presence as a naval mission engendered by Admirals Elmo Zumwalt and Stansfield Turner in the early 1970s. Thus, the contemporary era of U.S. Navy thought on peacetime presence operations began about five years prior to that on forward global wartime operational concepts. Both bodies of thought, however, built on the earlier literature of the late 1950s and 1960s on the role of the U.S. Navy in limited war.

While most of the items listed below focus on the U.S. Navy, there was a significant literature on the peacetime/crisis/"small war" activities of the Royal Navy and the Soviet Navy as well, some of the most important elements of which have been included here. In addition, certain of the white papers and defense reports published by various defense ministries around the world routinely highlighted the peacetime operations of their naval forces. Especially notable in this regard were the annual British "Defense Estimates" and Canadian "Annual Reports."

Joint Senate/House Armed Services Subcommittee. Hearings on *CVAN-70 Aircraft Carrier.* 91st Cong., 2nd sess. Washington, D.C.: U.S. Government Printing Office, 1970, 162–165. (Listing of uses of USN in wars/near-wars 1946–1969; takes negative view of same.)

Cable, James. *Gunboat Diplomacy: Political Applications of Limited Naval Force.* New York: Praeger, 1970. (First of a spate of useful books seeking to list, classify, and describe peacetime uses of navies. Surveys twentieth-century activities of all major navies. Updated in 1981.)

Howe, Cdr. Jonathan. *Multicrisis: Sea Power and Global Politics in the Missile Age.* Cambridge, Mass.: MIT Press, 1971. (The 1967 Mideast crisis, the 1958 Quemoy crisis, and the effectiveness of conventional naval forces as foreign policy instruments, by a future flag officer and political-military affairs subspecialist. Argues for a strong global naval posture, especially in the Mediterranean.)

Bull, Hedley. "Sea Power and Political Influence." In *Power at Sea: I. The New Environment.* Adelphi Paper Number 122. London: International Institute for Strategic Studies, 1974, 1–9. ("The period we are now entering will be one in which opportunities for the diplomatic use of naval forces, at least for the great powers, will be severely circumscribed.")

Moore, Capt. J. E., RN. "The Business of Surveillance." *Navy International* (June 1974): 9–10. (Rationale for peacetime surveillance operations at sea.)

McGruther, Lt. Cdr. Kenneth. "The Role of Perception in Naval Diplomacy." *Naval War College Review* (September–October 1974): 3–20. (Part of the initial Zumwalt-Turner new look at USN "Naval Presence" mission. Includes Indian Ocean case study and a "cookbook." By a future OP-603 staffer.)

McNulty, Cdr. James. "Naval Presence: The Misunderstood Mission." *Naval War College Review* (September–October 1974): 21–31. (Another reflection of the initial Zumwalt-Turner focus on presence.) See also Stansfield Turner, "Challenge": 1–2 in the same issue.

Luttwak, Edward N. *The Political Uses of Sea Power.* Baltimore: Johns Hopkins University Press, 1974. (Short treatment sponsored by Vice Admiral Turner. Typology and analysis based on concept of "suasion." Focus on the U.S. Navy in the Mediterranean.)

Young, Elizabeth. "New Laws for Old Navies: Military Implications of the Law of the Sea." *Survival* (November–December 1974): 262–267. (Forecasts the demise of naval diplomacy.)

Hill, Capt. J. R., RN. "Maritime Power and the Law of the Sea." *Survival* (March–April 1975): 69–72. (Takes issue with Young's article. Suggests that "in the turbulent future, maritime forces are likely to be more rather than less in demand both at home and away.")

McCGwire, Cdr. Michael, RN (Ret.). "Changing Naval Operations and Military Intervention." In *The Limits of Military Intervention*, by Ellen P. Stern. Beverly Hills, Calif.: Sage, 1977, 151–178 and reprinted in *Naval War College Review* (Spring 1977): 3–25. (Sees numerous constraints now in place on the "almost casual use of force which used to be the norm" in military intervention by sea.)

McCGwire, Cdr. Michael, RN (Ret.), and John McDonnell, eds. *Soviet Naval Influence: Domestic and Foreign Dimensions*. New York: Praeger, 1977. (See especially chapters by McCGwire, Booth, Dismukes, and Kelly.)

Booth, Ken. *Navies and Foreign Policy*. London: Croon Helm, 1977. (Magisterial treatment.)

Mahoney, Robert B., Jr. "U.S. Navy Responses to International Incidents and Crises, 1955–1975." Washington, D.C.: Center for Naval Analyses, 1977. (Survey of USN crisis operations and summaries of incidents and responses.)

Nathan, James A., and James K. Oliver. "The Evolution of International Order and the Future of the American Naval Presence Mission." *Naval War College Review* (Fall 1977): 37–59. (Sees political and technological changes as necessitating revision to contemporary thinking on naval presence, just when that thinking had begun to solidify.)

Eldredge, Capt. Howard S. "Nonsuperpower Sea Denial Capability: The Implications for Superpower Navies Engaged in Presence Operations." In *Arms Transfers to the Third World*, edited by Uri Ra'anan et al. Boulder, Colo.: Westview, 1978, 21–64. (Argues that growing sea-denial arsenals of littoral nations were complicating the risk calculations of the superpowers in using naval forces to further their interests. Focus on antiship missiles and submarine torpedoes.)

Blechman, Barry M., and Stephen S. Kaplan. *Force without War: U.S. Armed Forces as a Political Instrument*. Washington, D.C.: Brookings Institution, 1978. (Utility of USN vs. other U.S. armed forces.)

Congressional Budget Office. *U.S. Naval Forces: The Peacetime Presence Mission*. Washington, D.C.: 1978. (How it could allegedly be done with fewer CVs.)

Zakheim, Dov S. "Maritime Presence, Projection, and the Constraints of Parity." In *Equivalence, Sufficiency and the International Balance*. Washington, D.C.: National Defense University, August 1978, 101–118. (Argues for a combined-arms approach, vice solely naval focus, for U.S. maritime presence.)

Dismukes, Bradford, and James M. McConnell, eds. *Soviet Naval Diplomacy*. New York: Pergamon, 1979. (Comprehensive surveys and analyses.)

Madison, Cdr. Russell L. "The War of Unengaged Forces: Superpowers at Sea in an Era of Competitive Coexistence." *Naval War College Review* (March–April 1979): 82–94. (Thoughtful piece seeking to integrate naval peacetime and wartime missions into one framework—a "Theory of Unengaged Force Warfare.")

Smith, Edward Allen. "Naval Confrontation: The Intersuperpower Use of Naval Suasion in Times of Crisis." PhD diss., American University, 1979. (Examination of U.S. and Soviet use of their navies in six postwar crises. Heavily influenced by Luttwak's concept of "naval suasion.")

Allen, Capt. Charles D., Jr. USN (Ret.). *The Uses of Navies in Peacetime.* Washington, D.C.: American Enterprise Institute, 1980. Excellent short analysis, with typology. (Focus on postwar U.S. Navy and on escalation.)

Kaplan, Stephen S. *Diplomacy of Power: Soviet Armed Forces as a Political Instrument.* Washington, D.C.: Brookings Institution, 1981. (Does for the Soviets what Blechman and Kaplan did for the United States.)

Cohen, Raymond. *International Politics: The Rules of the Game.* London: Longman, 1981. 41–48. (One of the few general works on international relations by an academic political scientist to deal in any depth with the peacetime and crisis uses of navies. Navy force movements seen as part of the "vocabulary of international politics.")

Truver, Scott C. "New International Constraints on Military Power: Navies in the Political Role." *Naval War College Review* (July–August 1981): 99–104. (Sees regular employment of major naval combatants and large-deck carriers as becoming less tenable in Third World areas for the remainder of the century, for a variety of reasons.)

Neutze, Cdr. Dennis R., USN (JAGC). "Bluejacket Diplomacy: A Juridical Examination of the Use of Naval Forces in Support of United States Foreign Policy." *JAG Journal* (Summer 1982): 81–158. (By the legal advisor to the Deputy Chief of Naval Operations for Plans, Policy, and Operations. Very comprehensive examination of the lawfulness of the political uses of U.S. naval power in terms of domestic and international law, going back to the framers of the Constitution. Sees such political uses as expanding in the future.)

Wright, Christopher C., III. "U.S. Naval Operations in 1982." *Proceedings/Naval Review* (May 1983). Excellent survey and analysis. (Includes general introduction to USN concepts of operations, deployment patterns, and tempo of operations, as well as review of actual deployments. See also annual updates in subsequent *Naval Reviews.*)

Hickman, Lt. Cdr. William J. "Did It Really Matter?" *Naval War College Review* (March–April 1983): 17–30. (By a future OP-603 staffer. On limitations and misuses of U.S.

Navy naval presence operations. Indian Ocean case study is useful counterpoint to McGruther article a decade earlier, above.)

Barnett, Capt. Roger W. "The U.S. Navy's Role in Countering Maritime Terrorism." *Terrorism* 6, no. 3 (1983): 469–480. (A primary architect of *The Maritime Strategy* argues that while the U.S. Navy is well prepared against attacks on its own ships and installations, its role in deterring terrorist attacks on U.S. merchant ships or overseas facilities "cannot be suggested to be a large one.")

Zelikow, Philip D. "Force without War, 1975–82." *Journal of Strategic Studies* (March 1984): 29–54. (Updates Blechman and Kaplan book. Also provides listing of incidents when U.S. Navy was used.)

Cable, Sir James. "Showing the Flag." *Proceedings* (April 1984): 59–63. (The utility of ship visits.)

Luttwak, Edward N. *The Pentagon and the Art of War.* New York: Simon and Schuster, 1984, 222, 247–248. (Sees diminishing value of peacetime deployments.)

Howe, Rear Adm. Jonathan T. "Multicrisis Management: Meeting an Expanding Challenge." In *Security Commitments and Capabilities: Elements of an American Global Strategy*, edited by Uri Ra'anan and Robert L. Pfaltzgraff, Jr.. Hamden, Conn.: Archon Books, 1985, 125–137. (Reflections on America's ability to manage "multicrises," through naval as well as other means, by the U.S. naval officer who popularized the term fifteen years earlier.)

Martin, Laurence. "The Use of Naval Forces in Peacetime." *Naval War College Review* (January–February 1985): 4–14. (A lecture summarizing many contemporary themes on the subject.)

* U.S. Senate, Armed Services Committee. *Hearings on the Department of Defense Authorization for Appropriations for Fiscal Year 1986, Part 8.* 99th Cong. 1st sess. Washington, D.C.: U.S. Government Printing Office, 1986, 4409–4448. (Vice Adm. James A. Lyons on "Global Naval Commitments." 18 February 1985. The official policy enunciated by the Deputy Chief of Naval Operations for Plans, Policy and Operations [OP-06].)

Arnott, Cdr. Ralph E., and Cdr. William A. Gaffney. "Naval Presence: Sizing the Force." *Naval War College Review* (March–April 1985): 13–30. (Seeks to develop a rational structured approach to choosing a force tailored to respond to a particular crisis, so as to achieve the desired outcome with minimum effect on scheduled fleet operations.)

Lehman, John F., Jr. "An Absolute Requirement for Every American." *Sea Power* (April 1985): 13. (Secretary of the Navy argues that the high USN peacetime operating tempo is partly self-generated. See also *Washington Post* [6 October 1985]: A12, and *Virginia Pilot/Ledger Star* [27 October 1985]: A1.)

Daniel, Donald C., and Gael D. Tarleton. "The Soviet Navy in 1984." *Proceedings/Naval Review* (May 1985): 90–92, 361–364. (Snapshot of one year's Soviet global peacetime activity. See subsequent *Naval Reviews* for updates.)

Etzold, Thomas H. "Neither Peace Nor War: Navies and Low-Intensity Conflict." In *Future Imperative: National Security and the U.S. Navy in the Late 1980s,* by Harlan K. Ullman and Thomas H. Etzold. Washington, D.C.: CSIS, 1985. (Argues that low-intensity U.S. Navy contingencies and peacetime operations were on the increase.)

Levine, Daniel B. *Planning for Underway Replenishment of Naval Forces in Peacetime CRM 85–77.* Alexandria, Va.: Center for Naval Analyses, September 1985. (Concerns much more than underway replenishment. Examines U.S. Navy fleet exercises, crisis response, and surveillance operations. Analyzes them by ocean area, frequency, and number/types of combatants used.)

Harris, Cdr. R. Robinson, and Lt. Cdr. Joseph Benkert. "Is That All There Is?" *Proceedings* (October 1985): 32–37. (Contrasts peacetime and global war strategy requirements, with focus on surface combatants.)

Booth, Ken. *Law, Force, and Diplomacy at Sea.* London: George Allen and Unwin, 1985. (Peacetime naval strategy and the law of the sea, and much more. Rebuts Elizabeth Young arguments of a decade earlier: 66–68.)

Hill, Rear Adm. J. R., RN. *Maritime Strategy for Medium Powers.* Annapolis, Md.: Naval Institute Press, 1986. (Chapter 6, "Normal Conditions": 88–110, describes the various roles of navies, especially those of medium-sized countries, in peacetime. Chapter 7, "Low Intensity Operations": 88–131, covers operations somewhat higher up on the scale of violence.)

Parritt, Brigadier Brian. *Violence at Sea: A Review of Terrorism, Acts of War and Piracy, and Countermeasures to Prevent Terrorism.* Paris: ICC, 1986. (See especially Paul Wilkinson's "Terrorism and the Maritime Environment": 35–40, on the role of navies in combating terrorism and the kinds of naval force required.)

Mandel, Robert. "The Effectiveness of Gunboat Diplomacy." *International Studies Quarterly* (March 1986): 59–76. ("The most effective gunboat diplomacy involves a definitive, deterrent display of force undertaken by an assailant who has engaged in war in the victim's region and who is militarily prepared and politically stable compared to the victim.")

** Elliott, Frank. "Battleships Assume Some Carrier Duties." *Navy Times* (31 March 1986): 25, 28. (Role of battleships vis-à-vis carriers in the presence mission.)

Vlahos, Michael. "The Third World in U.S. Navy Planning." *Orbis* (Spring 1986): 133–148. (By a former Naval War College faculty member. Argues the U.S. Navy has recently refocused its attention on its contributions to a global allied campaign against the Soviets, to the detriment of planning for more likely and qualitatively different Third World contingencies.)

Cable, Sir James. "Gunboat Diplomacy's Future." *Proceedings* (August 1986): 36–41. (Forcefully argues that the days of gunboat diplomacy are by no means over. Denigrates those who have said otherwise.)

Coutau-Bégarie, Hervé. "The Role of the Navy in French Foreign Policy." *Naval Forces*, no. 6 (1986): 36–43. (By probably the most important contemporary French writer on naval strategy. The recent French global experience, one not often discussed in an English-language literature dominated by U.S., British, and Soviet examples.)

"Navy Cuts Carrier Presence in Mediterranean, Gulf Areas." *Washington Times* (24 November 1986): 4-D. (On adjustments to U.S. Navy routine forward presence posture to enhance Navy flexibility and reduce individual ship operating tempo.)

James, Lawrence. "Old Problems and Old Answers: Gunboat Diplomacy Today." *Defense Analysis* (December 1986): 324–327. (On its limitations, past and present.)

Bush, Ted. "Sailors Spending More Time at Home under PersTempo." *Navy Times* (February 1987): 3. (On naval presence and morale. The U.S. Navy tries to balance conflicting requirements.) See also Tom Philpott and John Burlage, "Stepped Up Operations May Cut Home Port Time." *Navy Times* (22 June 1987): 1, 8; and John Burlage, "CNO Trost: No Retreat on OpTempo." *Navy Times* (13 July 1987): 1, 26.

Cable, Sir James. "Showing the Flag: Past and Present." *Naval Forces,* no. 3 (1987): 38–49. (Update of Cable's thought on this particular aspect of peacetime naval operations.) Cf. his views in the April 1934 *Proceedings* cited above.

Jordan, Col. Amos A., USA (Ret). "A National Strategy for the 1990s." *Washington Quarterly* (Summer 1987): 15. (The president of the Center for Strategic and International Studies sees Third World peoples as increasingly uncowed by "gunboat diplomacy and other similar kinds of hollow threats.")

VIII. Fleet Balance: Atlantic vs. Pacific vs. Mediterranean

Geographic flexibility is one of the great strengths of naval power. Yet the U.S. Navy's *global* posture after World War II often looked like a series of hard-and-fast *theater* commitments, more appropriate to less flexible land-based types of forces. The articles and letters below illustrate the problems of implementing a balanced global maritime strategy with limited naval forces in the face of competing regional demands. They were selected because of their focus on the need for hard choices by the Navy regarding fleet balance; articles merely trumpeting the importance of an area or discussing regional priorities solely at the geopolitical level are omitted.

Booth, Ken. "U.S. Naval Strategy: Problems of Survivability, Usability, and Credibility." *Naval War College Review* (Summer 1978): 11–28. (Argues for withdrawal of Sixth Fleet.)

McGruther, Lt. Cdr. Kenneth R. "Two Anchors in the Pacific: A Strategy Proposal for the U.S. Pacific Fleet." *Proceedings/Naval Review* (May 1979): 126–141. (On reorienting the Pacific Fleet primarily northward for wartime operations, and secondarily westward, for peacetime presence. By a former OP-603 staffer.)

Etzold, Thomas. "From Far East to Middle East: Overextension in American Strategy since World War II." *Proceedings/Naval Review* (May 1981): 66–77. (On the need to make hard strategic choices, especially between the Pacific and Indian Oceans.)

Cole, Cdr. Bernard. "Atlantic First." *Proceedings* (August 1982): 103–106. Also "Comment and Discussion" (December 1982): 86–87.

Deutermann, Capt. Peter. "Requiem for the Sixth Fleet." *Proceedings* (September 1982): 46–49. Also "Comment and Discussion" (November 1982): 14; (January 1983): 17–20; (February 1983): 80–81; (March 1983): 12–17; (July 1983): 89.

Breemer, Jan S. "De-Committing the Sixth Fleet." *Naval War College Review* (November–December 1982): 27–32.

Jampoler, Capt. Andrew. "Reviewing the Conventional Wisdom." *Proceedings* (July 1983): 22–28. Also "Comment and Discussion" (December 1983): 26. (On refocusing the Atlantic Fleet from the Mediterranean to the North Atlantic.)

Ortlieb, Cdr. E. V. "Forward Deployments: Deterrent or Temptation." *Proceedings* (December 1983): 36–40. Also "Comment and Discussion" (February 1984): 22. (On reducing the Sixth and Seventh Fleets while increasing the Second and Third.)

Maiorano, Lt. Alan. "A Fresh Look at the Sixth Fleet." *Proceedings* (February 1984): 52–58. Also "Comment and Discussion" (July 1984): 28–33. (On reducing the U.S. Navy Mediterranean commitment, with U.S. Air Force and allied forces filling any gaps.)

Dismukes, Bradford, and Kenneth G. Weiss. "Mare Mosso: The Mediterranean Theater." In *The U.S. Navy: The View from the Mid-1980s*, edited by James L. George. Boulder, Colo.: Westview. (On timing reductions in U.S. Navy Mediterranean forces.)

Sestak, Lt. Cdr. Joseph. "Righting the Atlantic Tilt." *Proceedings* (January 1986): 64–71.

Kolodziej, Edward A. "The Southern Flank: NATO's Neglected Front." *AEI Foreign Policy and Defense Review* 6, no. 2 (1986): 45–56, especially: 48–50. (A leading political scientist endorses Captain Deutermann's views on reorienting U.S. naval concentration from the Mediterranean to the Atlantic.)

** Lee, Ngoc, and Lt. Cdr. Alan Hinge, RAN. "The Naval Balance in the Indian-Pacific Ocean Region." *Naval Forces,* no. 2 (1987): 150–175. (Views the U.S. Navy as understrength for warfighting in the Atlantic-Mediterranean threats, and overly strong in the Pacific and Indian Oceans. Essentially an update of Hinge's August 1986 article cited in section II above.)

IX. War Gaming

As is well discussed in previous sections, the U.S. and allied navies, other services, and joint and allied commands have a variety of means at their disposal in peacetime to test the wartime validity of aspects of *The Maritime Strategy,* besides debate and discussion. They participate in fleet exercises, advanced tactical training, and "real world" peacetime and crisis operations, and they conduct extensive operations analyses and war games. These avenues are generally inaccessible to the public, however, save one—gaming. There were in those years over a half-dozen commercial board and computer games available that could provide players with insights into maritime strategic, operational, and tactical problems and potential solutions, and thereby further enhance players' understanding of *The Maritime Strategy*. Like all simulations, however, each had its limitations, and even built-in inaccuracies (as the various reviews point out.) Thus they could not by themselves legitimately be used to "prove" validities or demonstrate "outcomes." Nevertheless, playing them was the nearest many students and theorists of maritime strategy could ever come to actually "being there."

A. Commentary

** Perla, Peter P. "Wargaming and the U.S. Navy." *National Defense* (February 1987): 49–53. (By a leading Center for Naval Analyses war gamer. "The Navy is continuing a process of using wargaming, exercises, and analysis to address the aspects of major issues for which they are best suited. . . . [A] classic example of this process can be seen at work in the 2nd Fleet. Taking the promulgated maritime strategy as his starting point, the commander, 2nd Fleet, proposed a concept for operating the NATO Striking Fleet in the Norwegian Sea. A war game was held at the Naval War College to explore this concept, and analysis was undertaken to quantify some of the issues raised by the game. Then an exercise was held in the area of interest, which confirmed some assumptions and raised new questions. A new series of games and analysis was capped by a second major exercise, as the process continues." See also his "What

Wargaming Is and Is Not," co-authored by Lt. Cdr. Raymond T. Barrett, *Naval War College Review* [September–October 1985]: 70–78, as well as "In My View" commentary—*Naval War College Review* [Autumn 1986]: 105–108.) See also "War Games, Analyses, and Exercises." *Naval War College Review* (Spring 1987): 44–52 (and endorsement from former CNO Adm. Thomas Hayward, USN (Ret.) in August 1987 *Proceedings*.

Connors, Lt. Cdr. Tracy D., USNR. "Gaming for the World." *Proceedings* (January 1984): 106–108. (On the Naval War College's Global War Game series, a principal research tool for identifying critical Navy, joint, and allied Maritime Strategy issues.) See also Robert J. Murray, "A War-Fighting Perspective. *Proceedings* (October 1983): 66–81; and Cdr. James Eulis, "War Gaming at the U.S. Naval War College." *Naval Forces,* no. 5 (1985): 96–103.

B. Games

Grigsby, Gary. *North Atlantic '86.* Mountain View, Calif.: Strategic Simulations, Inc., 1983 (Apple computer game). Reviewed by John Gresham and Michael Markowitz. *Proceedings* (July 1984): 116–117. (Entering premise is the initial failure of NATO, United States, and *The Maritime Strategy*: "The great war in Europe is over. As expected, Russia won; it now controls all of Germany and Norway. Its next plan: complete domination of the North Atlantic through the isolation of Great Britain.")

Nichols, W. J. *Grey Seas, Grey Skies.* Bridgewater, Nova Scotia: Simulations Canada, 1983, 1987 (Apple computer game). Reviewed by John Gresham and Michael Markowitz. *Proceedings* (July 1984): 116–117. (Seven "prebuilt" scenarios, including Japanese destroyers versus Soviet submarines in the Kurile Islands, a Soviet amphibious group versus West German forces in the Baltic, U.S. versus Soviet carrier battle groups off the North Cape, and similar clashes in the Western Pacific and the Mediterranean. Focus is more tactical than in the other games listed here.)

Nichols, W. J. *Fifth Escadra.* Bridgewater, Nova Scotia: Simulations Canada, 1984 (Apple computer game). (Soviets versus NATO in the Mediterranean. Five levels of conflict ranging from rising tensions to global nuclear war.)

Nichols, W. J. *Seventh Fleet.* Bridgewater, Nova Scotia: Simulations Canada, 1985 (Apple computer game). (Soviets versus United States and Japan. Includes Sea of Okhotsk, Sea of Japan, and South China Sea operations.)

** Balkoski, Joseph. *Sixth Fleet.* New York: Victory Games, 1986 (board game). Reviewed by U.S. Naval Historical Center historian Michael A. Palmer. *Strategy and Tactics* (January–February 1986): 51–52. ("The inclusion of random elements into the system, the addition of logistic rules, and the key role of Soviet naval aviation made the *Sixth Fleet* game an excellent operational level naval wargame.")

Balkoski, Joseph. *Second Fleet.* New York: Victory Games, 1986 (board game). Reviewed by U.S. Naval Historical Center historian Michael A. Palmer. *Proceedings* (March 1987): 160–162. ("Those of us without access to the War College's computers can test the waters north of the Greenland-Iceland–United Kingdom (GIUK) Gap and gain insight into the problems and opportunities inherent in the application of *The Maritime Strategy.*" Could be played simultaneously with *Sixth Fleet,* with forces shifted from one set of maps to the other, in a simulation of war in both northern and southern European waters and adjacent areas.)

Herman, Mark *Aegean Strike.* New York: Victory Games, 1986 (board game). Reviewed by U.S. Naval Historical Center historian Michael A. Palmer. *Strategy and Tactics* (1987). (The eastern Mediterranean. "Few, if any, games . . . better integrate the strengths and weaknesses of land, air, and naval assets.")

X. Antecedents

The general and historical literature on naval strategy is admittedly vast. What is presented here are only books that describe earlier strategies—conceptualized, planned, or implemented—that are analogous to key aspects of the U.S. Navy's Maritime Strategy. The materials are generally listed chronologically by historical period covered.

Till, Geoffrey. *Maritime Strategy and the Nuclear Age,* 2nd ed. New York: St. Martin's, 1984. (Basic one-volume historical and topical survey.)

Callwell, Maj. C. E., BA. *The Effect of Maritime Command on Land Campaigns since Waterloo.* Edinburgh: William Blackwood and Sons, 1897 (especially 178–182 and 196–197); Barker, A. J. *The War against Russia, 1854–1856.* New York: Holt, Rinehart and Winston, 1970; John Shelton Curtiss. *Russia's Crimean War.* Durham, N.C.: Duke University Press, 1979; and Norman Rich. *Why the Crimean War? A Cautionary Tale.* Hanover, N.H.: University Press of New England, 1985 (especially 124–126, 136–137, 158–159, 178, 201–202, 206–209). (Successful maritime global forward coalition strategy against Russia 130 years ago, with operations in Barents, Baltic, and Black Seas, and off the Kuriles and Kamchatka. Component of a larger military strategy, which blocked subsequent Russian expansion for over twenty years.)

** Mahan, Capt. Alfred Thayer. "The Problem of Asia." In his *The Problem of Asia and Its Effect upon International Politics.* Cambridge, Mass.: University Press, 1900, 1–146. (Mahan on "restraining Russia," the central problem of *The Maritime Strategy*: "The Russian centre cannot be broken. It is upon, and from, the flanks . . . that restraint, if needed, must come" [p. 26]; "Hence ensues solidarity of interest between Germany,

Great Britain, Japan and the United States" [p. 63].) See also Trofimenko, in section VI above; and Philip A. Crowl, "Alfred Thayer Mahan: The Naval Historian." In *Makers of Modern Strategy: From Machiavelli to the Nuclear Age*, edited by Peter Paret. Princeton, N.J.: Princeton University Press, 1986, 444–477, especially 477. (A Naval War College professor emeritus asserts *The Maritime Strategy* is antithetical to Mahan's teaching, especially as regards the role of other services, in a book that otherwise—and to its detriment—pays scant attention to makers of modern maritime strategy. Trofimenko gets the linkage between Mahan and *The Maritime Strategy* right. Crowl gets it wrong.)

Schilling, Warner R. "Admirals and Foreign Policy, 1913–1919." Ph.D. diss., Yale University, 1954. ("Maritime Strategy" of the 1980s was not the first time this century the U.S. Navy developed a coherent preferred strategy.)

Palmer, Alan. *The Gardeners of Salonika.* New York: Simon and Schuster, 1965: especially 226–247. (Southern Flank Maritime Strategy in action. World War I allies advance to the Danube from beachhead in Greece in 1918, knocking Austria-Hungary, Bulgaria, and Turkey out of the war. Gallipoli concept vindicated.)

Roskill, Stephen W. *Naval Policy between the Wars,* vol. 1, *The Period of Anglo-American Antagonism, 1919–1929.* New York: Walker, 1968: esp. chap. 3, "The War of Intervention in Russia, 1918–1920"; and Christopher Dobson and John Miller, *The Day They Almost Bombed Moscow: The Allied War in Russia, 1918–1920.* New York: Atheneum, 1986. 42–47, 72–73, 247–266, and 274–276. (Poorly devised global, allied, forward maritime operations against the Soviets seventy years ago, which, however, did achieve independence for the Baltic States.)

** Miller, Edward S. *War Plan Orange, 1897–1945: The Naval Campaign through the Central Pacific.* Annapolis, Md.: Naval Institute Press, 1988. (History's most successful prewar plan, with lessons for the complex problems of naval strategic planning of the 1980s.) See also Vice Adm. George C. Dyer, *On the Treadmill to Pearl Harbor: The Memoirs of Admiral James O. Richardson, USN (Ret.).* Washington, D.C.: Naval History Division, Department of the Navy, 1973: chap. 14, "War Plans"; and Cdr. Michael W. Shelton, CEC, "Plan Orange Revisited." *Proceedings* (December 1984): 50–56, and "Comment and Discussion" (March 1985): 73 and 79. (Draws false parallels between the western Pacific in 1941 and the Norwegian Sea of the 1980s—that is, between a purely naval, unilateral, theater problem and one portion of a joint, allied, global problem. Advocates ceding the Norwegian Sea, Norway, and Iceland to the Soviets. Bad history and worse strategy.)

** Vlahos, Michael. "Wargaming, an Enforcer of Strategic Realism: 1919–1942." *Naval War College Review* (March–April 1986): 7–22. (By a former Naval War College faculty member. How war gaming prepared the U.S. Navy for war in 1941 and how it was doing so again in 1986, including linkage between gaming and planning.)

** Reynolds, Clark G. "*The Maritime Strategy* of World War II: Some Implications?" *Naval War College Review* (May–June 1986): 43–50. (By a former Naval Academy faculty member. Gleans lessons and implications for today's Maritime Strategy from that of World War II.)

** Turner, Adm. Stansfield, USN (Ret.). "Victory at Sea: Bull Halsey at Leyte Gulf." *Washington Post Book World*, 15 December 1986: 1 and 13. (Review of E. B. Potter's *Bull Halsey*. Draws analogies to contemporary military problems, especially regarding "the offense and the defense." Of a piece with Turner's other writings.)

Erickson, John. *The Road to Stalingrad* (vol. 1) and *The Road to Berlin* (vol. 2). Boulder, Colo.: Westview, 1983. See especially vol. 1: 14, 55–57, 218, 237–240, 271–272, 295; vol. 2: 43, 132, 156. (Effect of Far East operations—or lack thereof—on the Central/East Europe Front in World War II.)

Spykman, Nicholas John. *The Geography of the Peace.* New York: Harcourt, Brace, 1944. (Basic geopolitical reference. See especially maps, 50–54.)

Love, Robert, B., Jr., ed. *The Chiefs of Naval Operations.* Annapolis, Md.: U.S. Naval Institute Press, 1980. (See sections on post–World War II CNOs' views on strategy, especially Rosenberg piece on Arleigh Burke.)

Rosenberg, David. "American Postwar Air Doctrine and Organization: The Navy Experience." In *Air Power and Warfare*, by A. F. Hurley, R. C. Ehrhart, et al. Washington, D.C.: U.S. Government Printing Office, 1970. (Antecedent naval postwar air strike strategies by a leading historian of U.S. Navy postwar strategy.)

Nimitz, Fleet Adm. Chester. "Future Employment of Naval Forces." *Vital Speeches* (5 January 1948): 214–217. (Also, in *Brassey's Naval Annual* [1948] and *Shipmate* [February 1948]: 5–6ff, as "Our Navy: Its Future." Argues for a projection strategy and a Navy capable of land attack early in a war.)

Cave Brown, Anthony, ed. *Dropshot, The American Plan for World War III against Russia in 1957.* New York: Dial, 1978. (1949 JCS study: good example of early post-war strategic thinking. See especially 161–165, 206–211, 225–235. Not to be read without examining the review by David Rosenberg and Thomas E. Kelly III, *Naval War College Review* [Fall 1978]: 103–106.)

** Palmer, Michael A. *Origins of The Maritime Strategy: American Naval Strategy in the First Postwar Decade.* Washington, D.C.: Naval Historical Center, 1988. (An important discussion of the similarities and differences in U.S. naval strategic thought between the first and fifth postwar decades, the two postwar eras most characterized by U.S. Navy concern with problems of naval warfighting vis-à-vis the Soviet Union itself.)

** Friedman, Norman. *The Postwar Naval Revolution.* London: Conway Maritime, 1986. See especially chapter 10, "Epilogue," 212–218. (On allied naval developments in the first post–World War II decade, including relationships to *The Maritime Strategy* developed three decades later.)

Huntington, Samuel P. "National Policy and the Transoceanic Navy." *Proceedings* (May 1954): 483–93. (Clearly foreshadows the basic outline of *The Maritime Strategy.* An analysis generally as relevant in the 1980s as then.)

Marolda, Edward J. "The Influence of Burke's Boys on Limited War." *Proceedings* (August 1981): 36–41. (By a prominent Navy Department historian on the influence of the Navy officer corps on national strategy a generation ago. "Between 1956 and 1960, the Navy added its considerable influence to the intellectual campaign within the national defense community for a reorientation in strategic policy.")

Wylie, Capt. J. C. "Why a Sailor Thinks Like a Sailor." *Proceedings* (August 1957): 811–817. (By the Navy's leading public strategist of the 1950s and '60s. Remarkably similar to the views expressed in *The Maritime Strategy* a generation later.)

** Rosenberg, David. *U.S. Navy Long-Range Planning: A Historical Perspective.* Washington, D.C.: U.S. Government Printing Office, 1988.

Wylie, Rear Adm. J. C. *Military Strategy.* New Brunswick, N.J.: Rutgers University Press, 1967. Reprinted with an intoduction by John B. Hattendorf and a postscript by Wylie in the Classics of Sea Power Series. Naval Institute Press, 1989. (Codification of views of U.S. Navy's most prominent postwar strategic theorist.)

Gray, Colin S. *The Geopolitics of the Nuclear Era: Heartland, Rimlands, and the Technological Revolution.* New York: Crane Russak, 1977. (Analyzes and updates geopolitical grand theory. Stresses maritime aspects of the Western alliance and global nature of Western security problems.)

Comptroller General of the United States. *Implications of the National Security Council Study "U.S. Maritime Strategy and Naval Force Requirements" on the Future Naval Ship Force.* PSAD-78-6A. Washington, D.C.: U.S. General Accounting Office, 7 March 1978. (Discusses in detail—and in highly unsympathetic terms—the classified National Security Council study often cited by Secretary of the Navy John Lehman as triggering his thinking on U.S. naval strategy and force levels.) See also Donald Rumsfeld. "Which Five-Year Shipbuilding Program?" *Proceedings* (February 1977): 18–25.

Lehman, John. *Aircraft Carriers: The Real Choices.* Beverly Hills, Calif.: Sage, 1978. (Codification of Lehman's thought on naval strategy before becoming Secretary of the Navy. Much more than carriers, especially chapter 2.) See also his March 1980 testimony in U.S. Senate, Committee on the Budget, *Hearings on National Defense: Alternative Approaches to the U.S. Defense Program.* 96th Cong., 2nd sess. Washington, D.C.: U.S. Government Printing Office, 1980, 208–253.

U.S. Navy. *Sea Plan 2000: Naval Force Planning Study* (unclassified executive summary). Washington, D.C.: 28 March 1978. (A progenitor of *The Maritime Strategy.* Whereas the latter stresses the role of the Navy in a global conventional war with the Soviets, the former tended more toward emphasizing the extent of the range of potential uses of naval power.)

Ryan, Capt. Paul, USN (Ret). *First Line of Defense.* Stanford: Hoover Institution, 1981. (Mainstream USN perspectives on postwar defense policies through the Carter administration.)

XI. Making Modern Naval Strategy: Influences

Snyder, Jack. *The Ideology of the Offensive: Military Decision Making and the Disasters of 1914.* Ithaca, N.Y.: Cornell University Press, 1984, chap. 1. (On how military strategy gets made, and why. Geopolitical, bureaucratic, and personal factors. Views military as predictably and unfortunately biased toward offensive strategies.) See also his "Perceptions of the Security Dilemma in 1914." In *Psychology and Deterrence*, edited by Robert Jervis et al. Baltimore: John Hopkins University Press, 1985, 162–164. (Summarizes the literature on the alleged "Military Bias for the Offensive.")

Sagan, Scott D. "1914 Revisited: Allies, Offense, and Instability." *International Security* (Fall 1986): 151–175. (An excellent piece. Takes issue with literature on the alleged "Military Bias for the Offensive": "Offensive military doctrines are needed not only by states with expansionist war aims but also by states that have a strong interest in protecting an exposed ally.") See also Jack Snyder and Scott D. Sagan, "Correspondence: The Origins of Offense and the Consequences of Counterforce" (Winter 1986–1987): 187–198.

Bartlett, Henry C. "Approaches to Force Planning." *Naval War College Review* (May–June 1985): 37–48. (By a Naval War College faculty member. Provides eight approaches to Force Planning, but each such "approach" can—and does—apply to the drafting of strategy as well. They are presented by the author as pure types, stark alternatives, but in actual practice [for example, in the development of *The Maritime Strategy*] their influence on the strategist is often simultaneous, to a greater or lesser degree. His list of approaches: "top-down," "bottom-up," "scenario," "threat," "mission," "hedging," "technology," and "fiscal." The first four were probably the most important influences on *The Maritime Strategy* of the late 1940s–early 1950s and the 1980s; "mission" and "hedging" were relatively more important from the late 1950s through the mid-1970s. "Threat" influences tended to be driven more by perceived *capabilities* in the 1940s through the 1970s and more by perceived *intentions* in the 1980s. Critics tend to focus on "technology" and "budget" influences. There is actually also a ninth approach, a "historical/academic" approach, which tends to focus the strategist on "lessons of history" or the great classics of military thought. All these approaches coexist with the organizational and psychological influences on war planning identified by Jack Snyder. The remaining citations in this section give examples drawn primarily from *The Maritime Strategy* debates.)

Johnson, Capt. W. Spencer. "Comment and Discussion." "Strategy: Ours vs. Theirs." *Proceedings* (September 1984): 107. (One of the initial drafters of *The Maritime Strategy* elaborates on the necessity, utility, and existence of a national military strategy from which *The Maritime Strategy* is derived. The "top-down" view of strategy-building written in response to McGruther's "threat-based" approach, cited below. See also "Comment and Discussion," *Proceedings* [April 1984]: 31.)

Hughes, Capt. Wayne, USN (Ret.). "Naval Tactics and Their Influence on Strategy." *Naval War College Review* (January–February 1986): 2–17. (The strategy-tactics interface. The "bottom-up" view of strategy-building.) See also his *Fleet Tactics Theory and Practice*, cited in section II above; and Rear Adm. C. A. "Mark" Hill, Jr., USN (Ret.). "Congress and the Carriers." *Wings of Gold* (Spring 1987): 6–8. But cf. "In My View: Tactical Skills." *Naval War College Review* (May–June 1986): 91—"The best plans are not those developed through top-down or bottom-up approaches. Strategists and tacticians need to keep in mind that the road to sound planning is a two-way, not a one-way, thoroughfare."

Jampoler, Capt. Andrew. "A Central Role for Naval Forces? . . . to Support the Land Battle." *Naval War College Review* (November–December 1984). (By a member of the 1983–1984 Strategic Studies Group at Newport. Argument is distilled from a "scenario" approach. See also fictional treatments by Clancy, Hackett and McGeoch et al., and Hayes et al., cited in sections I and II, above.)

McGruther, Cdr. Kenneth R. "Strategy: Ours vs. Theirs." *Proceedings* (February 1984): 339–344. (By a former member of the Strategic Concepts Group [OP-603.] Calls for a strategy based on defeating Soviet strategy, a "threat-based" approach. Unlike Bartlett, however, McGruther's approach is rooted in intentions as well as capabilities. Cf. Vlahos chapter, cited in section I above.)

Holloway, Adm. James L., III, USN (Ret.). "The U.S. Navy: A Functional Appraisal." *Oceanus* (Summer 1985): 3–11. (Focus on "mission" by the 1974–1978 CNO: "The organization of fleet battle strategy reflects the mission, functions, roles, and deployment of the U.S. Navy.") See also Cdr. John A. "Jay" Williams, USNR. "U.S. Navy Missions and Force Structure: A Critical Reappraisal." *Armed Forces and Society* (Summer 1981): 499–528; and Cdr. John Byron. "Sea Power: The Global Navy." *Proceedings* (January 1984): 30–33. (Alternative views of the Navy's "missions" by two officers who later contributed to *The Maritime Strategy*'s development. Also see "Commentary," *Armed Forces and Society* [Summer 1982]: 682–684 for official Navy response to Williams on the eve of Maritime Strategy development, and Williams's rejoinder. Williams's updated views are in "The U.S. and Soviet Navies: Missions and Forces." *Armed Forces and Society* [Summer 1984]: 507–528.)

Moodie, Michael, and Alvin J. Cottrell. *Geopolitics and Maritime Power.* Beverly Hills, Calif.: Sage, 1981. (A good example of a "hedging" focus. Regards Lehman's "major change" as not enough. Also wants greater naval activity in the Caribbean, periodic visits to the South Atlantic, an enhanced fleet in the Western Pacific, and continuing large-scale activity in the Indian Ocean. See also *Sea Plan 2000,* cited in section X above.)

** Froggett, Cdr. S. J. "*The Maritime Strategy*: Tomahawk's Role." *Proceedings* (February 1987): 51–54; Rear Adm. J. W. Williams, Jr. "In My View: Cross Training," *Naval War College Review* (March–April 1985): 96–97; and Dr. Donald D. Chipman and Maj. David Lay, USAF. "Sea Power and the B-52 Stratofortress." *Air University Review* (January–February 1986): 45–50. Good examples of the "technology" approach to strategy. Focus is on one system—the cruise missile, the nuclear submarine, and the land-based heavy bomber; arguments on strategy are built around it. But cf. Philip A. Taylor, "Technologies and Strategies: Trends in Naval Strategies and Tactics." *Naval Forces,* no. 6 (1986): 44–55. ("The consensus among senior military officers is that technology . . . has not, nor is it likely to, determine military strategy.")

** Ullman, Cdr. Harlan K., USN (Ret.). "Gramm-Rudman: A Fiscal Pearl Harbor." *Naval Forces,* no. 11 (1986): 10–11. (Congressional budget actions seen as potentially disastrous for both the 600-ship Navy and *The Maritime Strategy*. Exhibits all the pitfalls of a solely "fiscal" approach.) See also Harlan Ullman, *U.S. Conventional Force Structure at a Crossroads.* Washington, D.C.: Georgetown University CSIS, 1985; and the annual volumes issued by the Brookings Institution and the Committee for National Security, cited in sections I–III above.

Neustadt, Richard S., and Ernest R. May. *Thinking in Time: The Uses of History for Decision-Makers.* New York: Free Press, 1986. (Seeks to focus decision makers/users of the "historical" approach. Has direct relevance for strategists, a subcategory of "decision makers." For example, the "cases" highlighted in section X above and in its predecessor—the Crimea, Salonika, the Russian Intervention, World War II, etc.—can all be profitably examined using the Neustadt-May methodology.)

XII. Makers of Modern Naval Strategy: People and Institutions

The Maritime Strategy was originally drafted primarily—although certainly not exclusively—by U.S. naval officers for U.S. naval officers. Not only were agreed national, joint, and allied intelligence estimates and concepts of operations utilized as fundamental "building blocks," but great importance was also attached to long-held views of the U.S. Navy and Marine Corps leadership, to the concepts of operations of the fleet commanders in chief, and to the views of thinkers in uniform (active duty and reserve) at the Naval War College and the Center for Naval Analyses.

Much of *The Maritime Strategy* was hardly new and would have been directly recognizable to naval officers who developed U.S. and allied naval warfighting concepts in the late 1940s and 1950s. Likewise, elements from key strategy products of naval officers and civilian thinkers of the late 1970s—for example, the 1976 National Security Council *Maritime Strategy* study, naval reservist John Lehman's 1978 *Aircraft Carriers*, and the Navy's 1978 *Sea Plan 2000* and *Strategic Concepts of the U.S. Navy*, NWP 1 (Rev. A)—were also evident in *The Maritime Strategy* of the 1980s.

Much of what *was* new in *The Maritime Strategy* was the *linked, coherent discussion* of *global warfare*—rather than separate service and theater operations; *warfare tasks*—such as antisubmarine, anti-air, antisurface, strike, amphibious, mine, and special warfare—as opposed to traditional "platforms" or "unions"; the specific *geopolitical problems* facing the U.S. Navy—and other maritime elements—of the 1980s; and the contemporary conventional wisdom regarding *Soviet Navy* capabilities and intentions. This approach was largely driven by the primacy of the need for the strategy to satisfy current global operational requirements of fleet and other force commanders over the future requirements of competing bureaucracies in Washington. Its effect in fostering common reference points for all portions of the contemporary officer corps, especially junior officers, was soon felt.

While much of the robustness of *The Maritime Strategy* derived from its roots *throughout* the U.S. Navy and Marine Corps and elsewhere, both over space and over time, it owed a high degree of its utility to its initial approval and promulgation by successive Chiefs of Naval Operations in Washington and to its codification by their staffs (OPNAV.) These included especially the successive Deputy Chiefs of Naval Operations for Plans, Policy and Operations (OP-06), directors of the Strategy, Plans and Policy

Division (OP-60), heads of the Strategic Concepts Branch (OP-603), and staff officers in that branch. OPNAV was the one organization tasked to focus on maritime strategy, and to view it not only in a balanced global manner but also within the bounds of actual current national military planning parameters.

OPNAV's capabilities in this endeavor were due in part to the existence of the Navy Politico-Military/Strategic Planning subspecialty education, screening, and utilization system. This personnel system, while somewhat imperfect, had identified, trained, and used naval officers in a network of strategists—in Washington, Newport, the fleet, and elsewhere—for over a decade and a half by the 1980s.

Nevertheless, despite the clear postwar historical roots of *The Maritime Strategy* and its codification in and dissemination from Washington by some of the best minds in the national security affairs community, a number of publications appeared decrying a lack of strategic training and thinking in the Navy, past and present, and ignoring or misunderstanding the critical role in strategy development of naval officers in staff positions. This literature, as well as some counters to it, is briefly outlined below.

A. The Public Debate: Criticisms and Kudos

Brooks, Captain Linton F. "An Examination of Professional Concerns of Naval Officers as Reflected in their Professional Journal." *Naval War College Review* (January–February 1980): 46–56. (A future primary contributor to the development and articulation of *The Maritime Strategy* decries the paucity of articles on strategy in the Navy professional literature of the late 1960s. This era was admittedly dominated by Vietnam and an internal professional view of the Navy as primarily an infinitely flexible limited-war fire brigade, but the period did see the publication of Rear Adm. J. C. Wylie's *Military Strategy*, Rear Adm. Henry Eccles's *Military Concepts and Philosophy*, and Adm. Joseph J. Clark's coauthored *Sea Power and Its Meaning*.)

Buell, Cdr. Thomas B., USN (Ret.). "The Education of a Warrior." *Proceedings* (January 1981): 40–45. Also "Comment and Discussion" (February 1981): 21; (March 1981): 15; (April 1981): 21–23; (June 1981): 77–79; (July 1981): 78–80; (August 1981): 71–75; (November 1981): 84–87; (January 1982): 76; (March 1982): 27; (April 1982): 20. (Posed the question: "Where will we get our future strategists?" Implied that the Navy had no real answer to the question, a view shared by most of the eight "commenters and discussants" chosen for publication by the *Proceedings*, only one of whom was familiar with actual Navy practice in this area. Illustrative of the limited public visibility of true U.S. Navy strategic *thought* before 1981–1982.)

Woolsey, R. James. "Mapping 'U.S. Defense Policy in the 1980s.'" *International Security* (Fall 1981): 202–207. (By the 1977–1980 Under Secretary of the Navy. "The other side of the coin." A call to bring the "American academic intellectual establishment" and the military establishment more in touch with each other by focusing the efforts of the former on the actual "defense policy" problems of the latter, vice exclusively on "(a) the politico-military situation in the four corners of the globe and (b) nuclear and arms control theology.") For similar disconnects that have occurred even within the field of "nuclear theology" itself, see David Rosenberg, "U.S. Nuclear Strategy: Theory vs. Practice." *Bulletin of the Atomic Scientists* (March 1987): 20ff. ("Theorists and consultants have had little impact on the development of nuclear weapons policies. Rather, strategic planning should be seen as a governmental process, carried out largely by military officers and civilian bureaucrats.")

Bruins, Berend D. "Should Naval Officers Be Strategists?" *Proceedings* (January 1982): 52–56. Also "Comment and Discussion" (March 1982): 27; (April 1982): 20; (May 1982): 17. (The *Proceedings* throws three more retirees and an active-duty non-strategist into the public fray. Meanwhile, fleet plans staffs, the Strategic Studies Group at Newport, and the one intelligence officer and nine line officers—six with Ph.Ds.—assigned to OP-603 were at the time actively laying the groundwork for *The Maritime Strategy*. Illustrative of the limited public visibility of actual naval strategic thinkers before 1982–1983.)

Hanks, Rear Adm. Robert J., USN (Ret.). "Whither U.S. Naval Strategy?" *Strategic Review* (Summer 1982): 16–22. (An outstanding OP-60 director of the 1970s challenges the U.S. Navy to develop a coherent strategy, an activity being vigorously pursued even as the article was published.)

Lehman, John F., Jr., "Thinking about Strategy." *Shipmate* (April 1982): 18–20. (Secretary of the Navy's charge to the officer corps.)

Kennedy, Floyd D., Jr. "Naval Strategy for the Next Century: Resurgence of the Naval War College as the Center of Strategic Naval Thought." *National Defense* (April 1983): 27–30. (Covers the resurgence of the Naval War College, although without describing the linkages between that institution and the strategic planners in Washington, through which Naval War College thinking is actually translated into Maritime Strategy elements.) Also see 1983 Murray article cited in section I above.

Milsted, Lt. Cdr. Charles E., Jr. "A Corps of Naval Strategists." Master's degree thesis. Naval Postgraduate School, June 1983. (Based on the somewhat skewed open literature available during this period. As with Bruins, above, "strategy" and "long-range planning" not well differentiated. Proposed establishment of a network of specifically educated and trained naval strategists responsible for long-range planning. Following his own model, Milsted was assigned to OP-603 from 1983 to 1985; there he became a key contributor to the codification of *The Maritime Strategy*. Cf. U.S. Navy. *First Annual Long Range Planners' Conference* cited in section I above.)

Hattendorf, John et al. *Sailors and Scholars: The Centennial History of the U.S. Naval War College.* Newport, R.I.: Naval War College Press, 1984. (Chronicles the important supporting role of the Naval War College in the development and dissemination of U.S. Navy strategic thought. See especially 201–202, 237, 312–319.)

Crackel, Lt. Col. Theodore J., USA (Ret.). "On the Making of Lieutenants and Colonels." *Public Interest* (Summer 1984): 18–30. ("The services have produced no strategic thinkers at all." He is especially hard on war college faculties, including the Naval War College: "None of the war college faculties is in the forefront of development in any of the military disciplines they teach." Actually, no group was more in the "forefront of development" in the "discipline" of Maritime Strategy [Secretary of the Navy, the CNO, the OP-06 organization, and the Strategic Studies Group aside] than the Naval War College faculty, as evidenced by their prominence in this bibliography. Crackel is a military historian by training with little apparent experience in actual strategy—or policy making, and with an almost exclusively U.S. Army–oriented academic and operational record. Unlike most practicing U.S. naval strategists, he has apparently self-fulfilled his prophecy and "discovered that the think-tanks in and around Washington are a more congenial environment.")

"413 Named as Proven Subspecialists." *Navy Times* (9 September 1985): 58. (The Navy system for identifying the "pool" of naval strategists. Results of the *seventh* biennial U.S. Navy selection board that identifies "proven" subspecialists for further middle and high-level assignments in the eight fields of naval political-military/strategic planning. Earlier lists appeared in *Navy Times* back into the 1970s. Includes many of the builders of *The Maritime Strategy*. Note that these names constitute not only the "Corps of Naval Strategists" but also the Navy's Politico-Military and Regional Affairs experts.)

** Stavridis, Lt. Cdr. Jim. "An Ocean Away: Outreach from the Naval War College." *Shipmate* (November 1985): 8. (On the role of the Naval War College in contributing to OP-603's codification of *The Maritime Strategy* and in "getting the word out" to mid-grade naval officers. By a former OP-603 member.)

* Marryott, Rear Adm. Ronald F. "President's Notes." *Naval War College Review* (November–December 1985): 2–4. (By the 1985–1986 President of the Naval War College and 1983–1984 director of Strategy, Plans and Policy [OP-60], the Navy's principal global strategist. On development of *The Maritime Strategy* and the Naval War College's vital supporting contribution.)

** *CNA Annual Report: 1985.* Alexandria, Va.: Center for Naval Analyses, 1986: especially 7–12 and 29–30. (On CNA's contribution to the development of *The Maritime Strategy* and on its use of that strategy in planning its research programs. Also, CNA analysts' views on Soviet maritime strategy.)

Davis, Capt. Vincent, USNR (Ret.). "Decision Making, Decision Makers, and Some of the Results." In *The Reagan Defense Program: An Interim Assessment,* edited by Stephen Cimbala. Wilmington, Del.: Scholarly Resources, 1986, 23–62. (A somewhat anachronistic characterization of the contemporary Navy as one with "too few thinkers," riven by acrimonious debates among factions of naval officers. "Rancorous disputes simmer among its 'big three unions'—the carrier, submarine, and surface-warfare admirals." Thus the seminal thinker and writer on naval strategy and bureaucratic politics of the '40s, '50s, and '60s sees no essential change in the Navy of the mid-'80s—despite conscious Navy efforts to take his earlier counsel to heart in its development of a transcendent Maritime Strategy. Cf. articles by Vice Admirals Demars, Schoultz, and Dunn—leaders of the submarine and air warfare communities—and by Lieutenants Winnefeld, Peppe and Keller—the rising generation—cited in sections II and III above.)

** Bush, Ted. "Libyan Exercise Exemplifies New Navy Strategy." *Navy Times* (10 February 1986): 45–46. (OPNAV strategists illuminate a variety of aspects of *The Maritime Strategy* and its origins. Note that, unlike open-literature authors, actual practicing strategists usually remain nameless to the general public. This hardly means, however, that they are somehow less important.)

** Leibstone, Marvin. "U.S. Report." *Naval Forces,* no. 2 (1986): 94. (Alleges "an unusually large number of naval officers do not recognize fully the switch from 'defense' to 'offense' that the Navy's high command believes is necessary." But cf. "The United States Navy: On the Crest of the Wave." *The Economist* [19 April 1986]: 49, cited above: "What is certain is that an entire generation of junior and middle-grade naval officers now believes that the first wartime job of the navy would be to sail north and fight the Russians close to their bases.")

** Burdick, Capt. Howard "Sons of the Prophet: A View of the Naval War College Faculty." *Naval War College Review* (May–June 1986): 81–89. (On the Naval War College, its faculty, and *The Maritime Strategy,* by the Dean of Academics at the Naval War College.)

** Wirt, Robert T. "Strategic ASW." *Submarine Review* (July 1986): 50–56. (Calls for a comprehensive ASW plan, driven by submariners, to support *The Maritime Strategy.* Unionism was not quite dead.)

** Metcalf, Vice Adm. Joseph. "Metcalf Speaks Out: On the Navy's New Offense, Ship Design and Archimedes." *Navy News and Undersea Technology* (18 July 1986): 2. (The Deputy Chief of Naval Operations for Surface Warfare views maritime strategy as of little concern to Navy junior officers. Not a common view.)

** Gallotta, Capt. Richard USN (Ret.), et al. *Assessment of Maritime Strategy Education and Training in the Department of the Navy.* McLean, Va.: BDM, 31 December 1986. (A comprehensive balanced survey, with recommendations.)

Murray, Williamson. "Grading the War Colleges." *National Interest* (Winter 1986–1987): 12–19. (Antidote to Crackel. "The best of the war colleges, the Naval War College at Newport, sets the standard by which the other war colleges should be measured." "The strategy and policy curriculum has justifiably acquired a reputation as the premier course in the United States, if not the Western world, for the examination of strategy. So high is the Naval War College's reputation that over the course of the past few years it has attracted a number of the best young military historians and political scientists in national security affairs to Newport.")

** Clark, Charles S. "In Person: Fred H. Rainbow: Charting a Course for the Navy's Debates." *National Journal* (21 February 1987): 435. (On the role of the *Proceedings* in orchestrating "some heated forensics over the Navy's trumpeted Maritime Strategy [while] similar Air Force and Army journals often reflect the blandness of official restraints." The institute had come a long way in just a few short years. Like the Naval War College and the *Naval War College Review*, the Naval Institute and the *Proceedings* were clearly at the cutting edge of *The Maritime Strategy* debate.)

** Tritten, Cdr. James. "New Directions." *Naval War College Review* (Spring 1987): 94. (By the chairman of the Naval Postgraduate School National Security Affairs Department and a former OP-60 staffer. On the revitalization of naval history and strategy studies at the "PG School.")

** Hearding, Lt. Cdr. David. "A Requiem for the Silent Service." *Submarine Review* (July 1987): 73–78. (An important article, stressing the need for broader integration of U.S. Navy submarine officers into the Navy as a whole, in part as a result of the advent of *The Maritime Strategy*.)

B. The Public Record: OP-603

The primary U.S. Navy organization charged (in 1982) with codifying, refining, and articulating the consensus in the Navy regarding *The Maritime Strategy* was the OPNAV Strategic Concepts Group, OP-603. Organized by Vice Adm. William J. Crowe (then OP-06) and Rear Adm. Robert Hilton (then OP-60) in 1978, OP-603 evolved into an office of about a dozen post-graduate educated, trained, professional operator-strategists, including U.S. Army, Air Force, Marine Corps and Central Intelligence Agency officers.

Almost invisible to the general and national security affairs academic publics—especially in comparison to the Secretary of the Navy, the Chief of Naval Operations, OP-06 and OP-60, the operational commanders, the Strategic Studies Group and the Naval War College—these officers were principally responsible for the development of *The Maritime Strategy* as a unified, coherent, global framework and common U.S. and allied naval vision.

Like war planners, but unlike war college faculties, their output was largely classified. Nevertheless, they—and their superiors, OP-60 and OP-60B—often also achieved respectable open-publication records. Typically, their writings prior to assignment to OP-60/603 reflected their diverse operational and academic interests and achievements; their publications during and after their assignments as strategists usually reflected their work on *The Maritime Strategy*. (For the latter, see the entries cited earlier in this bibliography by Rear Admirals Hanks, Marryott, and Pendley; Captains Barnett, Brooks, Johnson, McGruther, and Swartz; Commanders Hickman, Kalb, and Milsted; and Lieutenant Commanders Pocalyko and Stavridis. For the former, see the entries below, which represent, admittedly, only a portion of the record, the products of officers who were *specifically* and *principally* assigned to codify *The Maritime Strategy*. These were generally the OP-603 "branch heads" and "Maritime Strategy action officers" serving from 1982 through 1986. They are provided only to illustrate the breadth of experience and depth of thought that members of the U.S. Navy's "corps of naval strategists" brought with them when they reported for duty.)

Weeks, Lt. Cdr. Stanley B. *United States Defense Policy toward Spain, 1950–1976.* Unpublished PhD diss. American University, 1977; and Lt. Cdr. William S. Johnson. "Naval Diplomacy and the Failure of Balanced Security in the Far East, 1921–1935," and "Defense Budget Constraints and the Fate of the Carrier in the Royal Navy." *Naval War College Review* (February 1972): 67–88 and (May–June 1973): 12–30. (Operators and international relations specialists as future strategists. By the OP-60 codrafters of the initial 1982–1983 U.S. Navy Maritime Strategy briefings and testimony.)

Barnett, Capt. Roger W. "Soviet Strategic Reserves and the Soviet Navy." In *The Soviet Union: What Lies Ahead? Military Political Affairs in the 1980s,* by Maj. Kenneth M. Currie and Maj. Gregory Varhall. Washington, D.C.: U.S. Government Printing Office, 1985, 581–605. (The operator and Sovietologist as future strategist. A 1980 paper by the 1983–1984 OP-603 Branch Head.) See also his "Their Professional Journal" (with Dr. Edward J. Lacey). *Proceedings* (October 1982): 95–101.

Seaquist, Cdr. Larry. "Memorandum for the Commander. Subject: Tactical Proficiency, and Tactics to Improve Tactical Proficiency." *Proceedings* (July 1981): 58–61 and (February 1983): 37–42. (The operator and tactician as future strategist. By a member of the 1983–1984 Strategic Studies Group and 1984–1985 OP-603 branch head.)

Parker, Lt. Cdr. T. Wood. "Thinking Offensively." *Proceedings* (April 1981): 26–31; "Theater Nuclear Warfare and the U.S. Navy." *Naval War College Review* (January–February 1982): 3–16; and "Paradigms, Conventional Wisdom, and Naval Warfare." *Proceedings* (April 1983): 29–35. (The operator and Naval War College student as future strategist. Three prizewinning essays by the 1984–1985 principal OP-603 Maritime Strategy action officer.)

Daly, Capt. Thomas M., and Cdr. Albert C. Myers. "The Art of ASW." *Proceedings* (October 1985): 164–165. (Operators and warfare specialists as strategists. The 1985–1986 OP-603 Branch Head and his primary Maritime Strategy action officer discuss their primary warfare specialty. See also Daly *Proceedings* articles on the Iran-Iraq War, July 1984 and May and July 1985, and on the Bikini A-bomb tests, July 1986.)

Epilogue: 1987–2003

This Epilogue is new for the fifth edition of the bibliography. It includes a short selection of the most important works on *The Maritime Strategy* to appear after mid-1987, the cutoff time for entries to the third edition.

The listing of entries in the new epilogue is nowhere near as comprehensive in its coverage as the listing of entries in the earlier editions of this bibliography. Also, the epilogue includes a few important but narrowly focused entries that in earlier editions would have been subsumed under specialized sections of the publication rather than listed with the more general works.

Ellmann, Ellingsen, ed. *NATO and U.S. Maritime Strategy: Diverging Interests or Cooperative Effort.* Oslo: Norwegian Atlantic Committee, 1987. (Contains an important set of graphics used by SacLant to explain *The Maritime Strategy* and its ties to NATO strategy.)

Kalb, Commander Richard W. "United States Maritime Strategy: Strengthening NATO's Deterrent Capability." *Atlantic Community Quarterly,* no. 25 (Spring 1987): 98–103. (By one of *The Maritime Strategy*'s many conceptualizers in the Office of the Chief of Naval Operations [OP-603].)

Friedman, Norman. *The US Maritime Strategy.* London and New York: Jane's, 1988. (An initial comprehensive look by a naval analyst close to the staffs of the Secretary of the Navy and the Chief of Naval Operations.)

Palmer, Michael A. *Origins of the Maritime Strategy: American Naval Strategy in the First Postwar Decade.* Washington, D.C.: Naval Historical Center, Department of the Navy, 1988. (Finds roots of the thinking behind *The Maritime Strategy* in the immediate post–World War II years.)

Lehman, John F. Jr. *Command of the Seas.* New York: Scribner's, 1988. (Memoirs of the Secretary of the Navy who catalyzed the Navy's *Maritime Strategy* efforts and much else. A second edition, published by the U.S. Naval Institute in 2001, contains a preface and an afterword with his post–Cold War views.)

Hattendorf, John B. "The Evolution of *The Maritime Strategy*: 1977–1987." *Naval War College Review* 41, no. 3 (Summer 1988): 7–28; reprinted with corrections in Hattendorf, *Naval History and Maritime Strategy: Collected Essays.* Malabar, Fla.: Krieger, 2000, 201–228. (How the Maritime Strategy was created, by a preeminent historian of naval strategy. Extracted for open publication from the more comprehensive classified study, originally commissioned by the Office of the Chief of Naval Operations [OP-603] to record the process.)

Gray, Colin S., and Roger W. Barnett, eds. *Seapower and Strategy.* Annapolis, Md.: Naval Institute Press, 1989. (A textbook on maritime strategy heavily influenced by *The Maritime Strategy*.)

Chernavin, Fleet Adm. Vladimir Nikolayevich. "Chernavin Responds." *Proceedings* (February 1989). The commander in chief of the Soviet Navy presents his views on *The Maritime Strategy* to a largely Western naval audience.

Winnefeld, Lt. Cdr. James A., Jr. "Winning the Outer Air Battle." *Proceedings* (August 1989): 37–43. (An example of the influence of *The Maritime Strategy* on thoughtful middle-grade U.S. naval officers of the period.)

Hartmann, Frederick H. *Naval Renaissance: The U.S. Navy in the 1980s.* Annapolis, Md.: Naval Institute Press, 1990. *The Maritime Strategy* and its context from the point of view of the then Chief of Naval Operations, Admiral James Watkins.

Perla, Peter P. *The Art of Wargaming: A Guide for Professionals and Hobbyists.* Annapolis, Md.: Naval Institute Press, 1990. (This book, by the dean of naval war-game thinkers, culminates years of analysis of war gaming—one of the chief tools the Navy used to validate *The Maritime Strategy*.)

Grove, Eric. *The Future of Sea Power.* London: Routledge, 1990. (Heavily influenced by the author's exposure to and analysis of *The Maritime Strategy*.)

Golightly, Lieutenant Neil L. "Correcting Three Strategic Mistakes." *Proceedings* (April 1990): 32–38. (As the world changes, a thoughtful junior officer challenges *The*

Maritime Strategy and its premises. A good example of the high level of internal debate that *The Maritime Strategy* had engendered by then in the fleet [and of eye-catching photography].)

FitzGerald, Mary C. "The Soviet Navy: Roles, Doctrines and Missions." In *The U.S. Stake in Naval Arms Control,* by Barry M. Blechman et al. Washington, D.C.: Henry L. Stimson Center, October 1990, 109–192. (An American Sovietologist describes and analyzes the public Soviet reaction to *The Maritime Strategy.*)

Oswald, Adm. Sir Julian. "NATO's Naval Forces Must Endure." *Proceedings* (November 1990): 35–38. (The Royal Navy's Chief of Naval Staff and First Sea Lord—a longtime advocate—weighs in heavily for the maintenance of a forward allied maritime strategy.)

Tamnes, Rolf. *The United States and the Cold War in the High North.* Aldershot, U.K.: Dartmouth, 1991. (An excellent analysis of the evolution of U.S. naval strategy on the northern flank of NATO.)

Grove, Eric, with Graham Thompson. *Battle for the Fiords: NATO's Forward Maritime Strategy in Action.* Annapolis, Md.: Naval Institute Press, 1991. (Exercising *The Maritime Strategy* and NATO's Concept of Maritime Operations [ConMarOps] in the Norwegian Sea.)

Secretary of the Navy H. Lawrence Garrett, III, Chief of Naval Operations Admiral Frank B. Kelso, II, and Commandant, U.S. Marine Corps General A. M. Gray. "The Way Ahead." *Proceedings* (April 1991): 36–47. (The first formal and public attempt by the U.S. Navy's leadership to replace *The Maritime Strategy* with a concept more in keeping with the times, noting that "*The Maritime Strategy* . . . remains on the shelf." With *The Maritime Strategy* as precedent, the Naval Institute also published this article as an individual supplement.)

Hegmann, Richard. "Reconsidering the Evolution of the U.S. Maritime Strategy 1955–1965." *Journal of Strategic Studies* 14 (September 1991): 299–336. (Demonstrates that offensive forward operations characterized U.S. Navy strategic thinking throughout the Cold War, not just at its beginning and its end.)

O'Rourke, Ronald. "The Future of the U.S. Navy." In *Fifty Years of Canada–United States Defense Cooperation: The Road from Ogdensburg,* edited by Joel J. Sokolsky and Joseph T. Jockel. Lewiston, N.Y.: Edwin Mellen, 1992, 289–331. (An informed assessment of the U.S. Navy at the end of *The Maritime Strategy* era by the leading congressional staff naval analyst of the period.)

Summers, Harry G., Jr. *On Strategy II: A Critical Analysis of the Gulf War.* New York: Dell, 1992. (A leading U.S. Army thinker argues that *The Maritime Strategy* prepared the Navy well for Operations DESERT SHIELD and DESERT STORM.)

Rosenberg, David A. "Process: The Realities of Formulating Modern Naval Strategy." In *Mahan Is Not Enough: The Proceedings of a Conference on the Works of Sir Julian Corbett and Admiral Sir Herbert Richmond,* edited by James Goldrick and John B. Hattendorf. Newport, R.I.: Naval War College Press, 1993, 141–175. (Analyzes the various strands that made up *The Maritime Strategy* efforts of the 1980s.)

Brooks, Ambassador Linton F. *Peacetime Influence through Forward Naval Presence.* Alexandria, Va.: Center for Naval Analyses, October 1993. An analysis of the element of the Cold War *Maritime Strategy* that would emerge as the centerpiece of immediate post–Cold War U.S. Navy strategic thought.

Crowe, Adm. William J. Jr. (Ret.), with David Chanoff. *The Line of Fire.* New York: Simon and Schuster, 1993, 279–287. (A former chairman of the U.S. Joint Chiefs of Staff—and only a tepid supporter of *The Maritime Strategy*—recounts the great fear of U.S. Navy offensive capabilities engendered by 1988 in Marshal of the Soviet Union Sergei F. Akhromeyev, Chief of the Soviet General Staff.)

Baer, George W. *One Hundred Years of Sea Power: The U.S. Navy, 1890–1990.* Stanford, Calif.: Stanford University Press, 1994. (A leading Naval War College historian and strategist sees *The Maritime Strategy* as a culmination of a century of American naval thought.)

Jan S. Breemer, "The End of Naval Strategy: Revolutionary Change and the Future of American Naval Power." *Strategic Review* 22 (Spring 1994): 40–53. (Sees *The Maritime Strategy* as the high-water mark of blue-water Mahanian thinking.)

Vistica, Gregory L. *Fall from Glory: The Men Who Sank the U.S. Navy.* New York: Simon and Schuster, 1995. (Full of useful details on the evolution of *The Maritime Strategy,* largely misinterpreted by the author.)

Brooks, Rear Adm. Tom (Ret.), and Capt. Bill Manthorpe (Ret.). "Setting the Record Straight: A Critical Review of *Fall from Glory.*" *Naval Intelligence Professionals Quarterly,* no. 12 (April 1996): 1–2. This ostensible book review is a brief but important description of the role played by intelligence analysis in shaping *The Maritime Strategy*—a role seldom discussed in public.

Small, Admiral William N. (Ret.). *Oral History: Interview by David F. Winkler.* Washington, D.C.: Oral History Program, Naval Historical Center, 1997. (Candid accounts of naval policy and strategy making by one of the major architects of *The Maritime Strategy*.)

Gaffney, H. H., et al. *U.S. Naval Responses to Situations, 1970–1999.* Alexandria, Va.: Center for Naval Analyses, December 2000. (Shows that while the focus of U.S. Navy Maritime Strategy plans and exercises may have been in the North Atlantic and North Pacific during the 1980s, the focus of its actual operations in response to real-world crises and situations was in the Middle East.)

Cote, Owen R., Jr. *The Third Battle: Innovation in the U.S. Navy's Silent Cold War Struggle with Soviet Submarines.* Newport Papers 16. Newport, R.I.: Naval War College Press, 2003. (The best public analysis to date of U.S. Navy forward submarine strategy, plans, and operations—a key element of *The Maritime Strategy.*)

Swartz, Capt. Peter M. (Ret.). "Preventing the Bear's Last Swim: The NATO Concept of Maritime Operations (ConMarOps) of the Last Cold War Decade." In *NATO's Maritime Power 1949–1990.* Piraeus, Greece: European Institute of Maritime Studies and Research (INMER), 2003: 47–61. (Traces the development and dissemination of NATO's complementary maritime strategic concept.)

Time Line

The Evolution of the U.S. Navy's Maritime
Strategy in the Context of Major Political
and Military Events of the Cold War,
1964–1991

Yuri M. Zhukov

	SOVIET UNION	UNITED STATES
1964	**14 January:** The project 1123 helicopter-carrying antisubmarine cruiser *Moskva* is launched; her sister ship, *Leningrad*, is laid down several months later in the Nikolayev Shipyard on the Black Sea.	
	25 July: Soviet Navy commander in chief Sergei Gorshkov announces that Soviet SSNs have operated in distant ocean regions, including equatorial waters and beneath the Arctic ice.	**2 August:** President Lyndon Johnson orders immediate retaliation for the attack on U.S. destroyers *Maddox* (DD-731) and *Turner Joy* (DD-951) in the Gulf of Tonkin, allegedly by North Vietnamese forces.
	15 October: Leonid Brezhnev and Alexei Kosygin replace Nikita Khruschev as General Secretary of the Communist Party and Soviet Prime Minister, respectively.	
	16 October: The People's Republic of China detonates its first atomic bomb.	
		3 November: Johnson is elected President.
1965	**17 February:** Former Chief of General Staff, Marshall Vasilii Sokolovskii, declares that the Soviet Union has achieved "virtual parity" with U.S. in nuclear-powered submarines and (for the first time) a smaller overall strength of armed forces: 2,423,000 Soviets vs. 2,690,000 Americans in uniform.	**18 February:** Secretary of Defense Robert McNamara reveals plans to terminate Atlantic and Pacific radar barrier patrols in an annual report to Congress.
		February–May: Operation SILVER LANCE, one of the largest-ever peacetime joint Naval/Marine Corps training exercises, is launched off the California coast, testing the mobility and strike capabilities of the U.S. Pacific Fleet; over 50 ships and 65,000 personnel participate.
		15 April: U.S. Naval and Marine Corps aircraft join the U.S. Army and Air Force, and the South Vietnamese Air Force in bombarding Viet Cong positions in South Vietnam.
	21–26 June: The Warsaw Pact War Game of 1965 is held; recently declassified documents show that its planners had access, through Warsaw Pact spies, to NATO's top-secret plans for war; the plans also presumed the destruction of Budapest and other Eastern European cities by NATO nuclear bombs, and displayed a preparedness to ignore the neutrality of Austria on the assumption that NATO would ignore it as well.	
	16 December: The R-36 Mod-3 intercontinental ballistic missile (ICBM), known in the West as the SS-9 Scarp/FOBS, is flight-tested; the missile had been allegedly developed to strike U.S. Minuteman ICBM Launch Control Centers, then the "Achilles heel" of the Minuteman system.	

	SOVIET UNION	UNITED STATES
1966	**21 January:** The state TASS news agency announces that a Soviet fishing flotilla has entered the Gulf of California for an experimental fishing expedition.	**21 January:** Two U.S. 6th Fleet destroyers conduct training exercises in Black Sea; Moscow condemns activities as "suspicious muscle flexing."
		10 March: French President Charles de Gaulle announces his country's intention to withdraw from NATO.
		1 May: The Office of Naval Material and the Bureaus of Naval Personnel and Medicine are placed under the direct command of the Chief of Naval Operations (CNO), as the Department of the Navy is reorganized into a unilinear framework.
	31 July: The project 1123 helicopter carrier *Leningrad* (Moskva-class) is launched.	
1967	**27 January:** The Outer Space Treaty, signed by the U.S., USSR, and 60 other nations, limits military uses of space.	
		2 February: Navy Secretary Paul Nitze announces that all strategic naval warfare activities have been placed under the authority of the Office of the CNO.
	5 June: The "Six Day" Arab-Israeli War begins as Israel launches a massive air strike against air bases in Egypt, Syria, and Jordan; an Israeli ground offensive into Sinai, Gaza, and the Golan Heights immediately follows.	
	June: Soviet naval force strength in the Mediterranean reaches 70 ships, including 2 cruisers, 15 destroyers, and 10 submarines, in support of Egypt and Syria during the "Six Day" Arab-Israeli War; the Soviet 5th Eskadra (Mediterranean Squadron) is formally established by the end of the month.	**June:** Significant U.S. Navy (USN) forces deploy to the Eastern Mediterranean and Red Sea in support of Israel during "Six Day" Arab-Israeli War.
	July: The helicopter-carrying project 1123 antisubmarine cruiser *Moskva* enters into service.	**1 September:** Paul R. Ignatius is sworn in as Secretary of the Navy.
		1 August: Admiral Thomas Moorer is appointed as CNO.
	October: Admiral Gorshkov is promoted to Admiral of the Fleet of the Soviet Union, a rank corresponding to that of Marshal of the Soviet Union.	**16 October:** A new NATO political headquarters is formally opened in Brussels.
	5 November: The Soviet Navy commissions the first of 34 project 667A SSBNs (Yankee-class), the K-137; this is the Soviet Union's first "modern" strategic missile submarine, fitted with 16 SS-N-6 Serb ballistic missiles.	**December:** The NATO Defense Planning Committee approves the Standing Naval Force Atlantic, to be implemented in January 1968.
1968		**22 January:** North Korean patrol boats fire upon the U.S. intelligence collection ship *Pueblo* (AGER-2) and imprison its crew, after the latter had entered the country's territorial waters.
	April: The Soviet Navy signs a five-year basing agreement with Egypt.	
	1 July: The Non-proliferation Treaty on Nuclear Weapons (NPT) is signed by representatives from over 60 countries.	

SOVIET UNION	UNITED STATES
August: Warsaw Pact forces invade Czechoslovakia to crush the Prague Spring, a socialist reform movement led by Czechoslovak President Alexander Dubcek.	

1969		**20 January:** Richard Nixon is inaugurated as the 37th President of the United States; Melvin R. Laird is sworn in as Secretary of Defense on 22 January, and John H. Chafee is sworn in as Secretary of the Navy on 31 January.
		March: The U.S. and South Vietnamese bombing of Cambodia begins.
		28 May: NATO establishes the Naval On-Call Force Mediterranean.
		20 July: Neil Armstrong and Edward "Buzz" Aldrin walk on the moon.
	August–September: Joint Soviet-Egyptian-Syrian naval exercises in the southeastern Mediterranean coincide with a successful military coup in Libya, led by Muammar Khadaffi.	**4 October:** Admiral Moorer establishes the Underwater Long-range Missile System, later renamed the Trident missile program.

1970	**5 March:** The NPT goes into force.	
		20 March: The first NATO military communications satellite, *NATO 1*, is launched from Cape Kennedy, Florida.
	16 April: The U.S. and Soviet governments begin Strategic Arms Limitation Talks negotiations in Vienna.	
	April: Worldwide OKEAN exercises are held, the largest peacetime naval operation in history; over 200 surface ships and submarines and hundreds of land-based aircraft take part. Exercises include anti-submarine warfare (ASW), anti-carrier, amphibious assault, and other operations in Northern, Pacific, and Mediterranean Fleet areas, and in the Indian Ocean.	**29 April:** U.S. and South Vietnamese ground invasion of Cambodia begins.
		1 July: The incoming CNO, Admiral Elmo Zumwalt, claims that the U.S. has only a 45–55% chance of winning a conventional war with the Soviet Union.
		3 August: USS *James Madison* (SSBN-627) carries out the first underwater launch of a Poseidon C-3 missile.
	September: The project 1143 *Kiev* aircraft carrier, the largest Soviet warship yet, at a displacement of 43,000 tons, is laid down in the Nikolayev Shipyard.	**23 September:** Admiral Zumwalt establishes the CNO Executive Panel, assigned with task of providing a "clear understanding of the navy's mission."

1971	**11 February:** U.S. and Soviet representatives sign the Seabed Arms Control Treaty, banning the intentional placement of nuclear weapons on ocean floor.	
		5 March: Admiral Zumwalt establishes the posts of Deputy CNO for Air, Surface, and Submarine activities.

SOVIET UNION	UNITED STATES
	18 March: Deputy Defense Secretary David Packard tells the House Appropriations Defense subcommittee that the USSR has achieved "rough overall parity" with the U.S. in strategic nuclear weapons.
19 April: Moscow launches the world's first orbiting space research station, the unmanned *Salyut 1.*	**March–May:** The USS *James Madison* SSBN holds its first patrol.
	August: The Minuteman III ICBM, with a multiple warhead capacity, enters service in United States.
September–December: Full-endurance trials are held on the first titanium-hulled submarine, the project 661 cruise missile-equipped K-162 (Papa-class); the boat achieves a world-record underwater speed of 44.7 knots.	**15 September:** President Nixon allegedly authorizes the U.S.-backed coup in Chile.
November: The *Soviet Diplomatic Lexicon*, edited by Foreign Minister Alexei Gromyko, demands that the Baltic Sea be closed to naval units of all non-Baltic powers.	**2 November:** The first U.S. Defense Satellite Communications System Phase II (DSCS II) satellites are launched.
15 November: The People's Republic of China joins the United Nations (UN).	
December: The first high-speed, deep-diving project 705 nuclear submarine (Alfa-class) is completed; the prototype has extensive technical problems.	

1972	**February:** Admiral Gorshkov publishes the first in a series of eleven articles in *Morskoi Sbornik*, bearing the earmarks of a new naval doctrine; he emphasizes Russia's destiny as a maritime power, the primarily defensive role of navy, the role of deterrence in wartime, the protection of SSBNs, and "coercive naval diplomacy."	
		4 May: John W. Warner is sworn in as Secretary of the Navy.
	22 May: Nixon arrives in Moscow, becoming the first U.S. President to visit the USSR.	
	25 May: Admiral Gorshkov and U.S. Navy Secretary John Warner sign the Incidents at Sea Agreement in Moscow, seeking to reduce the number of accidents between the two navies.	
	26 May: An interim Strategic Arms Limitation Talks (SALT) agreement on the Anti-Ballistic Missile (ABM) systems is signed in Moscow, restricting ABM development and freezing the numbers of ICBMs and submarine-launched ballistic missiles (SLBMs) in commission for a period of five years.	
	29 May: The "Basic Principles of Relations Between the USA and the USSR" agreement is signed by Nixon and Brezhnev, recognizing the Soviet Union as the primary military-political policeman of Eastern Europe, widening economic relations between the two countries, and marking the beginning of a new bilateral policy of "détente."	
	18 July: Egyptian President Anwar Sadat orders the immediate withdrawal of Soviet military advisers from Egypt and places Soviet air bases under exclusive Egyptian control.	**17 June:** The Watergate burglars break into the Democratic Party's National Committee offices.

SOVIET UNION	UNITED STATES
	September: NATO conducts its largest land, sea, and air exercise to date, Operation STRONG EXPRESS, involving more than 50,000 personnel and 300 ships from eleven nations, including NATO nonmember France.
14 October: The U.S. and USSR sign a three-year agreement to open 40 ports in each nation to visits by civilian-manned ships from each country.	
November: The Yak-36M Vertical/Short Take-off and Landing (VSTOL) aircraft is tested on the *Moskva* cruiser, marking the first time a plane successfully lands aboard a Soviet ship; the Yak-36 and its successor, the Yak-38, were designed to support submarines against NATO ASW operations after sea-based helicopters were deemed unfit for the task.	
15 November: U.S.-Soviet SALT II talks begin in Geneva.	
26 December: The *Kiev* aircraft carrier is launched; another ship of its class, the *Minsk* aircraft carrier (project 1143) is laid down in the Nikolayev Shipyard.	**17–31 December:** The U.S. launches the Linebacker II bombing of Hanoi and North Vietnam.
1973	**27 January:** The U.S.-Vietnamese cease-fire goes into effect.
	11 May: The NATO Standing Naval Force Channel is activated, later renamed Mine Countermeasures Force Northern Europe.
17 May: Formal diplomatic relations are opened between East and West Germany.	
	2 July: James R. Schlesinger is sworn in as Secretary of Defense; he will become an advocate of a 575-ship naval force.
3–7 July: The Conference on Security and Cooperation in Europe (CSCE) is opened in Helsinki.	
	10 August: The last USN submarine in the Atlantic-Mediterranean area fitted with the Polaris missile, the USS *Robert E. Lee* (SSBN-601), is transferred to the Pacific.
	17 August: Schlesinger announces that the Multiple Independently Targetable Re-entry Vehicle (MIRV) warhead system, similar to those of the United States, has been successfully tested by the Soviet Union.
6 October: Egypt and Syria launch a surprise attack against Israel on two fronts, inciting the "Yom Kippur" Arab-Israeli War.	
October–November: Soviet 5th Eskadra (Mediterranean Squadron) force strength grows to 96 ships during "Yom Kippur" Arab-Israeli War, as the Soviet Navy conducts massive air and sea-lift operations in support of Egypt and Syria.	**13 October:** The U.S. Air Force begins an airlift of munitions to Israel to offset the Soviet resupply effort to Egypt and Syria during "Yom Kippur" Arab-Israeli War.
24 October: Brezhnev threatens unilateral Soviet intervention in the Middle East to enforce a UN-brokered Arab-Israeli cease-fire, prompting Washington to place its armed forces on global nuclear alert.	**24 October:** Nixon orders a heightened readiness posture for the U.S. armed forces worldwide to Defense Condition Three (DEFCON 3) in response to Soviet threats of intervention in the Arab-Israeli conflict.

SOVIET UNION	UNITED STATES
25 October–3 November: The 5th Eskadra launches intense anti-carrier exercises in Mediterranean, using actual U.S. ships as live targets.	**19 November:** The Department of Defense announces that the U.S. 6th (Mediterranean) Fleet has been taken off alert.

1974

	10 January: Secretary Schlesinger announces plans to improve the accuracy of long-range missiles and to retarget them against select Soviet military, industrial, and civilian targets.
9 April: The first Soviet supertanker, the 150,500 deadweight ton *Krym,* is launched in the Black Sea.	**8 April:** J. William Middendorf is sworn in as Secretary of the Navy.
24 April: Anwar Sadat announces that Egypt will stop relying on Soviet arms in the interest of curtailing Soviet influence over his country's domestic politics.	
21 July: Brezhnev proposes a withdrawal of all U.S. and Soviet nuclear-armed naval forces from the Mediterranean.	**29 June:** Admiral James L. Holloway III is appointed CNO.
	9 August: Nixon resigns, hands presidency over to Vice President Gerald Ford.
	14 August: Greece withdraws its armed forces from the integrated military structure of NATO.
September: A compilation of Admiral Gorshkov's 1972–1973 *Morskoi Sbornik* articles is published in translation by the Naval Institute Press, titled *Red Star Rising at Sea.*	
23 November: During a conference with Gerald Ford in Vladivostok, over the course of which the U.S. and USSR sign an agreement placing limits on ICBMs, SLBMs, and heavy bombers, Brezhnev announces the construction of the Tayfun-class strategic missile submarine as a response to the U.S. Trident submarine program.	

1975

	22 January: President Ford signs the Geneva Protocol, prohibiting use of chemical weapons in war.
April–May: First factory tests of the project 1143 *Kiev* aircraft carrier are held; two Yak-36M VSTOL planes land on its deck.	**April:** Greece and the U.S. agree to close the U.S. Air Force base near Athens and end an agreement providing home port facilities to U.S. 6th Fleet.
April: Worldwide OKEAN 75 exercises are held, involving 220 ships in antisubmarine maneuvers, sea-lane interdiction, convoy escort, amphibious landings, and long-range aviation missions.	
May: The project 1143 *Minsk* aircraft carrier is launched.	**3 May:** The USS *Nimitz* aircraft carrier (CVN 68), the first nuclear-powered attack carrier designated for series production, is placed in commission in Norfolk, Va.
7 May: The first U.S.-Soviet warship visits are held in Leningrad and Boston.	

SOVIET UNION	UNITED STATES
	14 June: Vice Admiral Thomas Hayward is appointed Commander of the U.S. 7th Fleet (Western Pacific); over next two years, he develops the *Sea Strike Strategy*, promoting a central role for the Pacific Fleet in offensive naval war plans designed to distract the Soviets from the European front.
29 May: Beijing claims that Moscow has asked Saigon for use of the former U.S. naval base in Cam Rahn Bay in compensation for the Soviet aid delivered during the Vietnam War.	**2 July:** Schlesinger announces that the U.S. might consider a nuclear first-strike against select Soviet targets in some war scenarios.
1 August: The United States and Soviet Union sign the CSCE Helsinki Accords, pledging to accept European borders, protect human rights, and promote freer transnational trade and cultural exchanges.	
November: The project 1143 *Novorossiisk* aircraft carrier is laid down in the Nikolayev Shipyard.	**20 November:** Donald H. Rumsfeld is sworn in as Secretary of Defense; he will set the long-term naval force goal at 600 ships.
	2 December: Ex-CNO Zumwalt accuses the USSR of gross violations of the 1972 strategic arms limitation agreement in a testimony to the House Select Committee on Intelligence.
December: The USSR and Cuba increase assistance to rebel forces in Angola with military advisers, equipment, and troops.	
1976 Admiral Gorshkov's *Sea Power of the State* book is published by Voenizdat in the USSR this year; an English translation is published in the West by Oxford's Pergamon Press in 1979.	**24 January:** The U.S. agrees to withdraw its Poseidon submarines from Rota, Spain, by 1979; the submarine support facility begins moving to King's Bay, Ga., on 1 January 1979.
	16 February: The House Intelligence Committee learns that U.S. SSBNs have collided with nine Soviet vessels in Soviet territorial waters over preceding decade.
	26 March: U.S. agrees to give Turkey $1 billion in military aid in exchange for basing rights; a similar agreement is signed with Greece on 15 April.
April: Anwar Sadat cancels Soviet Navy access to Egyptian ports.	**April:** The keel of the first Trident strategic missile submarine, USS *Ohio* (SSBN 726), is laid down in Groton, Conn.
28 May: U.S. and Soviet officials sign the Peaceful Nuclear Explosions Treaty (PNET), limiting underground explosions and allowing U.S. inspections of some Soviet nuclear tests.	
July: Moscow cancels further U.S. port visits by sail training ships, following alleged poor treatment of crews in Newport, RI.	
July: *Kiev's* first tour of duty begins in the Mediterranean Sea after it passes through the Turkish Straits despite Montreux Treaty restrictions on aircraft carriers; it is subsequently reassigned to the Northern Fleet.	

SOVIET UNION	UNITED STATES
	27 September: Secretary Rumsfeld announces at a press conference that the Soviet nuclear buildup reflects an intention to win, not deter, a nuclear war.
	FY1976: Total U.S defense spending for this fiscal year is 24.8% of federal total; the lowest since 1940.
1977	**January:** A new National Intelligence Estimate, prepared with the participation of ex–Navy Secretary Paul Nitze, states that the USSR is striving for military superiority, not parity, with the United States.
	14 January: The 6th and 7th Fleets become home to all-nuclear-propelled task groups for the first time.
	20 January: Jimmy Carter is sworn in as the 39th U.S. President; Harold Brown is sworn in as Secretary of Defense the following day; he will set the long-term U.S. naval force goal at 425–500 ships.
	14 February: W. Graham Claytor, Jr., is sworn in as Secretary of the Navy.
14 April: A Tu-20 Bear naval surveillance plane flying near Charleston, S.C. carries out the closest flight by a Soviet aircraft to the U.S. East Coast ever recorded.	
June: U.S.-Soviet talks on the demilitarization of the Indian Ocean begin in Moscow.	
17 August: The Soviet nuclear icebreaker *Arktika* becomes first surface ship to ever break through the ice to the North Pole.	**7 September:** President Carter and Panamanian President Omar Torrijos sign treaties guaranteeing the neutrality of the Panama Canal in event of war, and agree to hand control of Canal over to Panama by 31 December 1999.
3 October: The SALT I agreement expires.	
	27 October: The USN admits to the highest desertion rate in its history during FY1977: 31.7 desertions per 1,000 enlisted personnel.
13 November: Somalia cancels Soviet use of its naval facilities, orders Soviet advisers to leave the country, and breaks off relations with Cuba.	
1978 **February:** The project 1143.4 *Baku* aircraft carrier is laid down in the Nikolayev Black Sea shipyard.	**1 February:** The first successful Tomahawk missile launch by a submerged submarine is carried out by the USS *Barb* (SSN-596) off the Californian coast.
	March: The *Sea Plan 2000* study completed; it predicts substantial constraints on U.S. naval power and flexibility over next 30 years; prescribes a shift to offensive mode to draw Soviet resources away from threatening Western sea-lanes; the U.S. General Accounting Office will criticize *Sea Plan 2000* in 1979 for being short-sighted and based on unrealistic funding assumptions.

SOVIET UNION	UNITED STATES
	30 May: Signaling an end to détente, Carter recommends to NATO to modernize and increase the alliance's military forces.
	1 July: Admiral Thomas B. Hayward is appointed CNO.
	17 August: Carter vetoes the FY1979 $36.9 billion defense bill, citing the inclusion in the bill of a $2 billion nuclear-powered aircraft carrier as the motive for the veto; Congress overrides the veto on 7 September.
	31 August: The 1978–1979 *Military Balance*, published by the International Institute for Strategic Studies, states that NATO no longer has the capacity to exert sea control in all areas of importance to the alliance at the start of a NATO–Warsaw Pact war.
29 September: The *Baltimore Sun* reports that a floating drydock, built by a Japanese shipyard to service *Kiev*-class aircraft carriers, is set for delivery to Vladivostok.	**17 September:** The Camp David Peace Accords are signed by Presidents Carter and Sadat and by Israeli Prime Minister Menachem Begin, calling for the return of Sinai to Egypt and the withdrawal of Israeli troops and settlements.
	20 October: Carter signs the 1979 Defense Authorization Act, making the Commandant of the Marine Corps a full member of the Joint Chiefs of Staff (JCS).
17 November: The first Soviet warship to visit Turkey in 40 years, the project 70-E cruiser *Dzerzhinskii* docks at Istanbul with the Black Sea Fleet Commander aboard.	**14 November:** GulfEx 79, an Atlantic Fleet exercise involving 20,000 Air Force, Navy, and Coast Guard personnel and almost 300 aircraft, begins in the Gulf of Mexico and western Caribbean.
December: The project 1143 *Novorossiisk* aircraft carrier is launched.	
1979	**1 January:** The United States and the People's Republic of China restore full diplomatic relations.
	January: Admiral Hayward and his Executive Assistant, Captain William Cockell, circulate the *CNO Strategic Concepts* memo, promoting greater force levels as part of a worldwide strategy capitalizing on Moscow's defensive mentality; Hayward briefs Congress, JCS, and others on his strategic concepts.
	16 January: The Shah of Iran, Mohammed Reza Pahlevi, flees his country as tensions there escalate.
	22 January: Carter allocates $6.1 billion from his FY1980 budget for 15 new Navy ships, including a $1.5 billion conventional aircraft carrier (which is ultimately never built).

SOVIET UNION	UNITED STATES
March: Soviet warships arrive at former U.S. bases of Da Nang and Cam Rahn Bay, Vietnam; two Tu-20 Bear reconnaissance aircraft land at Cam Rahn Bay the following month.	**10 April:** The first submerged launch of a Trident C-4 missile is carried out off the Floridian coast by the USS *Francis Scott Key* (SSBN 657).
15 May: Two Soviet maritime patrol planes fly dangerously close to the USS *Midway* aircraft carrier (CV 41) in the Arabian Sea, prompting U.S. protests under the Incidents at Sea Agreement.	**12 May:** The Solid Shield 79 exercise unfolds in the Atlantic with the participation of over 19,000 Army, Navy, Air Force, and Marine Corps personnel; Dawn Patrol 79, an eight-nation NATO Allied Southern Command exercise begins with nonmembers Greece and France taking part.
18 June: The SALT II agreement is signed by Carter and Brezhnev in Vienna, although it will be rejected by the U.S. Congress.	
	1 September: U.S. Department of State confirms intelligence reports that 2,000–3,000 Soviet troops remain in Cuba.
8 September: Soviet general intelligence vessels (AGIs) operate some 35 nautical miles off the California coast, the closest distance in years.	**September:** Two major NATO exercises begin: Display Determination 79 in the Mediterranean and Ocean Safari 79 in the Atlantic; Kernel Potlatch, a joint U.S.-Canadian exercise, begins in the northeastern Pacific, involving an amphibious landing on Vancouver Island.
10 September: Moscow signs an agreement with Greece for repairs of Soviet merchant and naval auxiliary vessels at the state-owned Neorion Shipyard; the first ships arrive for repairs at the Greek Island Siros on 6 October.	**1 October:** Carter announces the creation of the Caribbean Joint Task Force Headquarters in Key West, Fla., as a response to the continuing Soviet troop presence in Cuba; 1,800 U.S. Marines land in Guantánamo Bay two weeks later as a show of force.
	20 October: USS *Francis Scott Key* begins its first deterrent patrol with Trident C-4 missiles.
	24 October: Edward Hidalgo is sworn in as Secretary of the Navy.
	4 November: Iranian student revolutionaries storm the U.S. Embassy in Iran, taking 66 hostages.
	November: CrisEx 79, a joint U.S.-Spanish exercise, is held, involving a Marine landing on the Spanish coast on 4 November; Canus Marcor 79, a joint U.S.-Canadian exercise begins in the North Atlantic on 8 November.
	1 December: The U.S. Department of Energy reveals that 75% of Polaris A-1 ballistic missiles would not have functioned in the mid-1960s due to a mechanical defect.
	12 December: The deployment of hundreds of Pershing II launchers and ground-launched Tomahawk cruise missiles to Western Europe is announced by NATO ministers, as a response to domestic deployments of SS-20 intermediate-range nuclear missiles by Moscow.

SOVIET UNION	UNITED STATES
27 December: Soviet Speznaz commandos begin invasion of Afghanistan with a strike on the presidential compound in Kabul; in light of the invasion, the U.S. responds with sanctions, a grain embargo, decreased scientific and cultural exchanges, and a boycott of the 1980 Moscow Olympic Games.	

1980

SOVIET UNION	UNITED STATES
	1 January: The NATO Airborne Early Warning Force is established under Allied Command Europe.
	January: Admiral Hayward establishes the Long Range Planning Group (OP-00X) as a permanent fixture on CNO's staff; the group's primary mission is to assess resource limitations on future naval capabilities.
	February: Somalia, Kenya, and Oman agree to permit U.S. access to their naval and air bases.
	26 February: RimPac 80, the first of the year's many major naval exercises begins, this one a joint exercise with Canada, Australia, New Zealand, and Japan in the Pacific; Display Determination 80, a seven-nation NATO exercise involving nonmember France, begins in the Mediterranean on 29 September; Beacon Compass, a joint Ango-American exercise, begins in the Indian Ocean on 20 October.
	7 April: U.S. breaks off diplomatic relations with Iran; the Maritime Prepositioning Ship concept is launched the same day with Secretary Brown's announcement that seven U.S. ships will be deployed to the Indian Ocean with military equipment for contingency use by the Rapid Deployment Joint Task Force.
	29 May: The JCS announce that Carter's FY1981 defense budget is insufficient to counter Soviet advances.
July: The announcement of increases in meat prices sparks a wave of protests in Poland.	
28 August: A memorandum from the Central Committee of the Soviet Communist Party orders the Soviet Army to "requisition up to 100,000 military reservists and 15,000 vehicles from the civilian economy" and to place all regular units in military districts and Groups of Forces adjoining Poland on "full combat alert."	**22 August:** Secretary Brown announces major developments in stealth aviation technology.
4 September: Iran-Iraq war begins.	

SOVIET UNION	UNITED STATES
22 September: Solidarity, an independent and popularly-based trade union that would come to rival the Communist Party for political power, is formed in Poland under the leadership of Lech Walesa.	**12 October:** In testimony to Congress, Navy Under Secretary Robert Murray states that the USN is projected to suffer a severe shortfall in submarine officers in the following year.
	9 December: In response to a Soviet troop buildup in Poland, four U.S. Air Force E-3A Airborne Warning and Control System aircraft are deployed to West Germany.
30 December: The project 1144 nuclear-powered missile cruiser *Kirov*, the largest nonaircraft/helicopter carrier warship built since World War II, is commissioned.	

1981	
	20 January: Ronald Reagan is sworn in as the 40th President of the United States; Caspar Weinberger is sworn in as Secretary of Defense; Iran frees 52 Embassy hostages after 444 days.
26 January: Lech Walesa leads Polish workers in a week-long illegal strike.	**5 February:** John Lehman is sworn in as Secretary of the Navy, declares in testimony to the Senate Armed Services Committee that the U.S. must reestablish maritime superiority over the USSR, calling for a 600-ship navy with 15 aircraft carriers; Test Gate 81, a NATO exercise, begins the same day in the western Mediterranean.
	4 March: Secretary of Defense Caspar Weinberger announces a $57.8 billion defense budget for FY1981 and a $70.8 billion budget for FY1982, with proposals for extensive navy shipbuilding programs.
	April: Admiral Hayward announces plans for a Center for Naval Warfare Studies (CNWS) at the Naval War College (NWC), to serve as the center for strategic naval planning; the CNWS is established on 1 July.
	12 April: The space shuttle *Columbia* carries out its maiden orbital flight and successfully lands on a flight strip, thus obviating the need for ocean recovery of manned spacecraft by the USN.
	1 May: The Solid Shield 81 exercise begins in the Atlantic with the participation of over 27,000 personnel.
16 May: The U.S. Seventh Fleet Commander accuses the Soviet cruiser *Petropavlovsk* of slicing through the nets of a Japanese fishing vessel, following Japanese claims that the damage was inflicted by U.S. ships in a joint U.S.-Japanese exercise.	**17 June:** The U.S. General Accounting Office, in a report to the House Appropriations Committee, calls for a higher budget priority for naval mine warfare programs.

SOVIET UNION	UNITED STATES
7 July: An amphibious troop landing in Syria occurs as part of a Soviet Mediterranean Squadron training exercise, the first such landing in the eastern Mediterranean known at that time to have occurred.	**August:** The CNO Strategic Studies Group (SSG) I is assembled at CNWS.
1 September: A Soviet task group, including a Kara-class missile cruiser, two frigates, and a replenishment ship, comes within 230 nautical miles of the Oregon coast.	**August–October:** Ocean Venture 81, the largest U.S.-led naval exercise in years, takes place in the South Atlantic, Caribbean, and Baltic Seas; forces from fourteen nations take part, comprising 250 ships, 1,000 aircraft and some 120,000 personnel.
4–12 September: ZAPAD 81 exercises are held in the Baltic Sea, involving the *Kiev* aircraft carrier and the RSD-20 medium-range strategic missile complex.	
6 October: Egyptian President Anwar Sadat is assassinated.	
	October–November: The CNO SSG I holds two war games, emphasizing the idea of preventing Soviet escalation by prolonging the conventional phase of war, part of a "long war" strategy.
November: Bear reconnaissance aircraft begin nearly continuous use of airfields in San Antonio de los Banos, Cuba.	**11 November:** The first Ohio-class Trident submarine, the USS *Ohio* (SSBN 726), is placed in commission at Groton, Conn.
	19 November: Reagan proposes the "zero option" to Moscow, proposing the elimination of an entire class of weapons—intermediate-range nuclear missiles.
13 December: In an attempt to quell the Solidarity movement, martial law is imposed in Poland by the Military Council for National Salvation, led by Prime Minister General Wojciech Jaruzelski.	**November:** An Interagency Intelligence memorandum on *Soviet Intentions and Capabilities for Interdicting Sea Lines of Communication in a War with NATO* is completed; the memo argues that in the event of war, the majority of Soviet naval forces would be deployed closer to USSR to defend the country's SSBN force.
1982	**17 January:** The first submerged launch of a Trident C-4 missile is carried out by the USS *Ohio* submarine off the Florida coast.
16 March: Brezhnev announces a moratorium on the deployment of mid-range SS-20 missiles in the eastern Soviet Union, contingent in a move similar to the U.S. regarding the Pershing II missiles.	**2 April–14 June:** The Falklands War begins when Argentine forces land in the Falkland Islands in an initially successful invasion; the Argentineans surrender to British troops ten weeks later.
	9 May: President Reagan outlines the U.S. Strategic Arms Reduction Treaty (START) proposal, with which to reach a verifiable bilateral agreement to reduce ICBMs and other strategic nuclear weapons on both sides.

SOVIET UNION	UNITED STATES
	6 June: The 6th Fleet goes on alert as Israeli troops cross into southern Lebanon to root out some 15,000 Palestinian Liberation Army (PLO) militants, eventually encircling and blockading Beirut; the U.S. Embassy in Beirut comes under rocket attack on 7 June.
30 June: The U.S.-Soviet START negotiations are opened in Geneva.	
	30 June: Admiral James Watkins is appointed CNO.
	25 August: 6th Fleet amphibious ships facilitate a landing by the 32nd Marine Amphibious Unit in Beirut to help withdraw the families of some 12,000 PLO members.
	August: During the academic year 1982–83 at NWC, the CNO SSG II adopts tenets of forward defense as the foundation of deterrence in peacetime and applies these concepts to Southern European and Pacific theaters.
	August: Vice CNO Admiral William Small signs a memorandum sent to all four flag officers concerned with preparation of the Program Objective Memorandum (POM), calling on an integration of analyses into a coherent war-winning strategy; action on the memo is passed to the Strategic Concepts Branch (OP-603), to be carried out by Lt. Commander Stanley Weeks and Commander W. Spencer Johnson.
	29 September: 1,200 Marines join 2,200 French and Italian troops on the ground in Lebanon to preserve order.
	26–29 October: Admiral Watkins convenes an annual conference of Navy commanders in chief at NWC, stressing "deterrence to the last" as the naval objective during periods of rising tensions; the Weeks-Johnson Maritime Strategy briefing is presented to the conference.
10 November: Leonid Brezhnev dies; he is succeeded two days later by Yuri Andropov as General Secretary of the Communist Party.	
1983 **January:** The first full-deck Soviet aircraft carrier, the project 1143.5 *Tbilisi* (later renamed *Admiral Kuznetsov*), is laid down in the Nikolayev shipyard.	**1 January:** The commander in chief U.S. Central Command replaces the Rapid Deployment Joint Task Force in the Middle East; will draw on forces from U.S. Atlantic and Pacific Commands as needed.
	1 February: USN ships participate in the joint U.S.-Honduran Ahuas Tara exercise in Honduras.

SOVIET UNION	UNITED STATES
	23 March: Reagan addresses the nation in support of the Strategic Defense Initiative (SDI), an anti-strategic missile defense also known as the "Star Wars" program.
	February: The Maritime Strategy briefing presented in full to the Subcommittee on Seapower and Strategic and Critical Material of the House Armed Services Committee.
	20 April: Deputy CNO Vice Admiral Robert Walters testifies to the House Appropriations Committee that Navy programs to counter the Soviet threat in mine warfare are dangerously underfunded.
21 July: Martial law is lifted in Poland.	**26 July:** In response to Soviet arms shipments to Nicaragua, the USS *Ranger* (CVA 61) carrier attack group deploys off that country's Pacific coast.
	August: In the academic year 1983–84 at NWC, the CNO SSG III expands forward defense strategy to include employment of naval forces in handling outlying Soviet client states before a NATO–Warsaw Pact war, focusing on cases of Libya, Cuba, and Southwest Asia.
1 September: A Su-17 Flagon fighter jet shoots down a Korean Airlines airliner over the Kamchatka Peninsula, killing all 269 aboard, including 61 U.S. citizens.	**September:** The Maritime Strategy, as modified by new Action Officer Commander Peter Swartz, is presented to Admiral Watkins and six former CNOs in Newport.
	1 October: Navy Secretary John Lehman announces the creation of a Navy Space Command to support existing Navy space programs.
	23 October: 241 U.S. servicemen are killed in a truck bombing of the U.S. Marine compound in Beirut; Secretary Weinberger announces a month later that the attack had been executed by Syrian-backed Iranian nationals.
	24 October: Operation URGENT FURY, under the command of Vice Admiral Joseph Metcalf III, USN, and his deputy, Maj. Gen. Norman Schwartzkopf, USA, begins in Grenada to overthrow the country's new Communist government; the goals are accomplished within days.
	October: The Maritime Strategy, with added discussion on the USN's role in peacetime, is presented to CNO Executive Panel.
	22 November: The U.S. deploys Pershing II missiles to West Germany after a protracted political fight.

SOVIET UNION	UNITED STATES
December: Moscow suspends the START negotiations.	**December:** Exchanges of fire between artillery positions in Syrian-occupied Lebanon and locally deployed U.S. 6th Fleet ships intensify after surface-to-air missiles (SAMs) are launched against U.S. reconnaissance aircraft on 3 December.
1984	**19 January:** Navy Secretary John Lehman and Admiral Watkins present the Maritime Strategy briefing to Secretary of Defense Weinberger.
9 February: Soviet General Secretary Yuri Andropov dies; he is succeeded by Konstantin Chernenko on 13 February.	**2 February:** Amidst the withdrawals of Italian and British ground forces from Lebanon, USN ships launch the heaviest bombardment yet of Syrian artillery positions near Beirut; the U.S. Marine withdrawal occurs on 21 February, after which only the French contingent remains in significant numbers.
21 March: A Soviet Victor-class SSN collides with the carrier USS *Kitty Hawk* in the Sea of Japan.	**9 April:** Marking a new phase in anti-submarine warfare, a new submarine detection system supplementing the existing seafloor Sound Surveillance System (SOSUS)—the Surveillance Towed Array Sensor System (SURTASS)—goes into service in the Military Sealift Command, fitted on the surveillance ship USS *Stewart* (DE 238).
	2 May: The first of 84 USN Landing Craft Air Cushioned (LCAC), a new type of high-speed amphibious ship, is launched.
May: A quarter to a third of the Northern Fleet's SAM stockpile is destroyed when a week-long series of fires and explosions ravages weapons magazines in Severomorsk.	**4 May:** Admiral Watkins signs the final FY1984 version of *The Maritime Strategy* for publication in classified and unclassified forms.
29 June: Moscow issues a statement calling for the resumption in September of U.S.-Soviet negotiations on anti-satellite, strategic, and intermediate-range nuclear weapons reductions; Washington agrees to hold talks.	
	2 July: Cobra Gold 84, a joint U.S.-Thai naval exercise in the Gulf of Thailand, begins, involving 10,000 personnel in minelaying, minesweeping, and amphibious landing operations.
August: The Soviet Navy joins the U.S., U.K., Italy, France, the Netherlands, and Egypt in a mass de-mining operation in the Suez Gulf, after mines allegedly laid by the Islamic Jihad inflict damage to passing Soviet merchant ships; mines subsequently discovered by a U.K. ship are determined to be of Soviet manufacture and laid by a Libyan freighter.	**August:** In the academic year 1984–85, the CNO SSG IV examines deterrence in the context of the *Maritime Strategy*, recommending demonstrations of NATO solidarity, interoperability, and sustainability in forward defense to aggravate Soviet fears of prolonged conventional war.
24 September: Reagan proposes a broad "umbrella" framework for U.S.-Soviet arms talks to the UN General Assembly.	
	5 November: The first-ever joint U.S.-Egyptian naval exercise begins in the eastern Mediterranean.

SOVIET UNION	UNITED STATES
22 November: President Reagan's National Security Adviser, Robert McFarlane, announces that Washington and Moscow have agreed to hold new negotiations on nuclear and space issues.	
	26 November: Washington resumes diplomatic ties with Iraq for the first time since the 1967 Arab-Israeli War.

1985	**10 March:** General Secretary Konstantin Chernenko dies; Mikhail Gorbachev succeeds him on the following day.	
	12 March: The U.S.-Soviet Nuclear and Space Talks (NST) open in Geneva, based on the START proposals of 1983.	
		9 April: The Space and Naval Warfare Systems Command is established in the Navy as the Naval Material Command is disestablished, eliminating a bureaucratic layer above the naval systems commands.
		20 May: The most significant case of espionage involving USN personnel is unraveled as retired Chief Warrant Officer John Walker, Jr., is arrested for having spied for Moscow since 1968.
		5 July: Operation BRIGHT STAR 85, the largest U.S. training exercise to date in the Middle East, is held in Egypt, Jordan, and Somalia; OCEAN SAFARI '85, the largest NATO exercise ever held, begins on 29 August, involving 157 ships and 70,000 personnel from ten nations.
		August: In the academic year 1985–86, the CNO SSG V focuses on the employment of naval forces in support of peacetime foreign policy objectives.
	30 September: Moscow presents a START proposal, which accepts the principle of deep reductions in strategic offensive forces for the first time.	**November:** Admiral Watkins formally signs the third version of the *Maritime Strategy*.
	21 November: At the Geneva Summit, Reagan and Gorbachev issue a joint statement on cooperation in arms reductions, setting the goal at 50% reduction of nuclear arms.	
	December: The *Tbilisi* carrier is launched; the *Varyag* aircraft carrier, also known as project 1143.5, is laid down in the Nikolayev Shipyard.	
	5 December: Gorshkov is replaced as commander in chief of the Soviet Navy by Admiral of the Fleet Vladimir Chernavin, a former nuclear submarine commander; Gorshkov had held the post since 1956.	

1986	**15 January:** Gorbachev proposes the elimination of all nuclear weapons by the year 2000, contingent on Washington's cancellation of SDI; Reagan does not change his position.	**24 March:** Operation PRAIRIE FIRE begins with strikes on Libyan missile ships and shore-based missile installations after several SAMs are launched against U.S. aircraft operating near Libyan territorial waters.

SOVIET UNION	UNITED STATES
	11 April: Admiral Watkins becomes the first U.S. Navy CNO to visit the People's Republic of China.
	15 April: 6th Fleet carrier groups launch strikes against ground targets in Libya, ten days after a U.S. soldier is killed in a Libyan-backed bombing of a West Berlin discotheque.
26 April: Fire and an explosion at reactor no. 4 of the Chernobyl Nuclear Power Plant contaminate large areas of Ukraine and Belarus.	**1 July:** Admiral Carlisle Trost is appointed CNO.
6 October: The project 667-AU nuclear submarine K-219 (Yankee-class), on patrol with 15 nuclear-tipped SS-N-6 missiles, sinks east of Bermuda, 40 hours after a missile propellant explosion.	**1 October:** The Goldwater-Nichols Defense Reorganization Act is passed into law, adding the post of Vice Chairman of the JCS at the four-star level, and placing the Chairman of the JCS in the chain of command between the Secretary of Defense and the unified commanders.
11–12 October: At the Reykjavik Summit, U.S.-Soviet arms talks stall over Reagan's refusal to limit SDI research and testing to the laboratory.	
	5 November: The first U.S. Navy ship visits to China since 1949 take place.
	23 November: Frank Carlucci is sworn in as Secretary of Defense.
	22 December: The Peacekeeper ICBM becomes operational.
1987 **1 January:** Gorbachev addresses Soviet citizens on the dangers of the arms race; on the same day, President Reagan uses Voice of America to announce to Soviet citizens the unprecedented imminence of a bilateral nuclear arms reduction agreement.	**January:** President Reagan delivers to Congress a public and unclassified statement of the *National Security Strategy of the United States*, developed by Rear Admiral W. A. Cockell.
	1 May: James Webb is sworn in as Secretary of the Navy.
	5 May: Nationally televised hearings on the Iran-Contra scandal open before the House and Senate; Colonel Oliver North, former National Security Adviser John M. Poindexter, and Iranian-American arms dealer Albert Hakim are indicted 15 March 1988 on charges of diverting Iranian arms sales proceeds to Nicaraguan Contras.
26 August: West German Chancellor Helmut Kohl announces Germany's intention to destroy its Pershing missiles given that the United States and Soviet Union agree to destroy their own intermediate-range nuclear missiles.	
15 September: The U.S. and USSR sign the Nuclear Risk Reduction Center Agreement, promoting communication and confidence-building measures.	
8 December: Gorbachev and Reagan sign the Intermediate-range Nuclear Forces (INF) treaty in Washington, eliminating a full class of weapons and granting an unprecedented level of access to inspectors of sites in both countries.	
1988 **January:** The project 1143.5 *Varyag* aircraft carrier is launched.	

SOVIET UNION	UNITED STATES
5 January: A Soviet nuclear submarine is transferred to another nation for the first time, as a project 670 (Charlie I-class) cruise missile submarine is leased by Moscow to the Indian Navy.	**22 February:** Navy Secretary Webb resigns in protest of Secretary of Defense Frank Carlucci's lack of support for a 600-ship Navy.
	28 March: William L. Ball is sworn in as Secretary of the Navy.
15 April: After seven years of peace talks, Moscow agrees to withdraw all its forces from Afghanistan by 15 February 1989.	
18 May: Soviet troops begin withdrawal from Afghanistan.	
29 May–1 June: At the Moscow Summit, Reagan and Gorbachev reaffirm their commitment to concluding the START treaty.	
28 June: Gorbachev reports to the 19th All-Union Conference of the Communist Party that key elements of Communist doctrine are outdated, defending his proposals for Perestroika reforms.	**3 July:** USS *Vincennes* (CG 49) mistakenly shoots down an Iran Air commercial airliner, killing 290.
16 August: Pro-Solidarity strikes in Poland demand the granting of a legal status to the union.	
20 August: A cease-fire ending the Iran-Iraq War is announced.	
7 December: Gorbachev announces a unilateral withdrawal of 50,000 Soviet troops from Eastern Europe and a 10% reduction in the Soviet armed forces.	
1989 **1 January:** Remaining Soviet troops in Afghanistan cease fire a day after Moscow announces that it will halt arms shipments to the Kabul government.	**20 January:** George Bush is sworn in as the 41st President of the United States.
7 February: Deputy Foreign Minister Igor Rogachev announces a complete withdrawal of Soviet troops from Afghanistan by 15 February as another official announces that 15,000 Soviet servicemen had been killed since the start of the conflict.	**21 March:** Richard Cheney is sworn in as Secretary of Defense.
5 April: Poland grants legal status to the Solidarity union.	
7 April: 42 submariners die after a fire sinks the project 685 *Komsomolets* nuclear submarine (Mike-class) near the Norwegian coast.	**15 May:** Henry L. Garrett III is sworn in as Secretary of the Navy.
	3 June: After the occurrence of seven aircraft mishaps in the first half of the year, the U.S. Marine Corps announces a two-day operational stand-down for all Marine aviation units.
3–4 June: The Chinese army attacks students protesting in Tiananmen Square, killing hundreds.	

SOVIET UNION	UNITED STATES
21 July: Three Northern Fleet ships under the flag of Vice Admiral I. V. Kasatonov, the First Deputy commander in chief of the Northern Fleet, dock in Norfolk, Va., in the first such naval port visit since 1975; two USN ships reciprocate by visiting Black Sea Fleet headquarters in Sevastopol two weeks later.	
22–23 September: The U.S. and USSR sign the "Reciprocal Advance Notice of Major Strategic Exercises Agreement" as part of the Wyoming Ministerial, pledging to prevent inadvertent conflict caused by provocative military exercises.	
1 November: *Admiral Kuznetsov/Tbilisi* (the country's first full-deck carrier and the largest Soviet warship ever built) goes to sea; aboard the carrier, the first conventional aircraft landing on a Soviet ship is carried out by test pilot Viktor Pugachev.	
14–21 November: The Berlin Wall is dismantled.	
2–3 December: Speaking at the Malta Summit, President Bush proposes to accelerate START negotiations.	
	20 December: Operation JUST CAUSE is launched by 24,000 U.S. troops against the government of Panamanian president General Manuel Noriega.

1990	**12 February:** NATO and Warsaw Pact officials meet in Ottawa to discuss the "Open Skies" concept of inspection of countries by reconnaissance aircraft.	
		29 June: Admiral Frank Keslo III is appointed CNO.
	2 August: The Iraqi invasion of Kuwait begins.	
		August–November: Operation SHARP EDGE, a mass evacuation of U.S. and other citizens from war-torn Liberia, is launched.
		7 August: Operation DESERT SHIELD begins as President Bush orders U.S. forces to Saudi Arabia to protect that country from Iraqi invasion.
	9 September: Gorbachev and Bush meet in Helsinki and declare unconditional support for UN sanctions against Iraq.	
	12 September: The Two-Plus-Four Treaty is signed by U.S., Soviet, British, and French representatives, recognizing the creation of a united post–Cold War German state.	
		1 October: U.S. forces formally end their presence in West Berlin.
	12 December: Lech Walesa is elected President of Poland.	**14 December:** Navy Secretary H. Lawrence Garrett III signs a memorandum establishing Air, Surface, Undersea, and Command, Communications, and Ocean Surveillance Warfare Centers, and reorganizing the Navy's research, development, test, and evacuation activities.

1991		**4 January:** Operation EASTERN EXIT begins as two USN amphibious ships conduct an evacuation of U.S. citizens from Somalia, during that country's escalating civil war.

SOVIET UNION	UNITED STATES
	7 January: The development of the Navy's long-range strike aircraft ends with the cancellation of the planned A-12 Avenger carrier-based attack plane.
17 January: Operation DESERT STORM begins as U.S. and coalition aircraft launch strikes against Iraqi targets.	
21 January: The *Tbilisi* aircraft carrier enters naval service.	**27 February:** Bush announces the suspension of all offensive combat operations by U.S. and coalition forces in the Persian Gulf.
3 March: Iraq accepts cease-fire terms and the Gulf War is over.	
31 July: Bush and Gorbachev sign the START treaty, pledging to destroy thousands of strategic nuclear weapons.	
18 August: Gorbachev is placed under house arrest by the KGB in his Yalta dacha, as hard-line coup conspirators announce a state of emergency in the Soviet Union; Boris Yeltsin and other leaders of the Russian Soviet Federated Socialist Republic (RSFSR) demand Gorbachev's release a day later as armed citizens take up positions to defend the Parliament building against tanks and troops deployed by coup supporters; mass anti-coup demonstrations erupt in Leningrad and Moscow; troops withdraw from Moscow on 21 August, following the deaths of three civilian protestors; Gorbachev's bodyguards arrest coup plotters on the same day and Gorbachev calls President Bush, reaffirming his control of the country.	
24 August: Gorbachev resigns as General Secretary of the Communist Party, effectively ending 74 years of Communist rule.	
2 September: The Soviet Union is voted dissolved by the Congress of People's Deputies, an act Gorbachev denounces as betrayal; power shifts to Russian President Boris Yeltsin.	
11 September: Gorbachev announces that Moscow will hold talks with Cuba over the withdrawal of Soviet forces from that country.	
27 September: A missile misfires on a project 941 (Typhoon-class) SSBN carrying several nuclear weapons.	**27 September:** Bush proposes sweeping nuclear reductions, including the unilateral cancellation of MX rail-garrison and short-range attack missile (SCRAM II) programs, the worldwide withdrawal of all Army ground-based tactical nuclear weapons and Navy tactical nuclear weapons, and an end to the 24-hour alert status of B-1B and B-52 bombers; he urges Gorbachev to reciprocate.
5 October: Gorbachev announces the removal of all tactical nuclear weapons from warships and the abolition of short-range Soviet nuclear weapons.	
6 October: Poland, Czechoslovakia, and Hungary express a desire to join NATO.	
27 December: Gorbachev hands nuclear codes to Russian Federation President Yeltsin; he resigns on 30 December, declaring the USSR to be defunct.	

Sources

This timeline draws on information collected from various unclassified U.S., Russian, and other primary and secondary source materials.

Electronic resources extensively exploited for the creation of this chronology included websites maintained by the Federation of American Scientists (http://www.fas.org/man/dod-101/ops/cold_war.htm), the Woodrow Wilson School's Cold War International History Project (http://wwics.si.edu/index.cfm?topic_id=1409&fuseaction=topics.home), the Parallel History Project on NATO and the Warsaw Pact (http://www.isn.ethz.ch/php/), the CIA's Center for the Study of Intelligence (http://www.cia.gov/csi/books/19335/art-1.html), and the National Security Archives (http://www.gwu.edu/~nsarchiv/).

Western printed materials that proved indispensable in the creation of this work included two outstanding volumes edited by Norman Polmar—*Chronology of the Cold War at Sea 1945–1991* (Annapolis, Md.: Naval Institute Press, 1998) and *The Naval Institute Guide to the Soviet Navy*, 5th edition (Annapolis, Md.: Naval Institute Press, 1991). Various other secondary sources, press reports, research databases, as well as *Jane's Fighting Ships* and back issues of U.S. Naval Institute *Proceedings* were accessed to verify select events.

Among the Russian language print sources of much value were Ivan Kapitanets's *Na Sluzhbe Okeanskomu Flotu* [On Service to the Ocean-going Fleet] (Moscow: Izdatel'stvo Andreevskii Flag, 2000), I. V. Kasatonov's *Flot Vyhodit v Okean* [The Fleet is Going to the Ocean] (Saint Petersburg: Astra-Lyuks, 1995), Gennadii Panatov's *Morskaya Aviatsiya na Sluzhbe Rossii* [Marine Aviation Serving Russia] (Moscow: Restart+, 2000), Igor Drogovoz's *Bolshoi Flot Strany Sovetov* [The Large Fleet of the Country of Soviets] (Minsk: Kharvest, 2003), and G. G. Kostev's *Voenno-Morskoi Flot Strany 1945–1995: Vzlety i Padeniya* [The Country's Navy 1945–1995: Take-offs and Falls] (Saint Petersburg: Nauka, 1999). Numerous Russian online resources were exploited to verify select events.

The dates mentioned in the above chronology were confirmed using two or more sources. Where possible, information taken from U.S. or NATO sources was verified with Russian or ex–Warsaw Pact materials and vice versa.

TABLE OF ABBREVIATIONS

AGI	Auxiliary General Intelligence Vessel
ABM	Anti-Ballistic Missile Treaty
ASW	Anti-submarine Warfare
CNO	Chief of Naval Operations
CNWS	Center for Naval Warfare Studies
CSCE	Conference on Security and Cooperation in Europe
DEFCON	Defense Condition/Readiness Posture
DSCS	Defense Satellite Communications System
FOBS	Fractional Orbital Bombardment System
ICBM	Intercontinental Ballistic Missile
INF	Intermediate-range Nuclear Forces Treaty
JCS	Joint Chiefs of Staff
LCAC	Landing Craft Air Cushioned
MIRV	Multiple Independently-targeted Reentry Vehicle
NATO	North Atlantic Treaty Organization
NPT	Non-proliferation Treaty on Nuclear Weapons
NST	Nuclear and Space Talks
NWC	Naval War College
PLO	Palestinian Liberation Army
PNET	Peaceful Nuclear Explosions Treaty
POM	Program Objective Memorandum
RSFSR	Russian Soviet Federated Socialist Republic
SALT	Strategic Arms Limitation Talks
SAM	Surface-to-air Missile
SDI	Strategic Defense Initiative
SLBM	Submarine-launched Ballistic Missile
SOSUS	Sound Surveillance System
SSG	Strategic Studies Group
SSN	Nuclear-powered Attack Submarine
SSBN	Nuclear-powered Ballistic Missile Submarine
SURTASS	Surveillance Towed Array Sensor System
START	Strategic Arms Reduction Treaty
UN	United Nations
USN	United States Navy
VSTOL	Vertical/Short Take-off and Landing

Index

About the Authors

Professor John B. Hattendorf, chairman of the Naval War College's new Maritime History Department, has served since 1984 as the College's Ernest J. King Professor of Maritime History. His service to the U.S. Navy extends over three decades—as an officer with combat experience at sea in destroyers, at the Naval Historical Center, and as both a uniformed and a civilian Naval War College faculty member. He earned his master's degree in history from Brown University in 1971 and his doctorate in war history from the University of Oxford in 1979. Kenyon College, where he earned his bachelor's degree in 1964, awarded him an honorary doctorate in 1997, and the National Maritime Museum, Greenwich, awarded him its Caird Medal in 2000 for his contributions to the field of maritime history. Since 1988 he has directed the Advanced Research Department in the Center for Naval Warfare Studies. He is the author, coauthor, editor, or coeditor of numerous articles and more than thirty books on British and American maritime history, including *Sailors and Scholars: The Centennial History of the Naval War College,* studies on Alfred Thayer Mahan and Stephen B. Luce, and *America and the Sea: A Maritime History.* His most recent works include coediting *War at Sea in the Middle Ages and the Renaissance* (2002) and a major exhibition catalog for the John Carter Brown Library, *The Boundless Deep: The European Conquest of the Oceans, 1450–1840* (2003).

Peter M. Swartz is a senior analyst at the Center for Strategic Studies of the CNA Corporation (CNAC), in Alexandria, Virginia. He has been an analyst and manager at CNAC since 1993, specializing in studies analyzing the development over time of fleet deployment strategy, naval homeland defense, NATO naval relationships, and the role of the U.S. Navy in operations other than war. Before joining CNAC, he was a career officer in the navy, retiring as a captain. His navy assignments included duty as Special Assistant to the Chairman of the Joint Chiefs of Staff, General Colin Powell, during the First Gulf War, and Director of Defense Operations at the U.S. Mission to NATO in Brussels during the Warsaw Pact collapse. Throughout the early and mid-1980s, he was a principal author of and spokesman for *The Maritime Strategy,* serving for part of that time on the staff of Secretary of the Navy John Lehman. During the late 1960s he had been an advisor with the Vietnamese Navy in the western Mekong Delta and in Saigon. He holds a B.A. with honors in international relations from Brown University, an M.A. in international affairs from the Johns Hopkins Nitze School of Advanced International Studies, and an M.Phil. in political science from Columbia University. He lectures widely at military and civilian institutions and is the author of numerous journal articles.

Yuri Zhukov, who produced the time line appendix for this Newport Paper, is a technical research adviser/translator (with native fluency in Russian) with Science Applications International Corporation. Since earning a B.A. with honors in international relations at Brown University in Providence, Rhode Island, he has been a research assistant for the Naval War College, the Watson Institute for International Studies at Brown, and Action Without Borders, Inc.

Titles in the Series

The Third Battle: Innovation in the U.S. Navy's Silent Cold War Struggle with Soviet Submarines, by Owen R. Cote, Jr. (2003).

The Limits of Transformation: Officer Attitudes toward the Revolution in Military Affairs, by Thomas G. Mahnken and James R. FitzSimonds (2003).

Military Transformation and the Defense Industry after Next: The Defense Industrial Implications of Network-Centric Warfare, by Peter J. Dombrowski, Eugene Gholz, and Andrew L. Ross (2003).

Forthcoming in 2004

China's Nuclear Force Modernization, edited by Lyle Goldstein.

Global War Game: Second Series, 1984–1988, by Robert H. Gile.